AF599226

OH!

WHAT FUN WE HAD

·

GAVIN WATSON

EDITED BY

RINI GIANNAKI

There was a time before the so-called Digital Era when fun was quantified in a different system of measurement.
Online presence or number of followers didn't exist; you didn't need a fashion week to trigger an outfit change; music was something that you had to go out and find for yourself and physical space was something to claim.
Through good times and hard. With mates by your side and time on our side.
Growing up in 1980s rural Italy my own reality was defined by what I could immediately surround myself with. Anything outside that was often welcome but rarely understood. The black-and-white chequer, a pattern that came hand-in-hand with some of the best bands of those times, like Madness or The Specials, made little sense to me even though I embraced it wholeheartedly. It would take decades before I would meet people whose own personal account would help me attach some sense to the past. And Gavin continues to be one of those friends.
The essence of Gavin's photography is something that you can only experience today via movies and nostalgic editorials.
Authenticity is something difficult to define in a world of instantaneity and Gavin's eyes are one of the few living

The last few years have been hilarious for me. I don't think I've ever laughed or had my faith restored in humanity so much, since the rise of the meme.

For my younger dyslexic self, it would have been a dream to be able to communicate with images and knock-around graphics that actually affect the fabric of society. As young rebels at the time our actions had no real impact – except for the clothes we wore and the triggering they provoked. Those years, 1979-84, it all happened on such a localised scale that we were easily ignored.

To see the same hysterical nut jobs that lied about white laces meaning you were anti-pakistani being the same people that suggested a badly drawn cartoon frog "was literally Hitler." Or that a blonde blue-eyed Swede would take over the world. Or that we would remember that we are an island. Or hearing a world leader actually saying this...

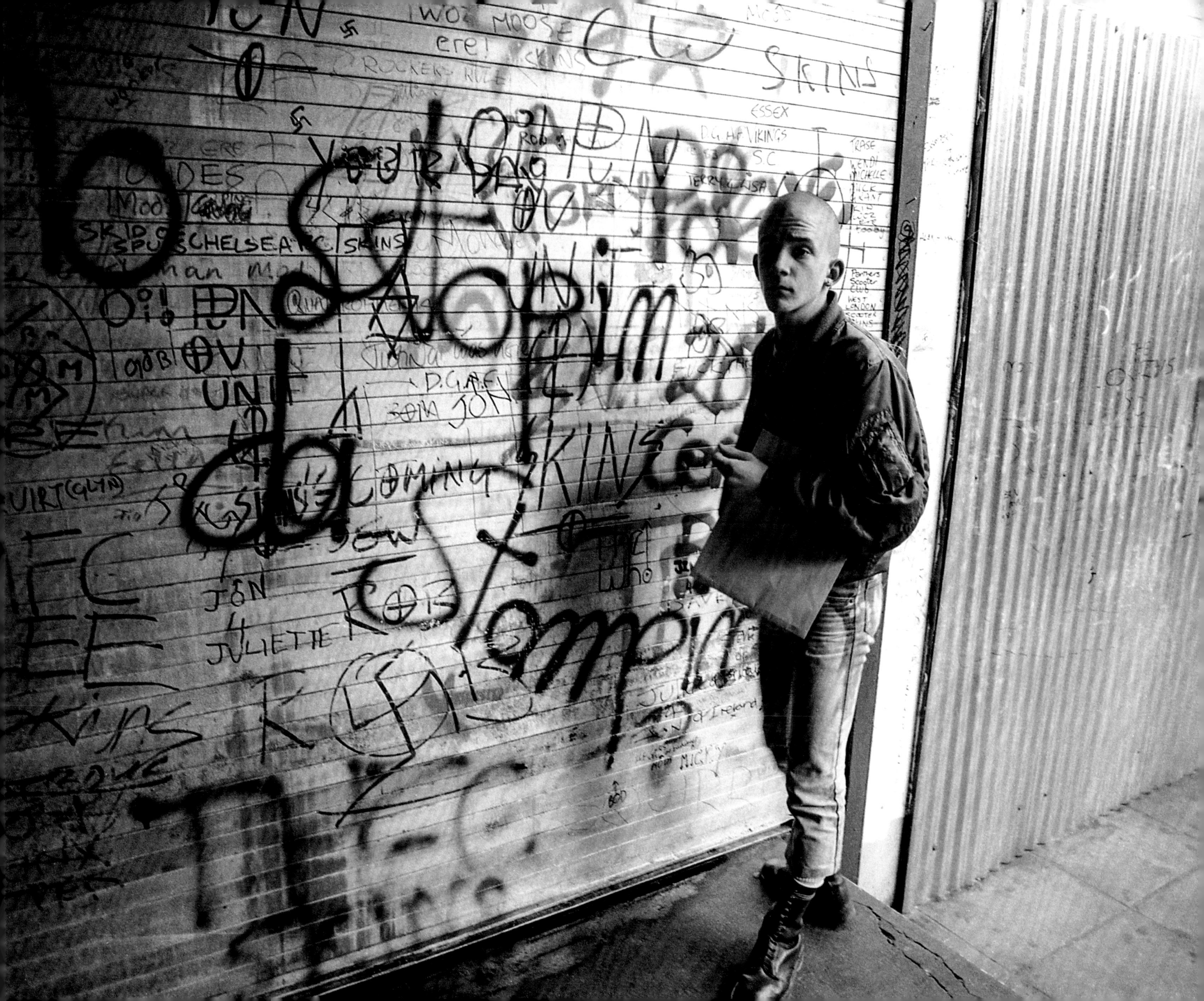

I WOZ ere!
MOOSE
SKINS
ROCKERS RULE
ESSEX
D.G.H. VIKINGS
SC
TERRY & LISA
SKINS
CHELSEA F.C.
SKINS
Oi!
Panthers Scooter Club
WEST LONDON SCOOTER BOYS
D.G.H.
BON JON
COMING
SKINS
The Who
JON 4 JULIETTE
Stompin
Ireland

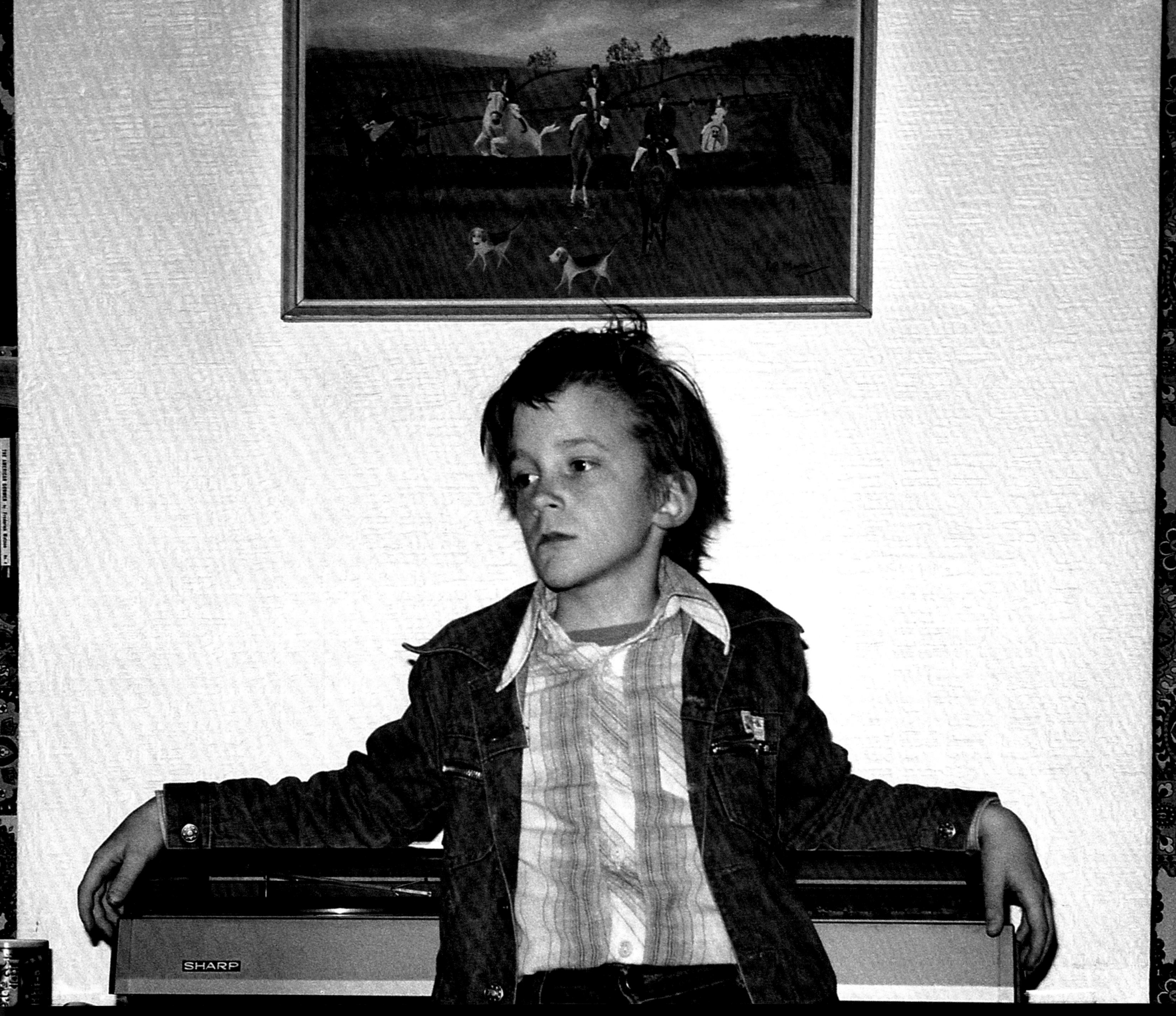
SHARP

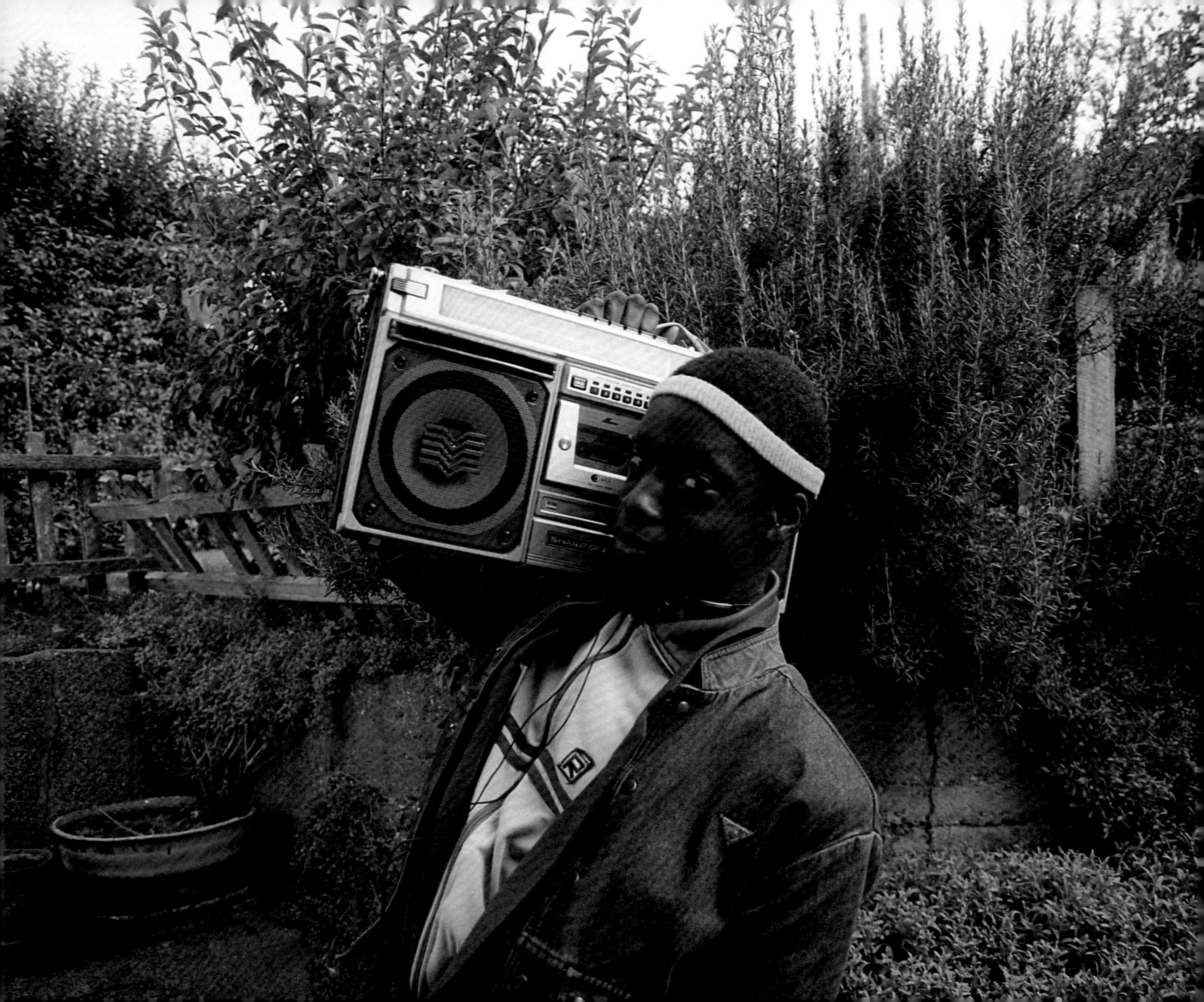
SHARP

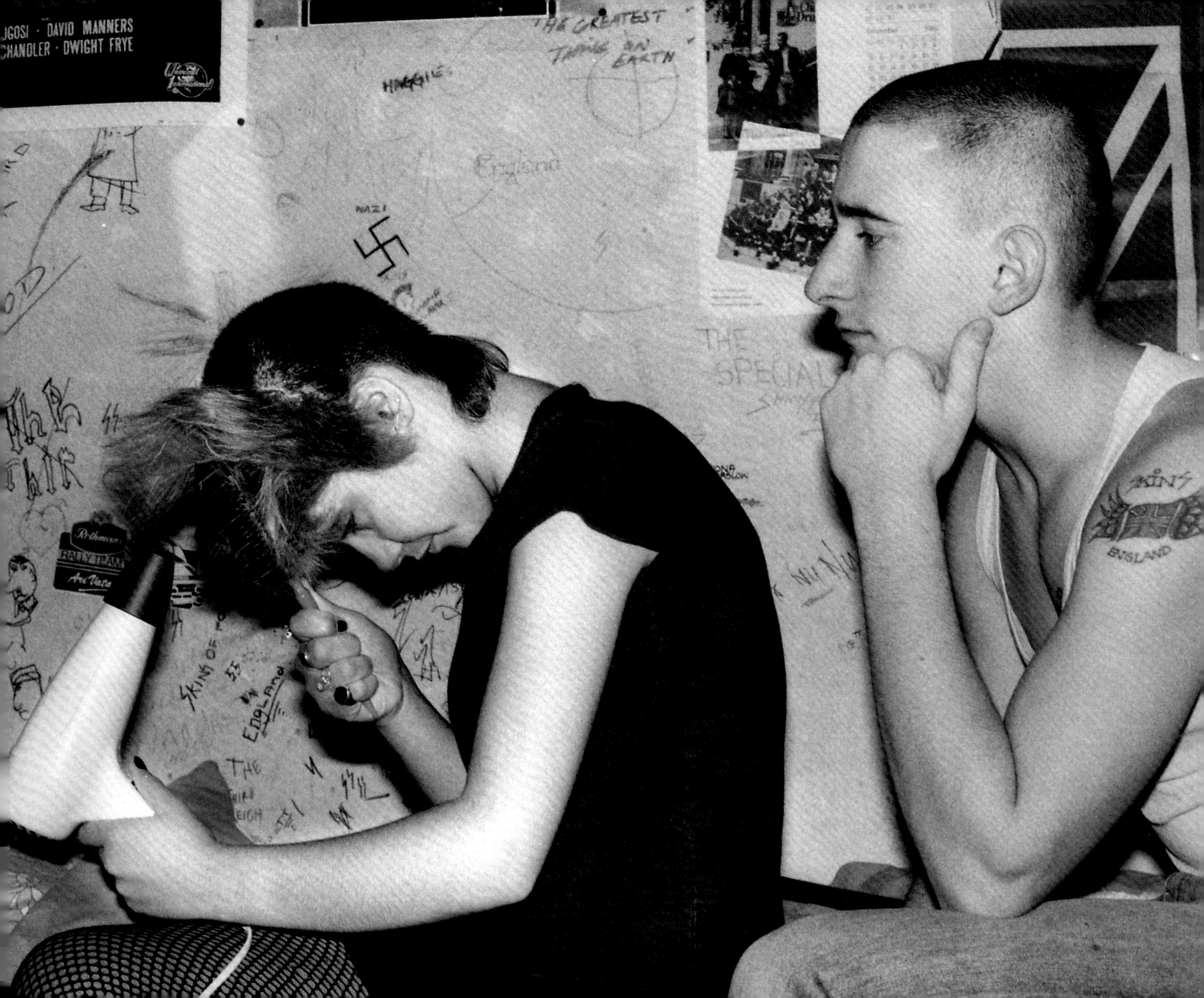
UGOSI · DAVID MANNERS
CHANDLER · DWIGHT FRYE
THE GREATEST THING ON EARTH
England
NAZI
THE SPECIAL
Rothmans
SKINS
ENGLAND

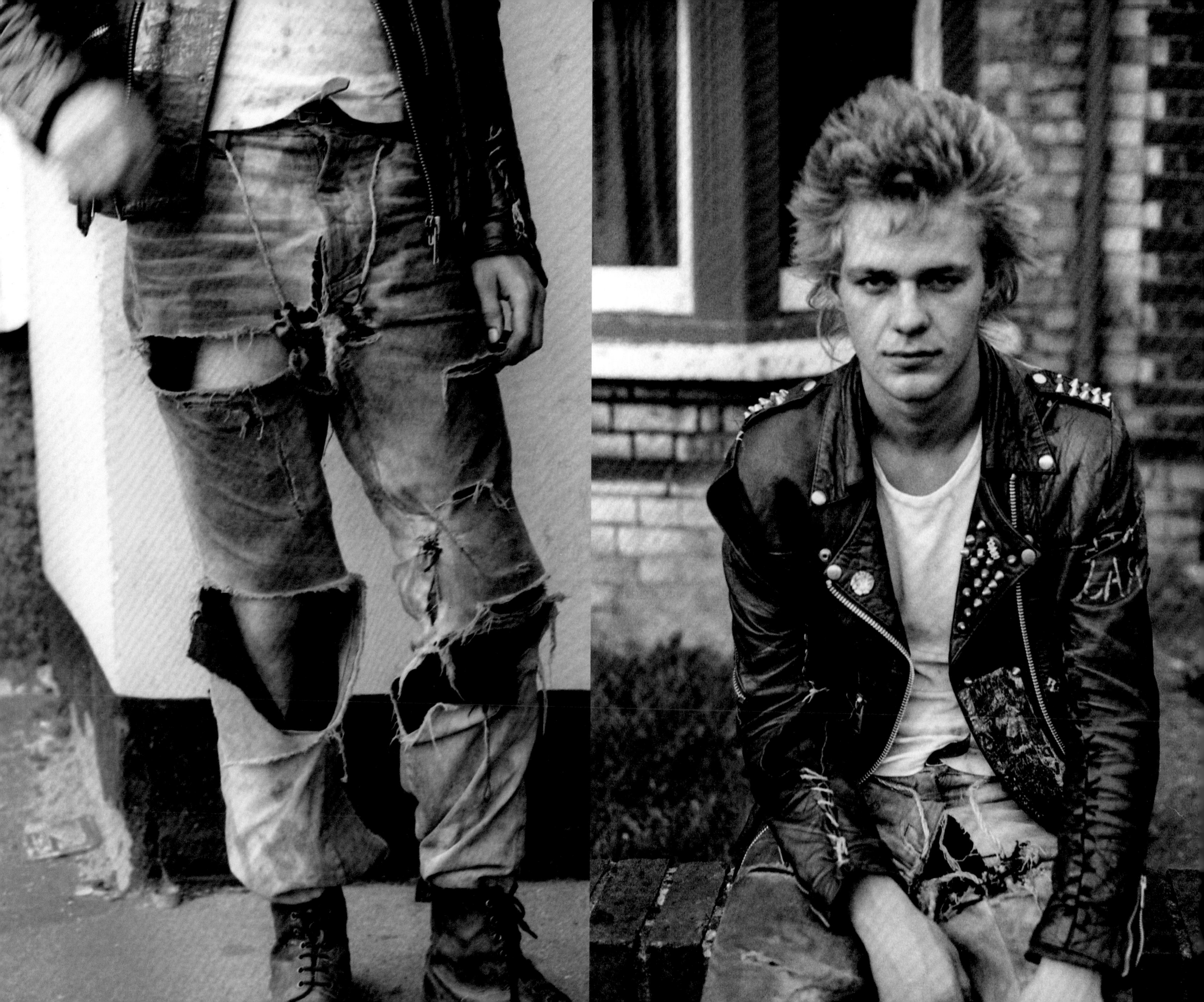

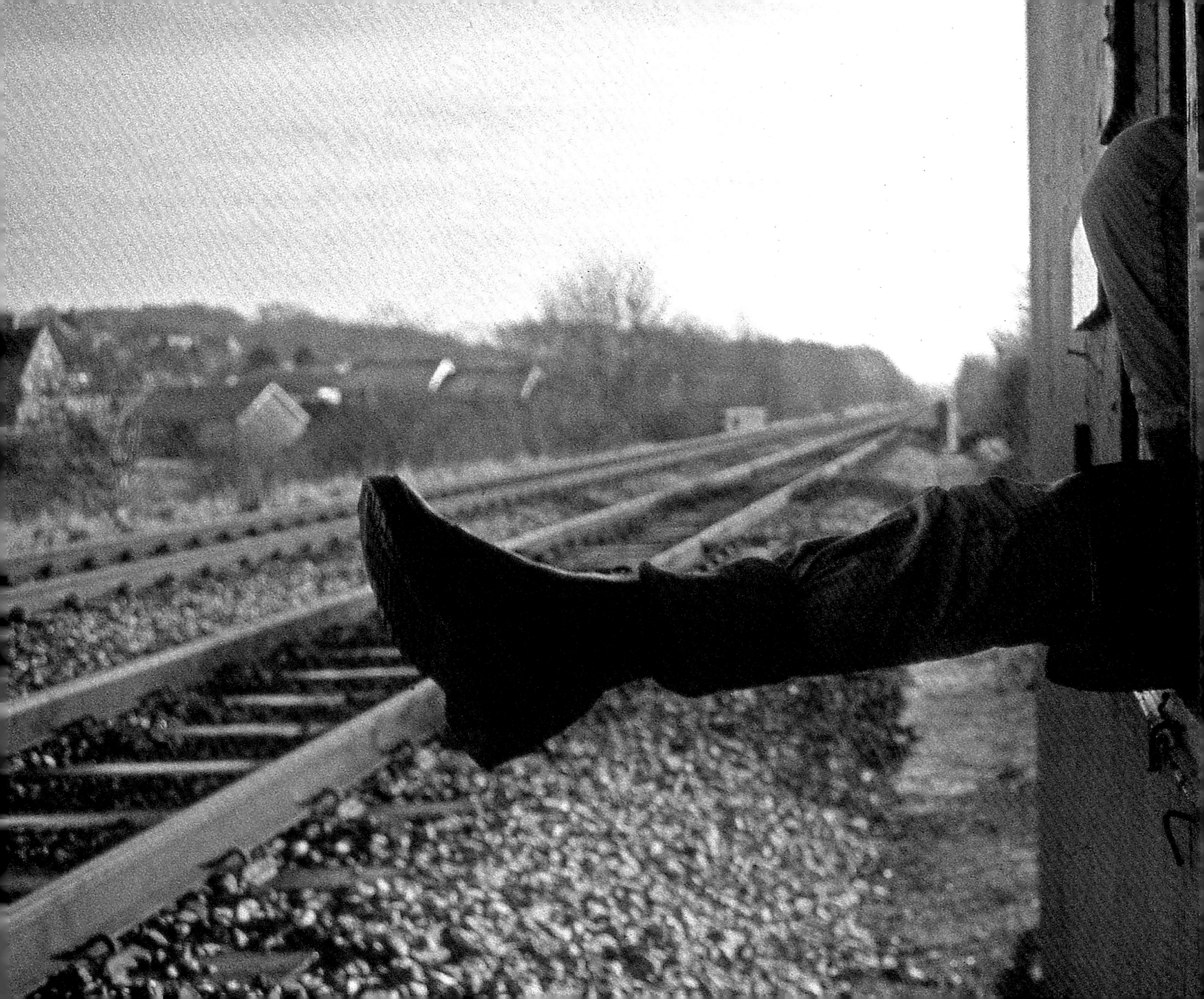

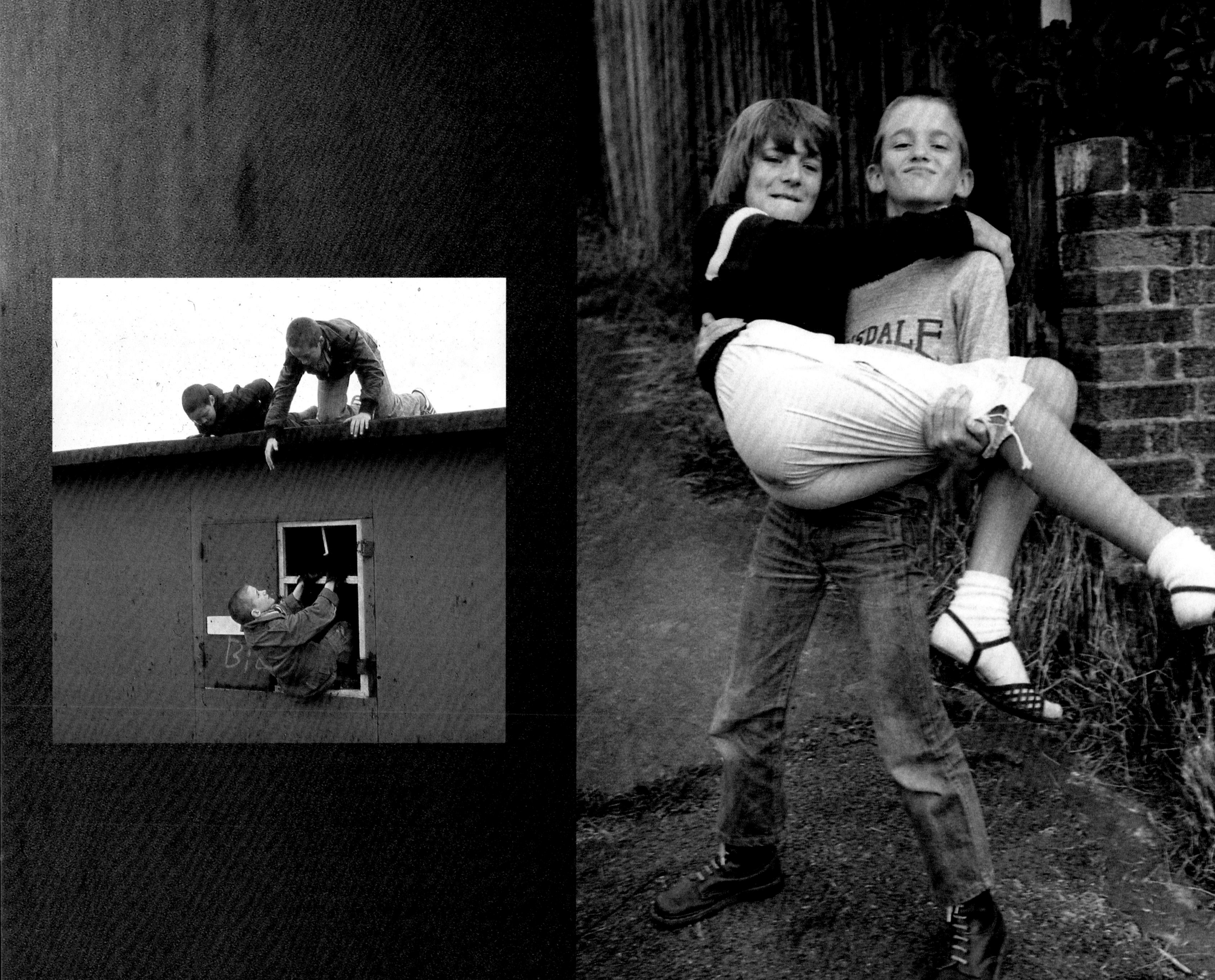
SDALE

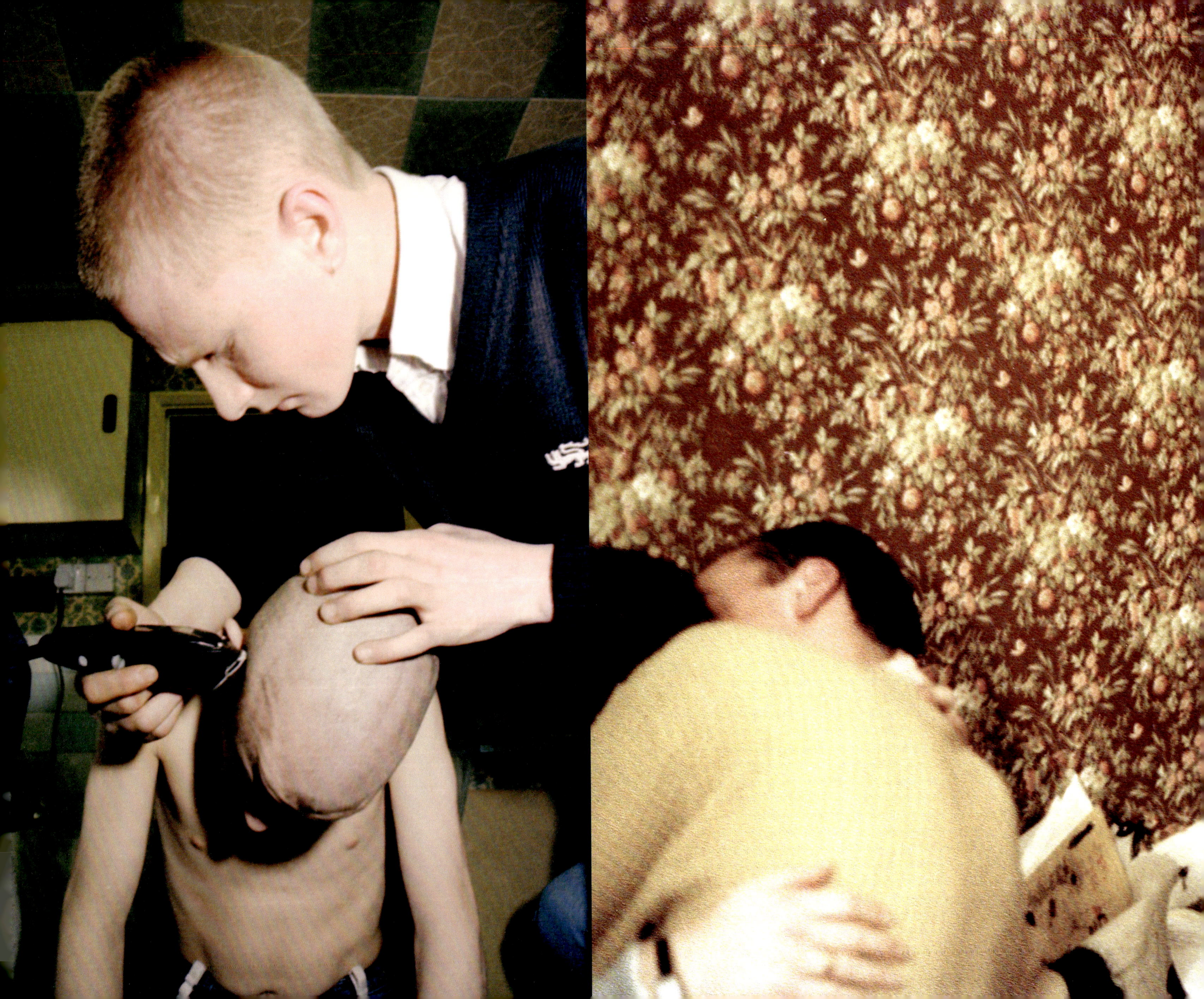

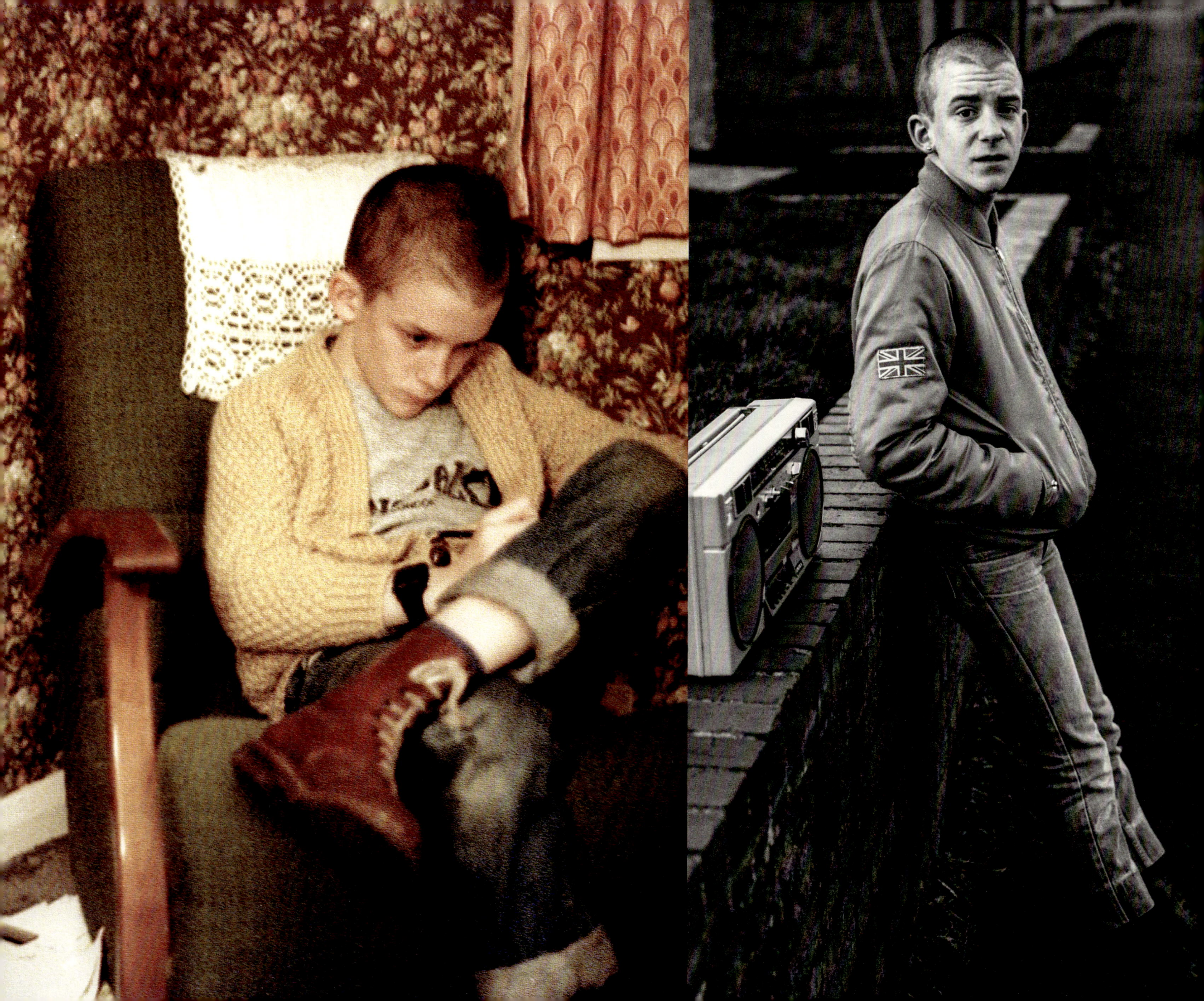

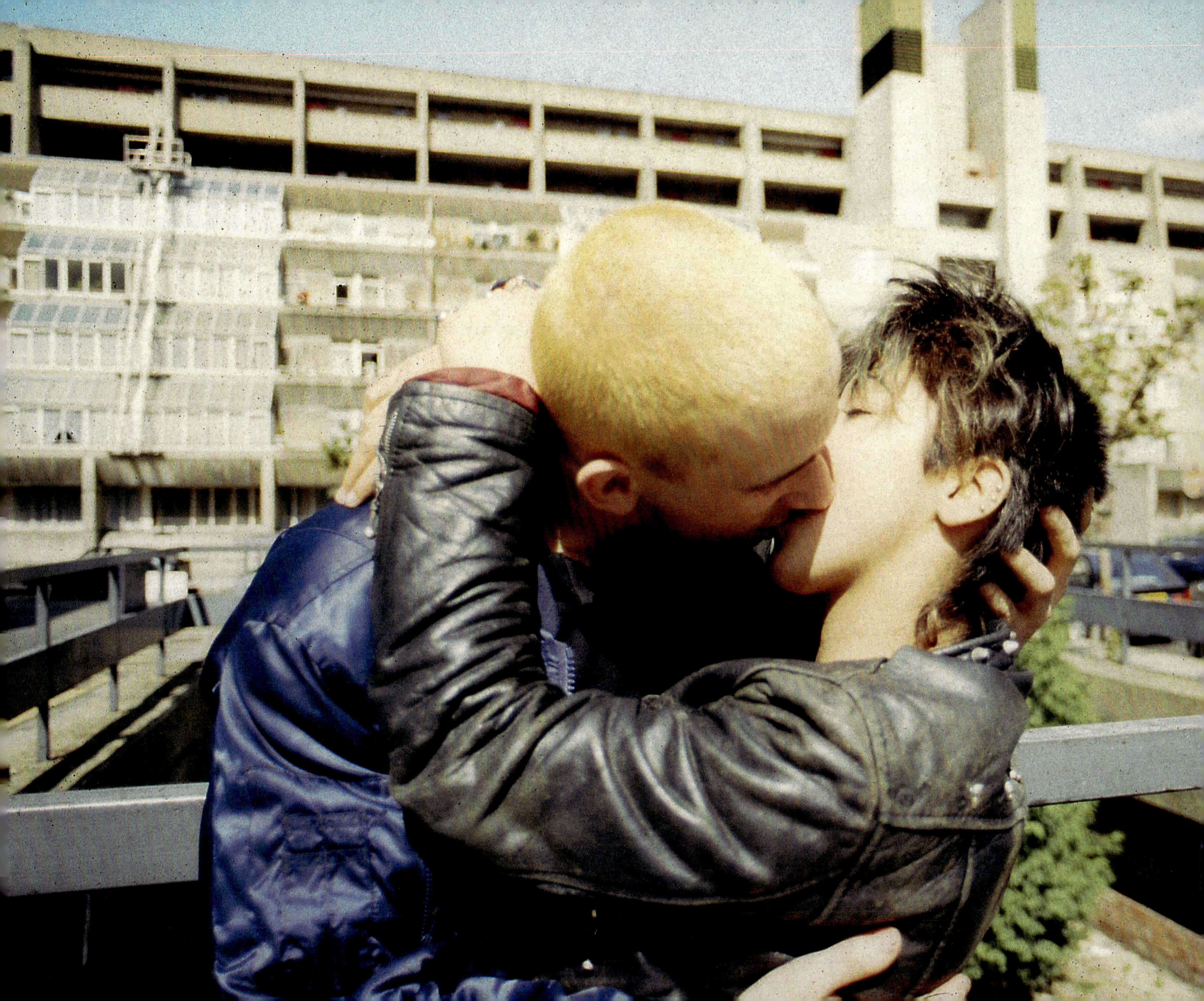

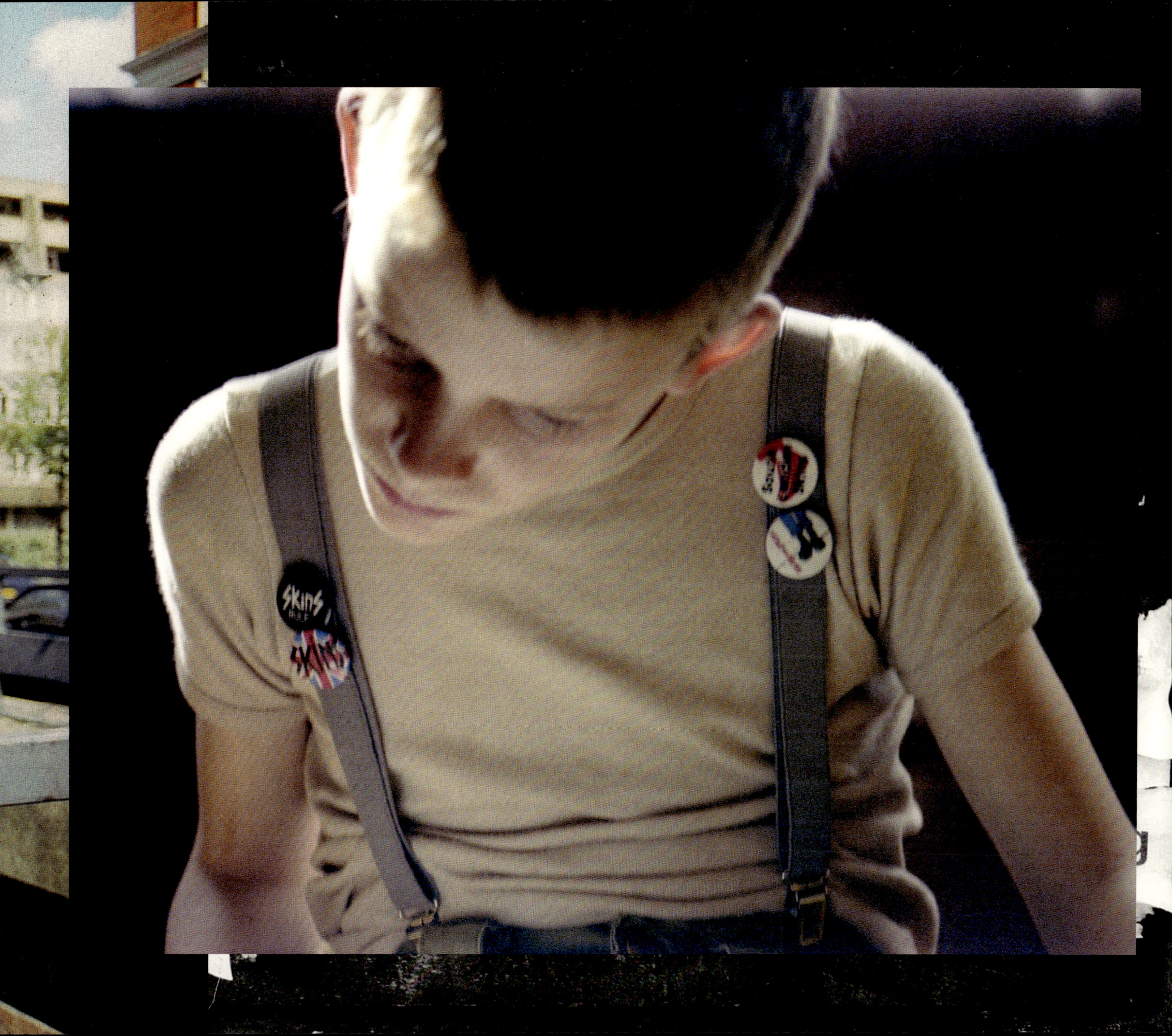
Skins

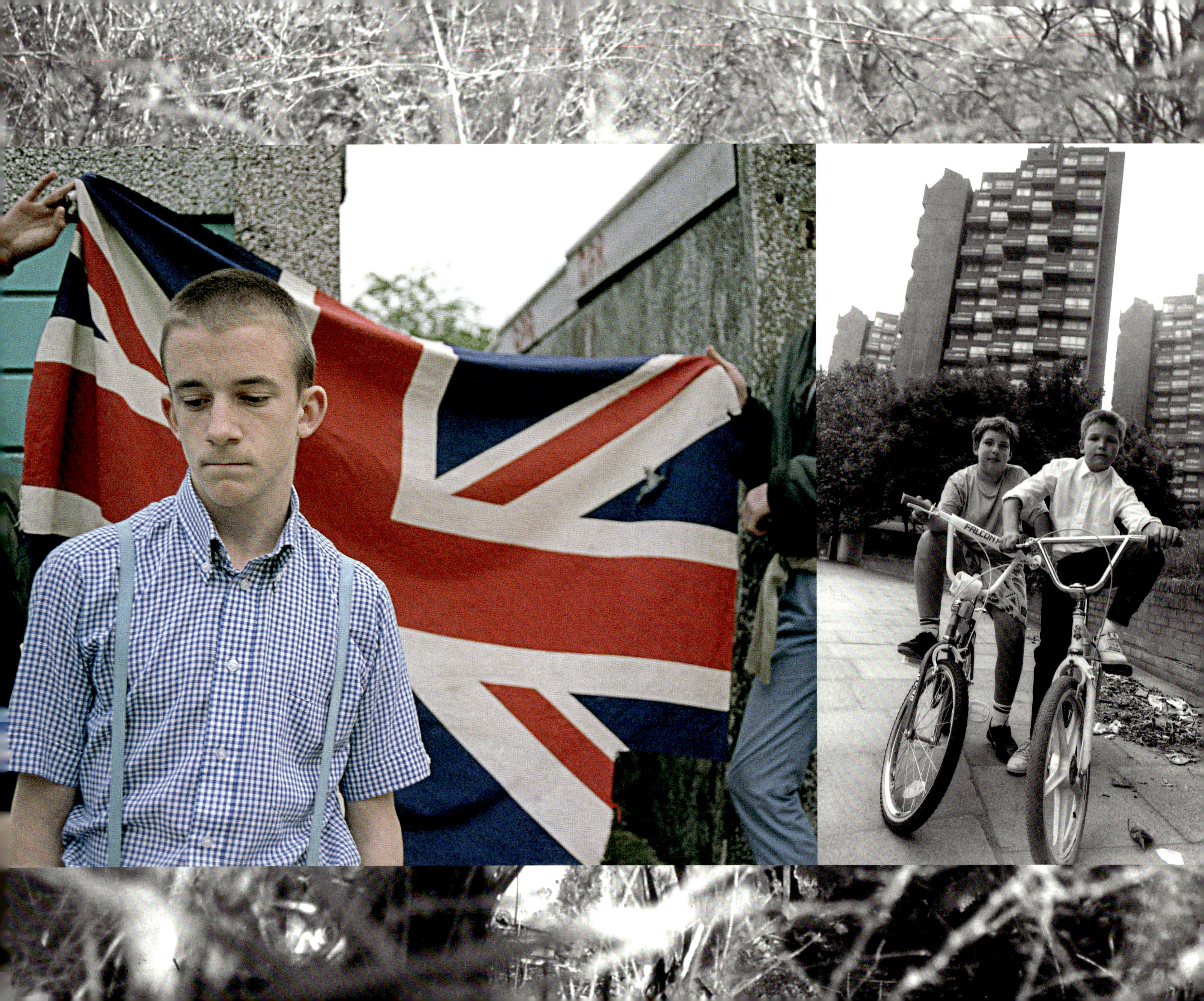
FALCON

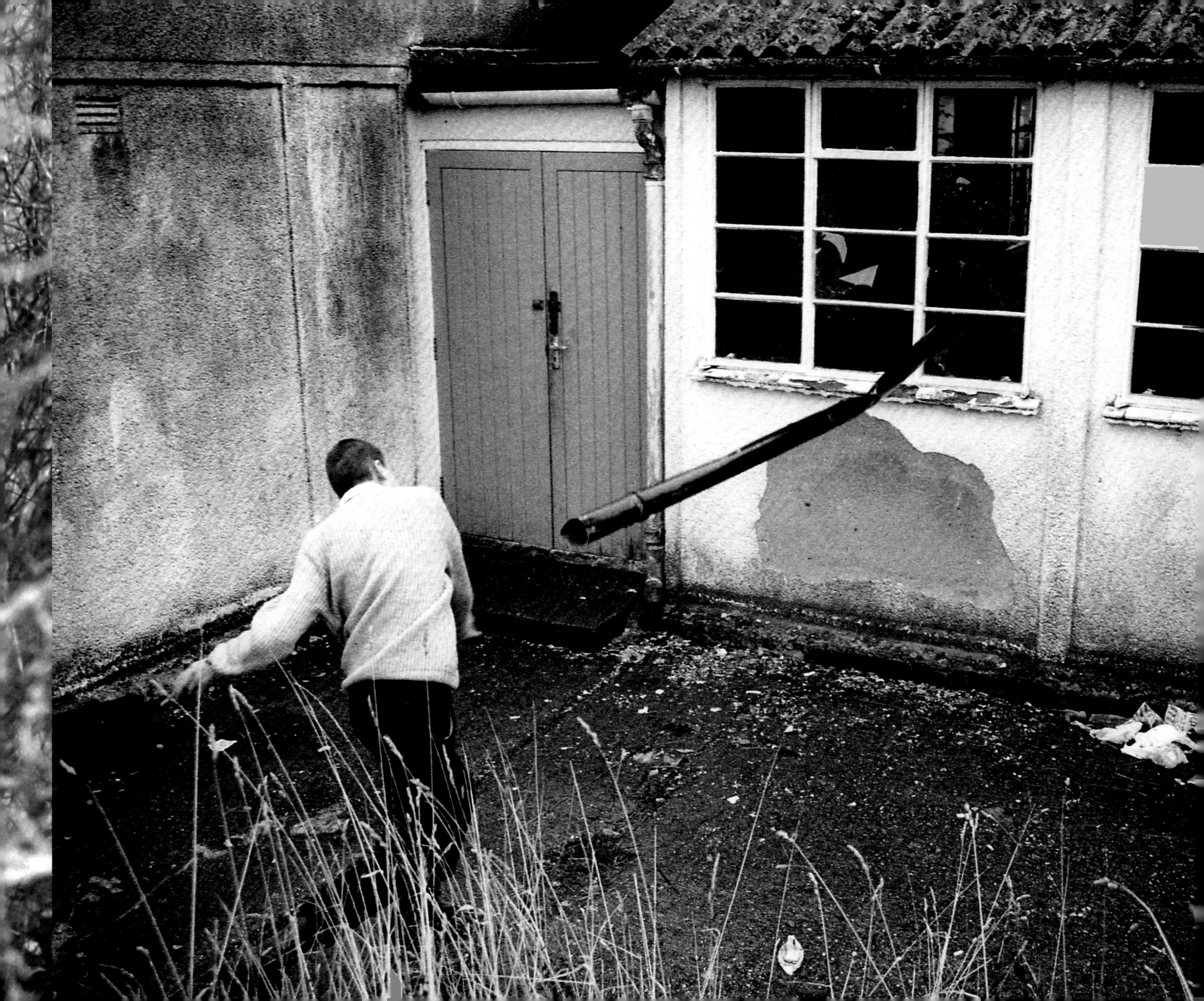

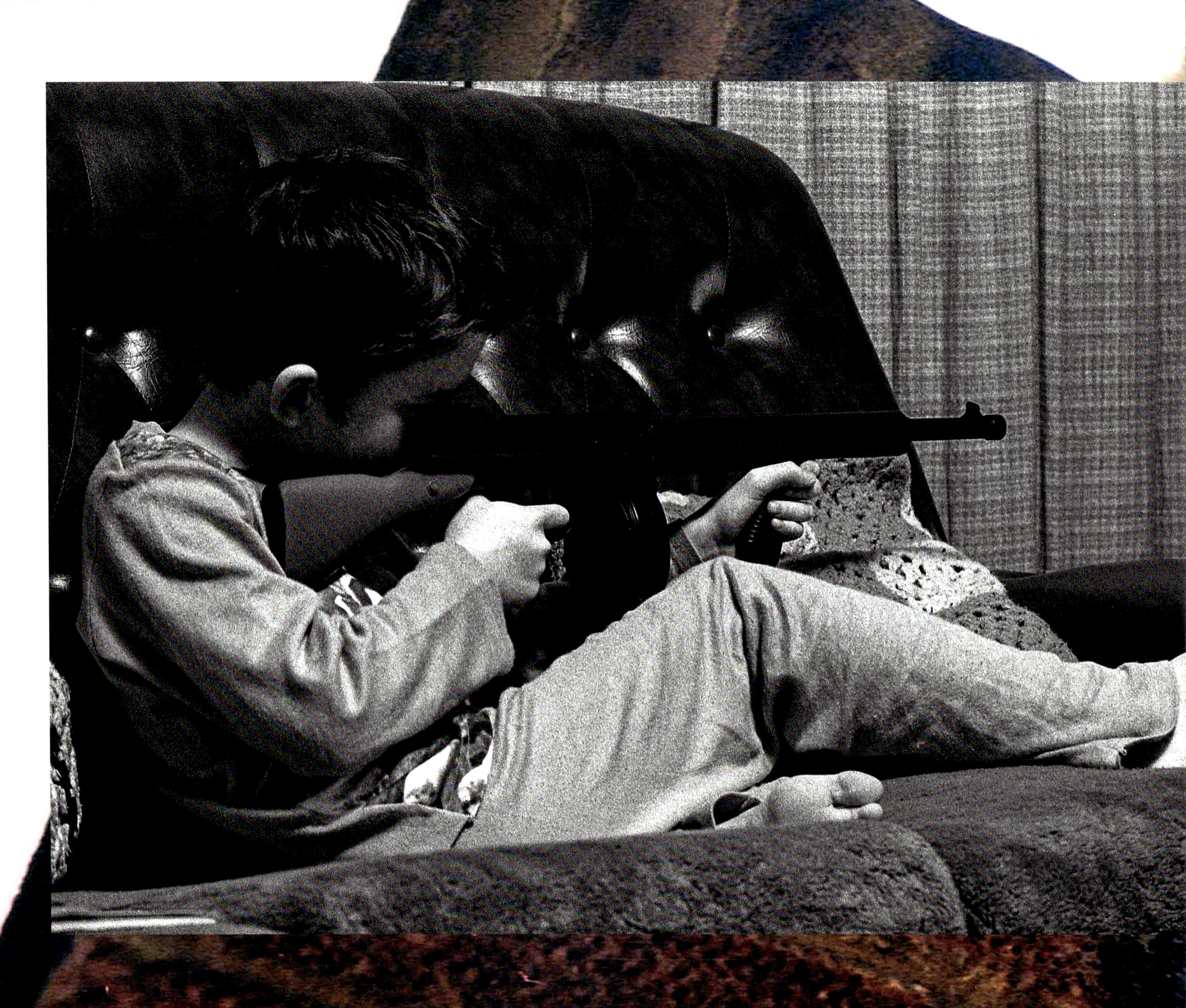

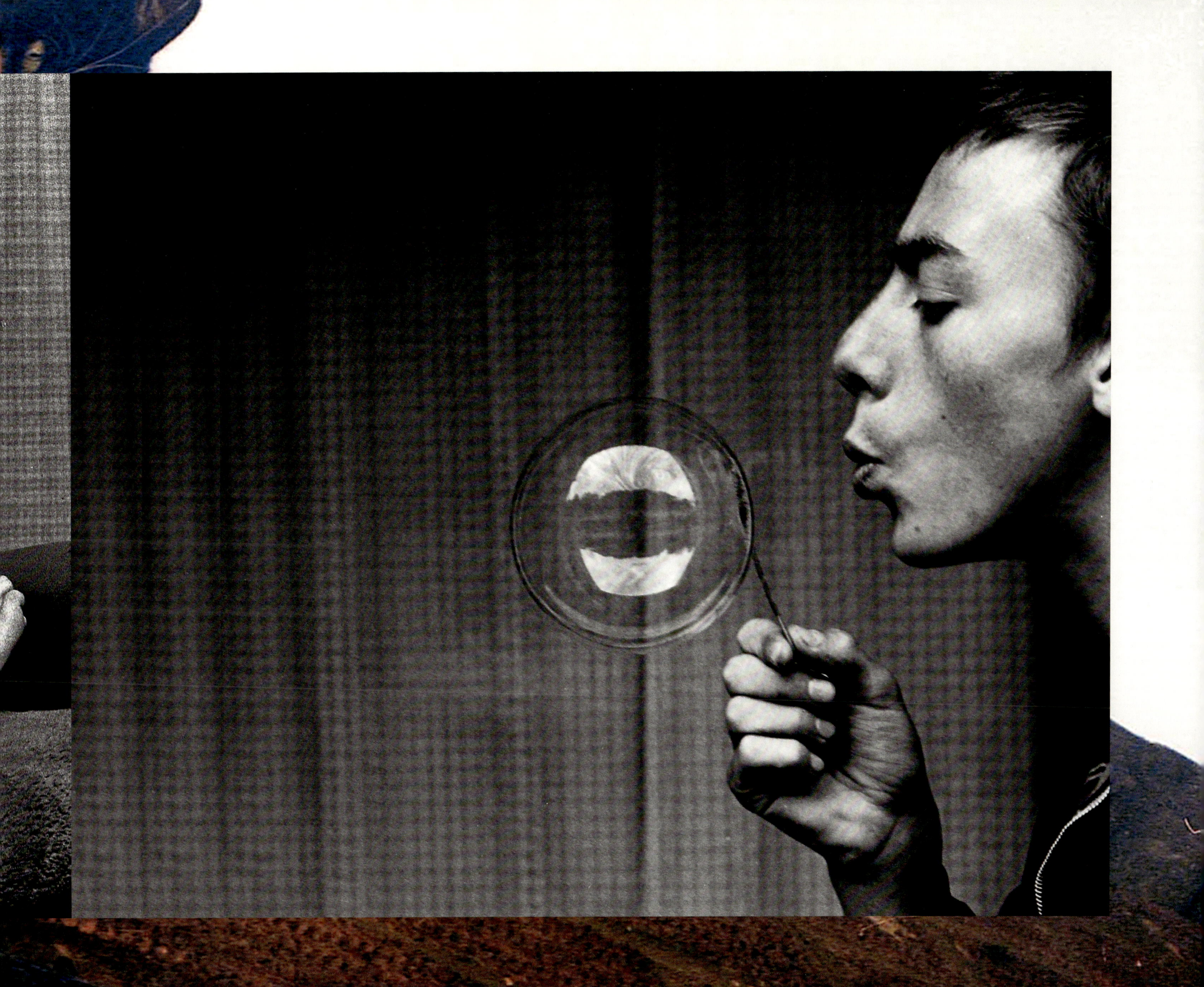

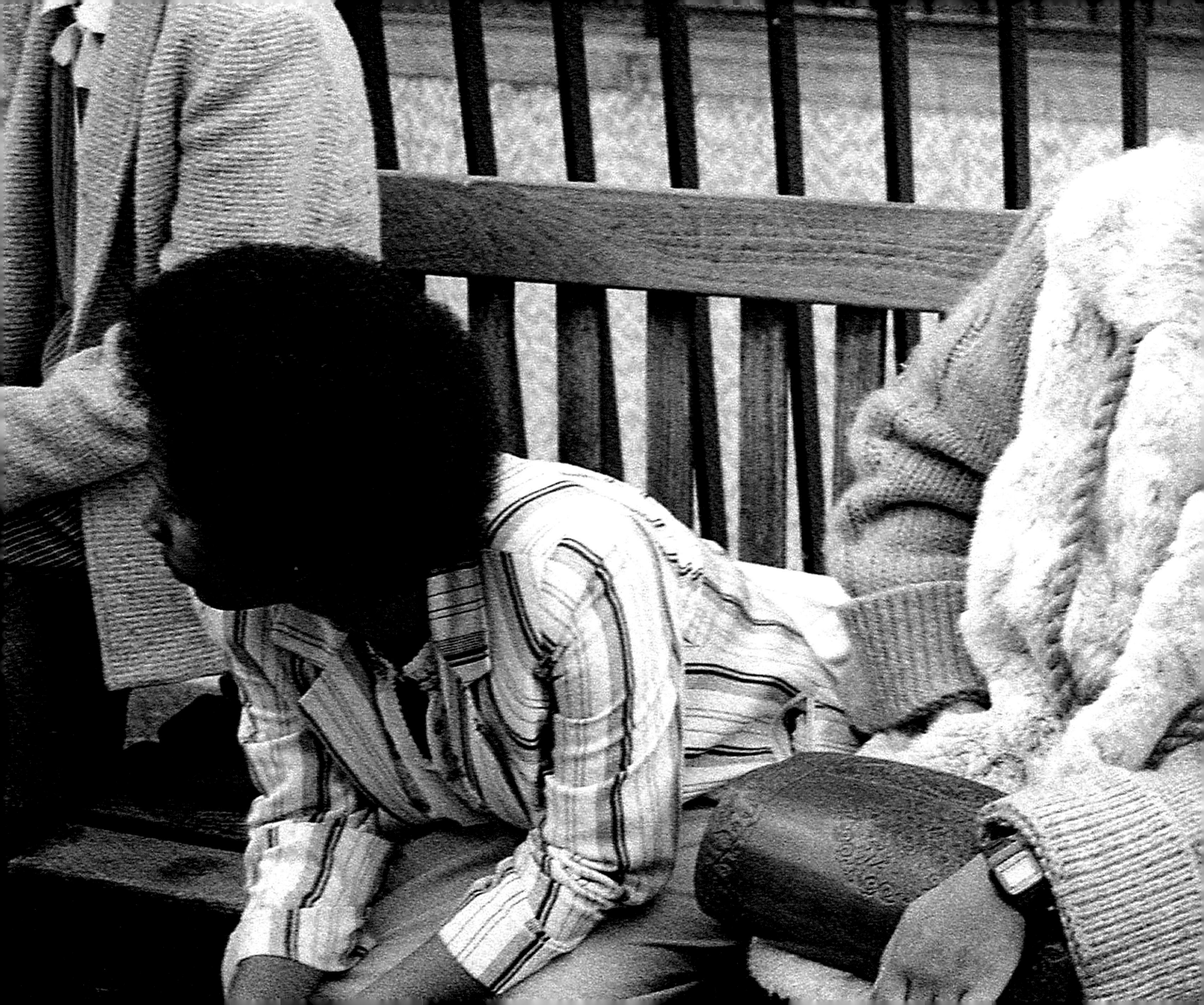

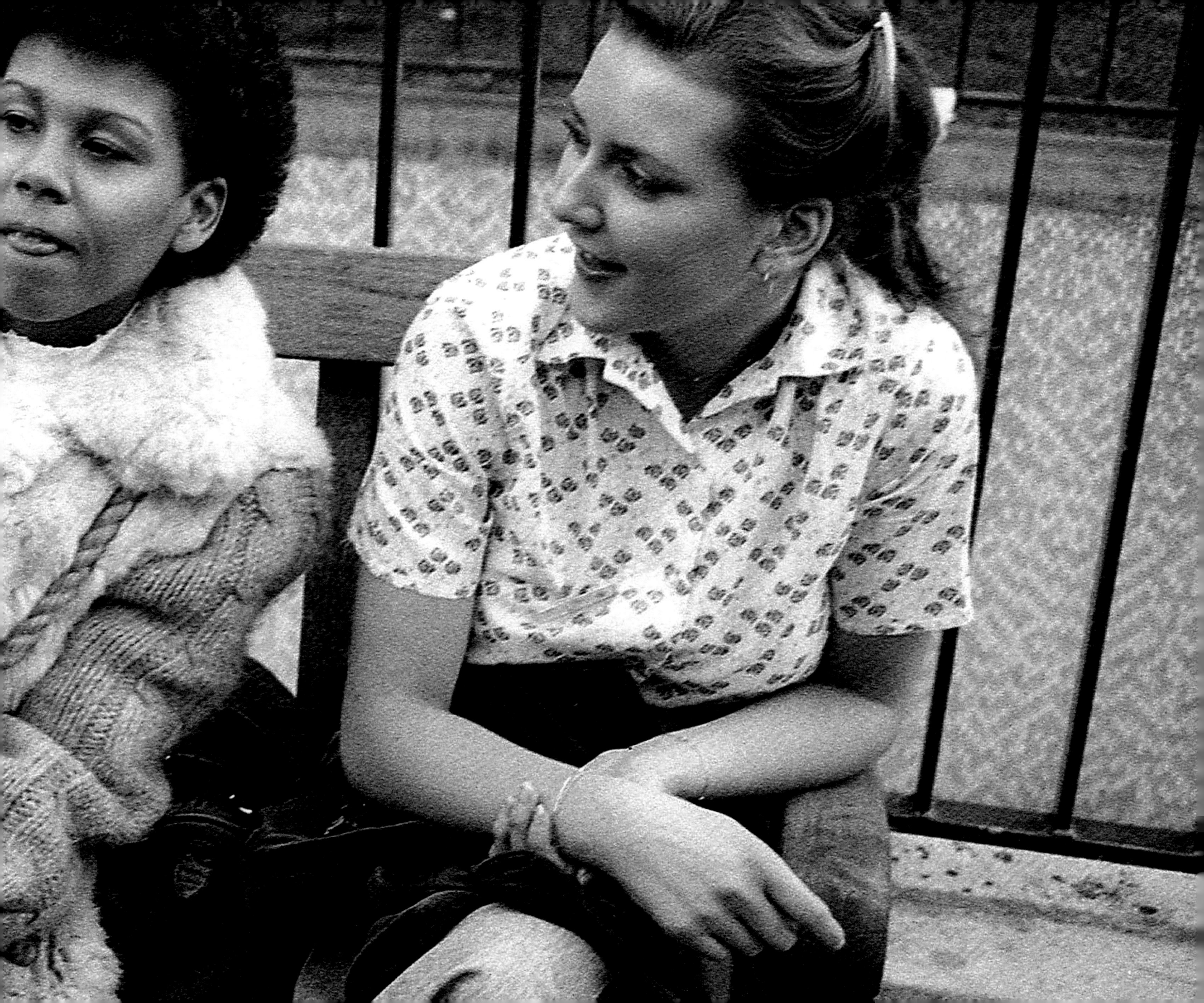

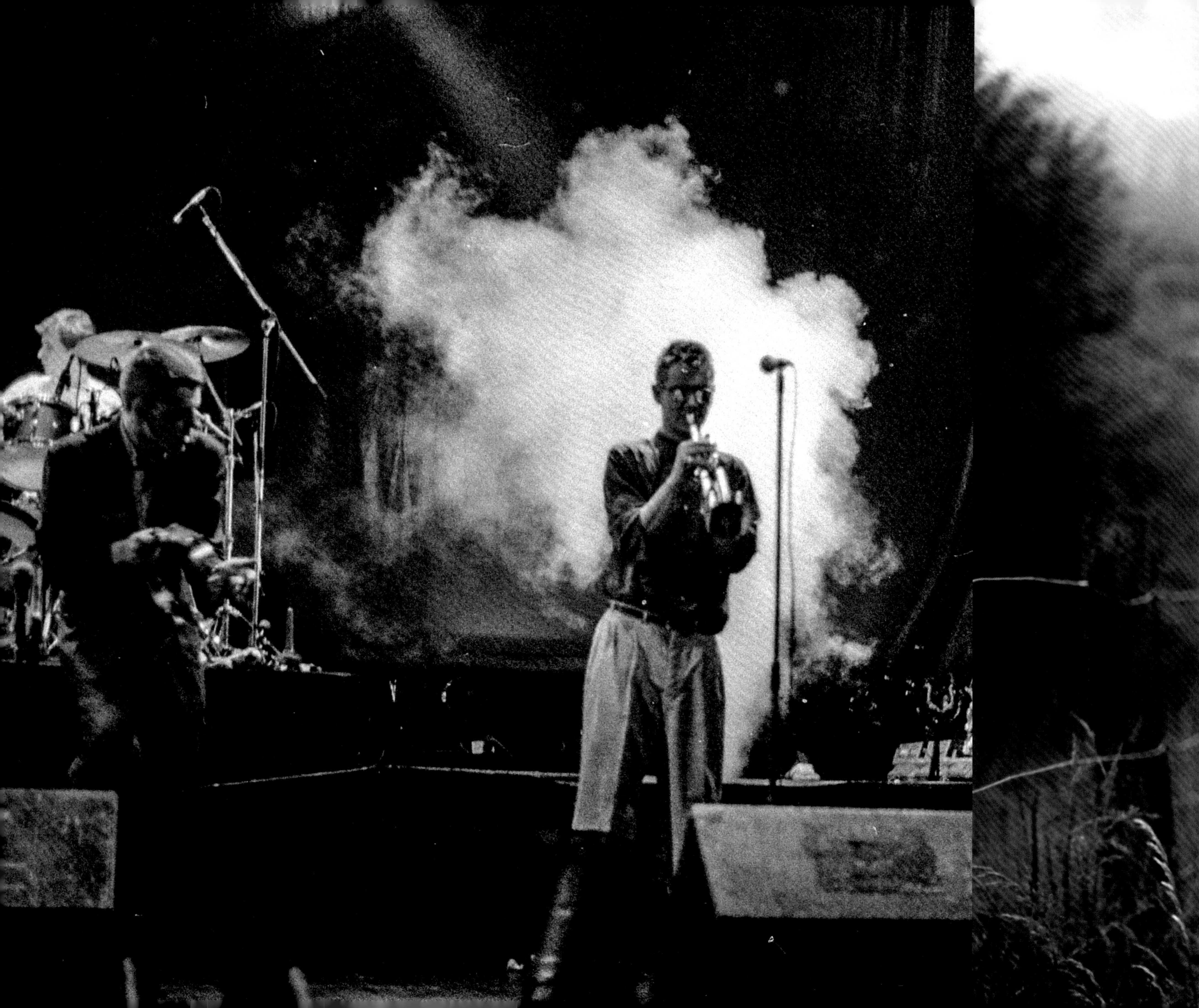

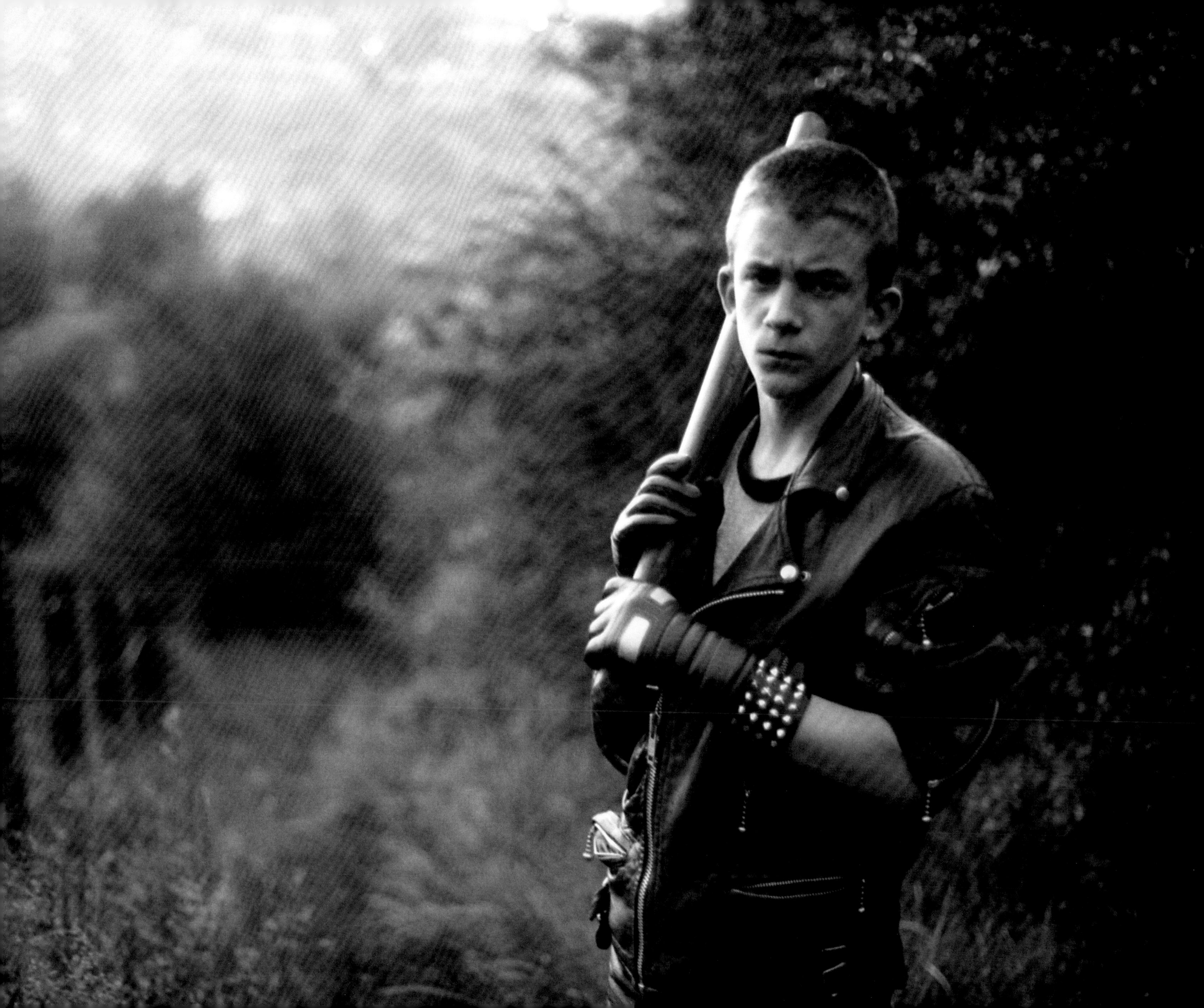

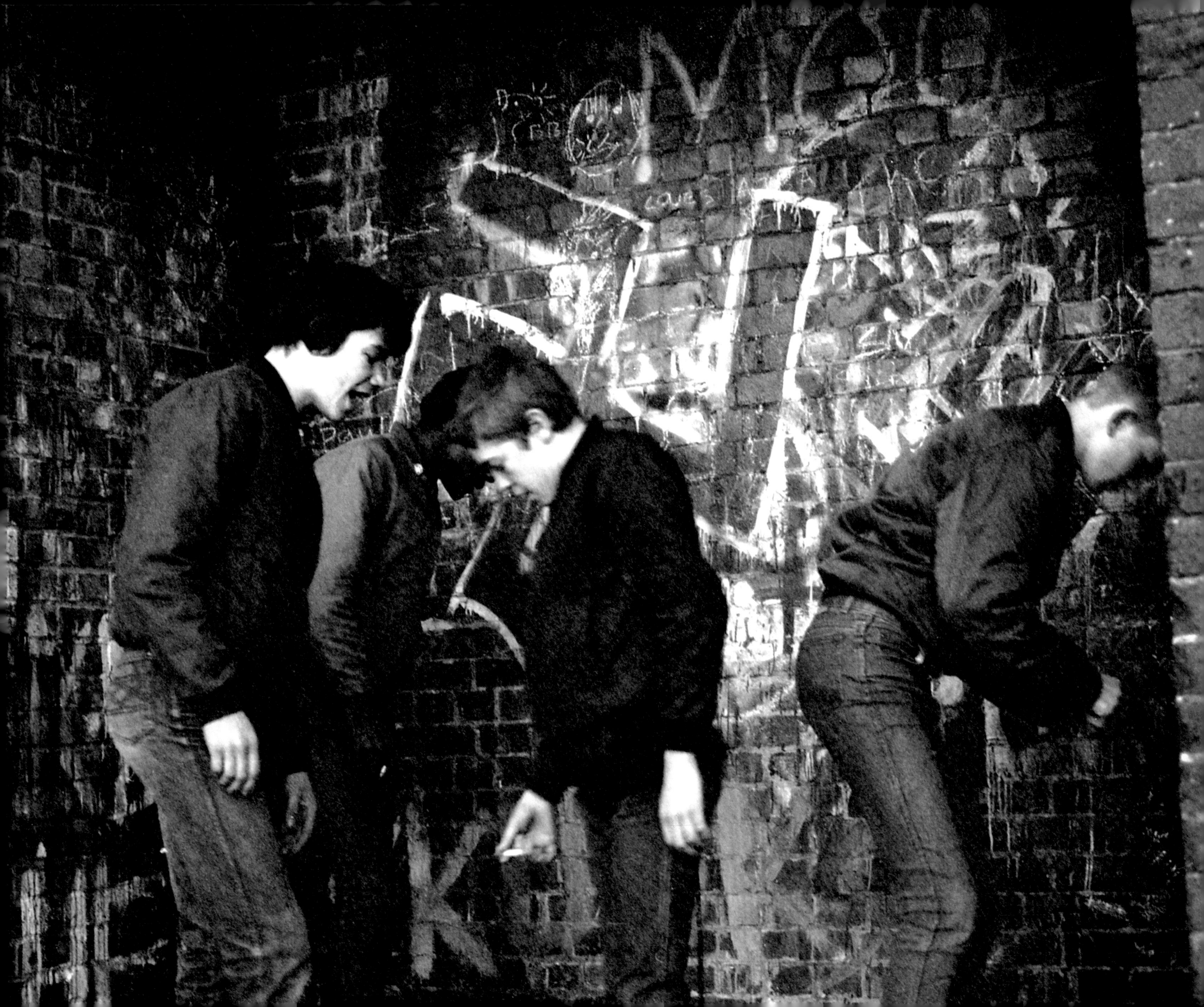

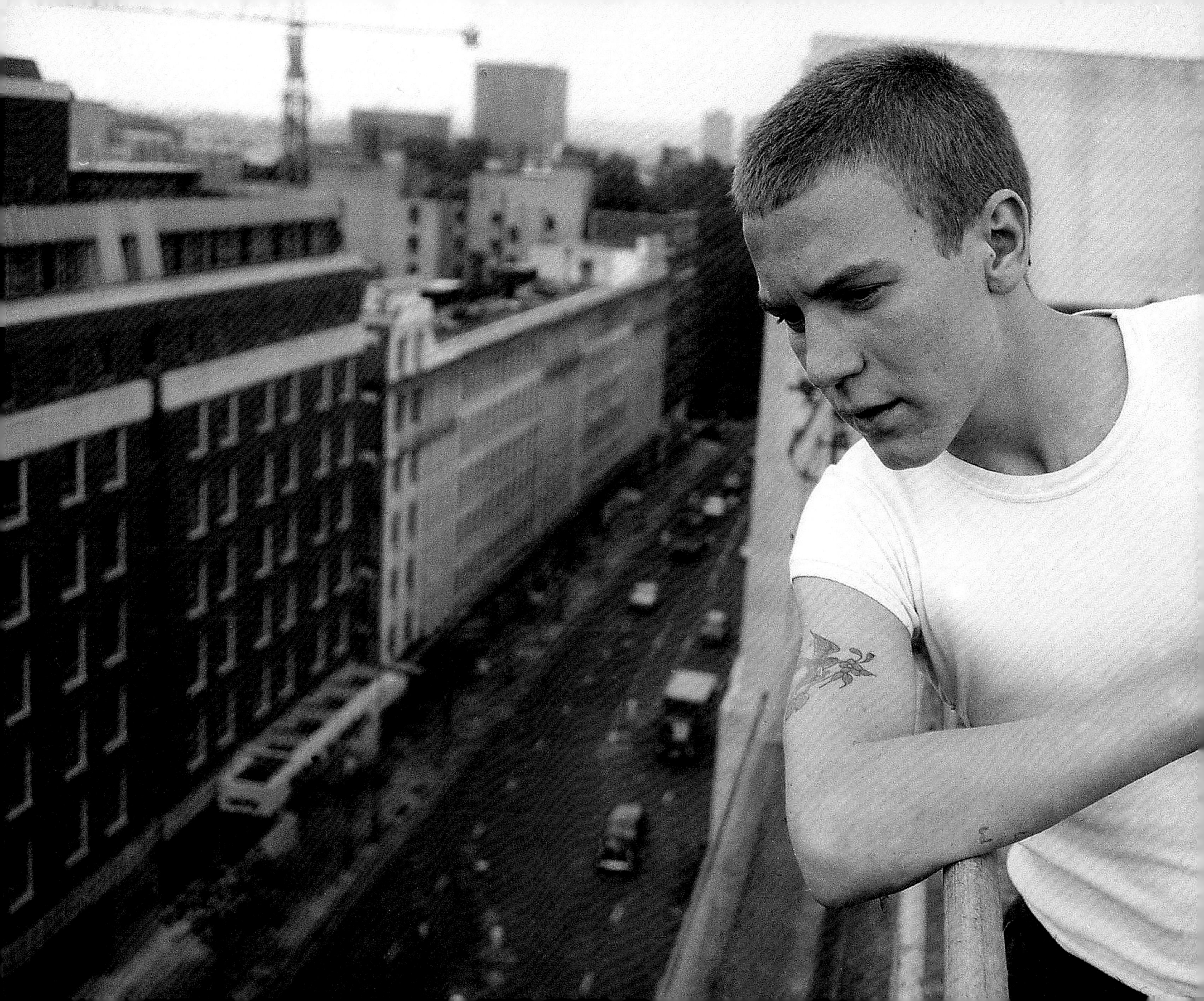

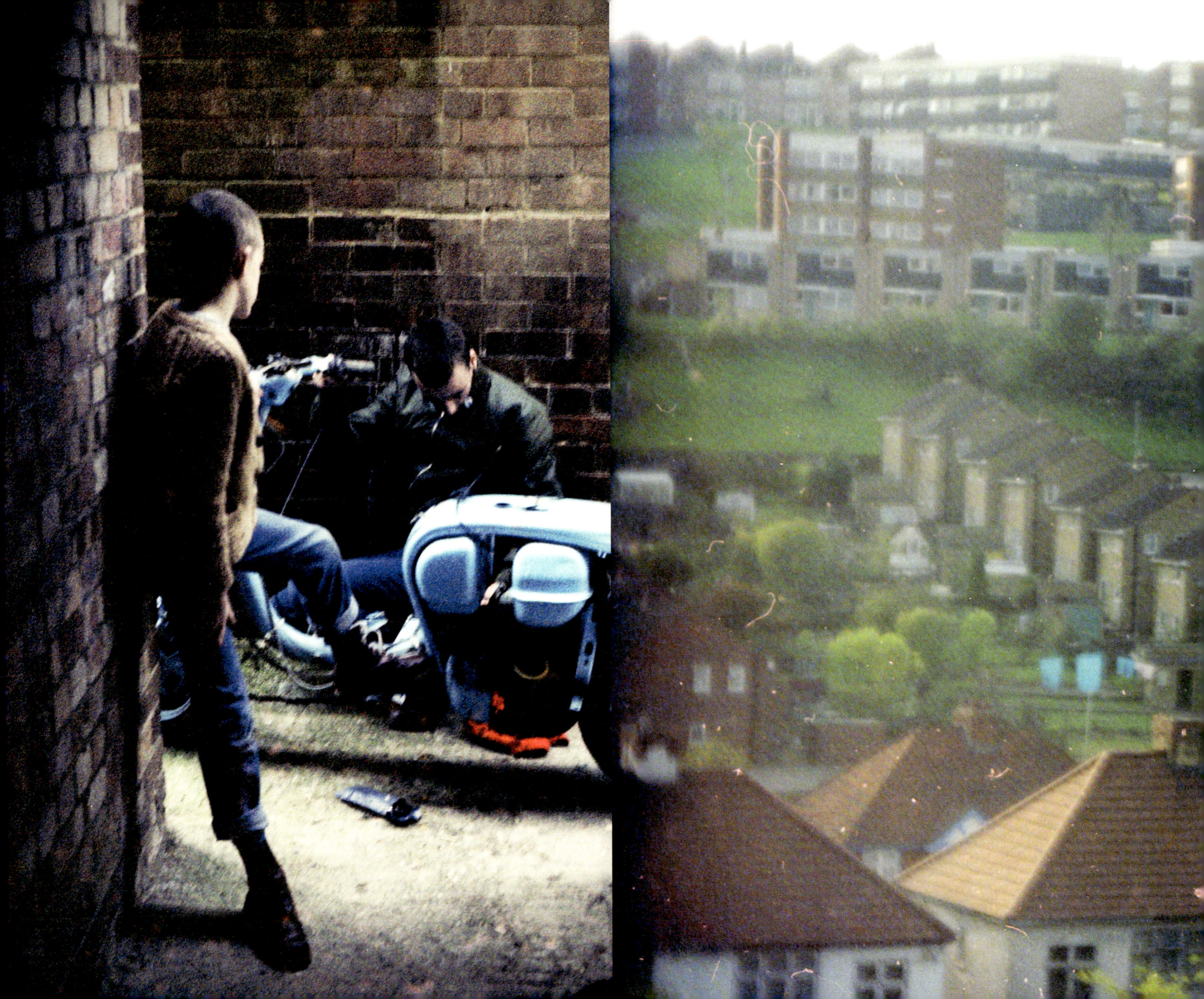

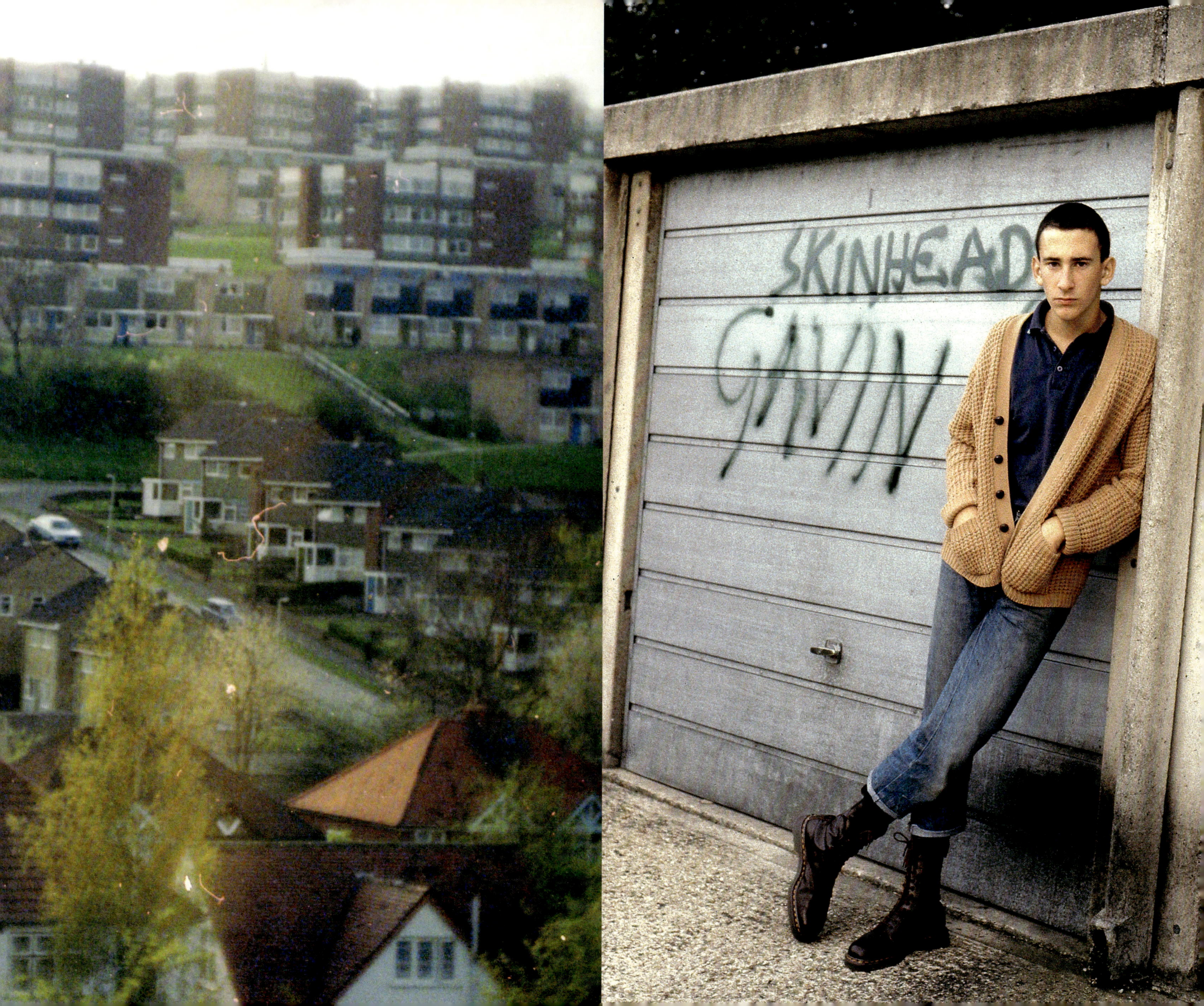
SKINHEAD
GAVIN

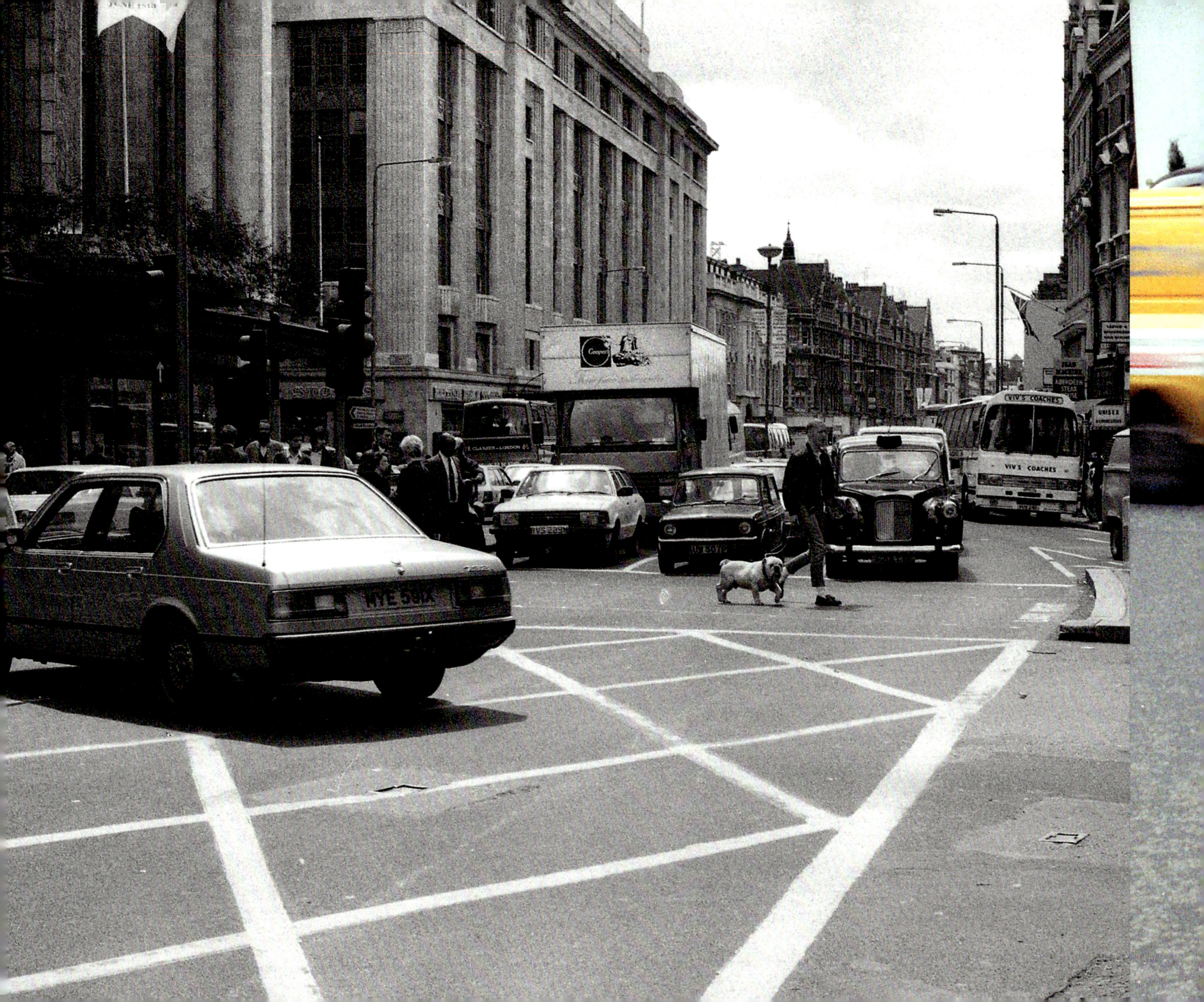
VIV'S COACHES
VIV'S COACHES
UNISEX
WYE 581X

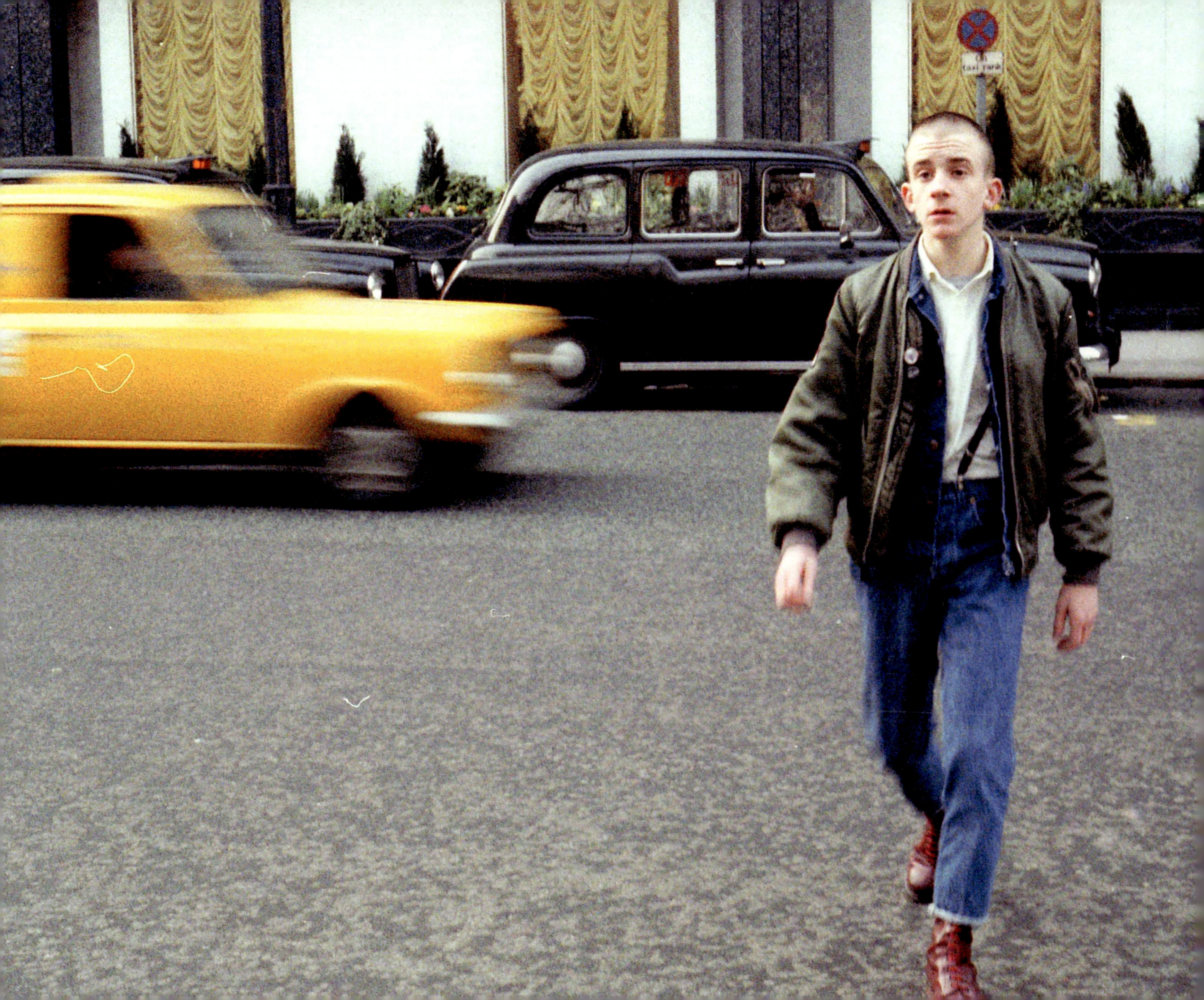

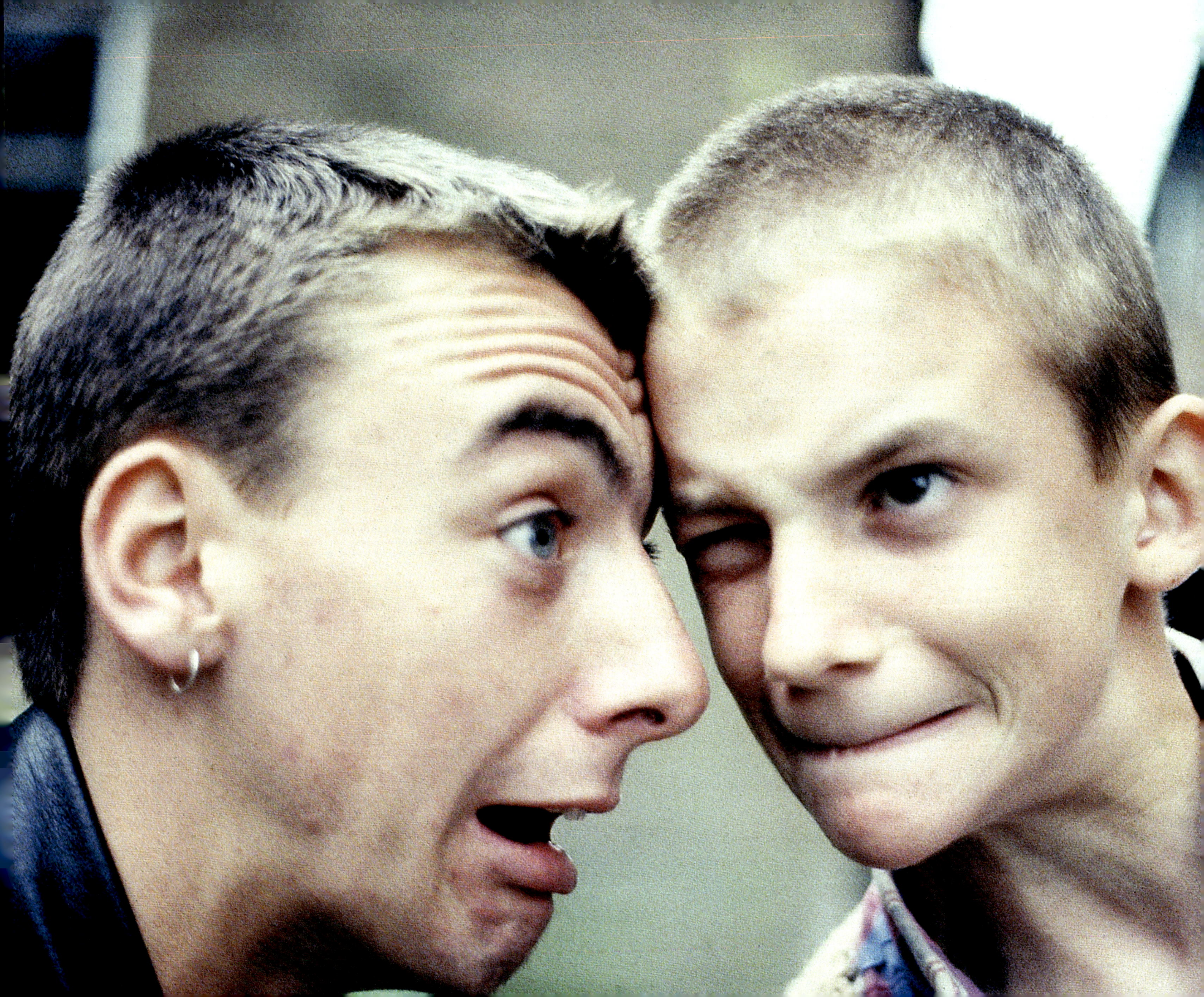

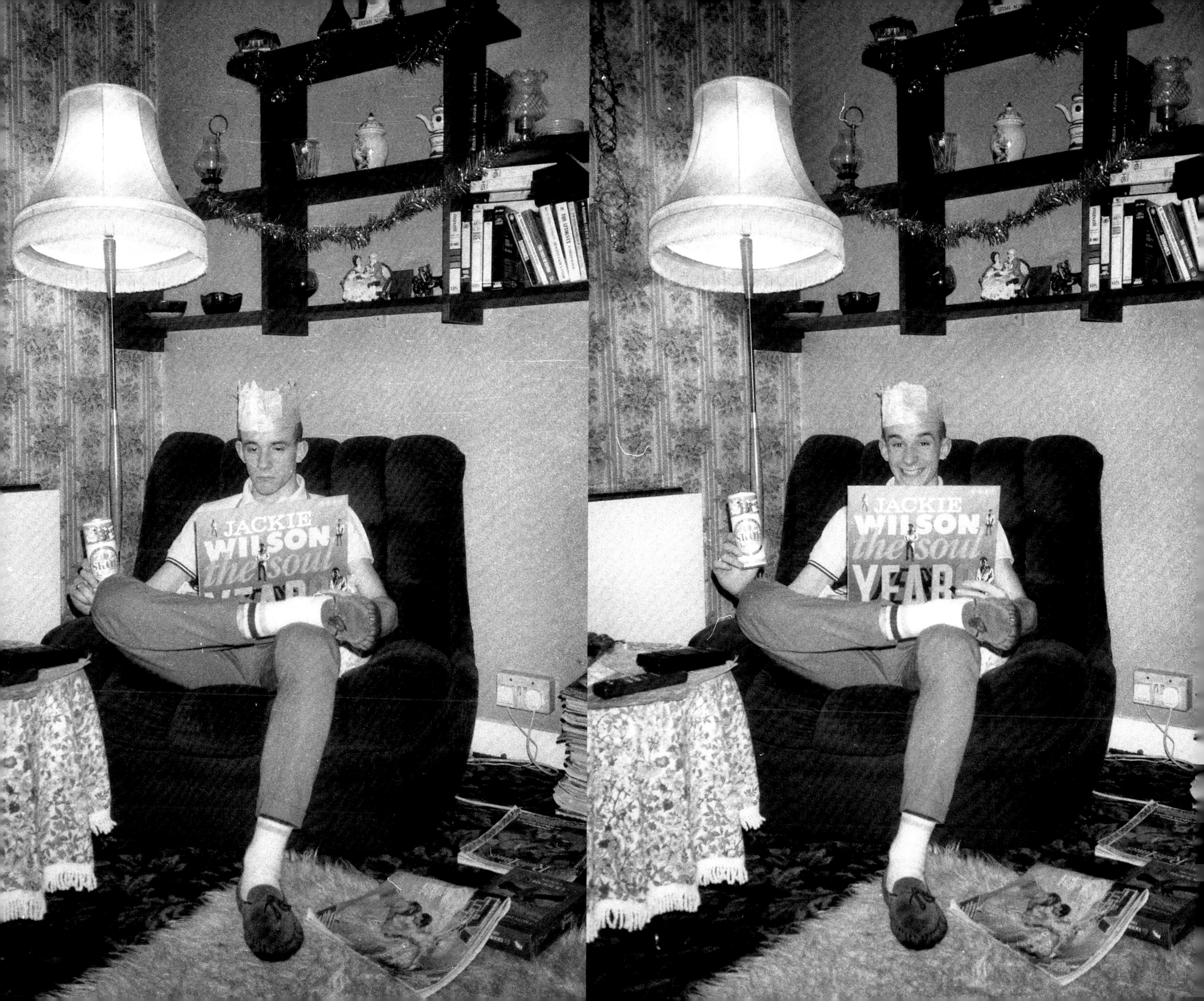
JACKIE
WILSON
the soul
YEAR

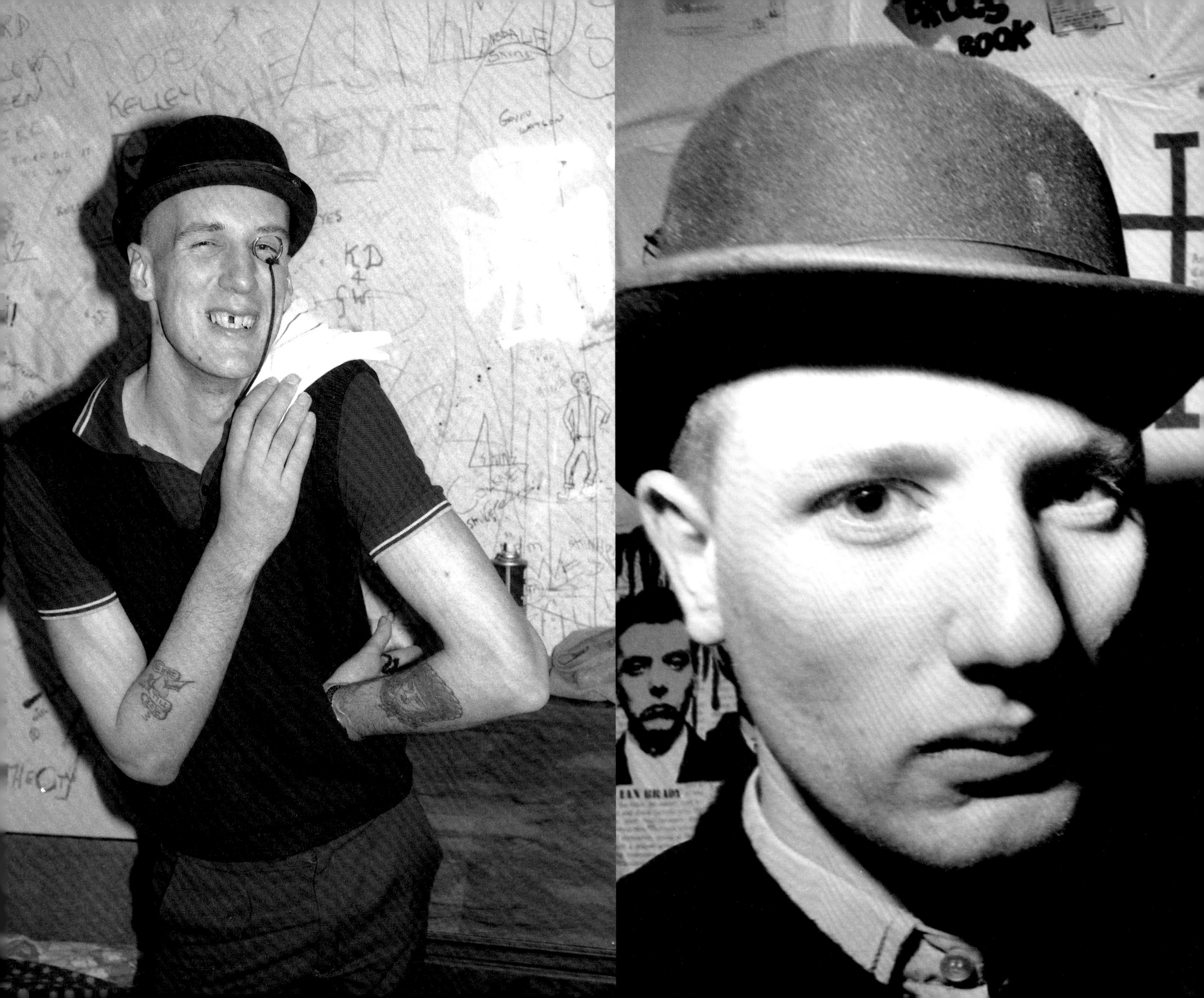

KELLEY
IAN BRADY

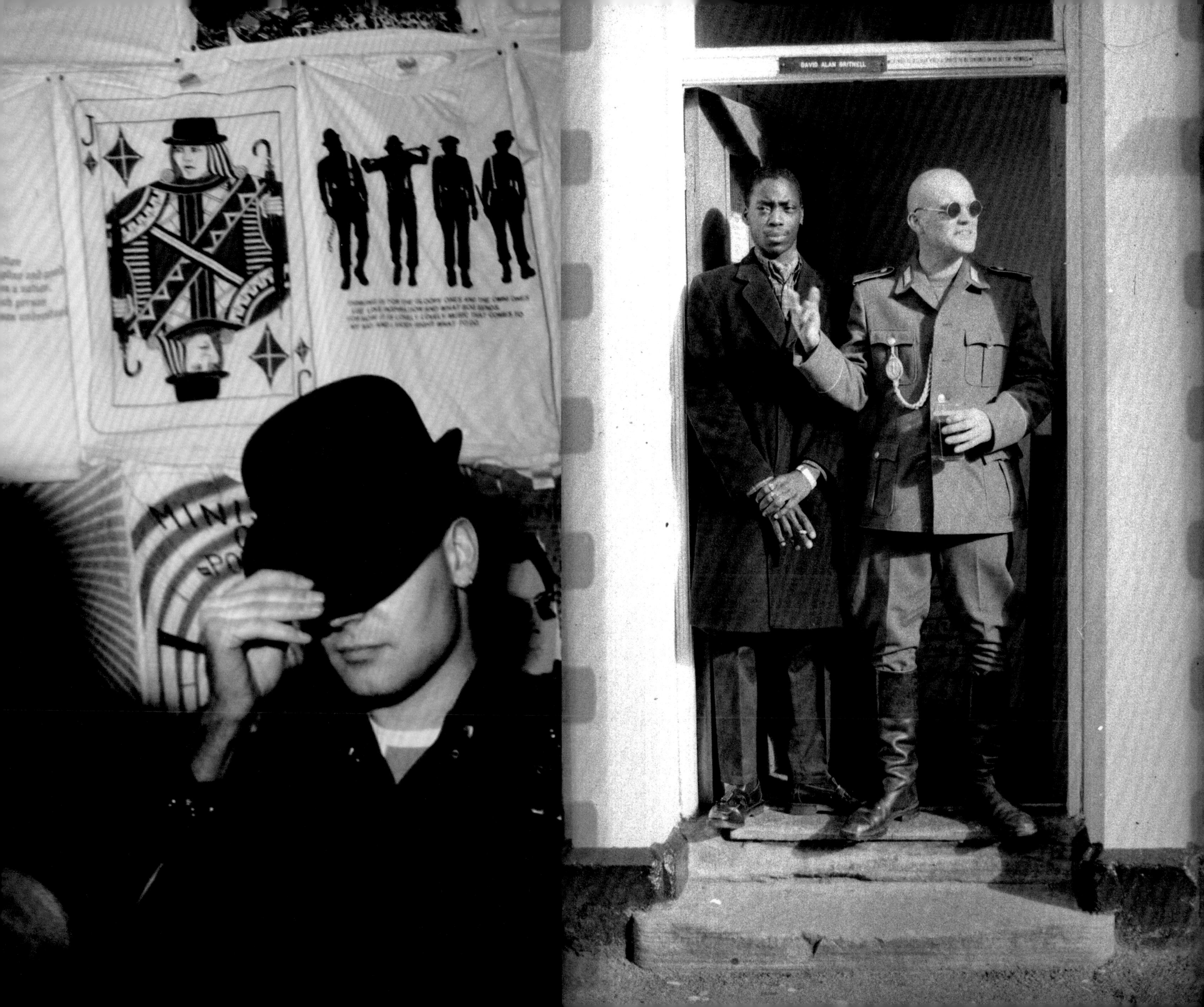
DAVID ALAN BRITNELL

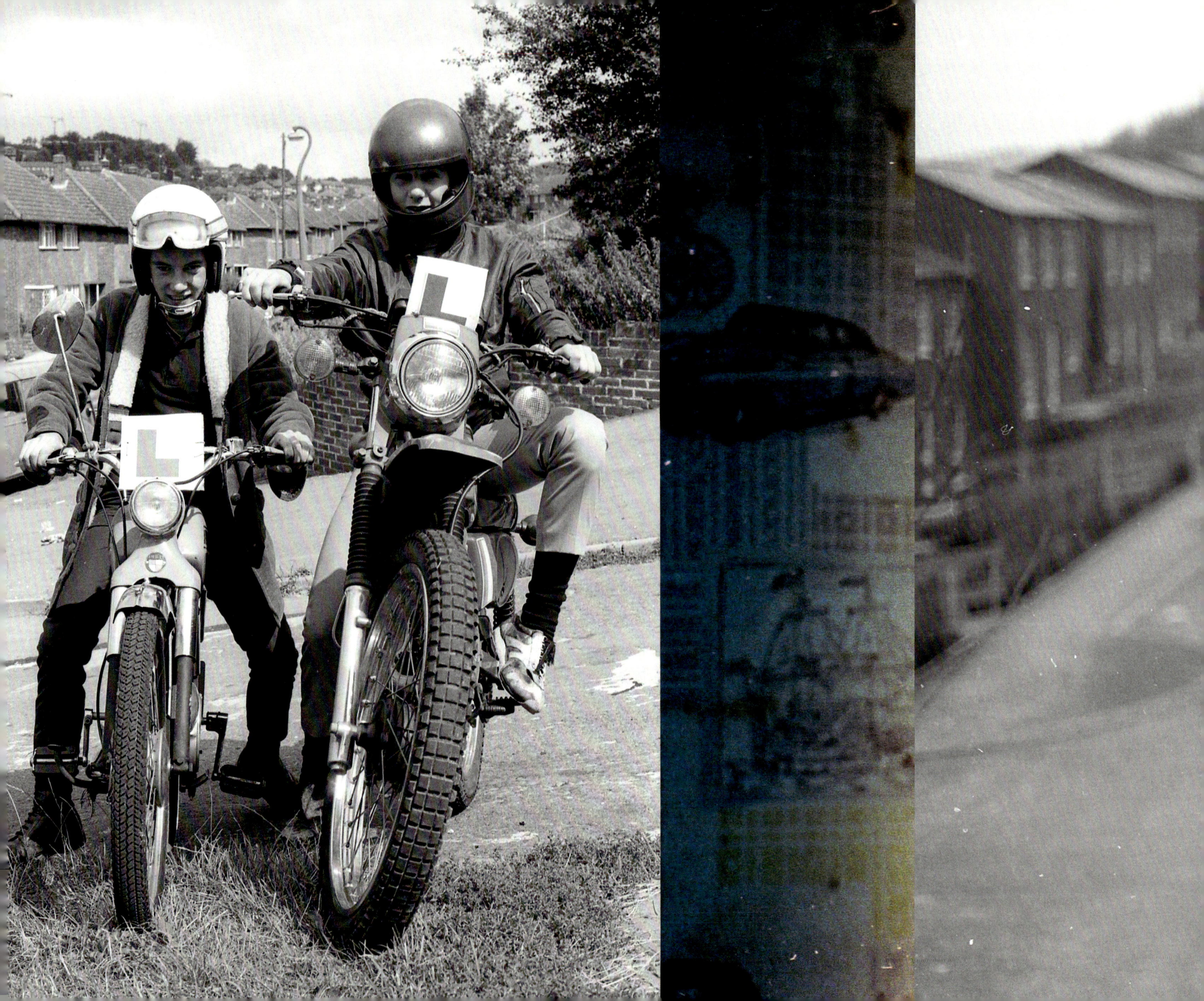

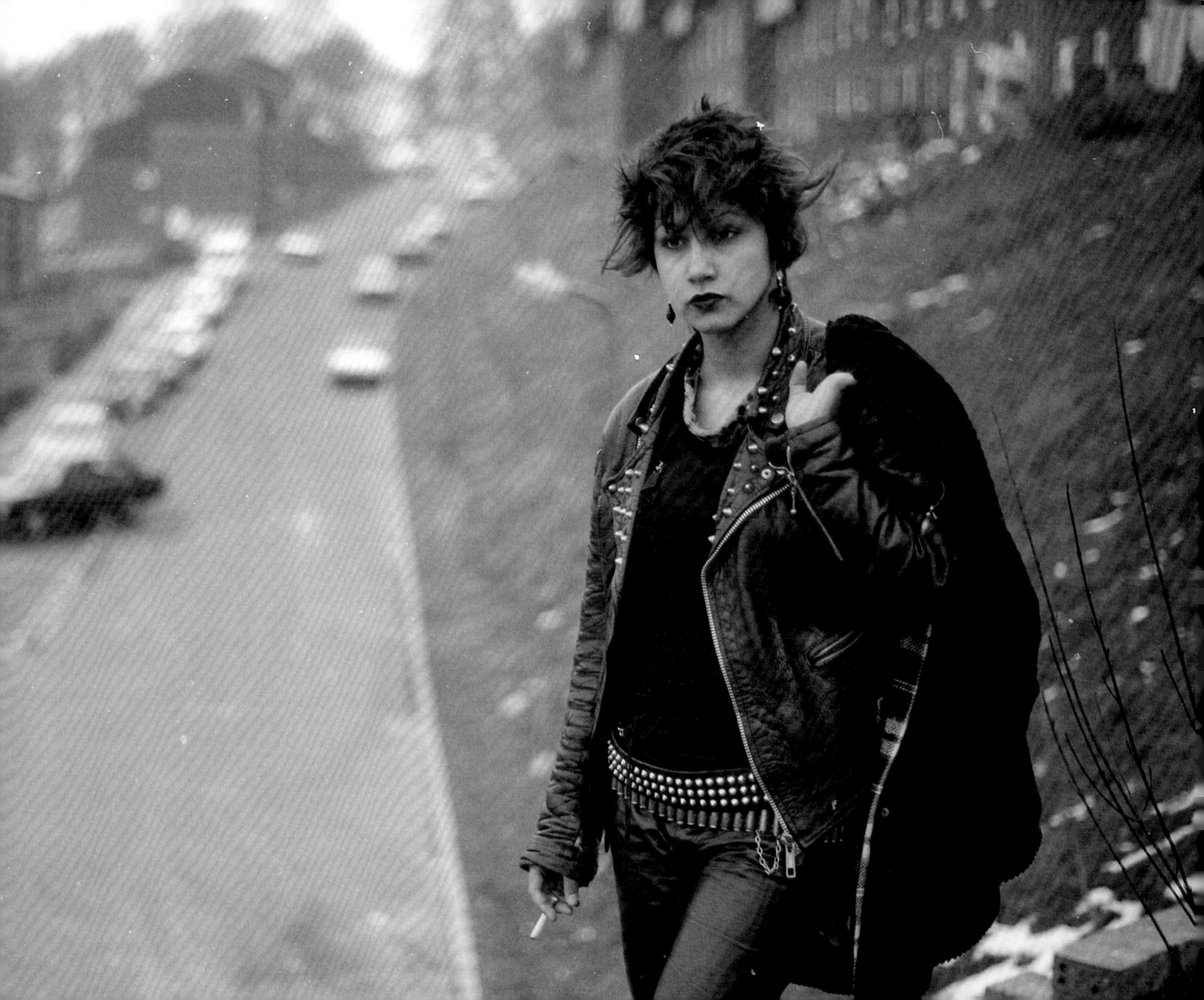

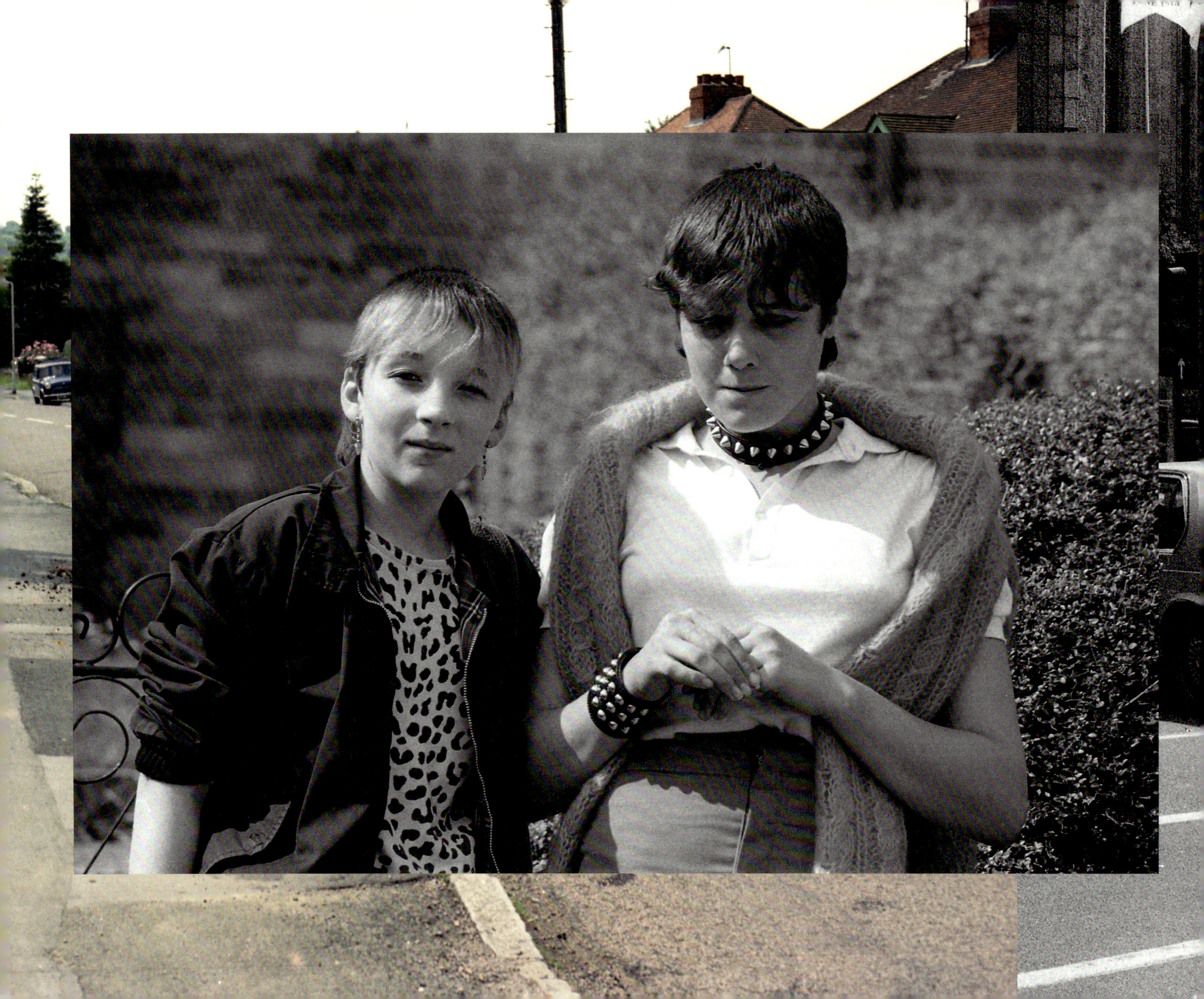

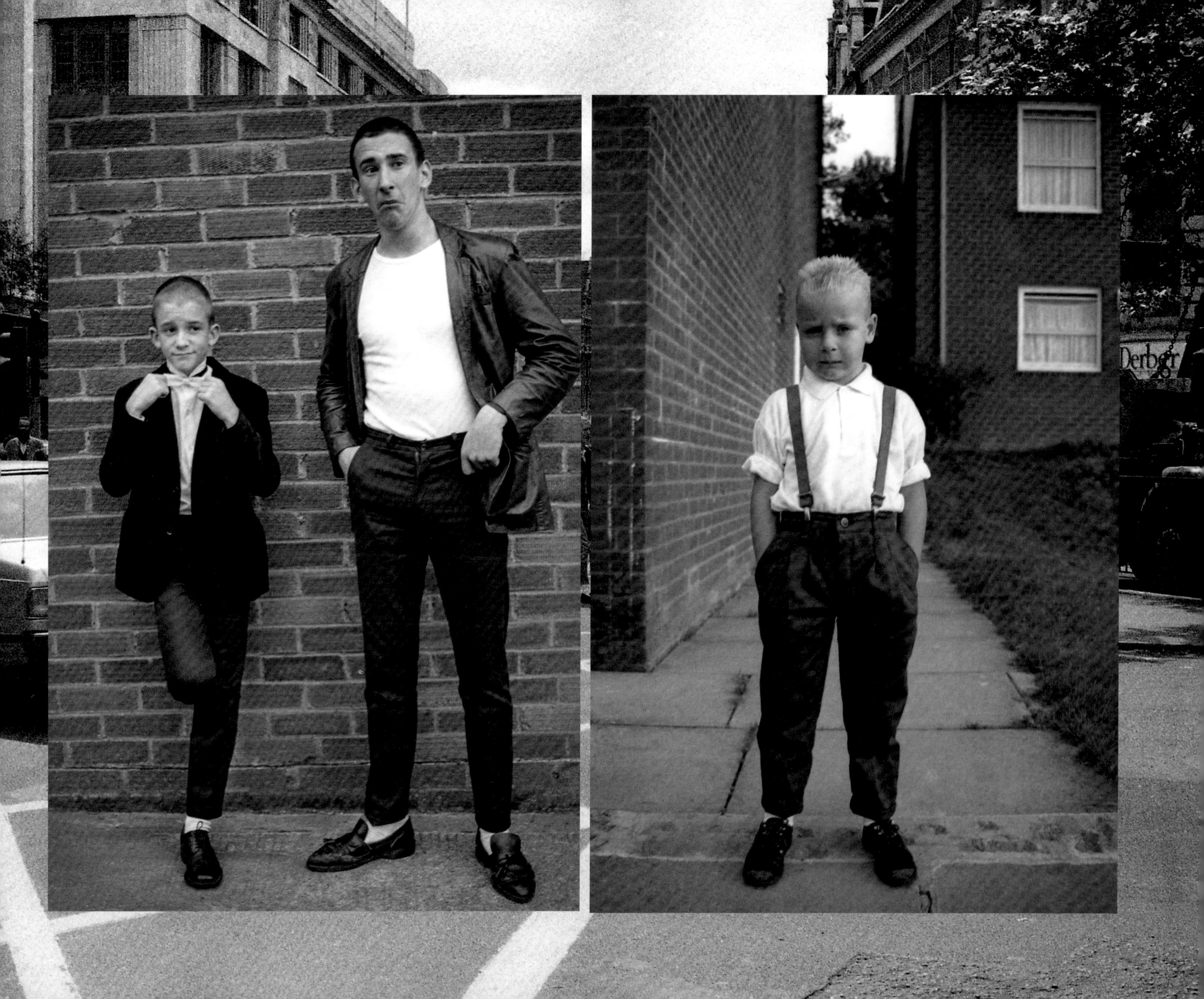

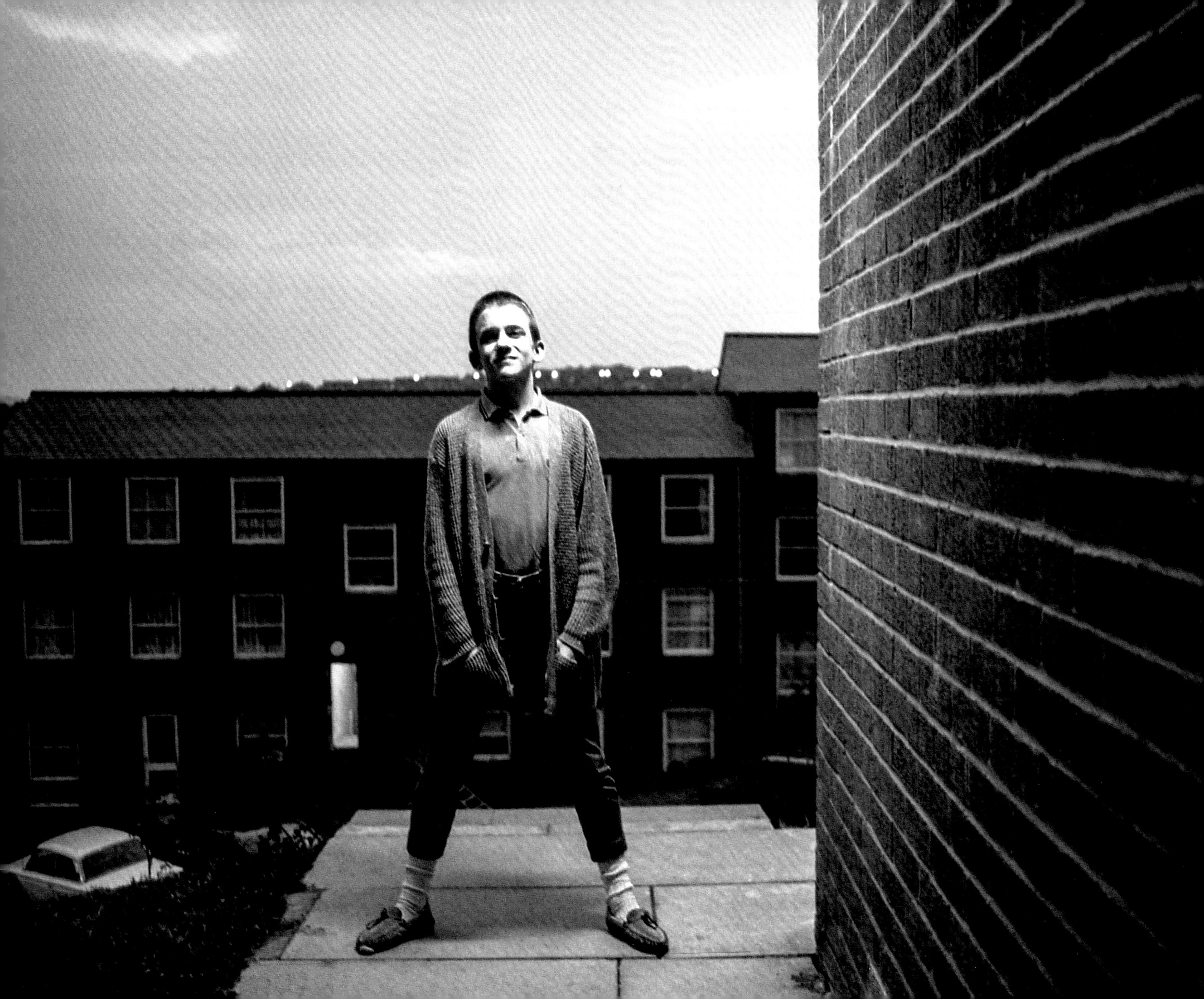

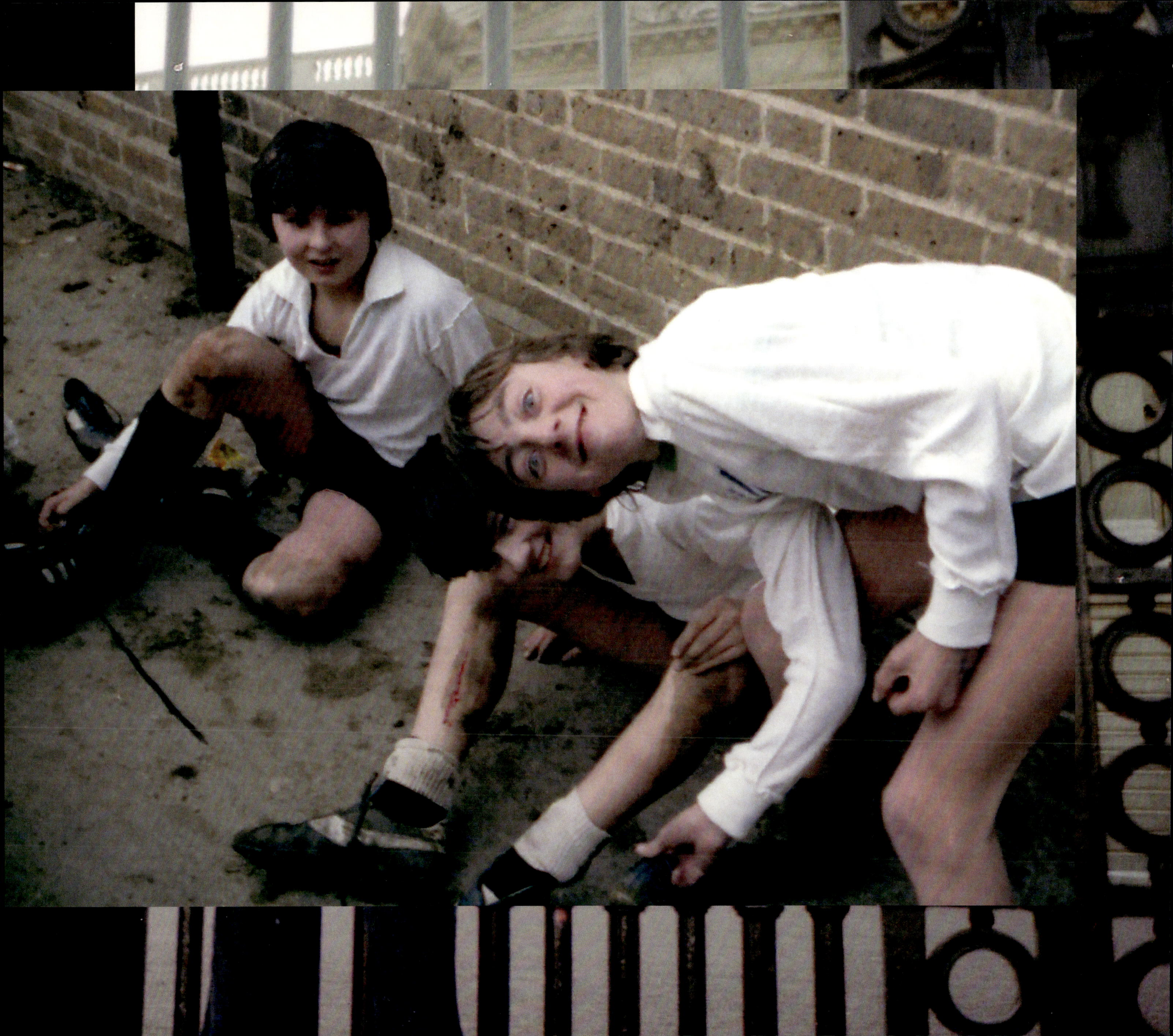

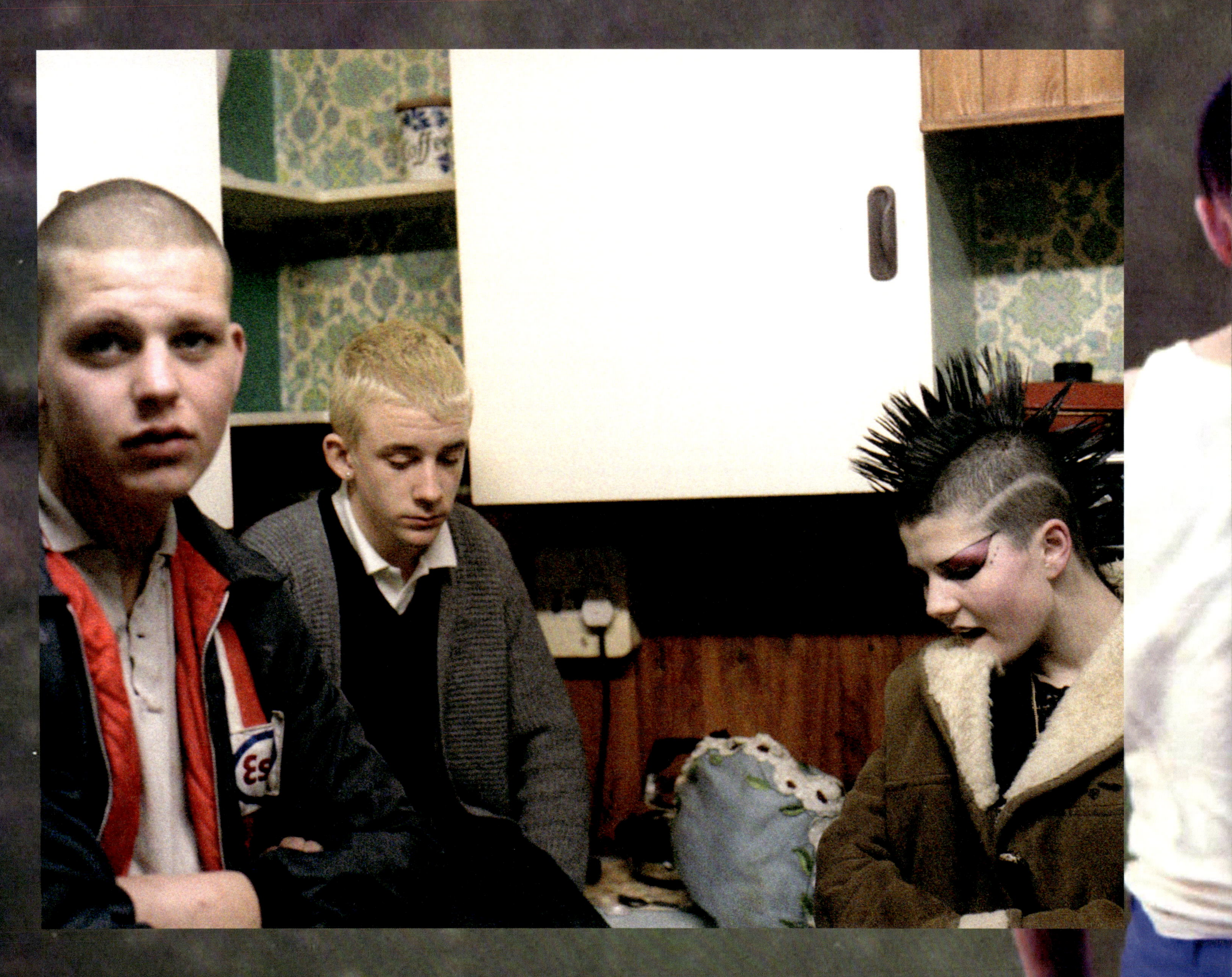

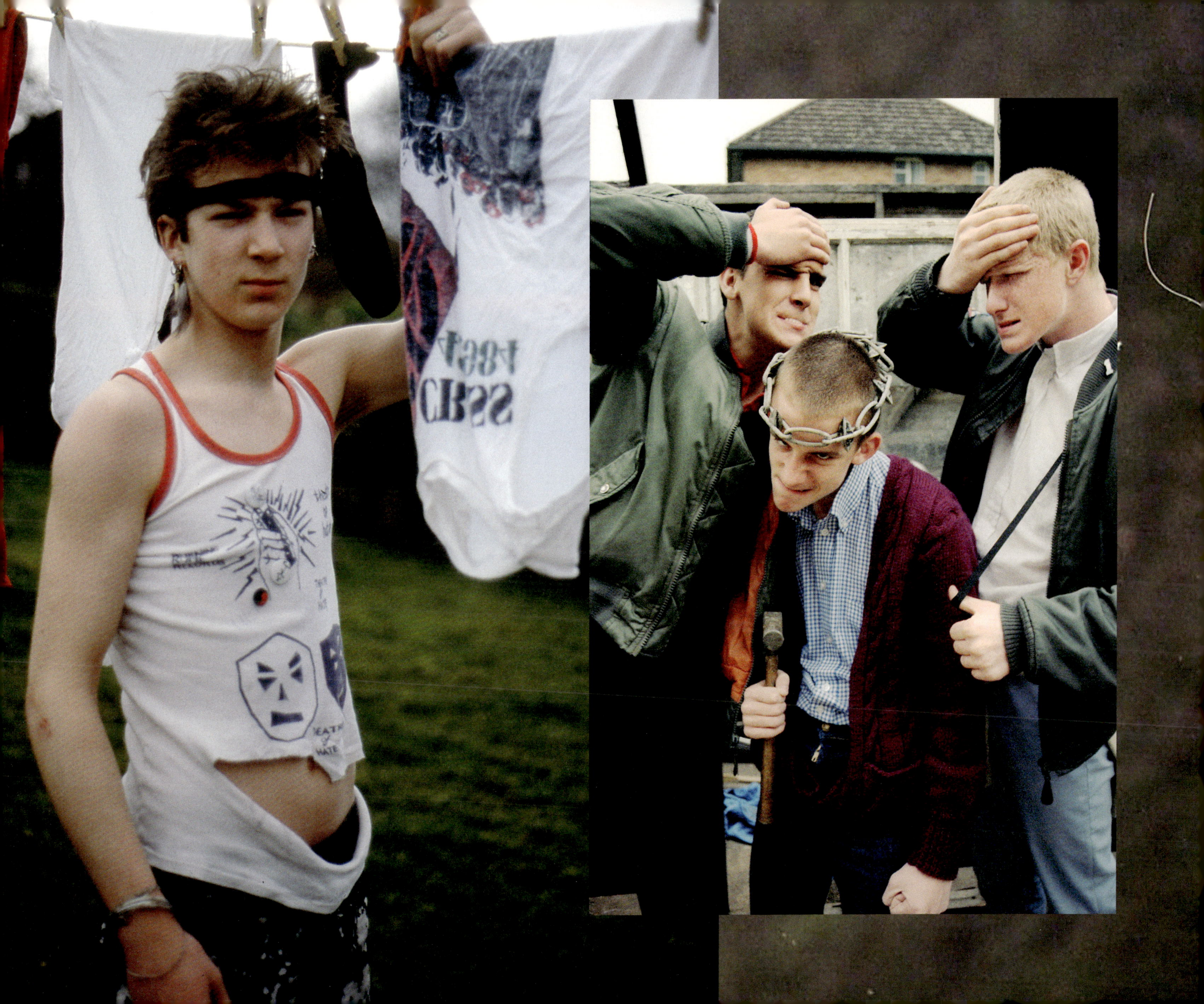

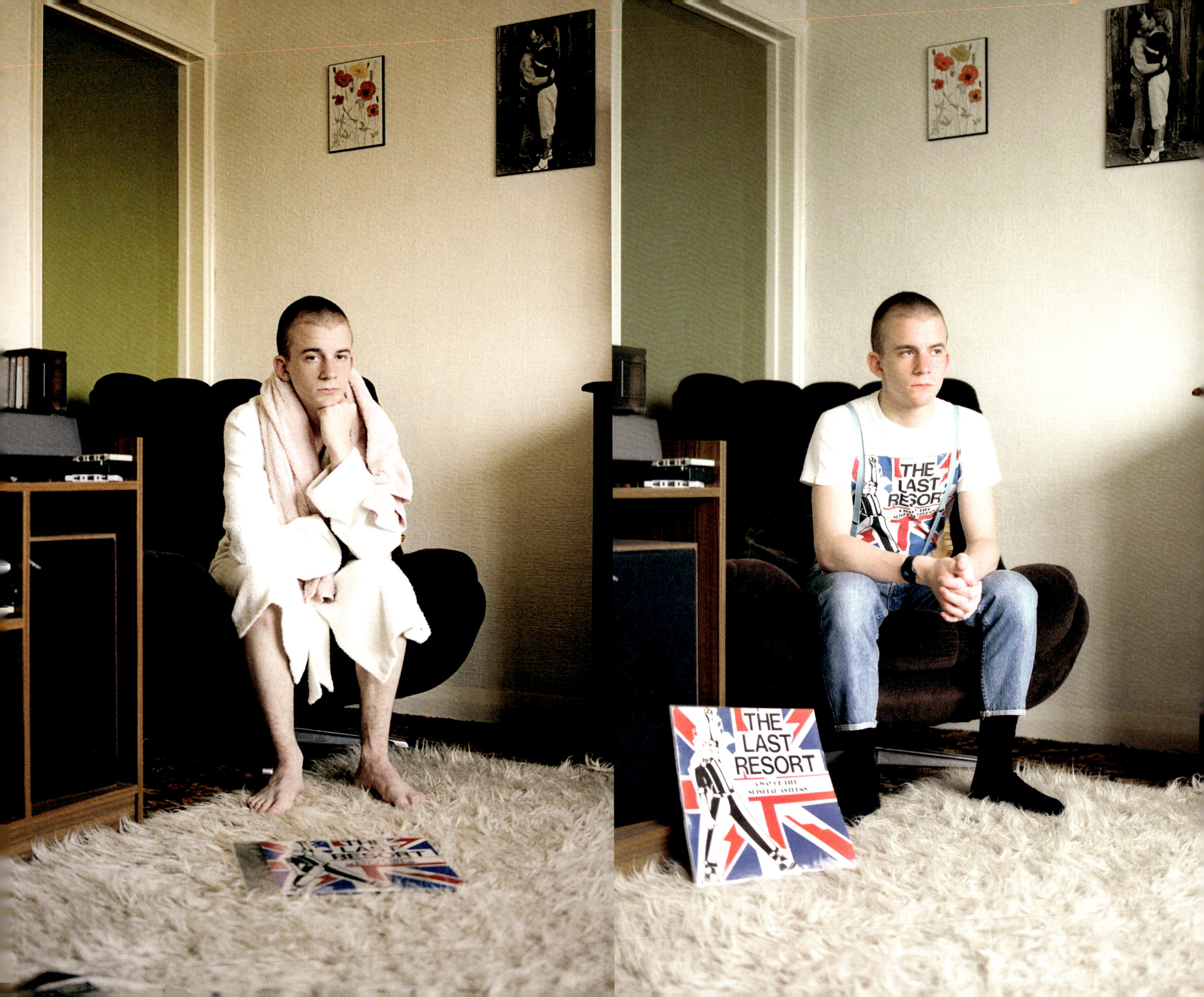
THE LAST RESORT

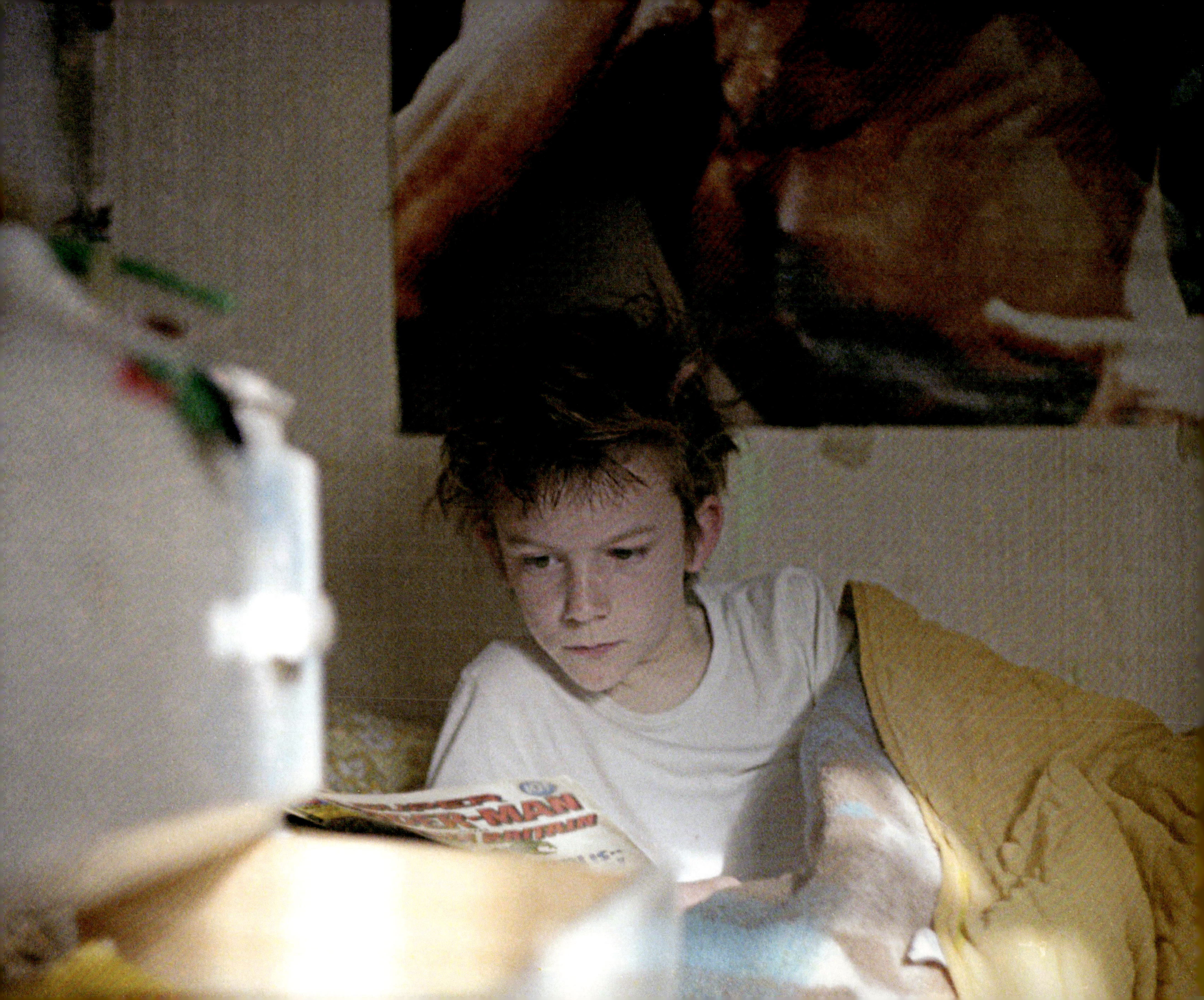

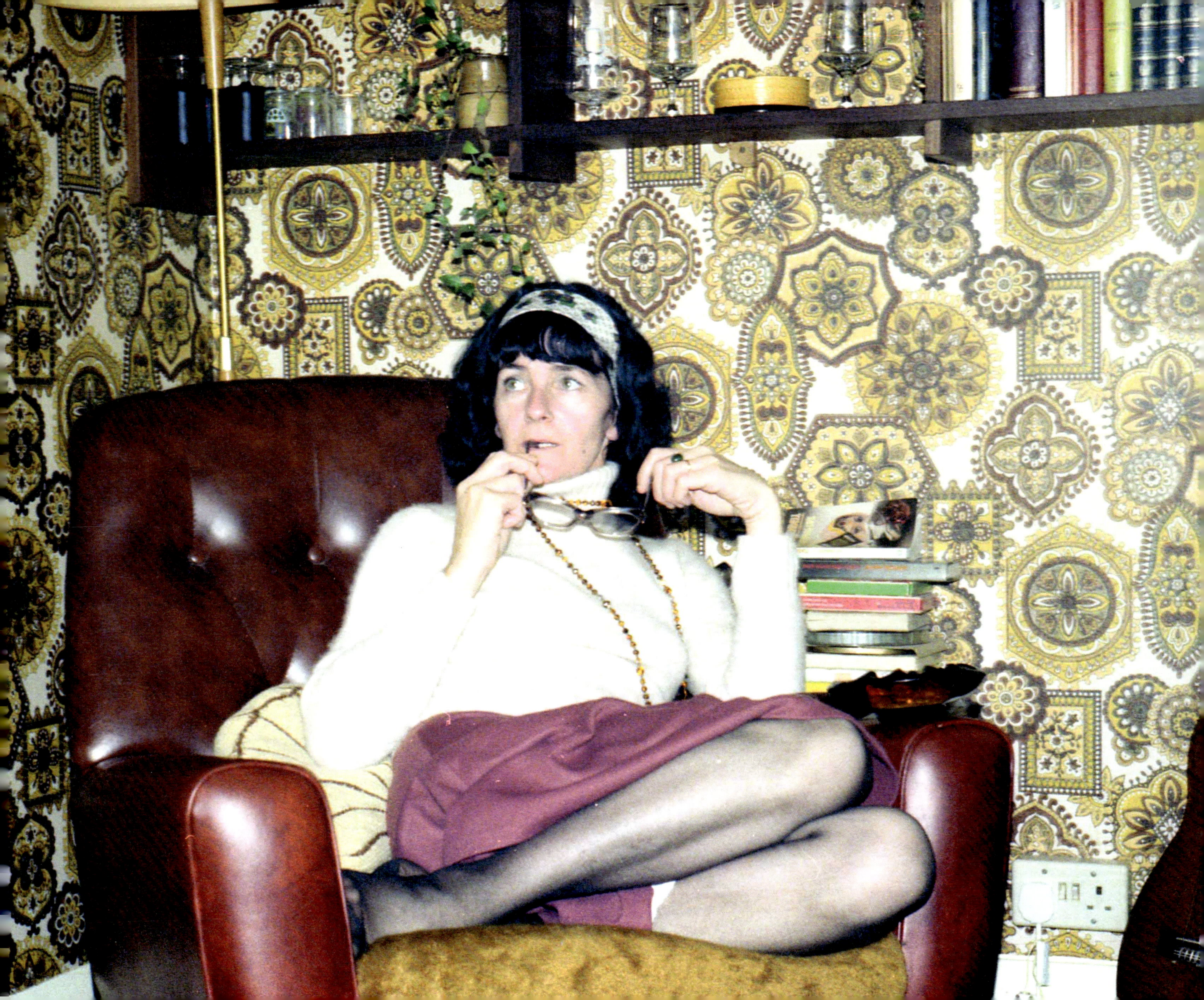

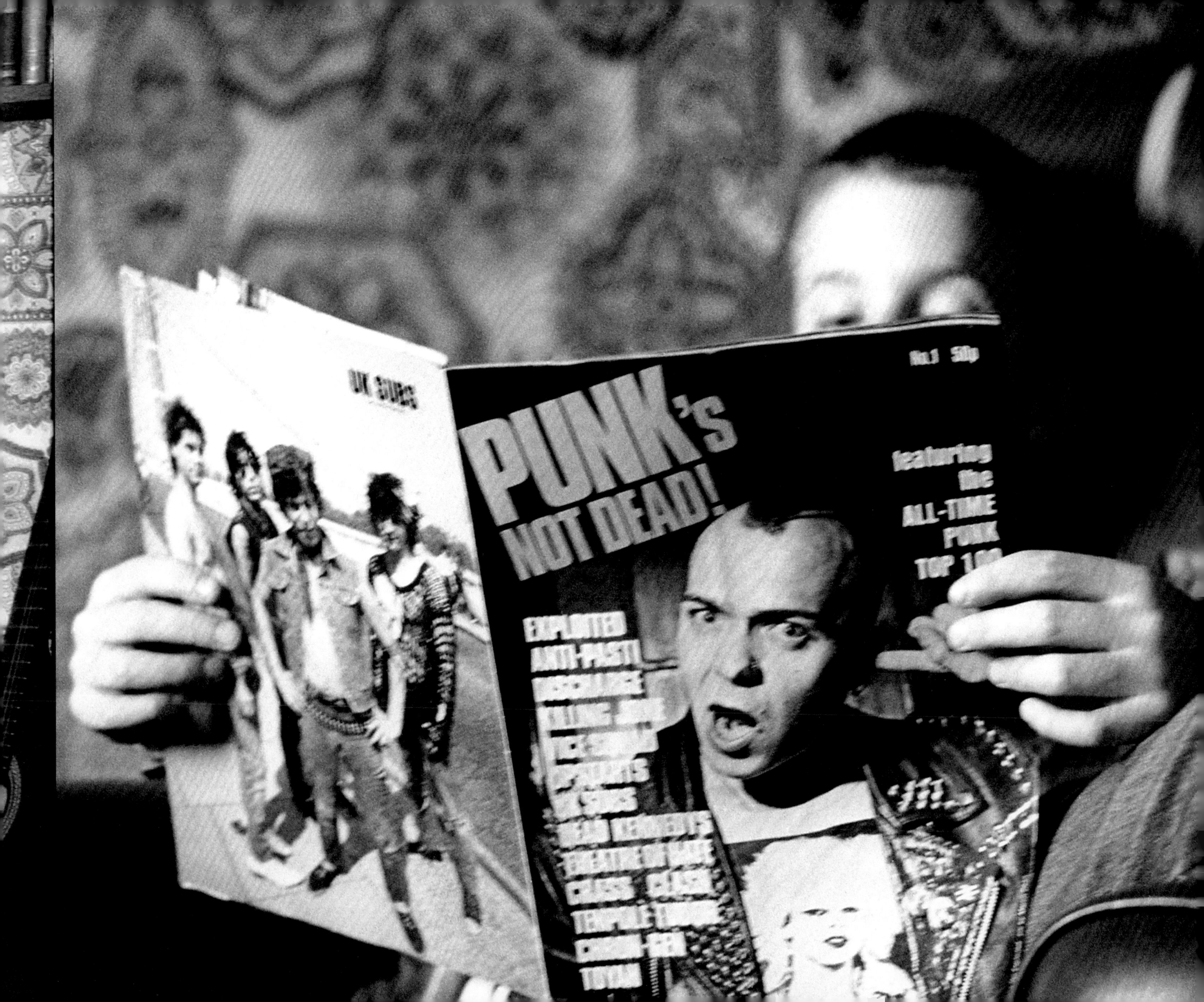
UK SUBS
No.1 50p
PUNK's NOT DEAD!
featuring the ALL-TIME PUNK
EXPLOITED
ANTI-PASTI
UK SUBS
DEAD KENNEDYS
CRASS CLASH
TOYAH

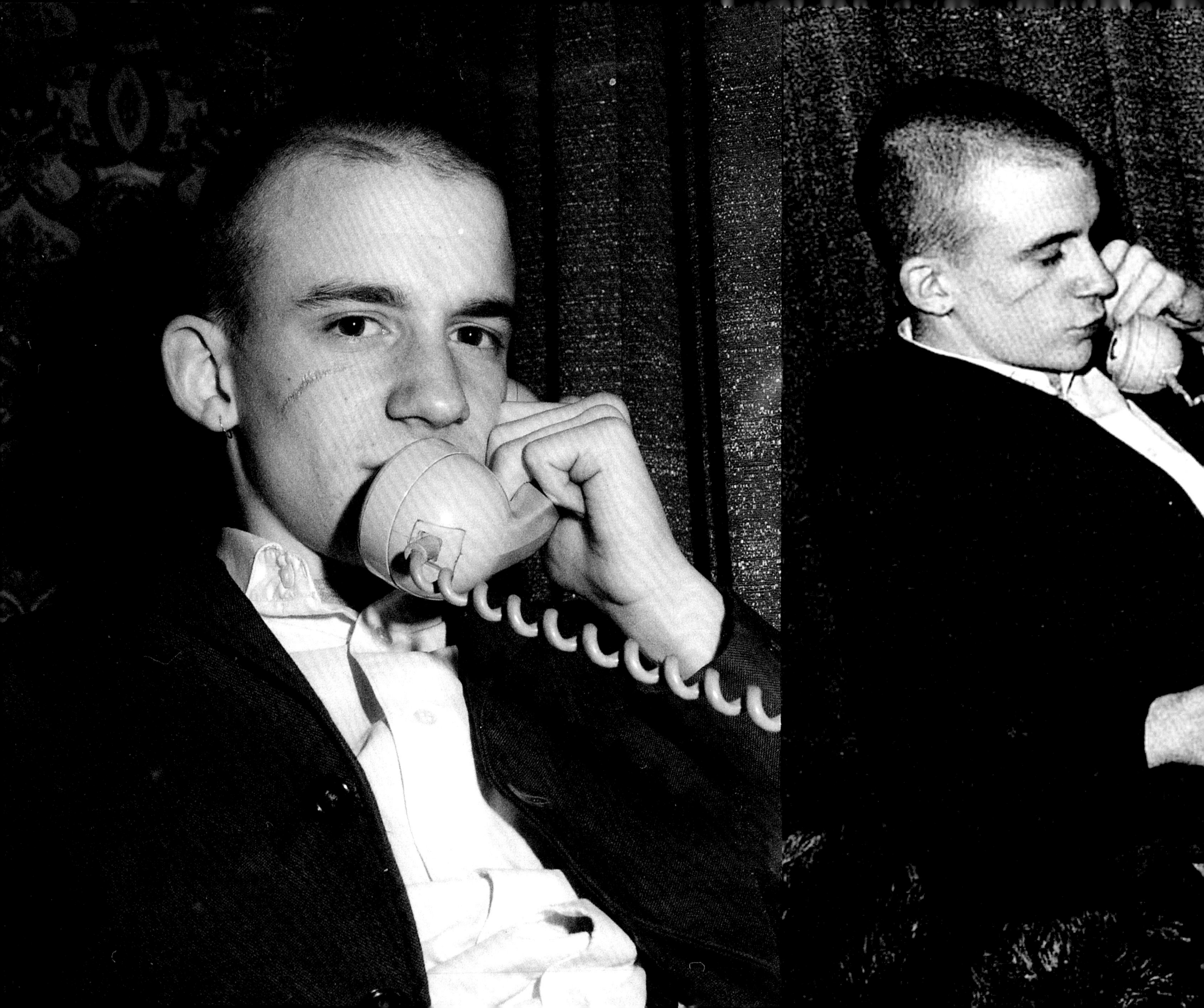

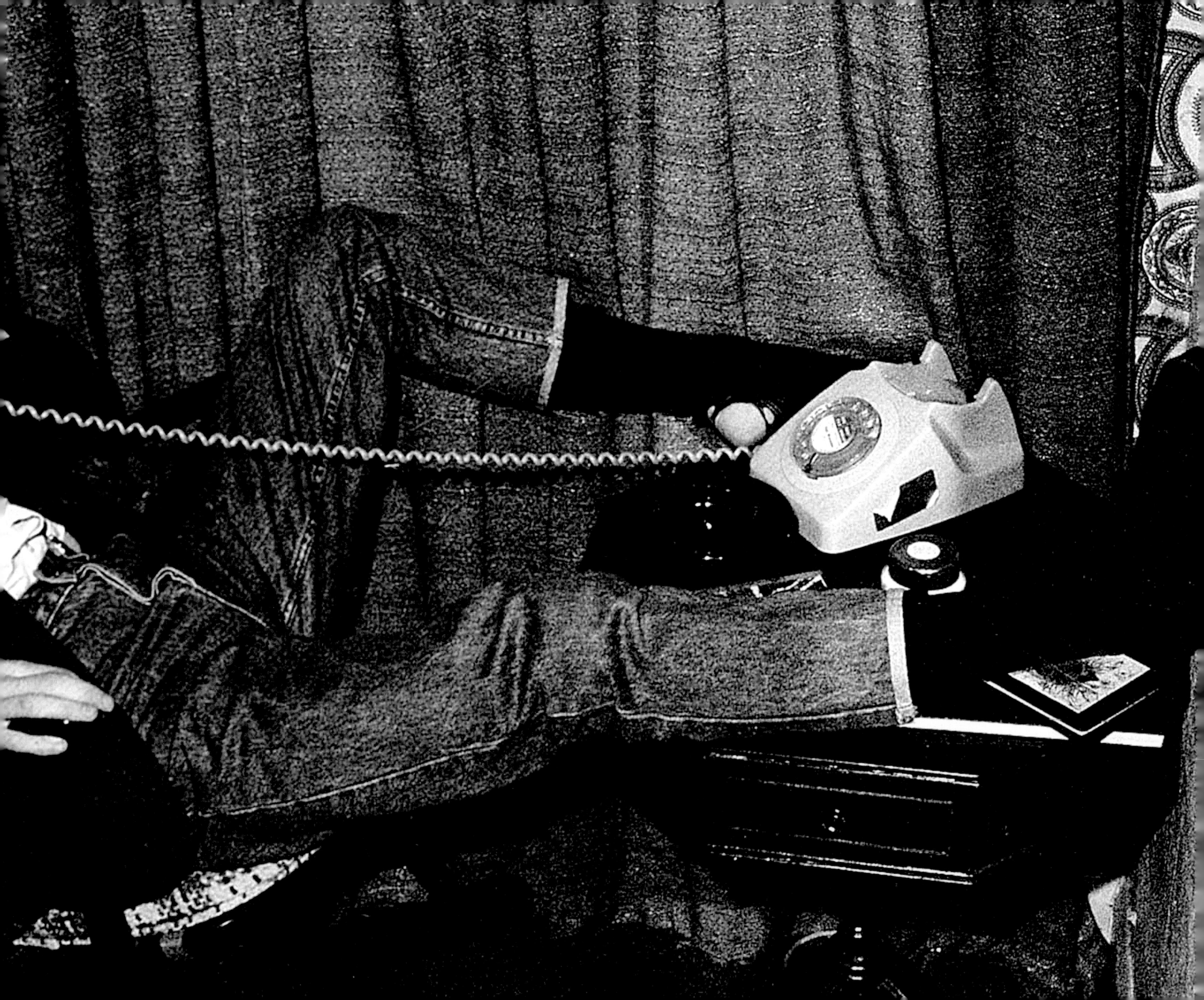

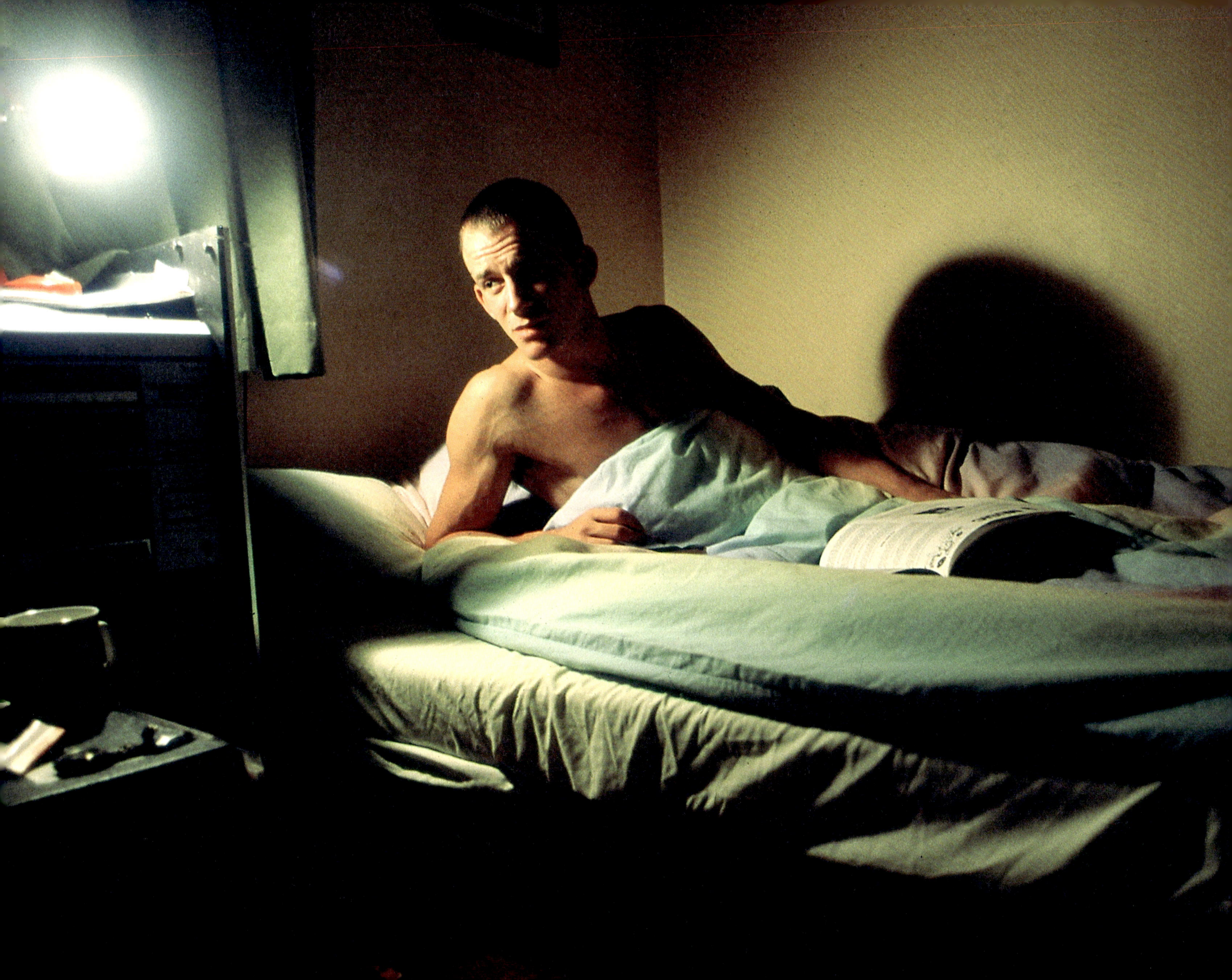

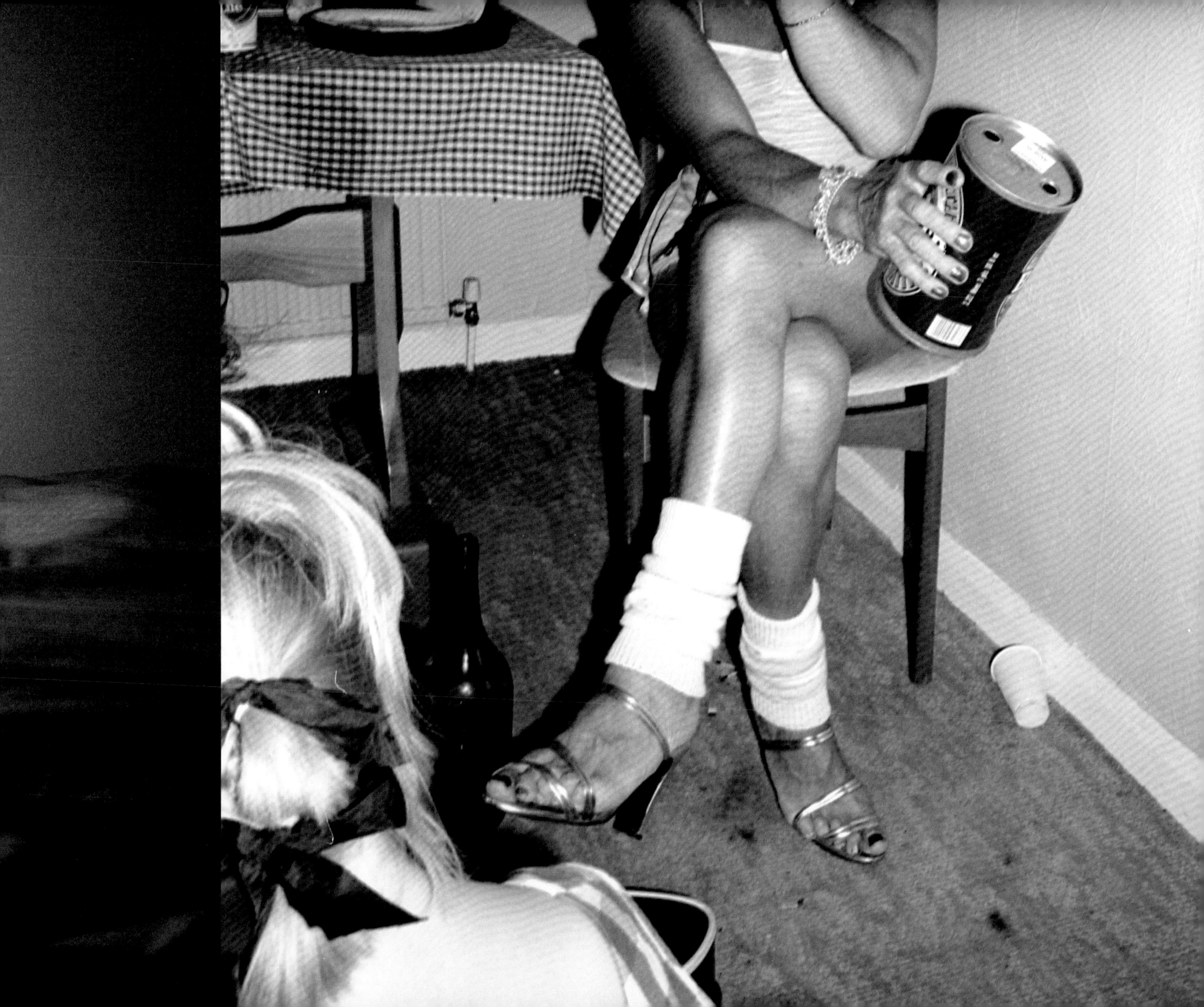

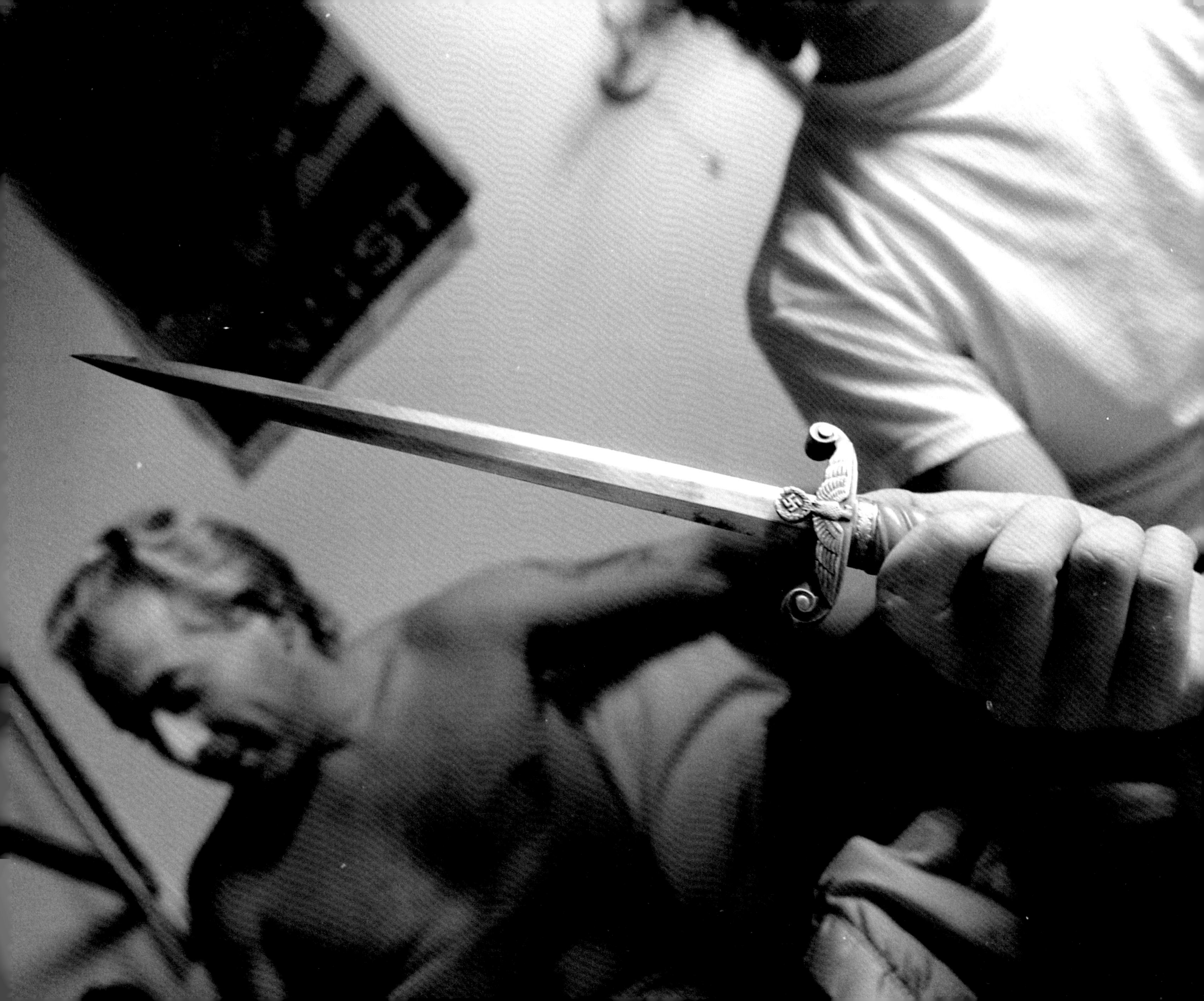

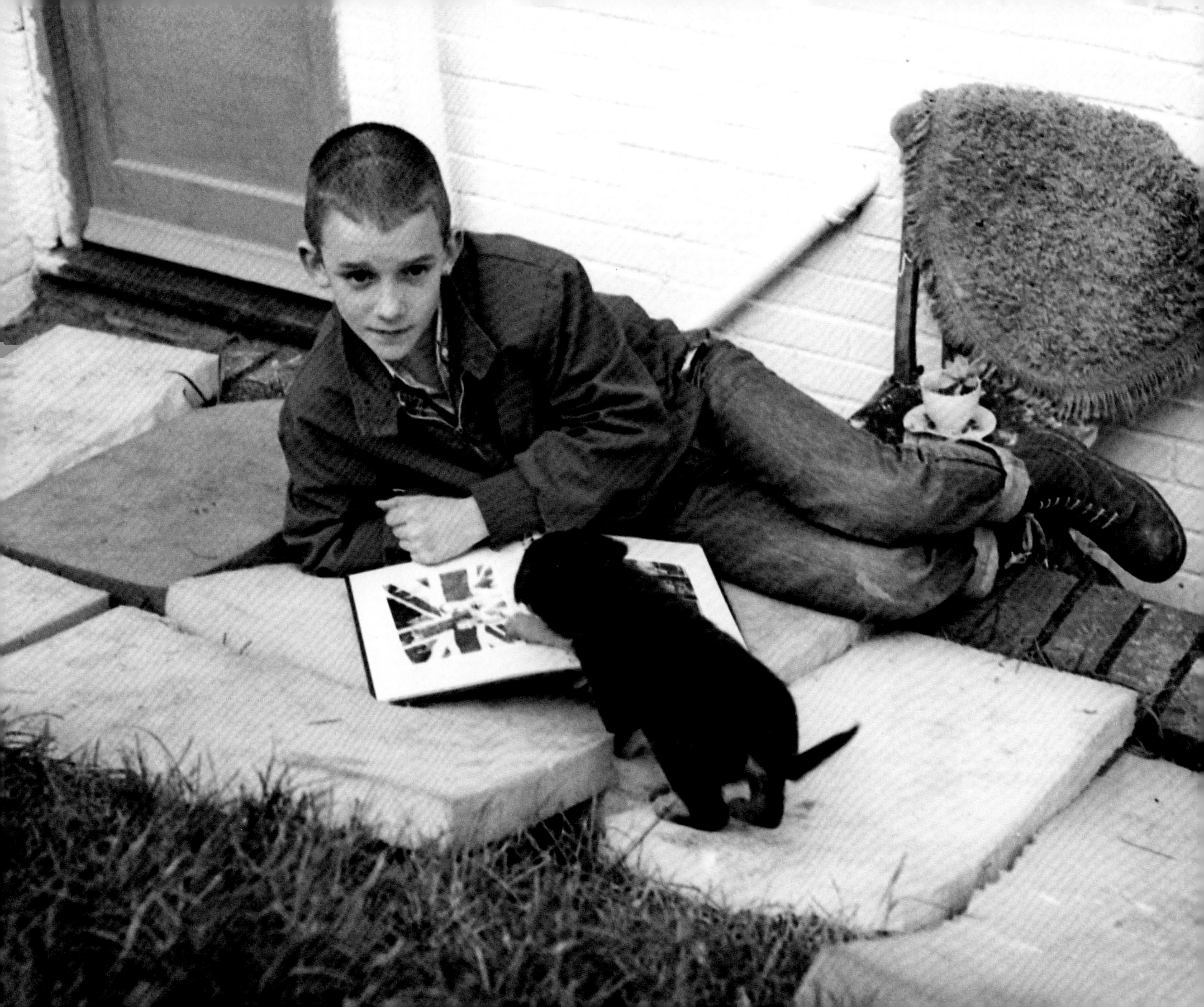

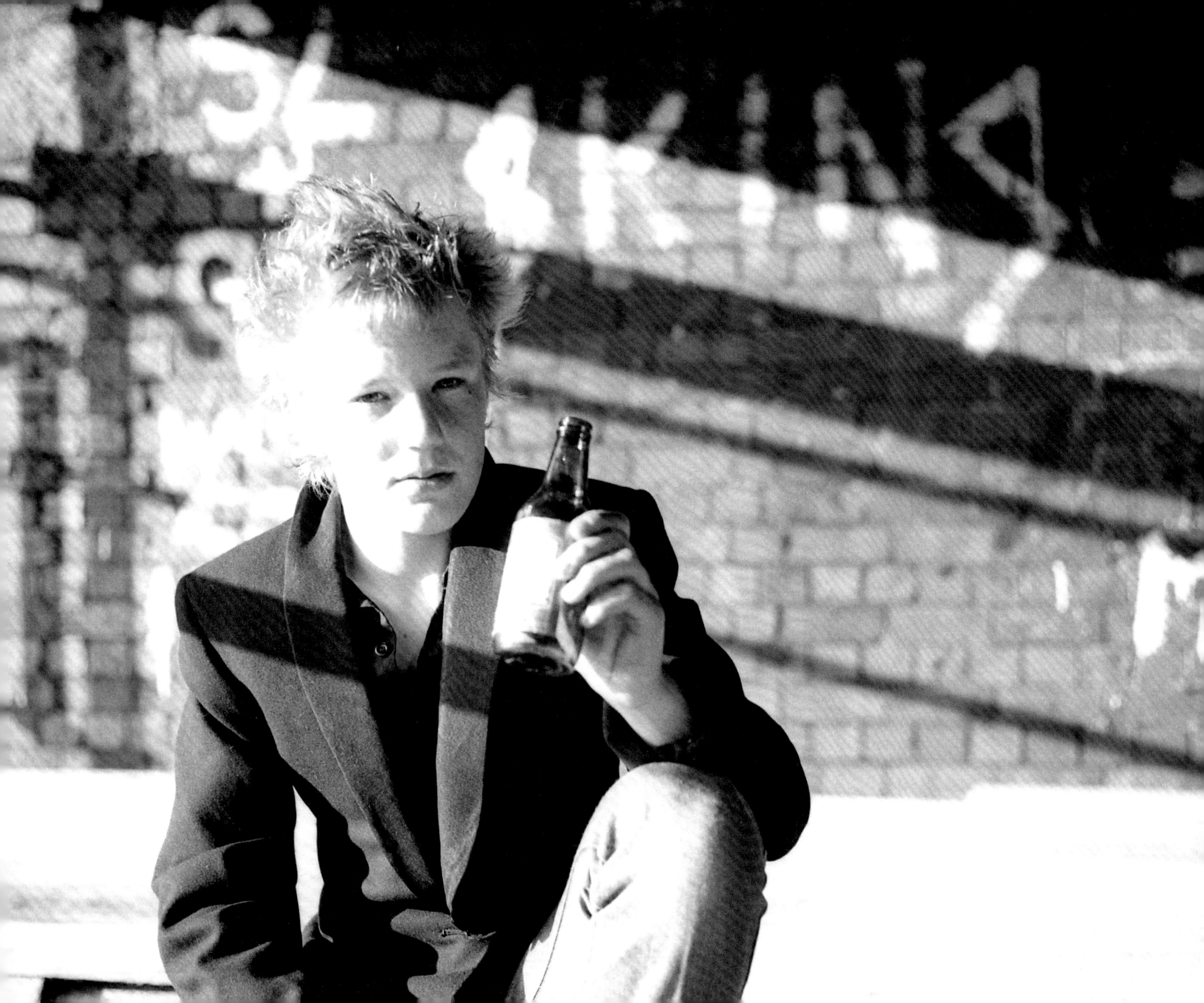

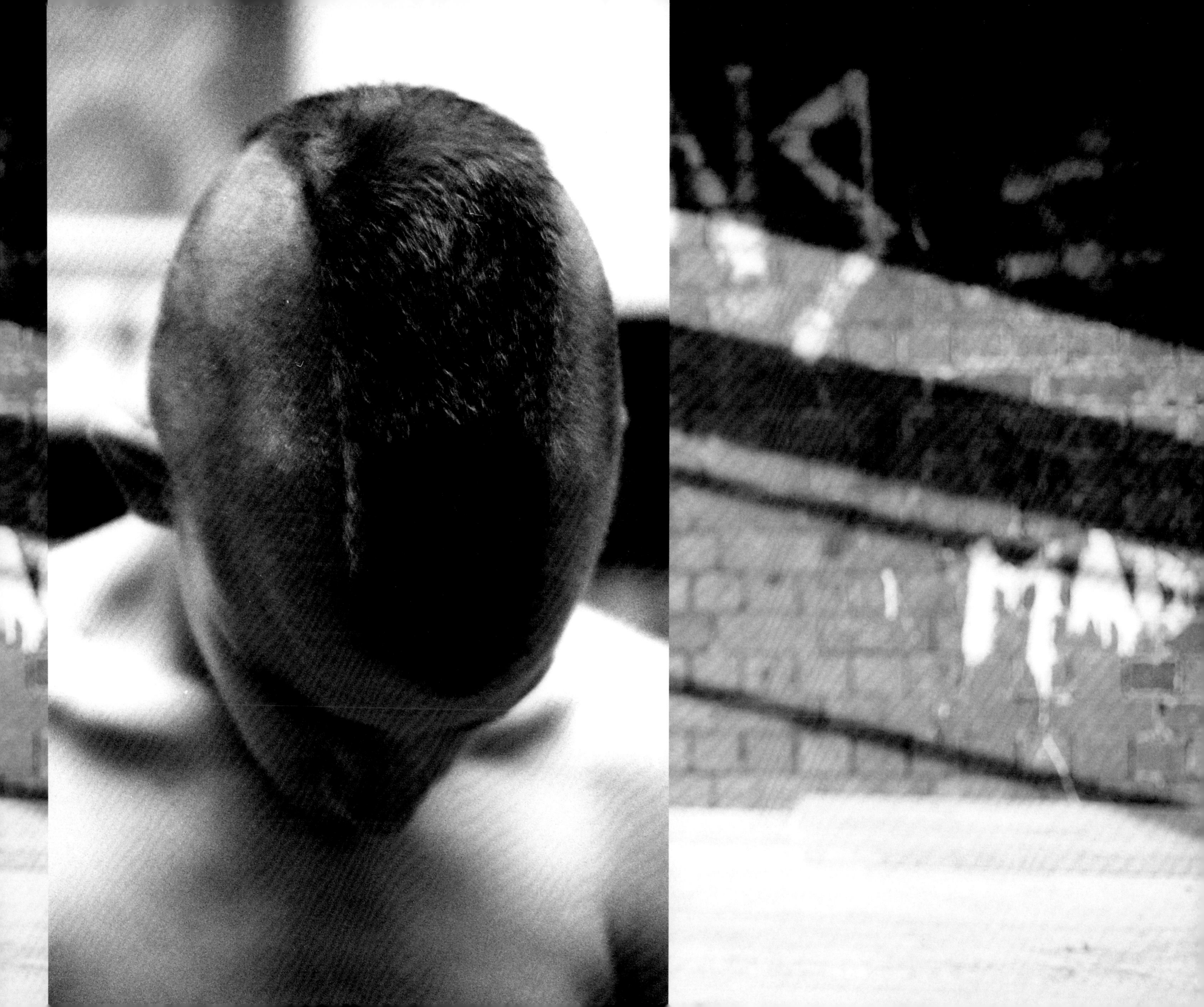

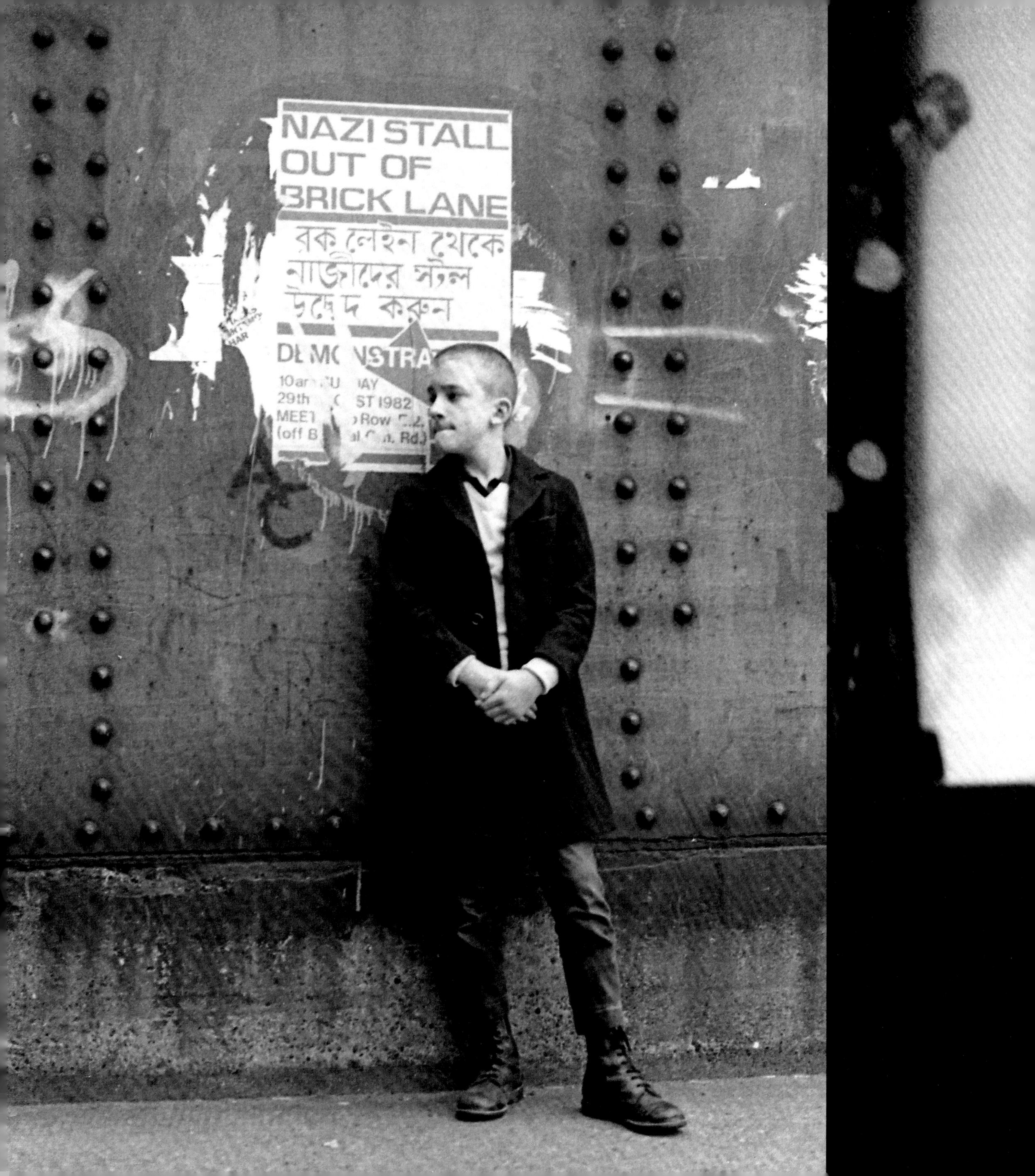

NAZI STALL
OUT OF
BRICK LANE

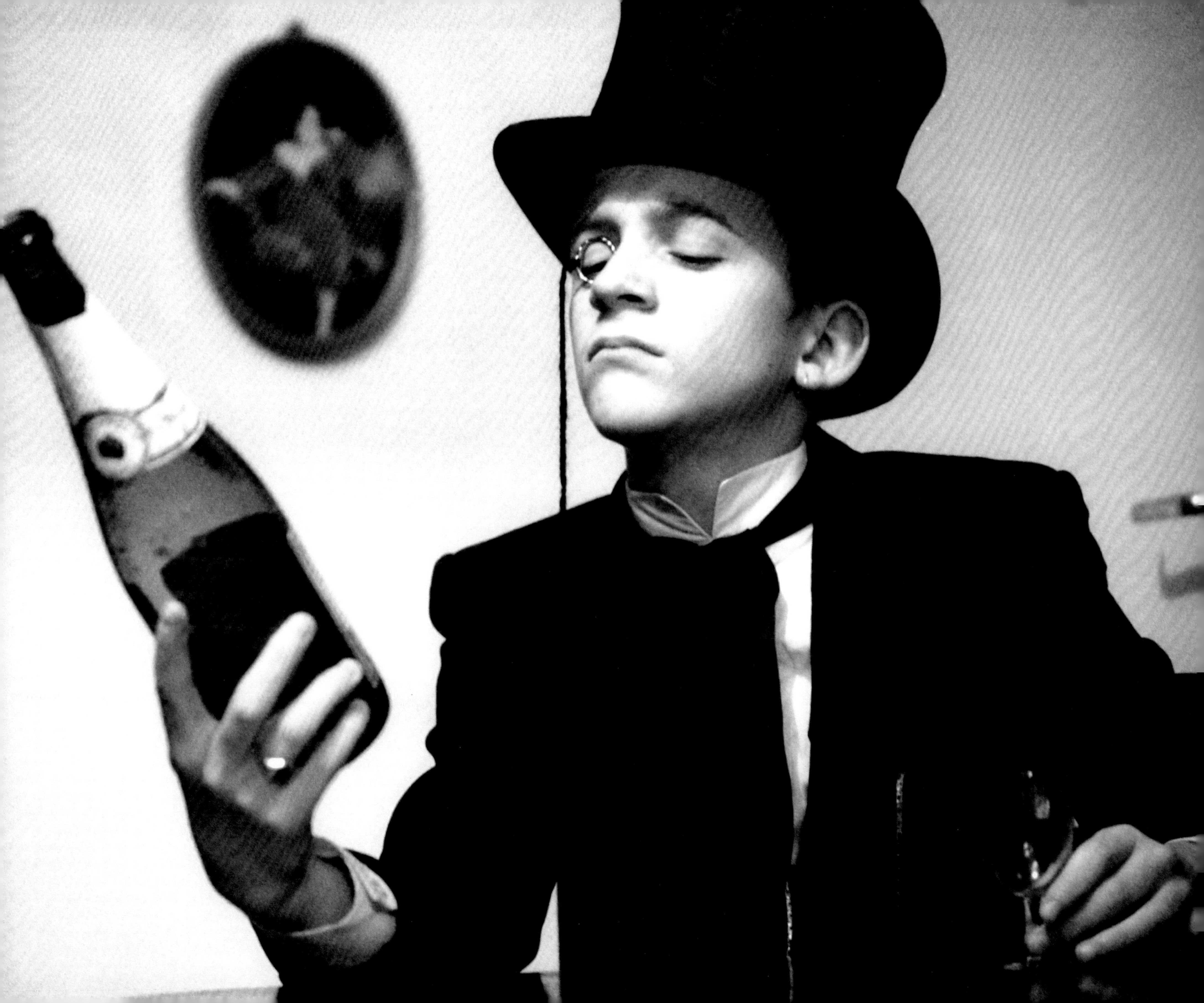

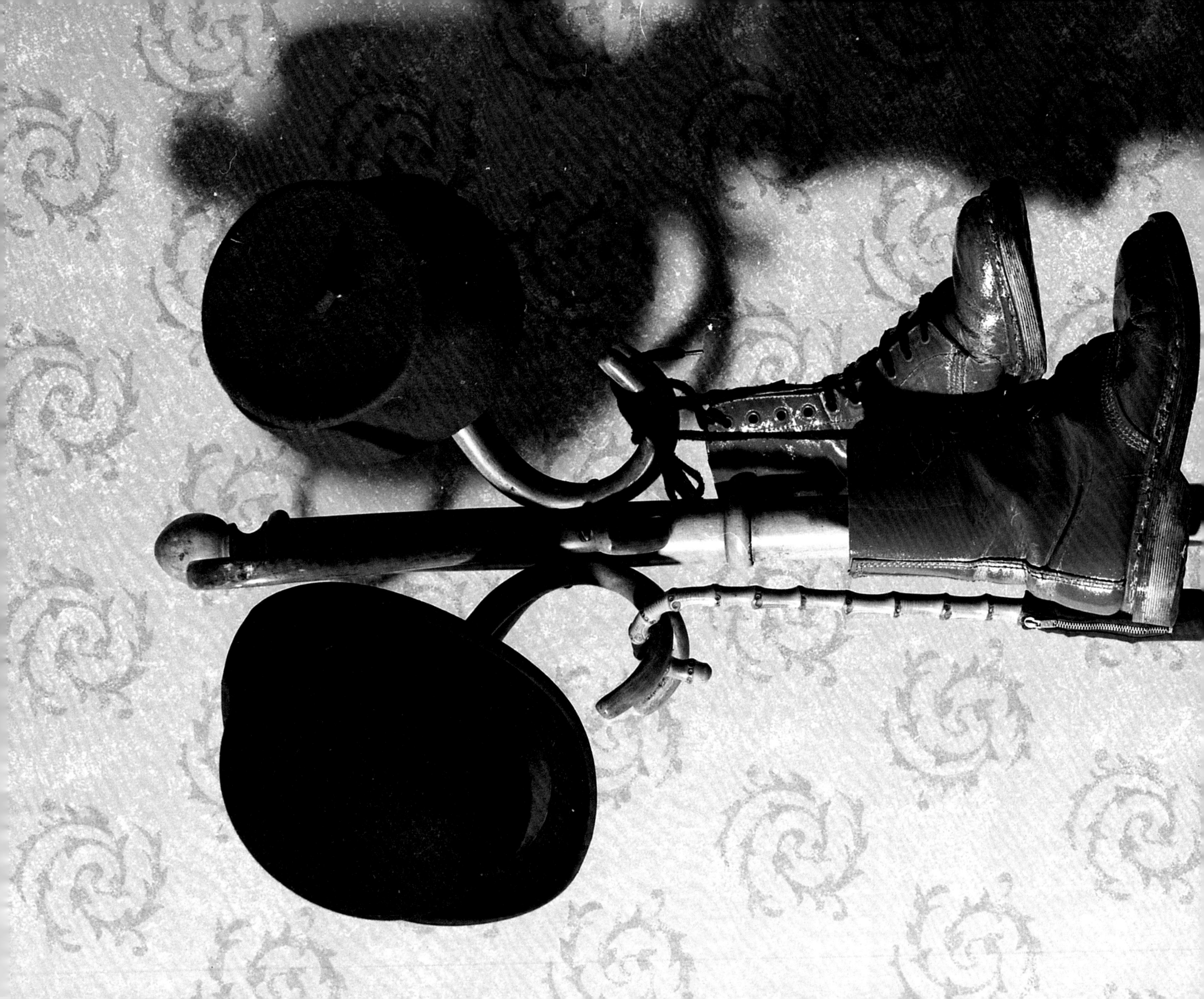

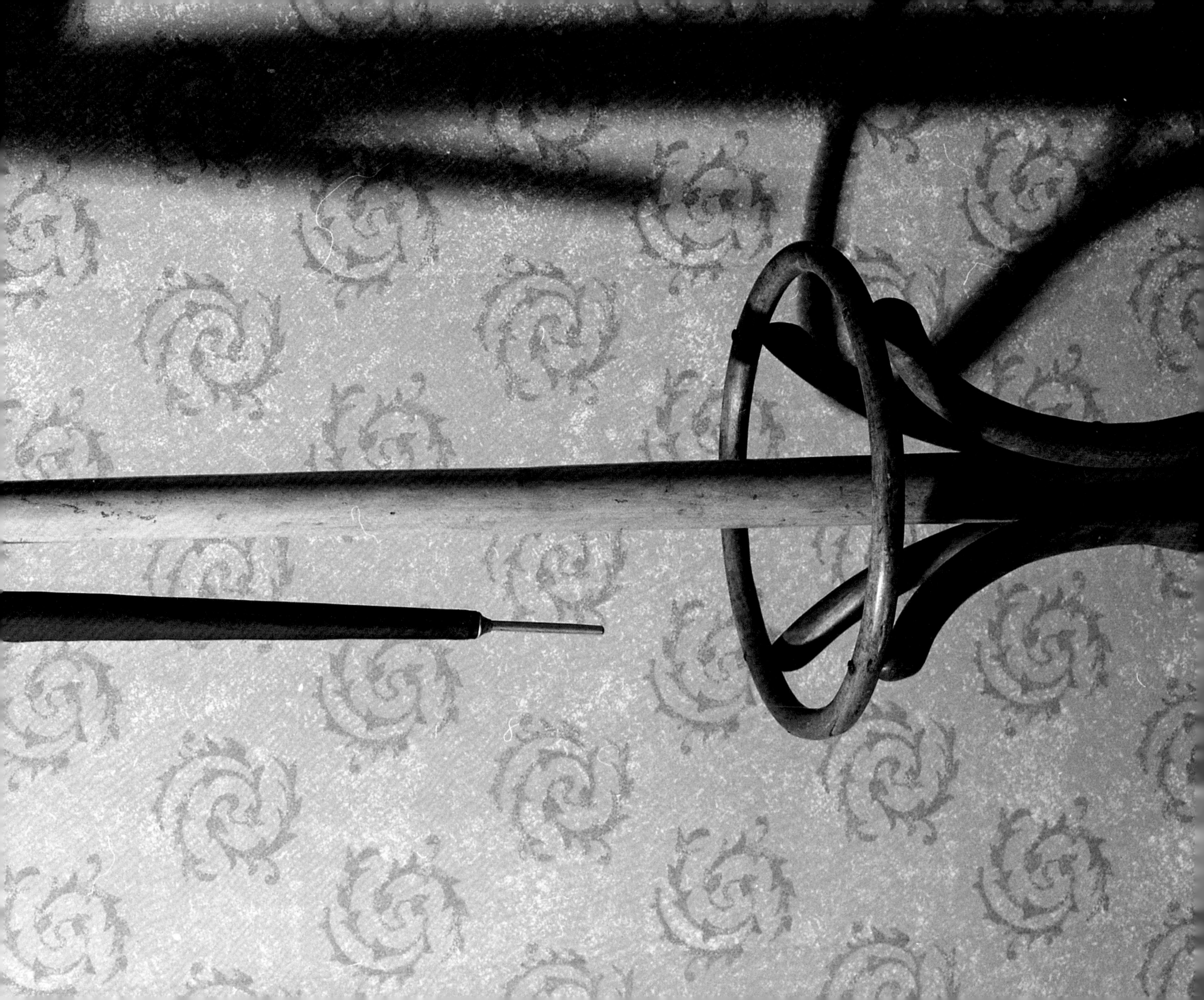

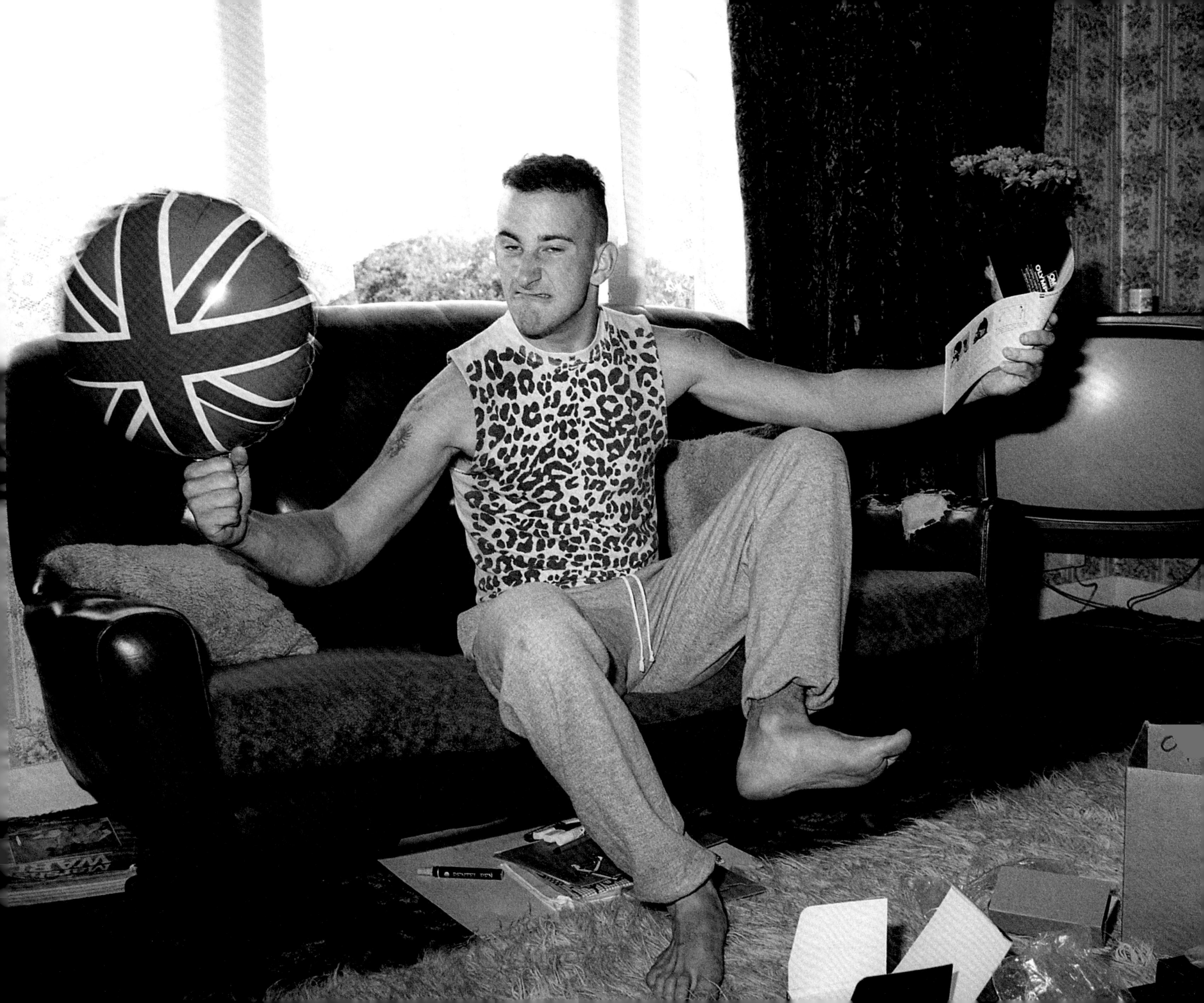
PENTEL PEN

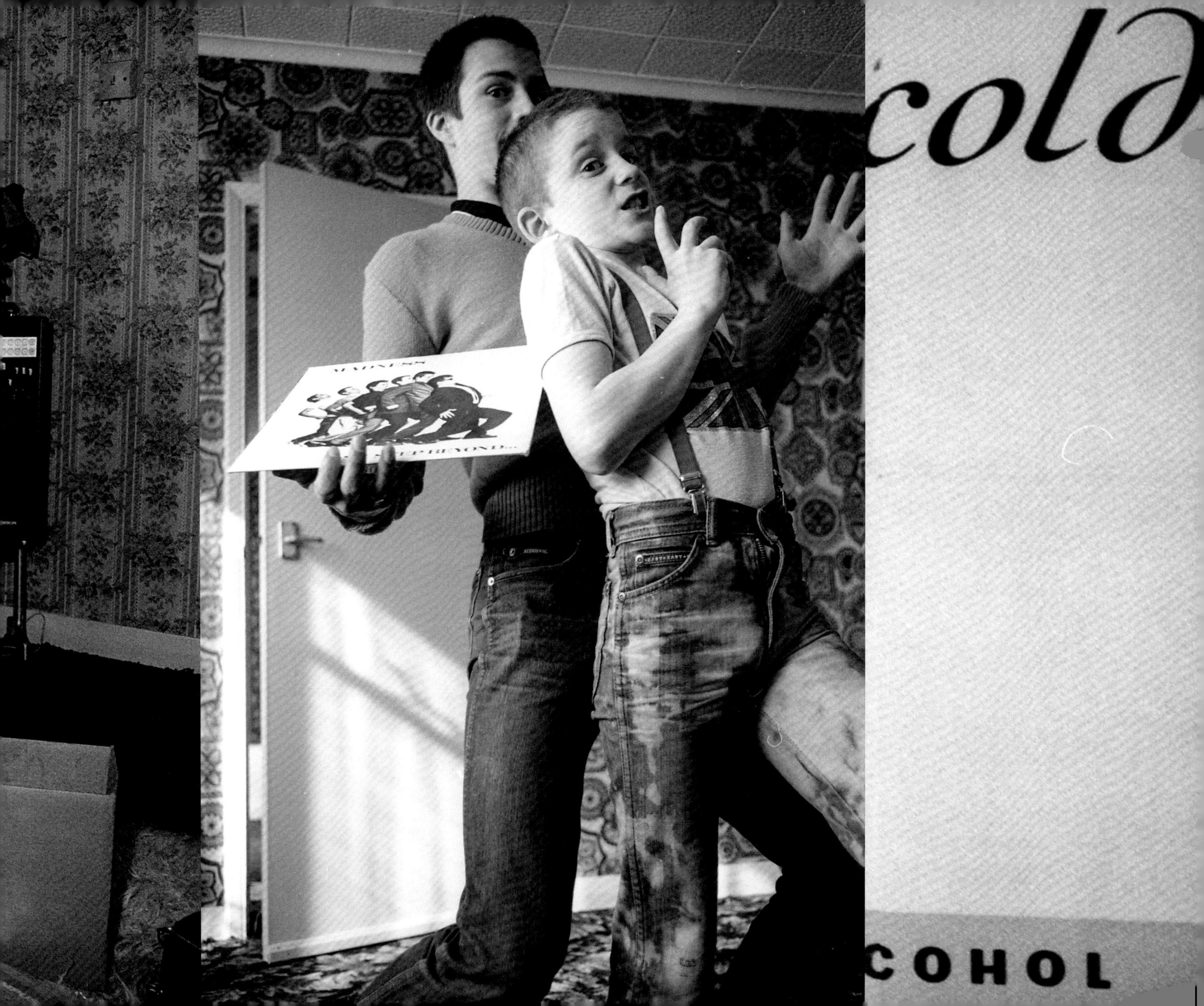

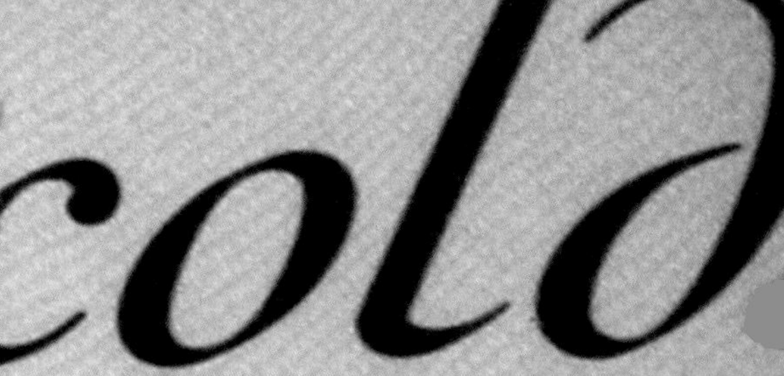
cold
COHOL

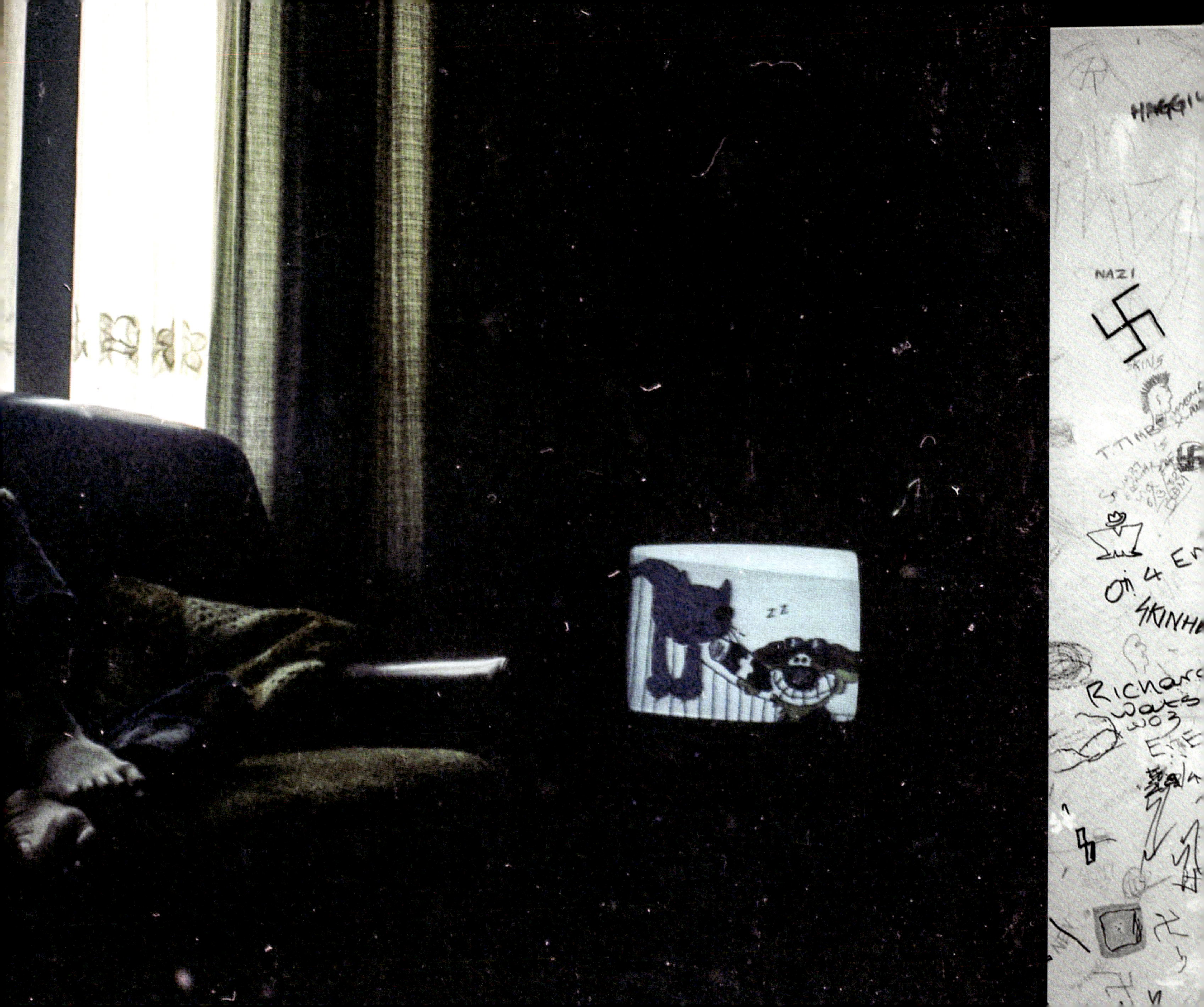
NAZI
Oi 4

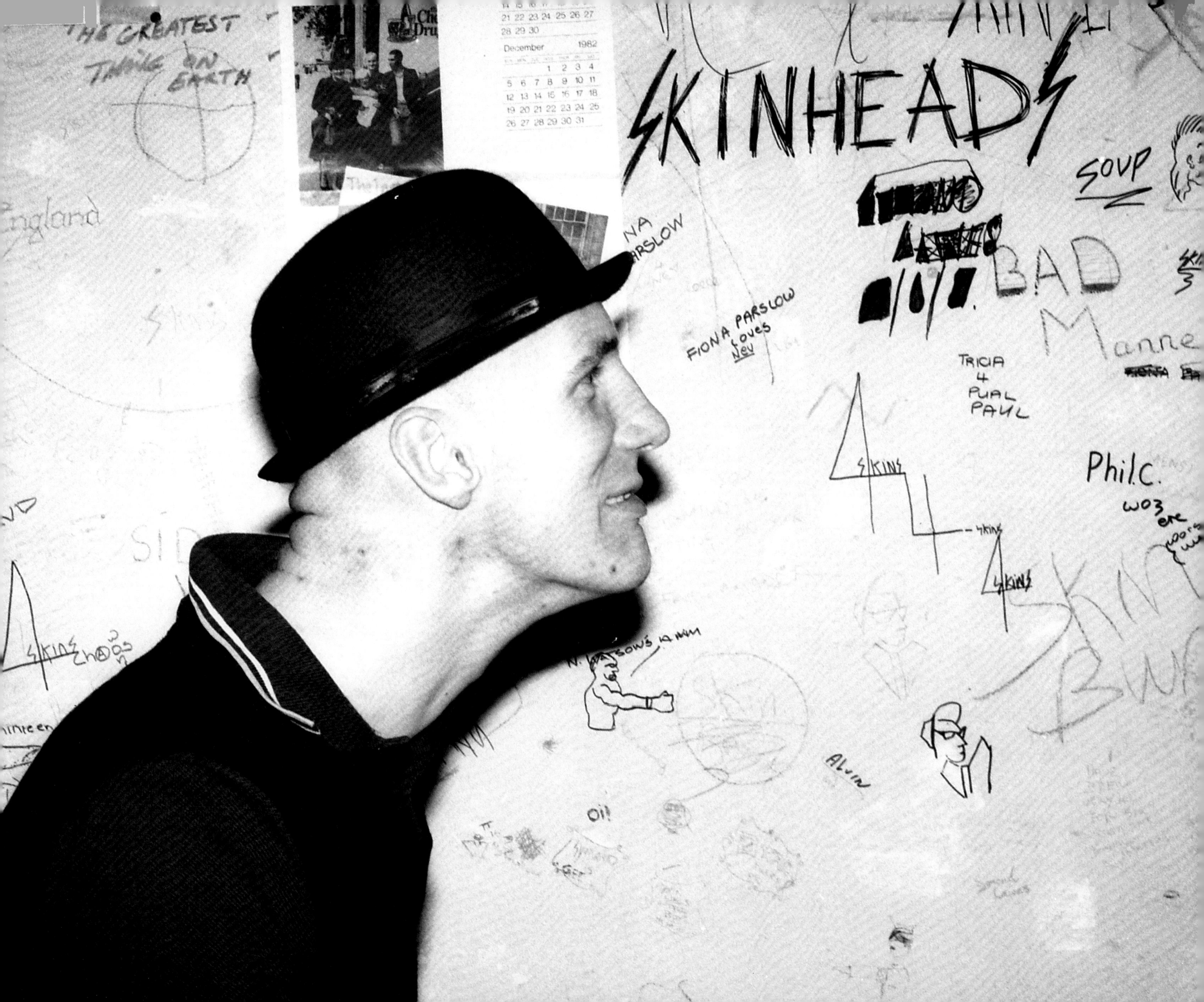

THE GREATEST THING ON EARTH
England
December 1982
SKINHEADS
SOUP
BAD
FIONA PARSLOW Loves Nev
TRICIA 4 PUAL PAUL
Phil.C.
4 SKINS
Alvin
Oi!

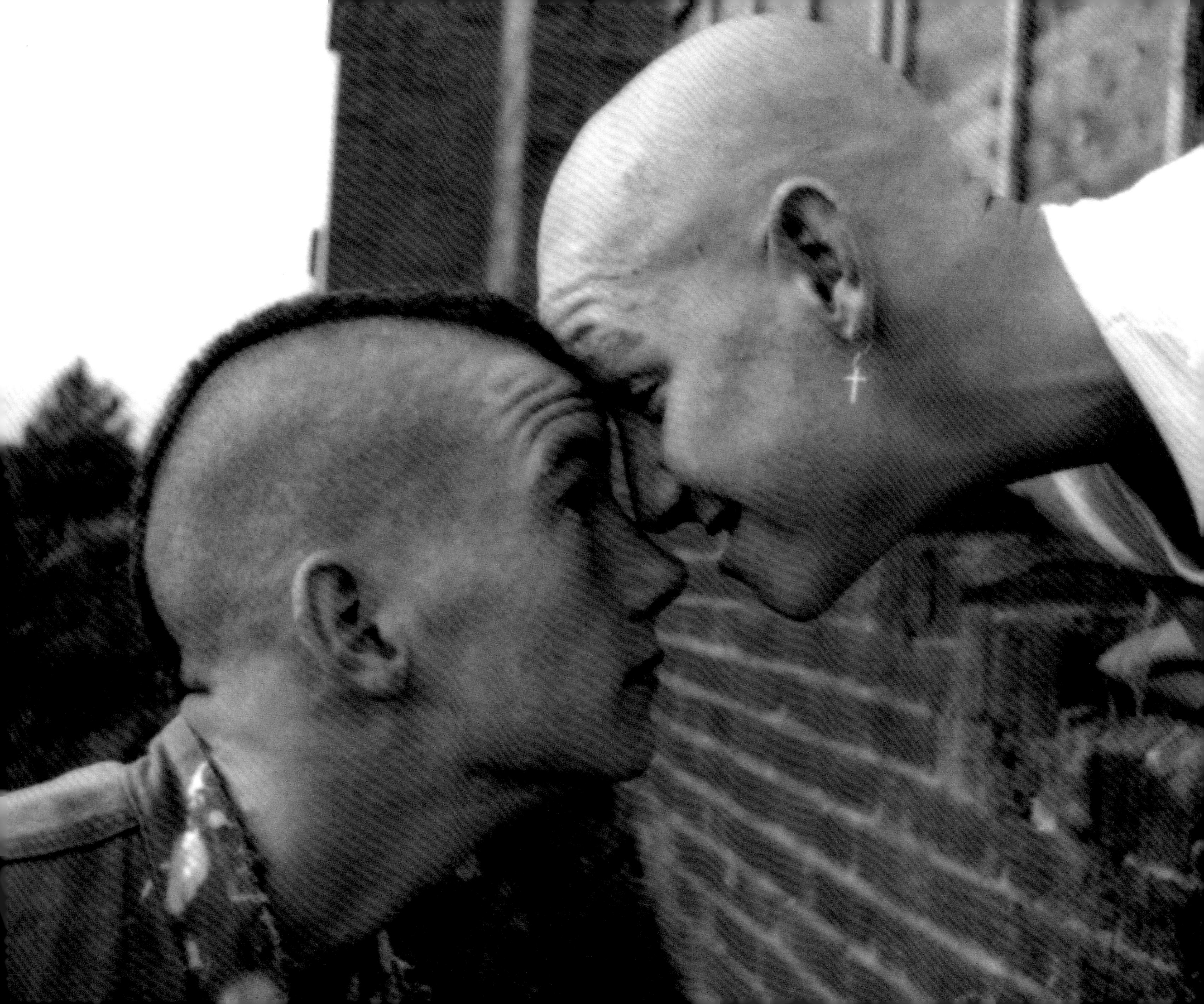

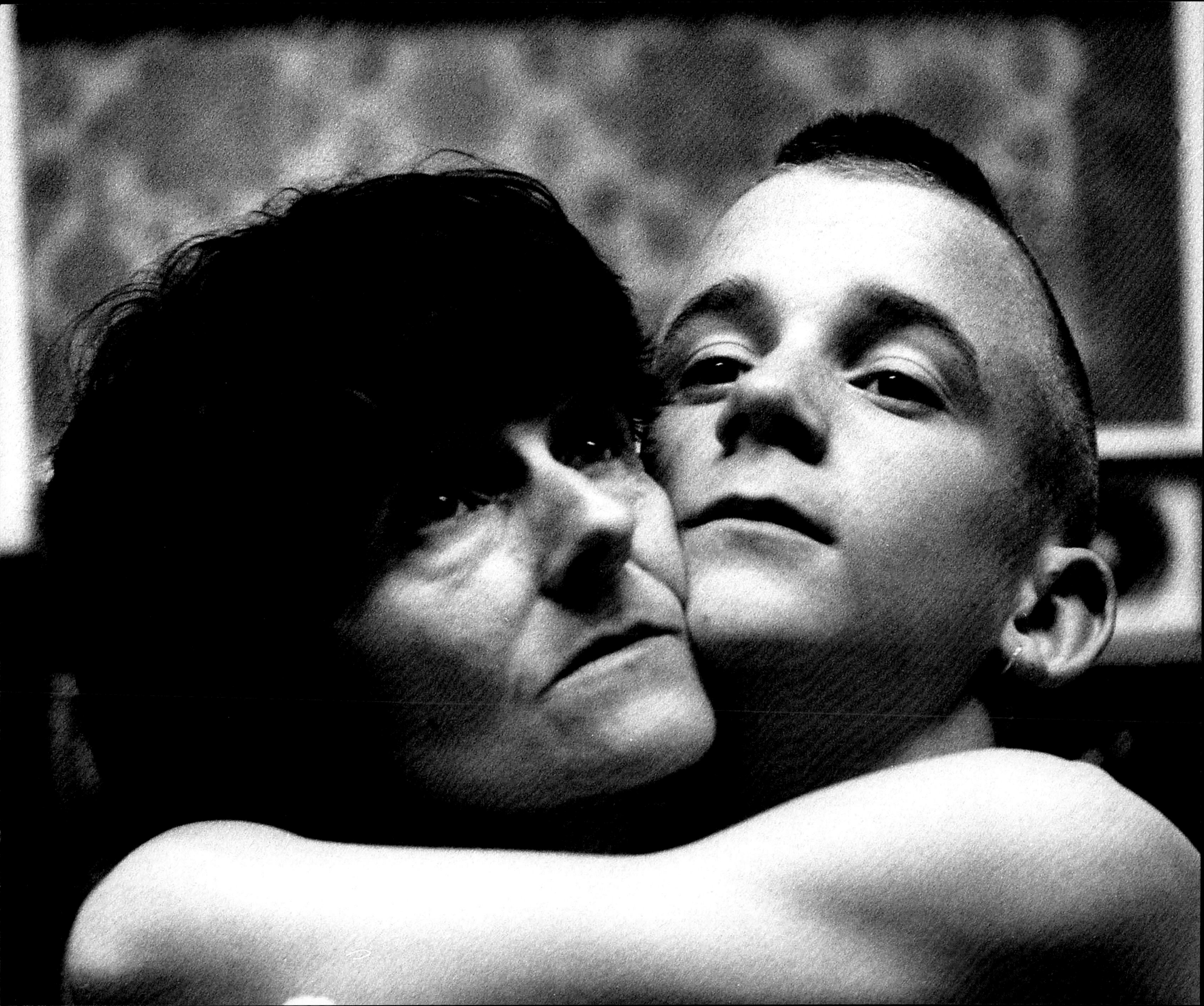

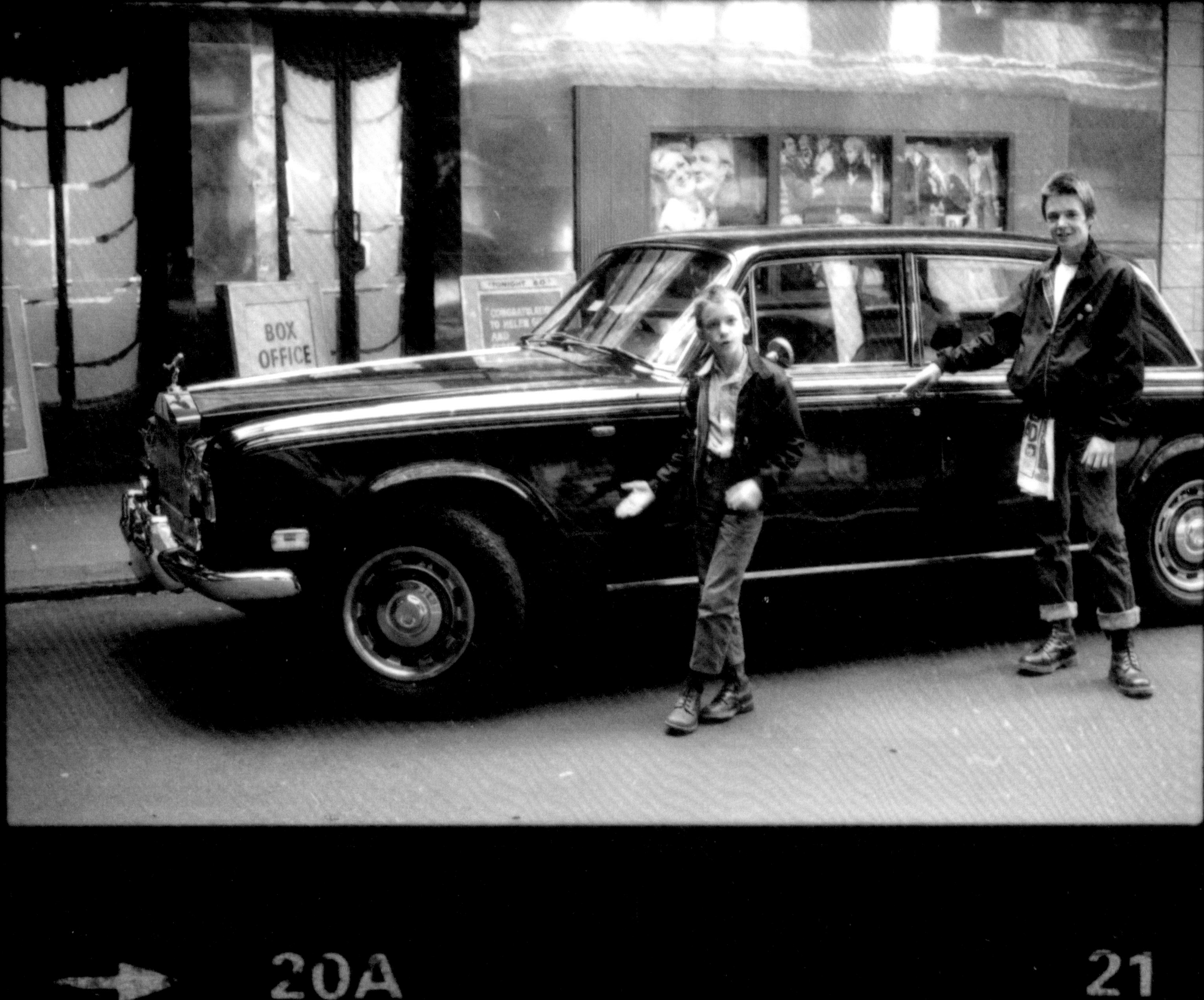

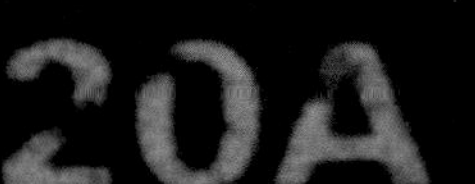
BOX
OFFICE
20A
21

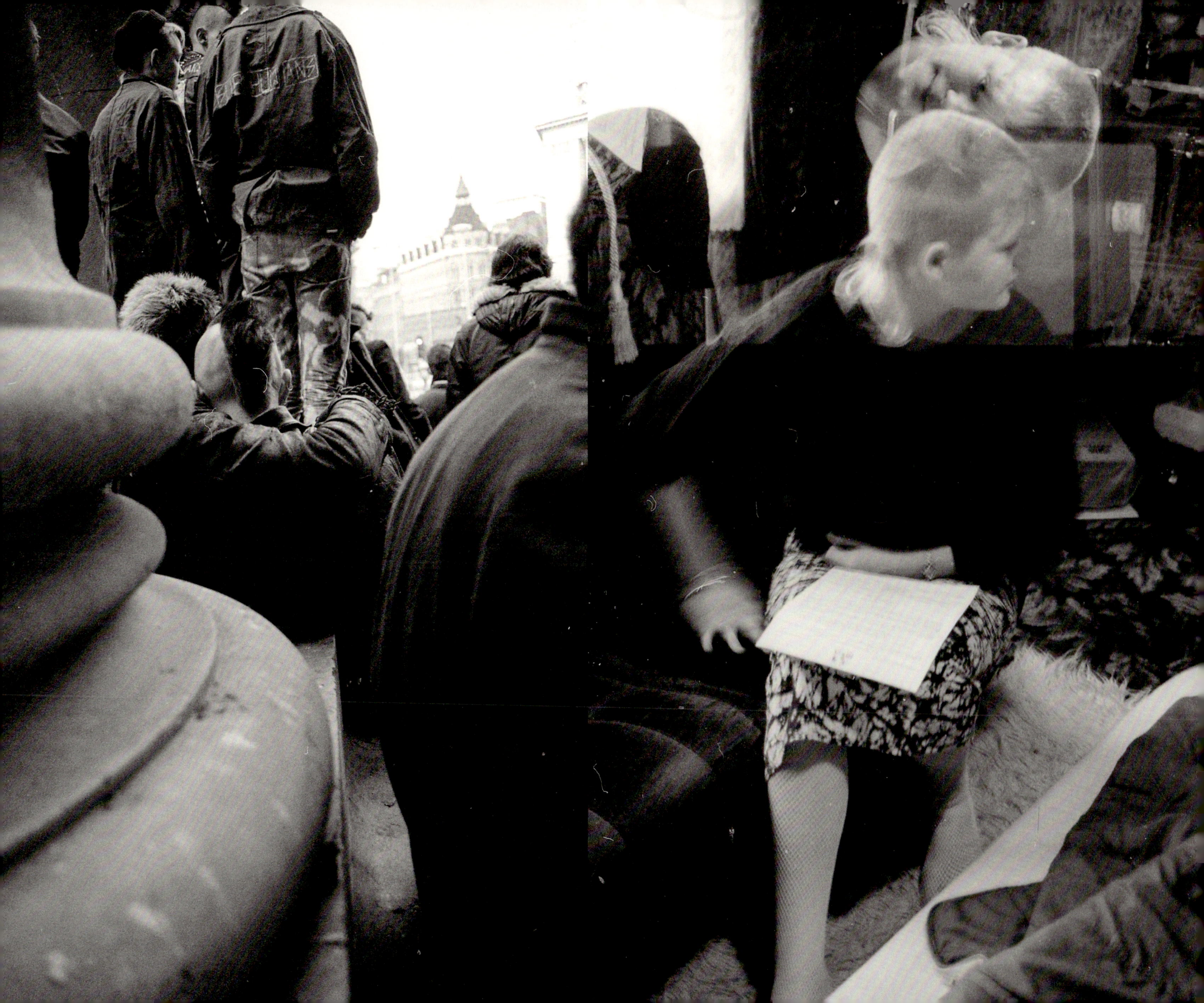

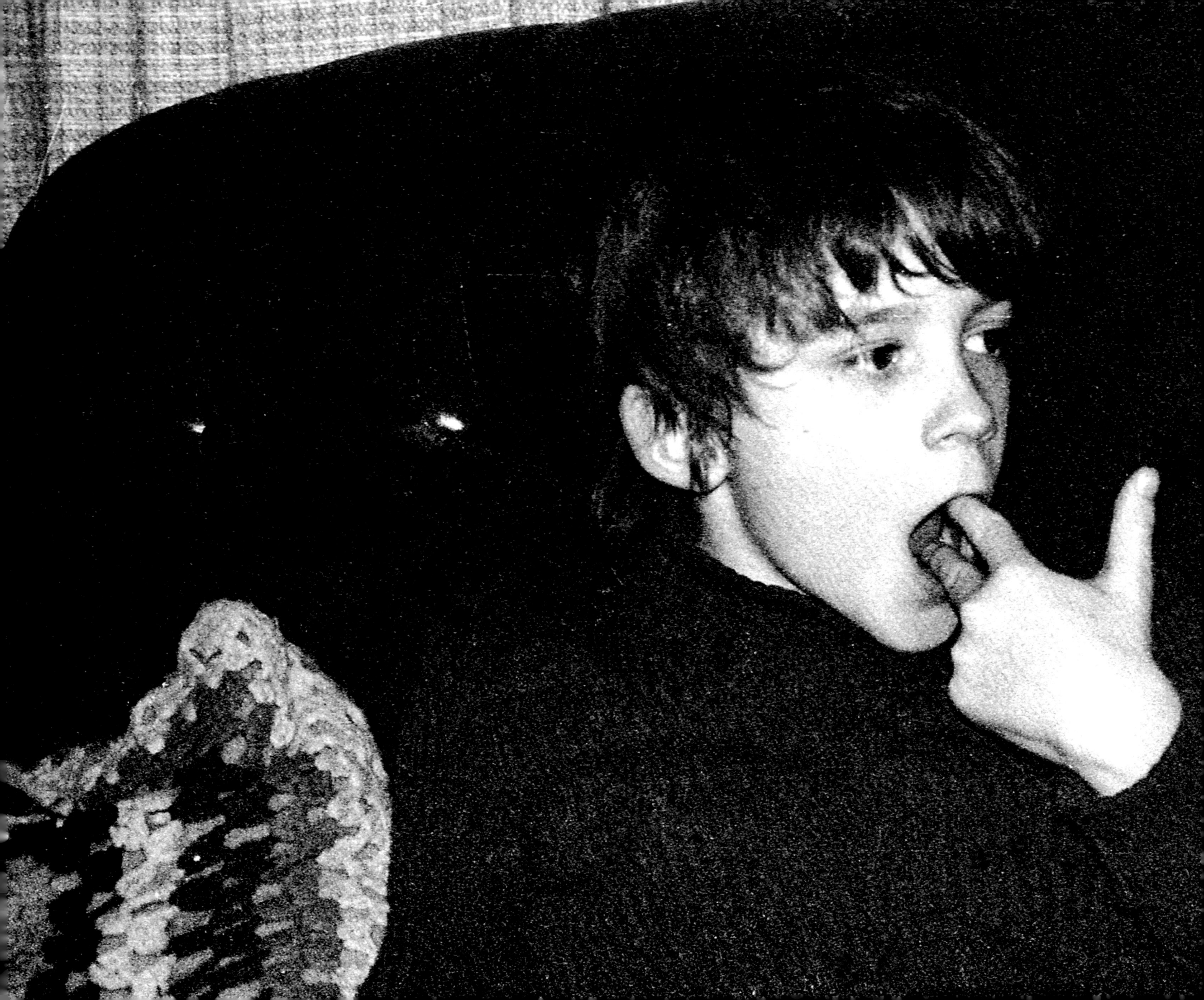

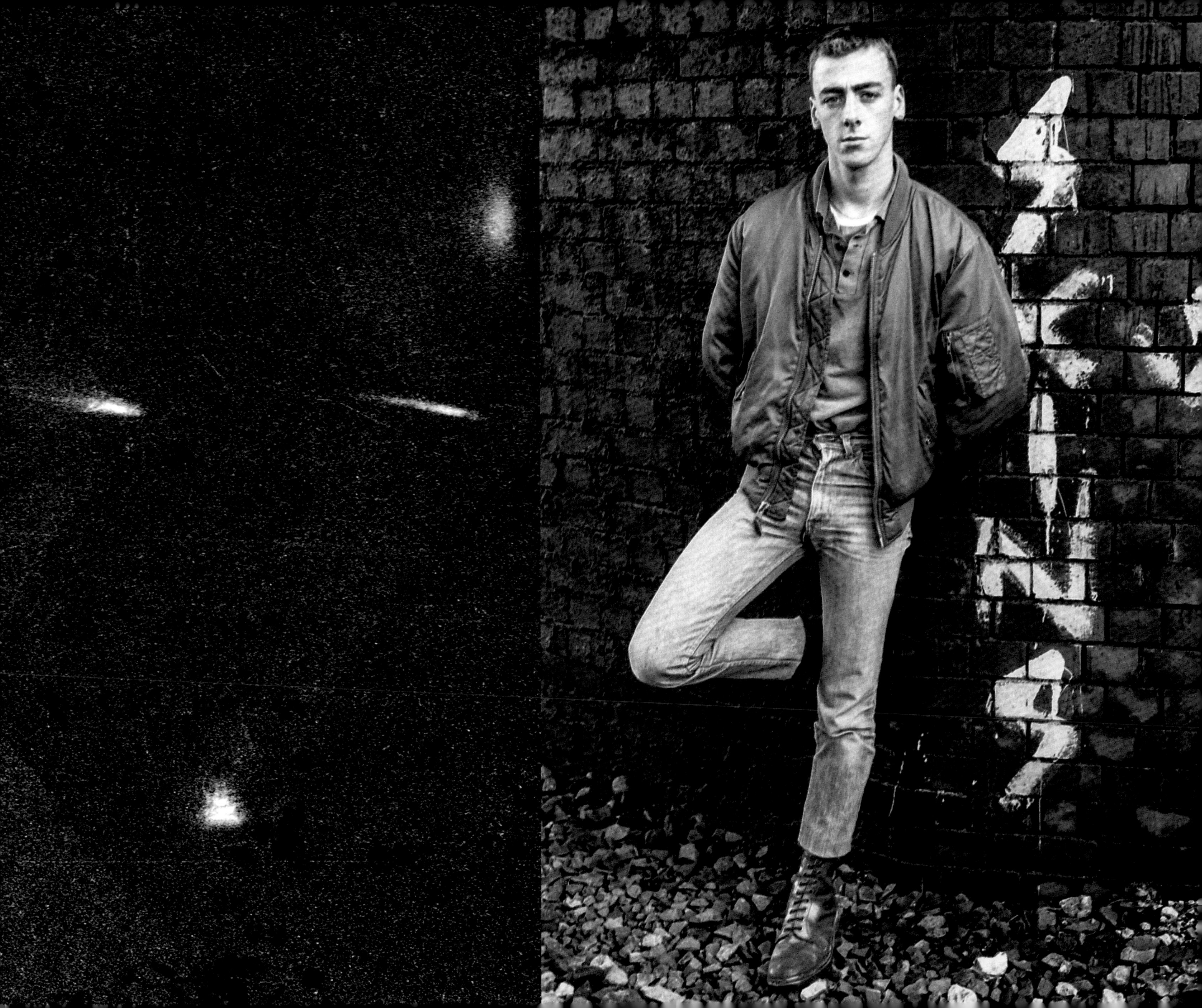

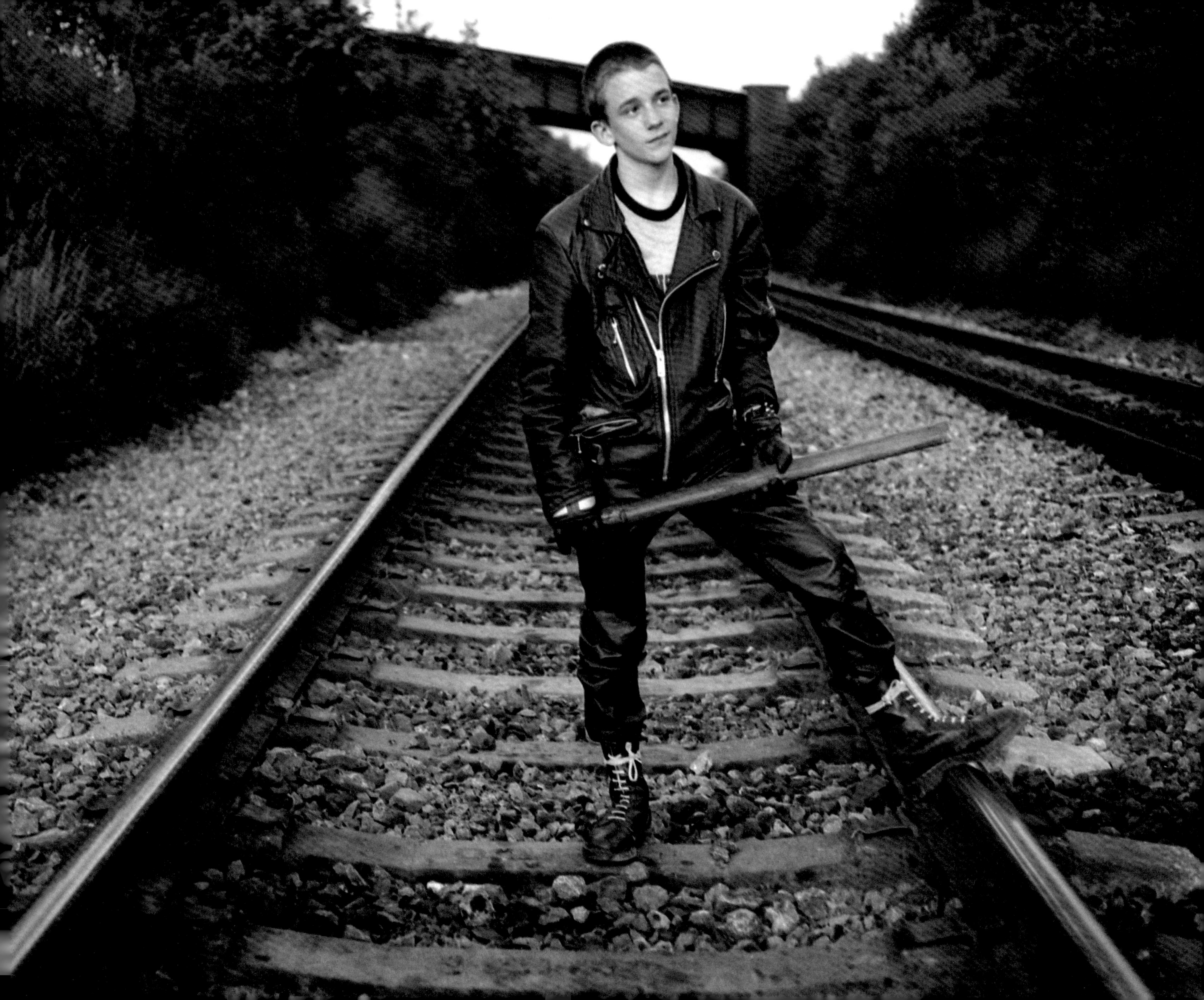

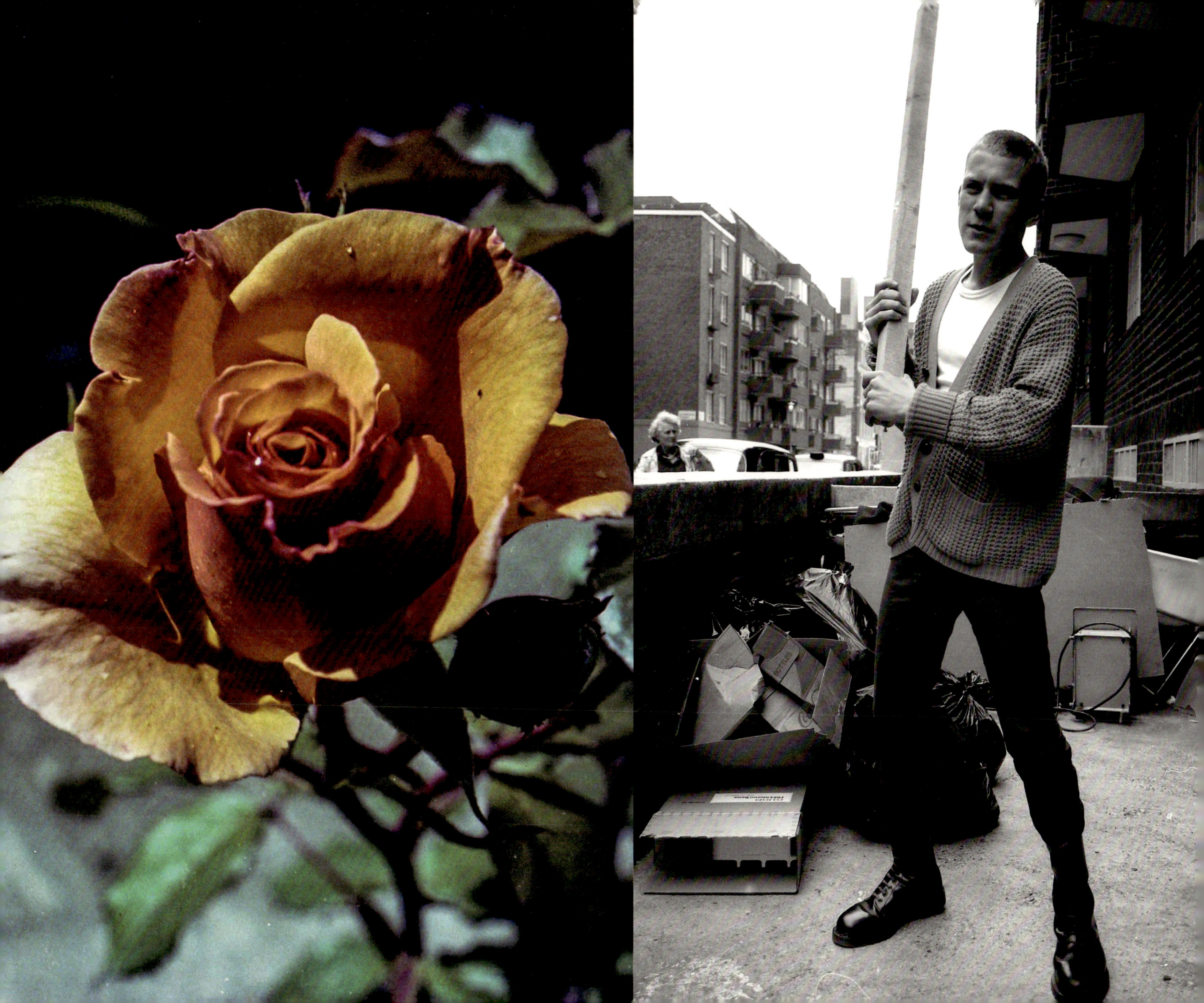

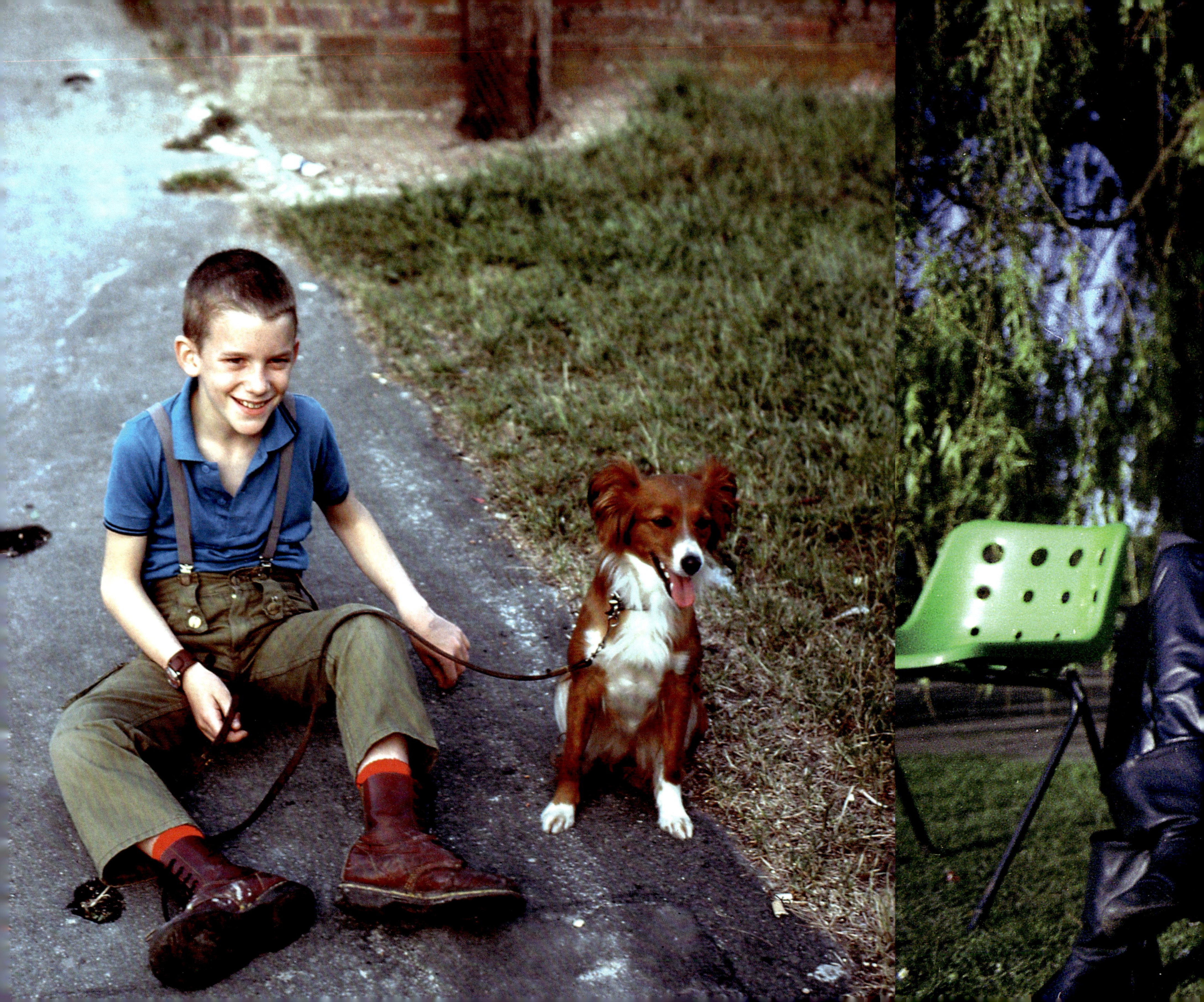

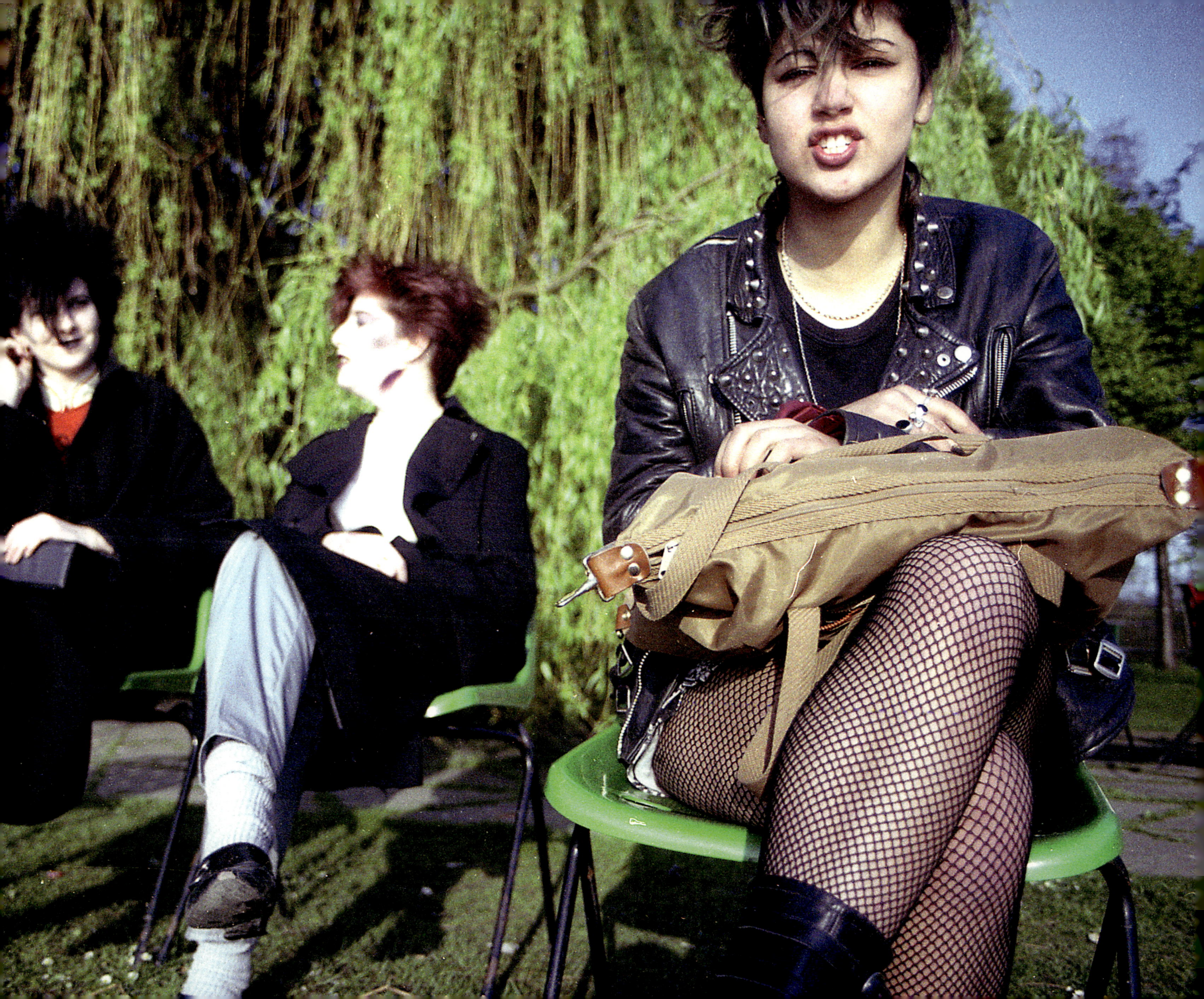

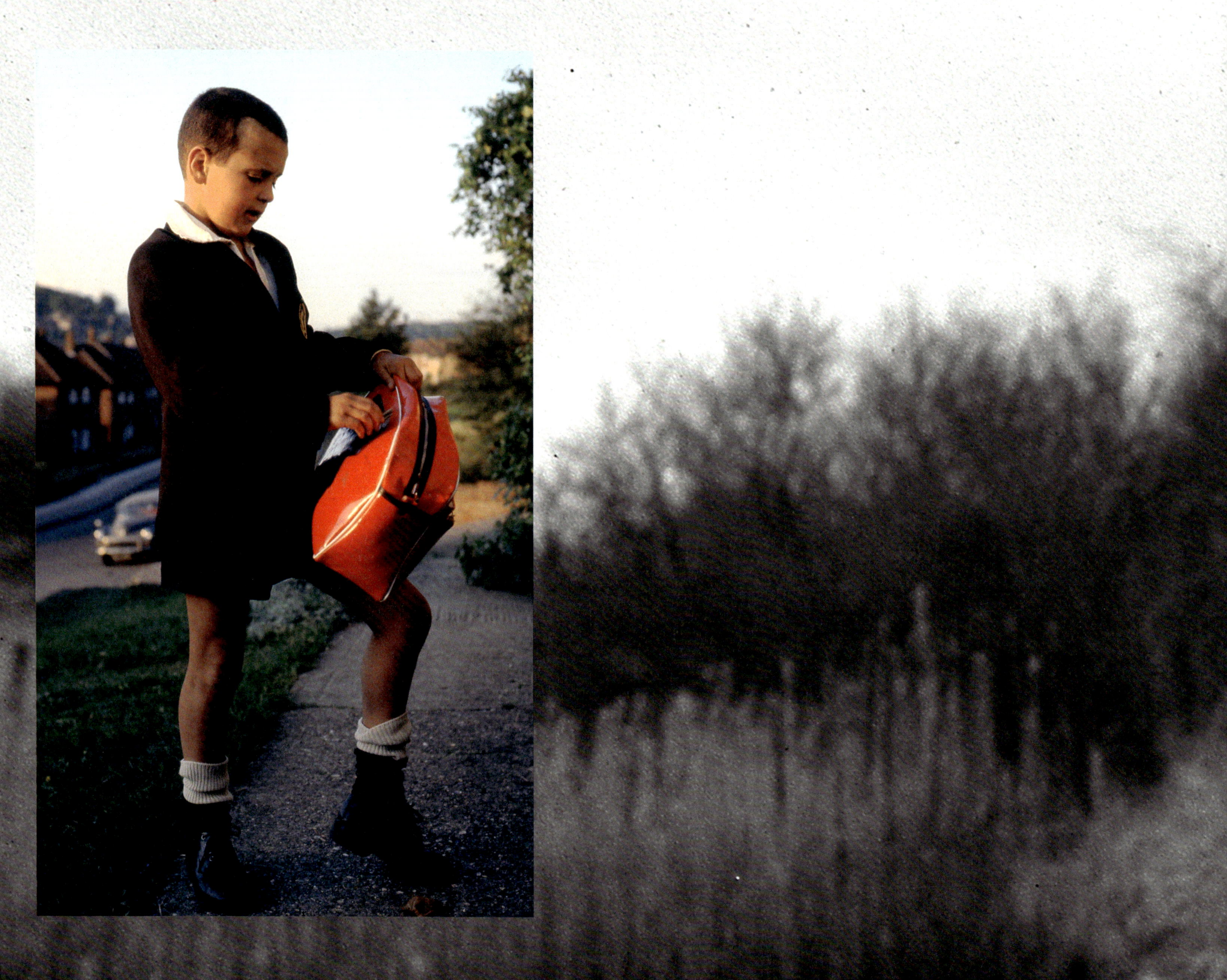

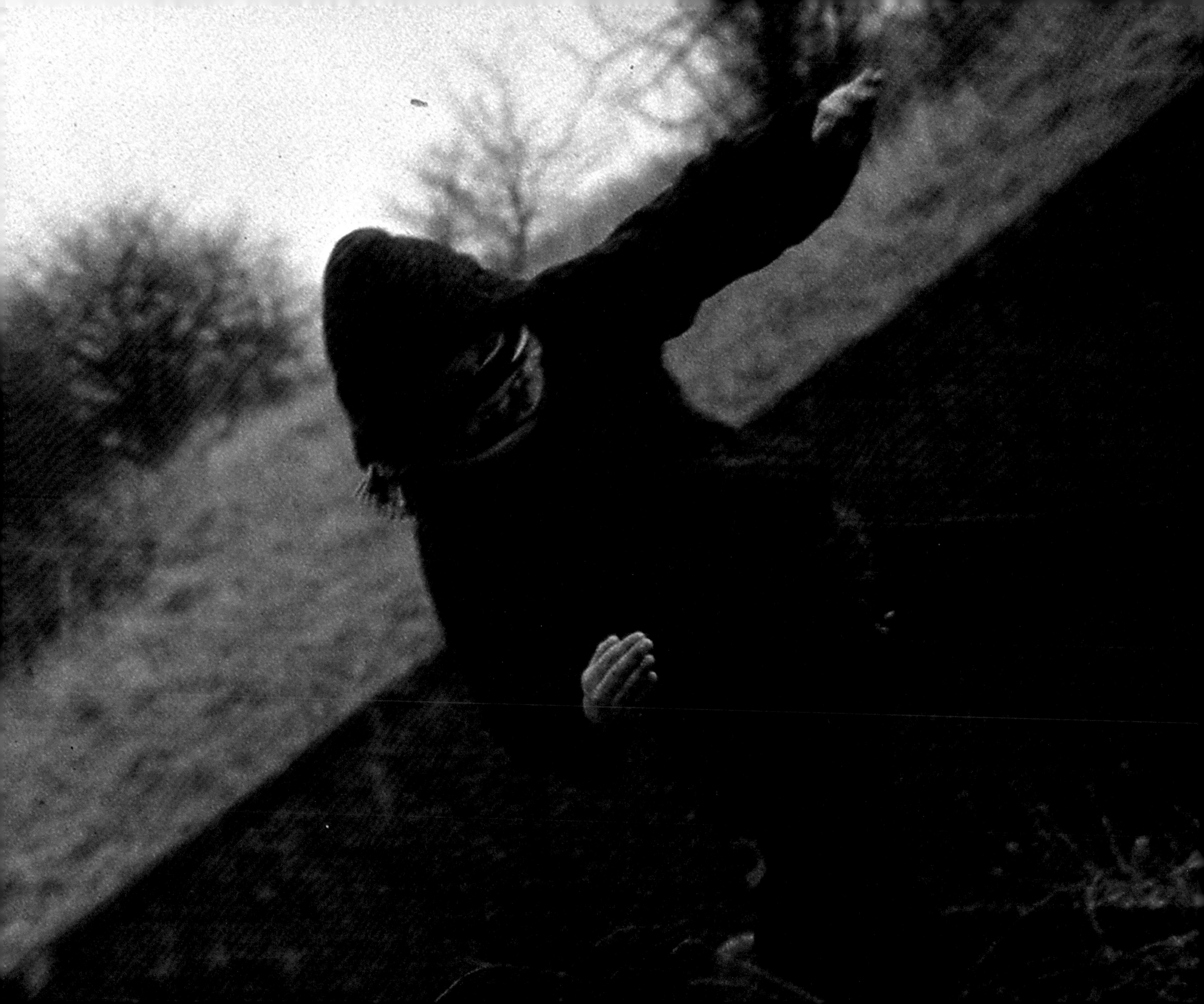

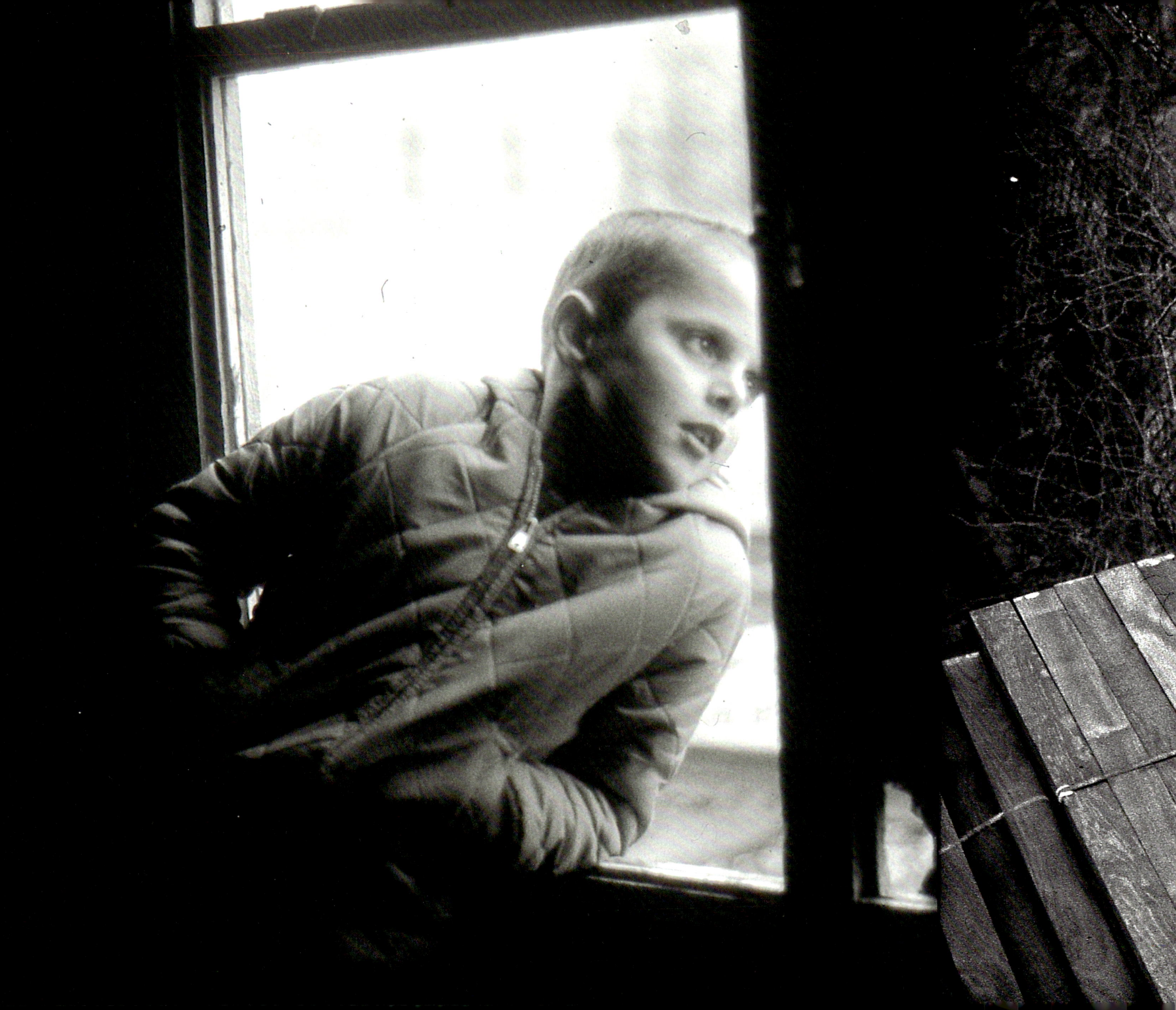

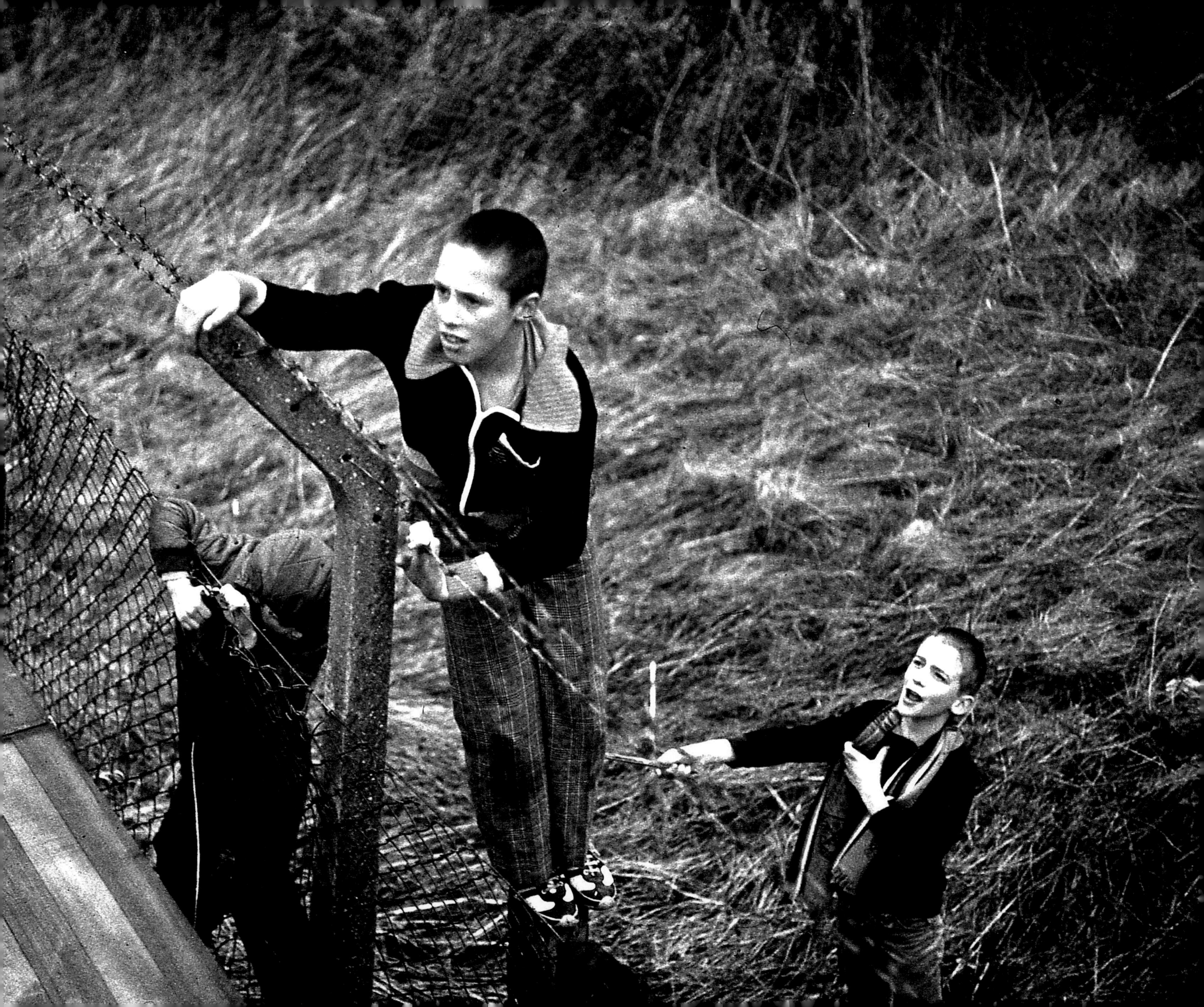

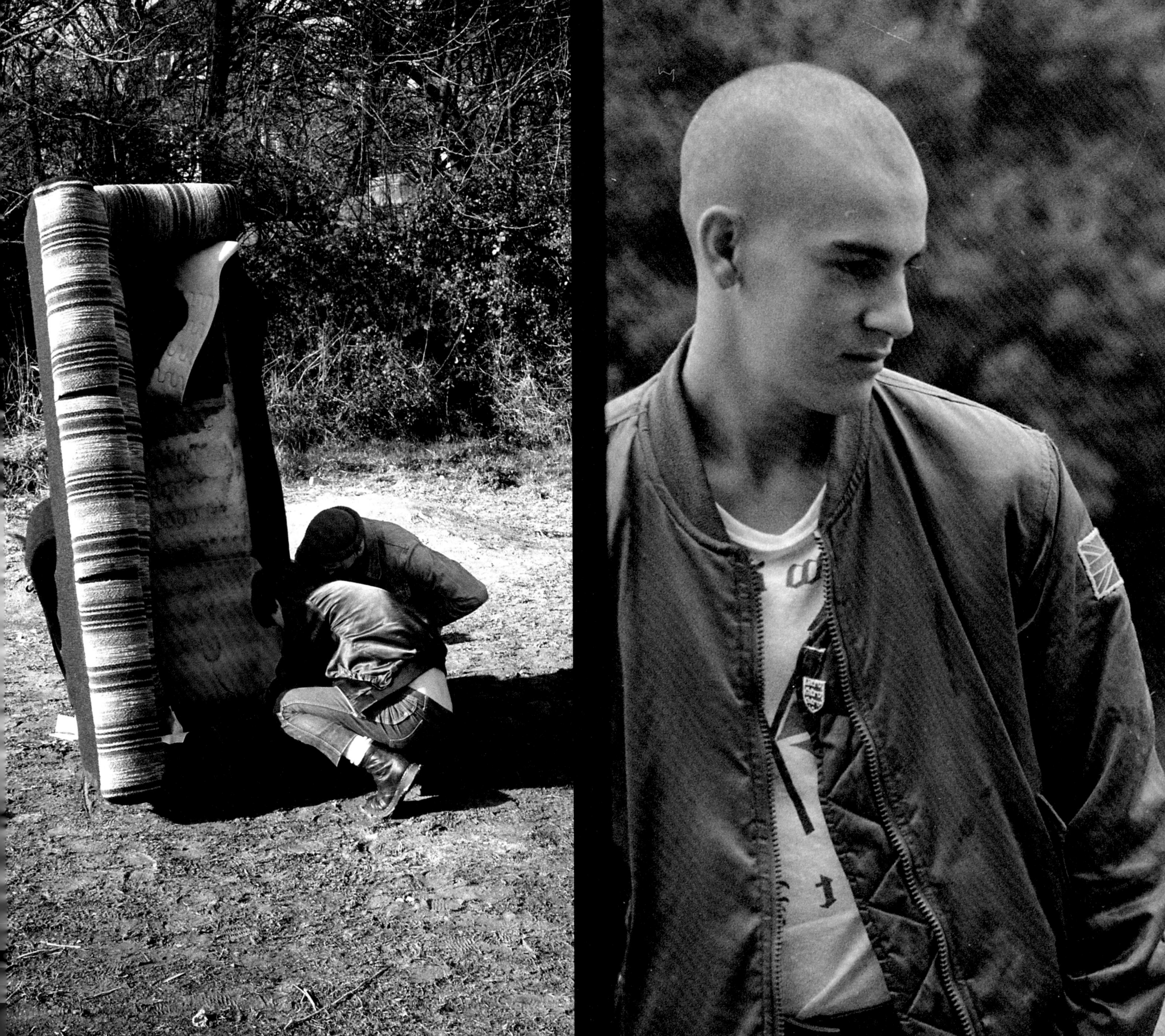

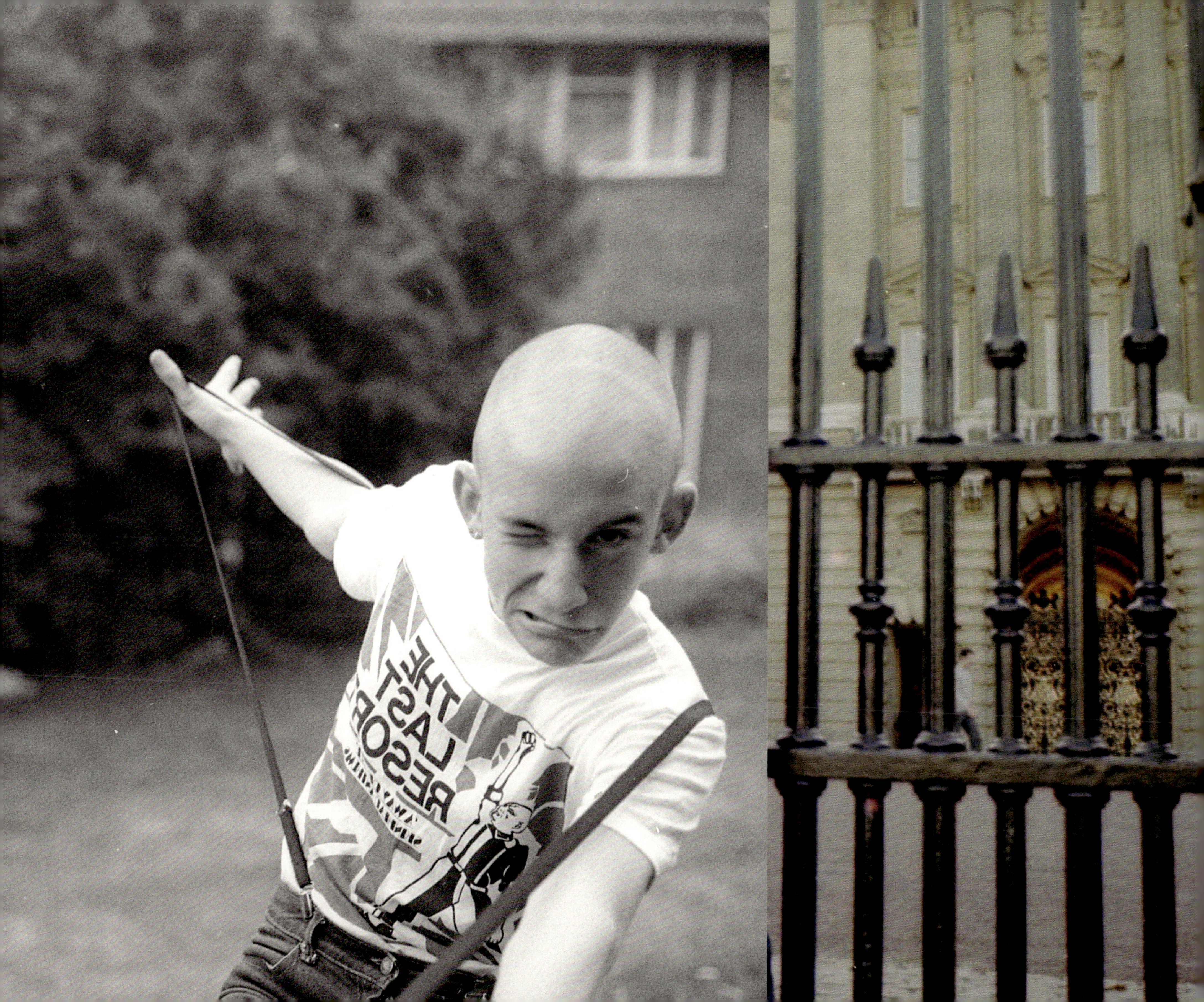
THE
LAST

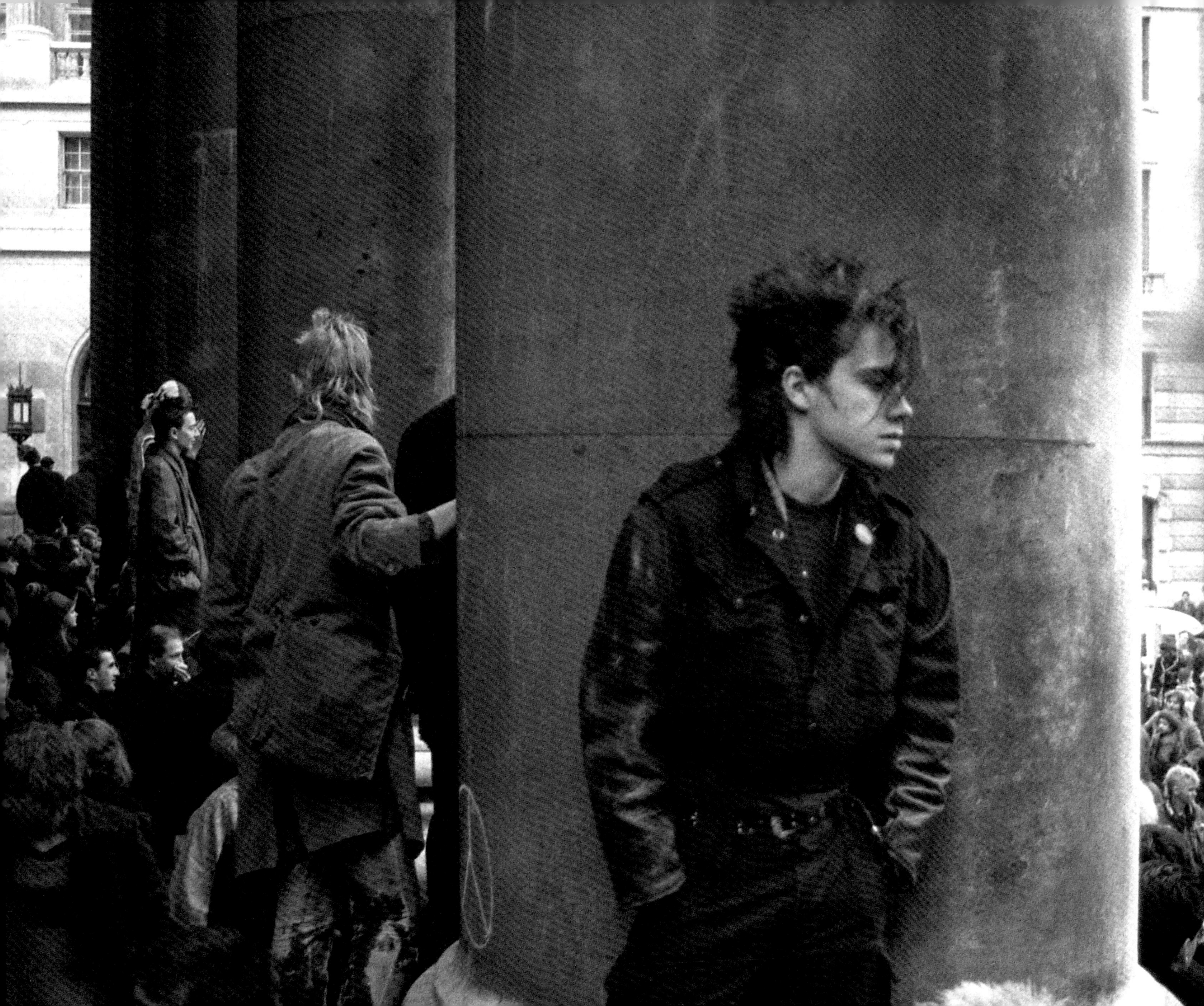

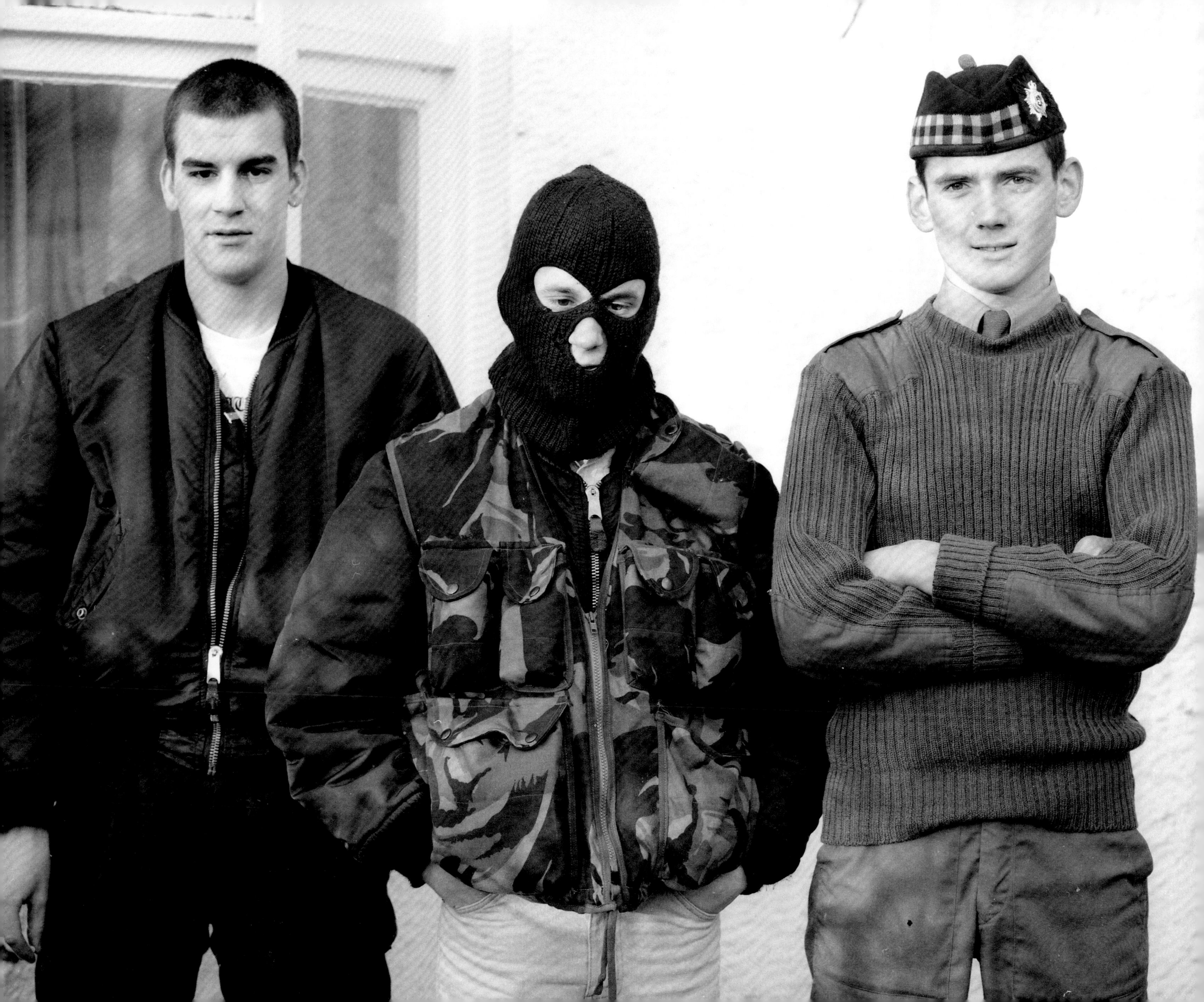

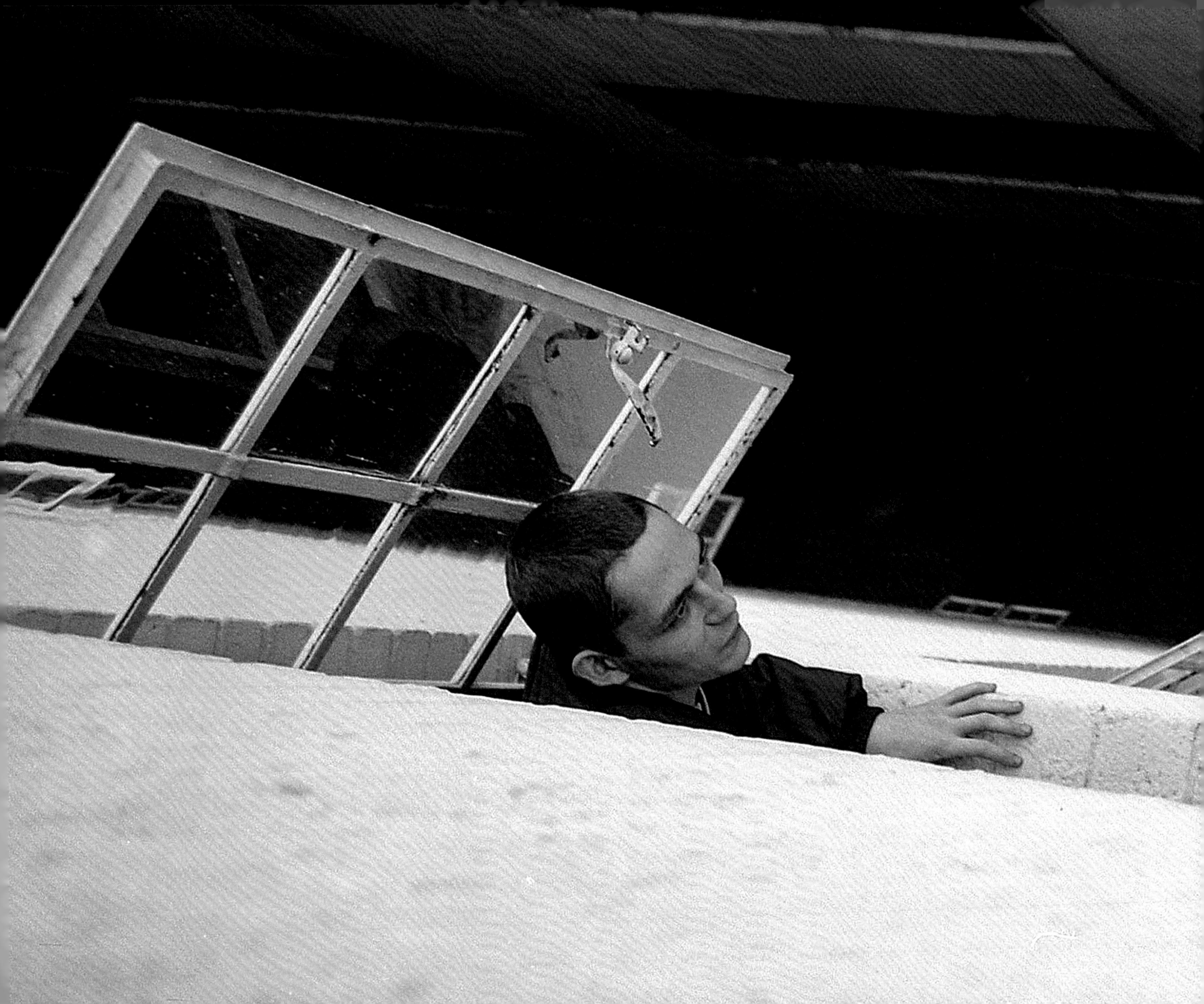

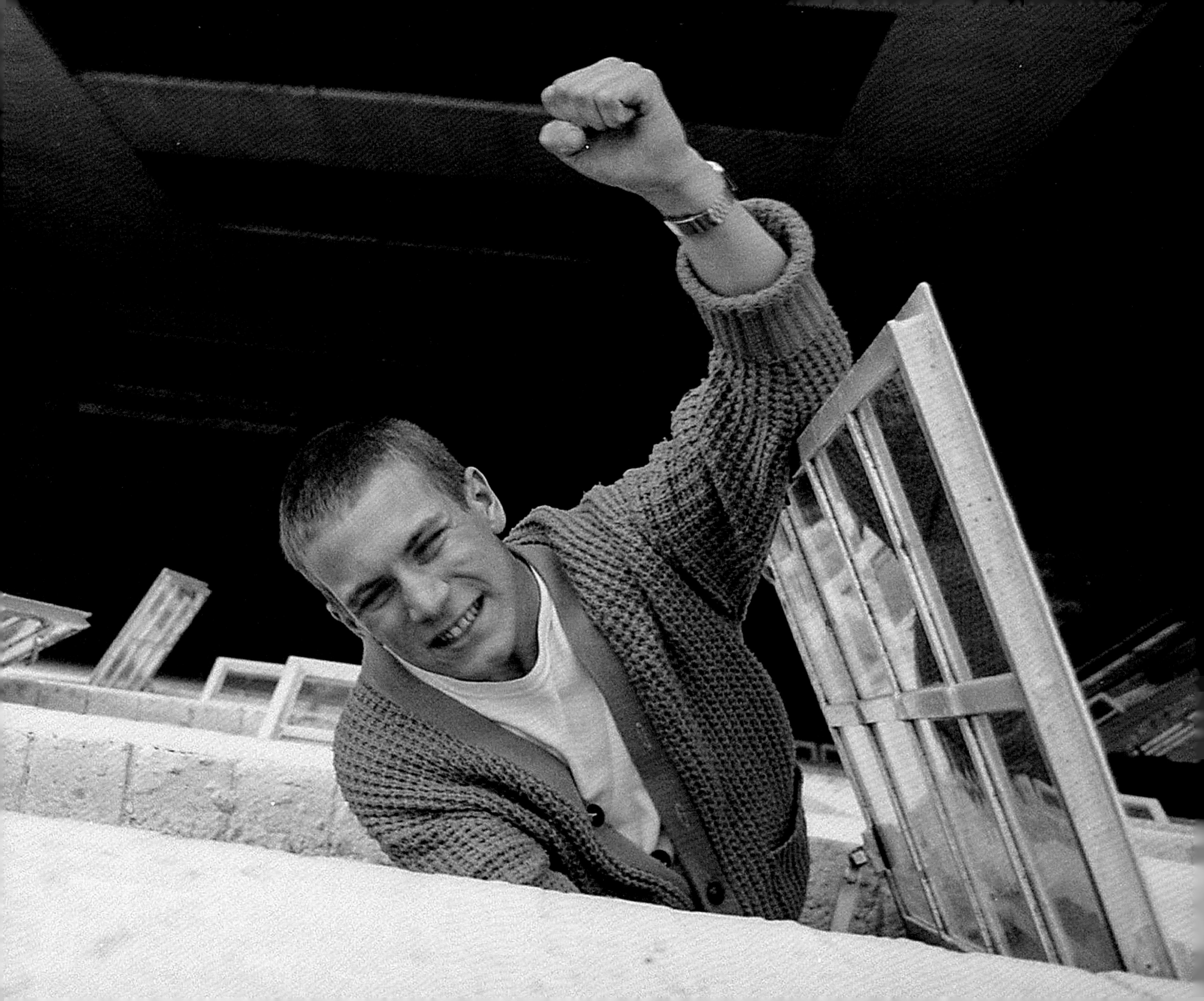

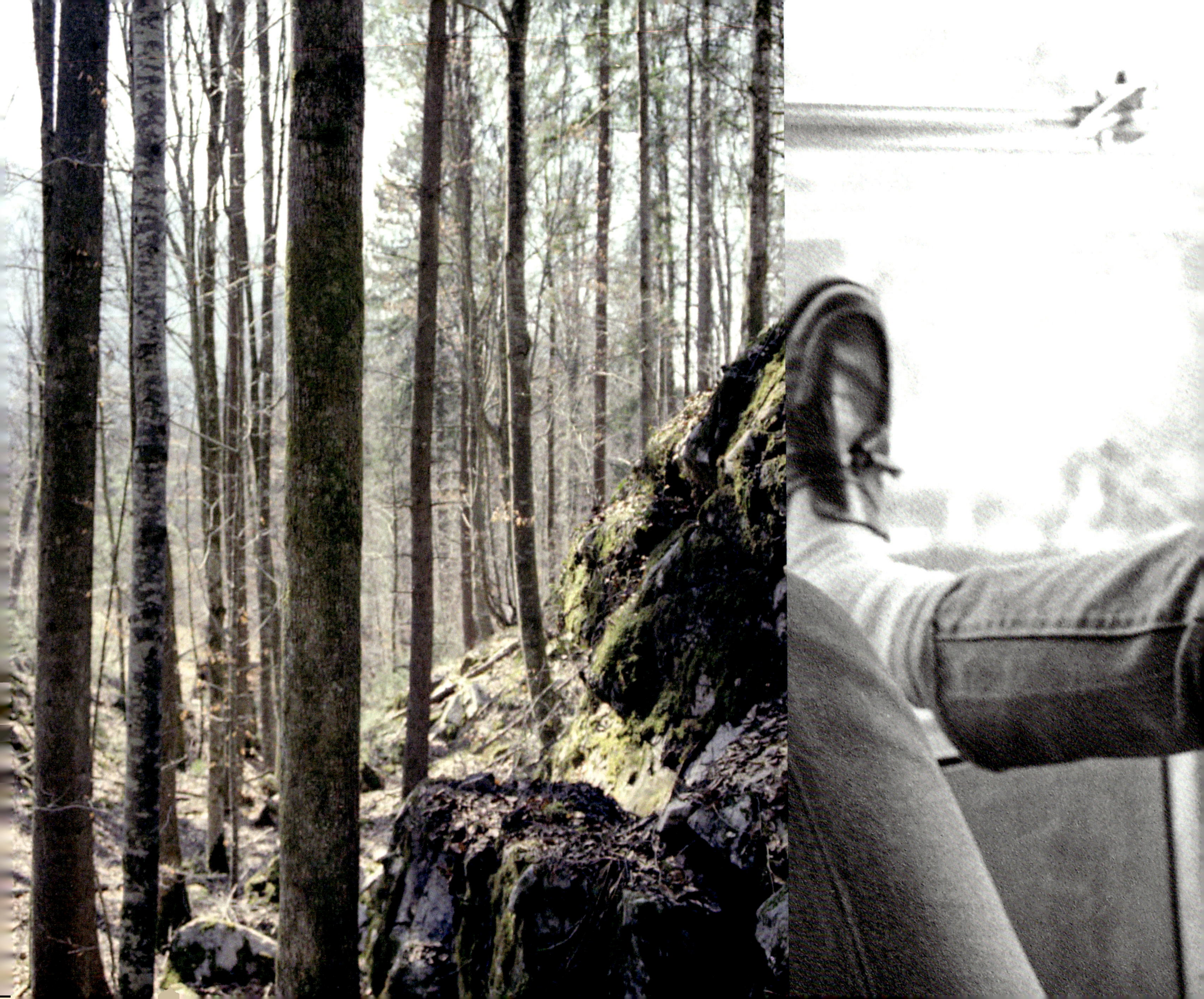

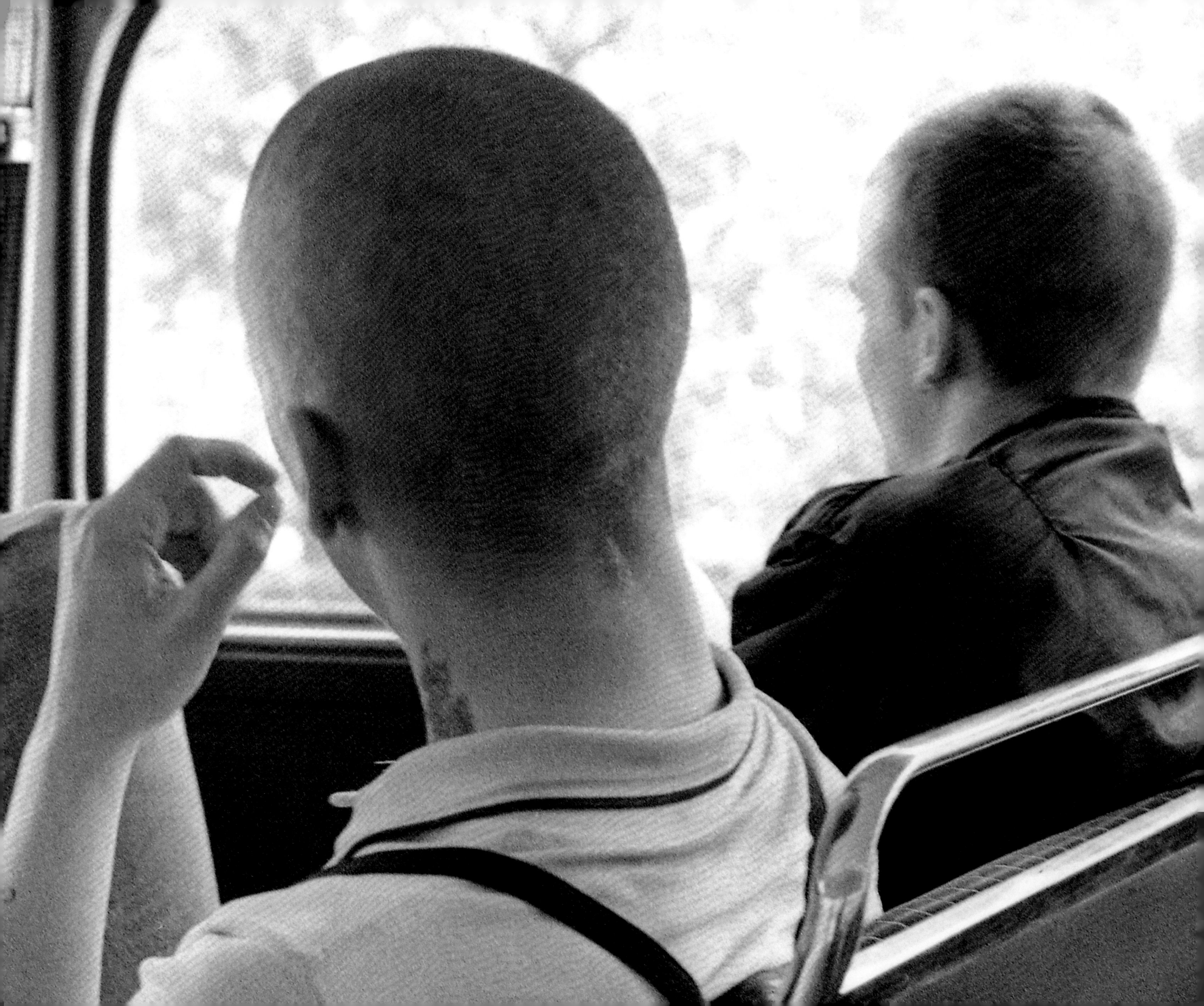

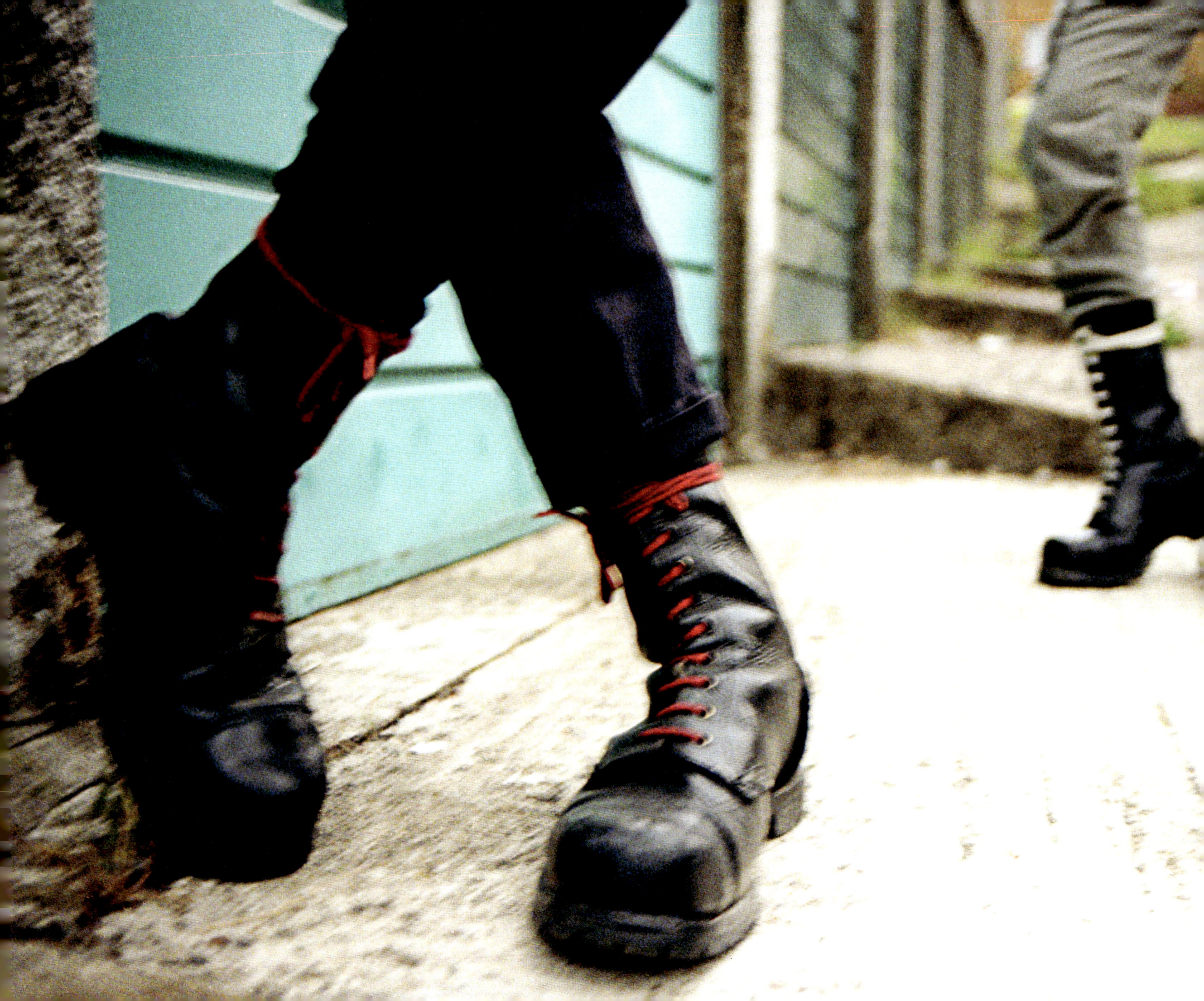

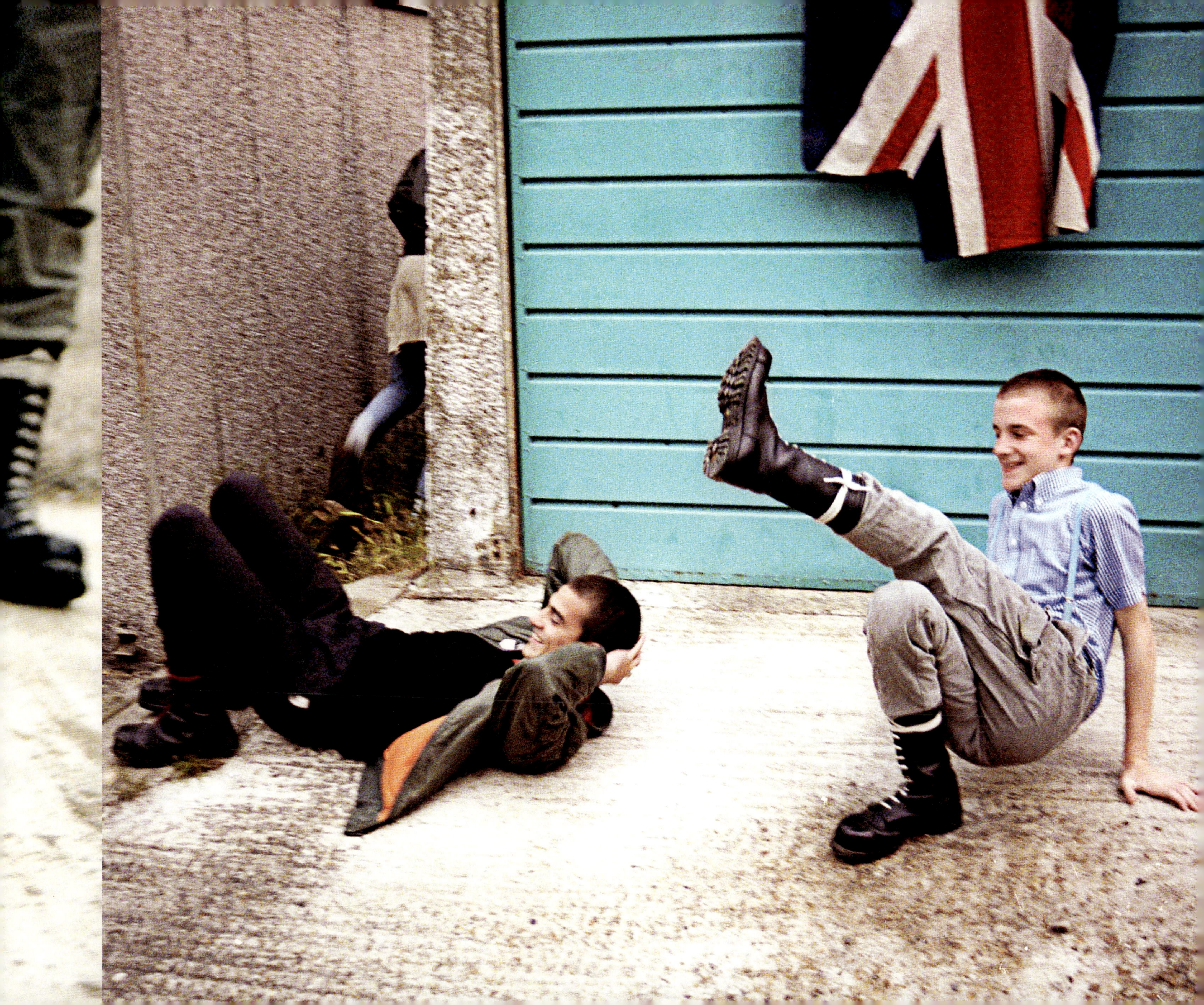

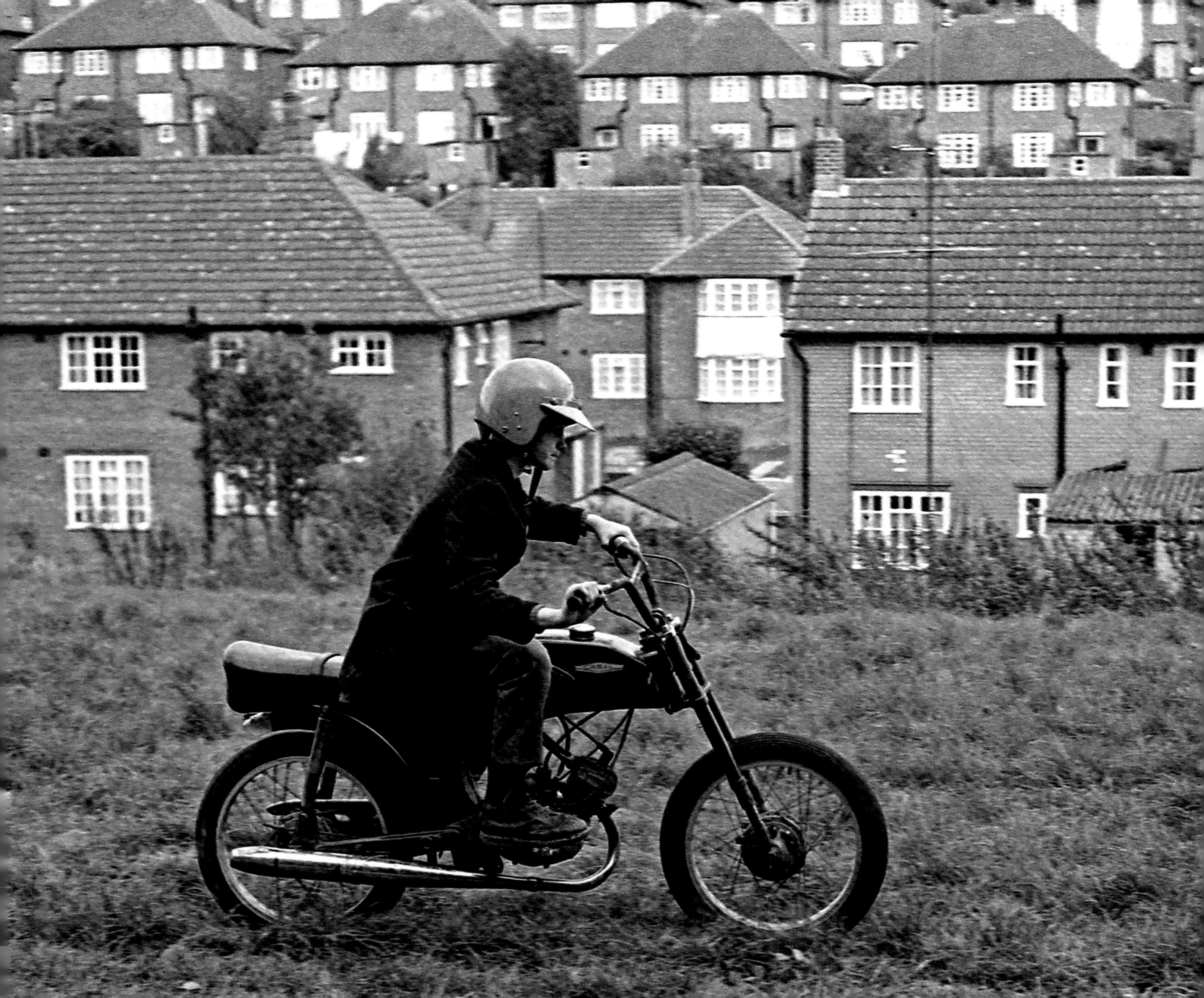

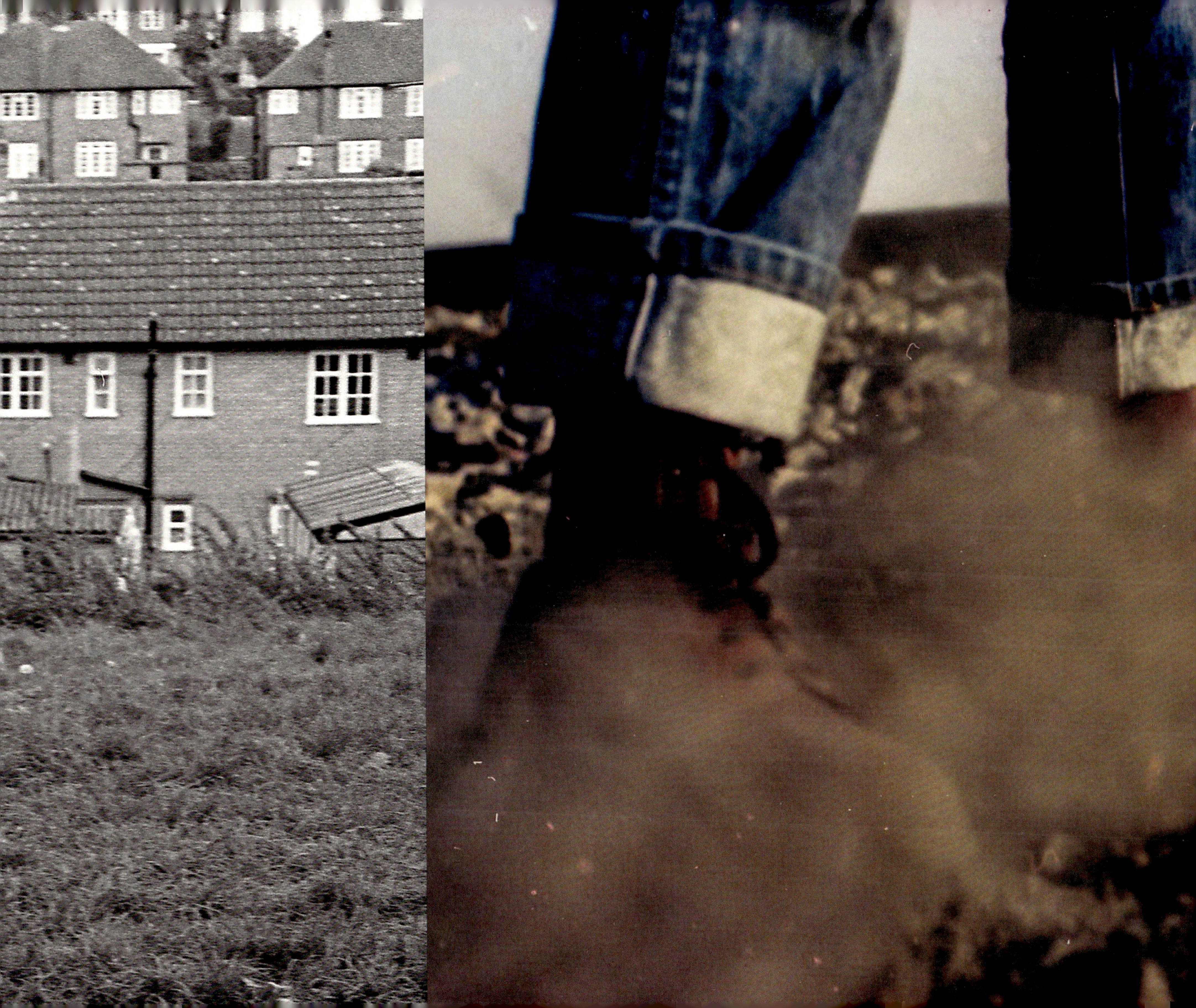

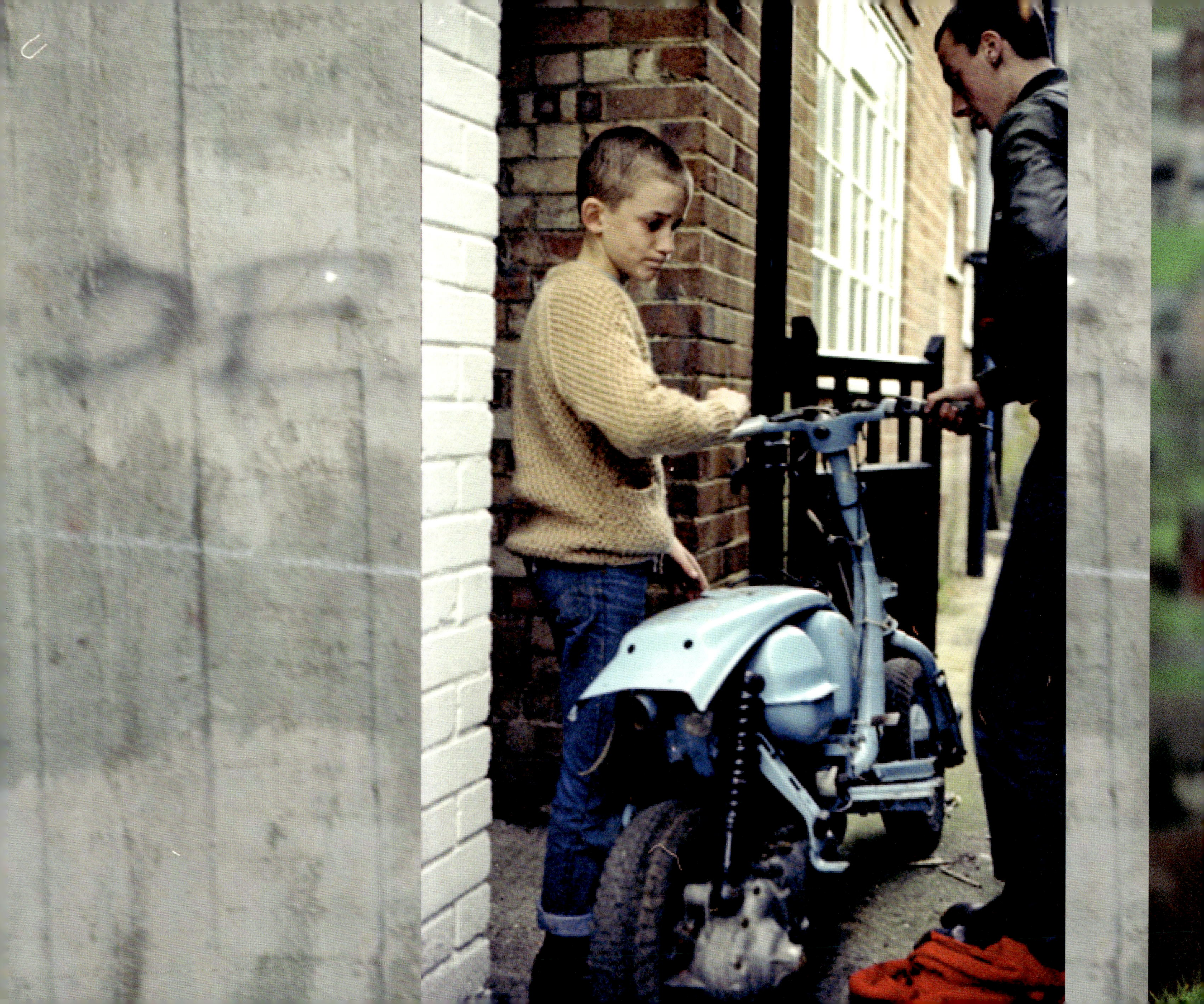

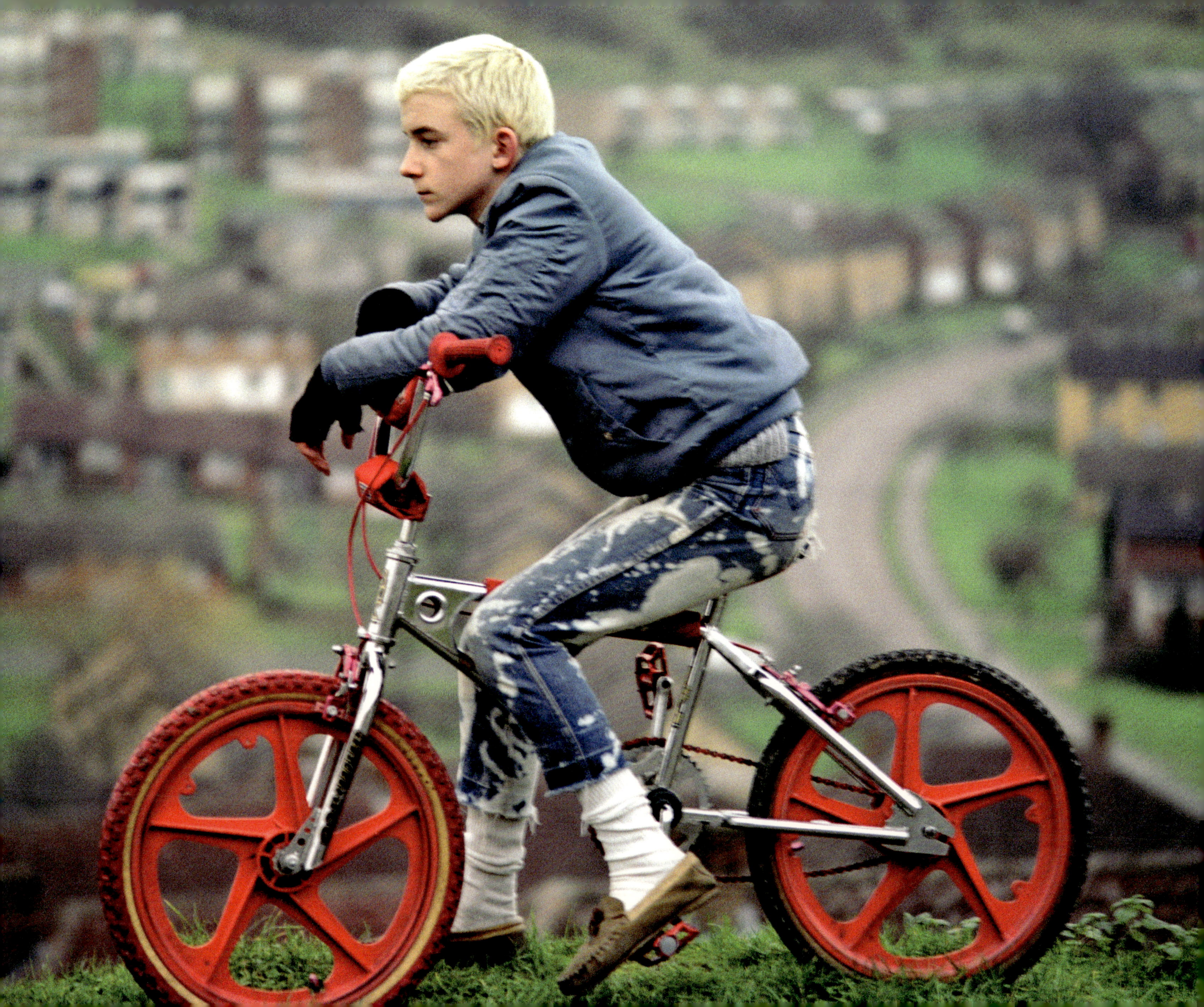

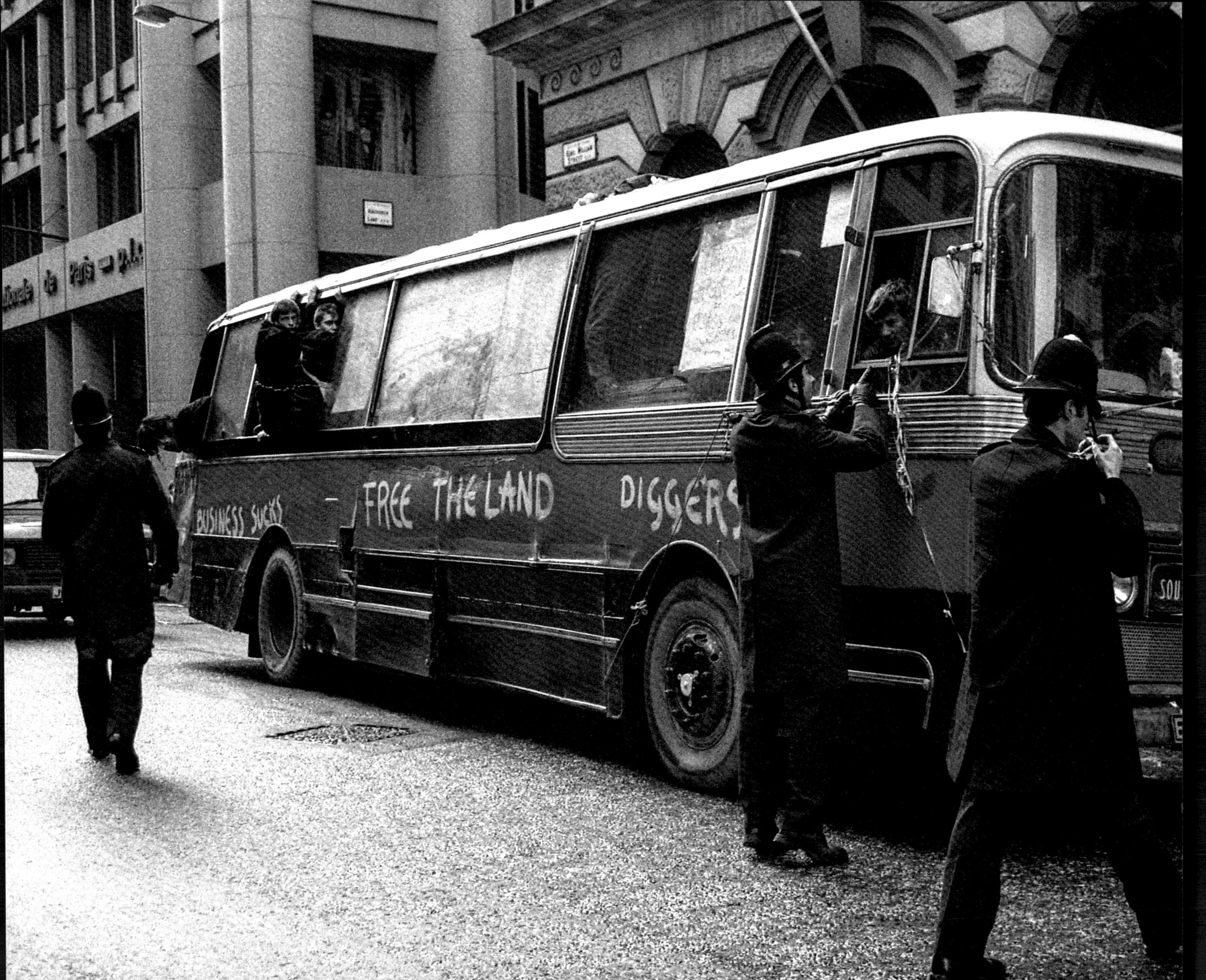
BUSINESS SUCKS
FREE THE LAND
DIGGERS

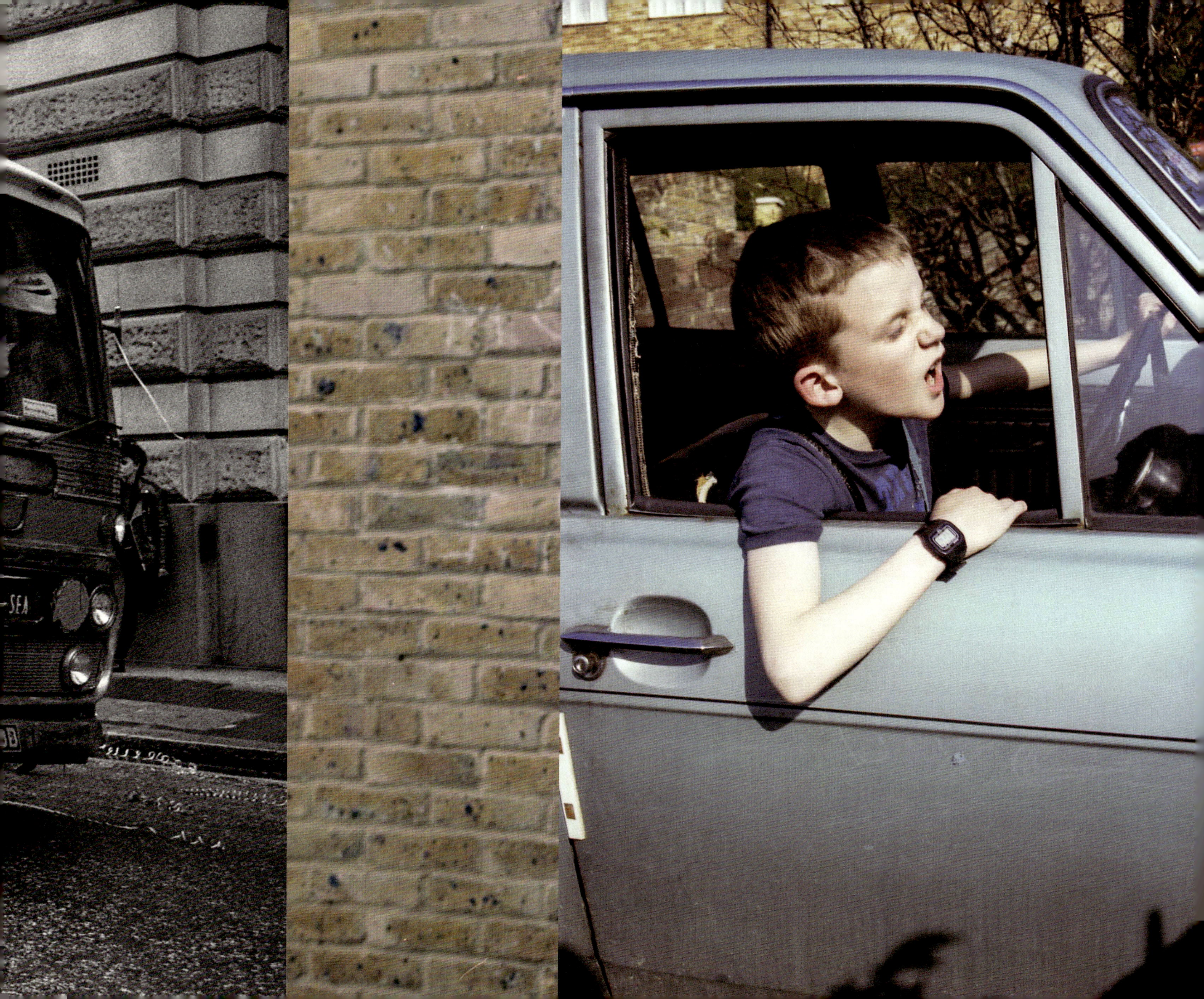

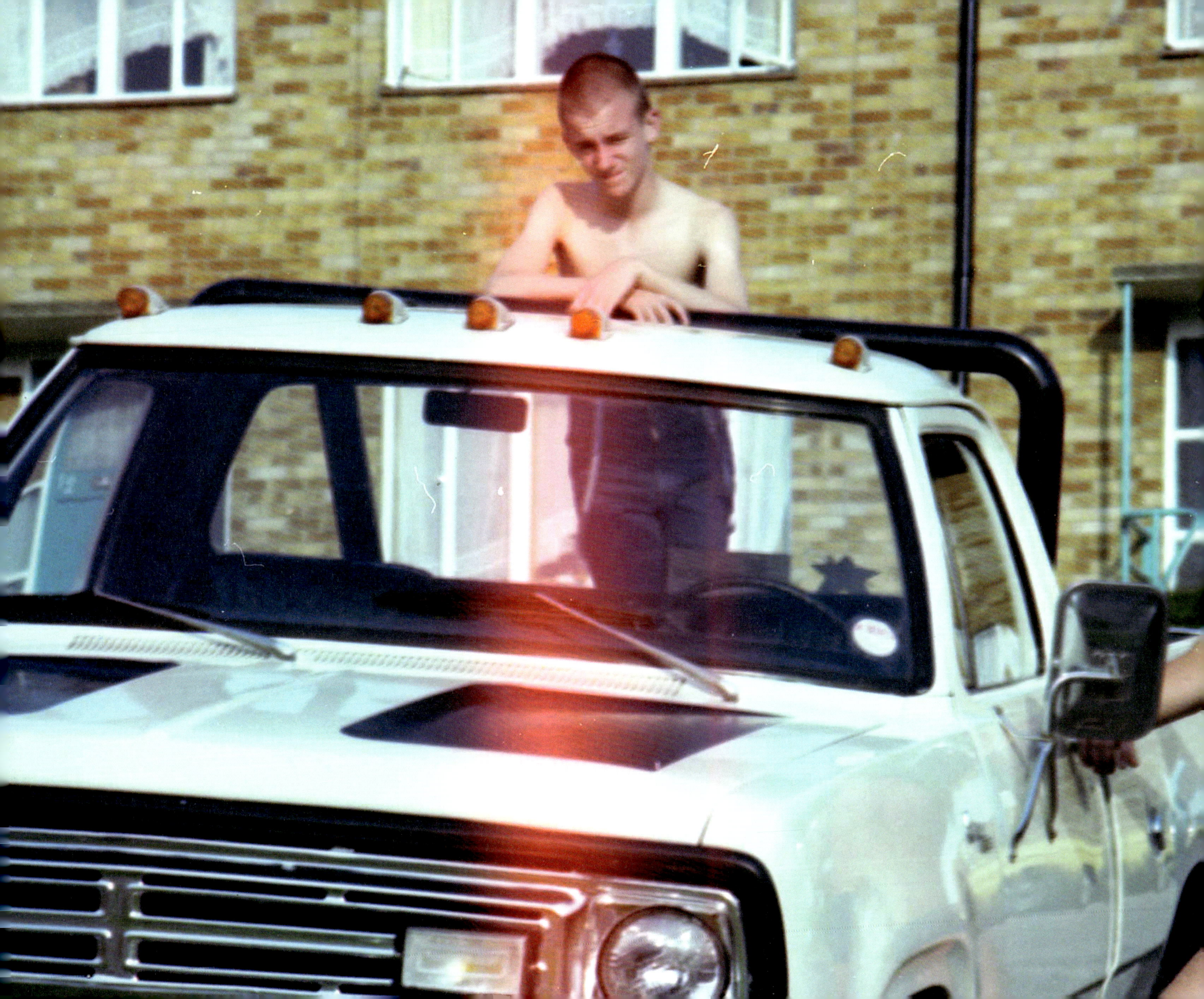

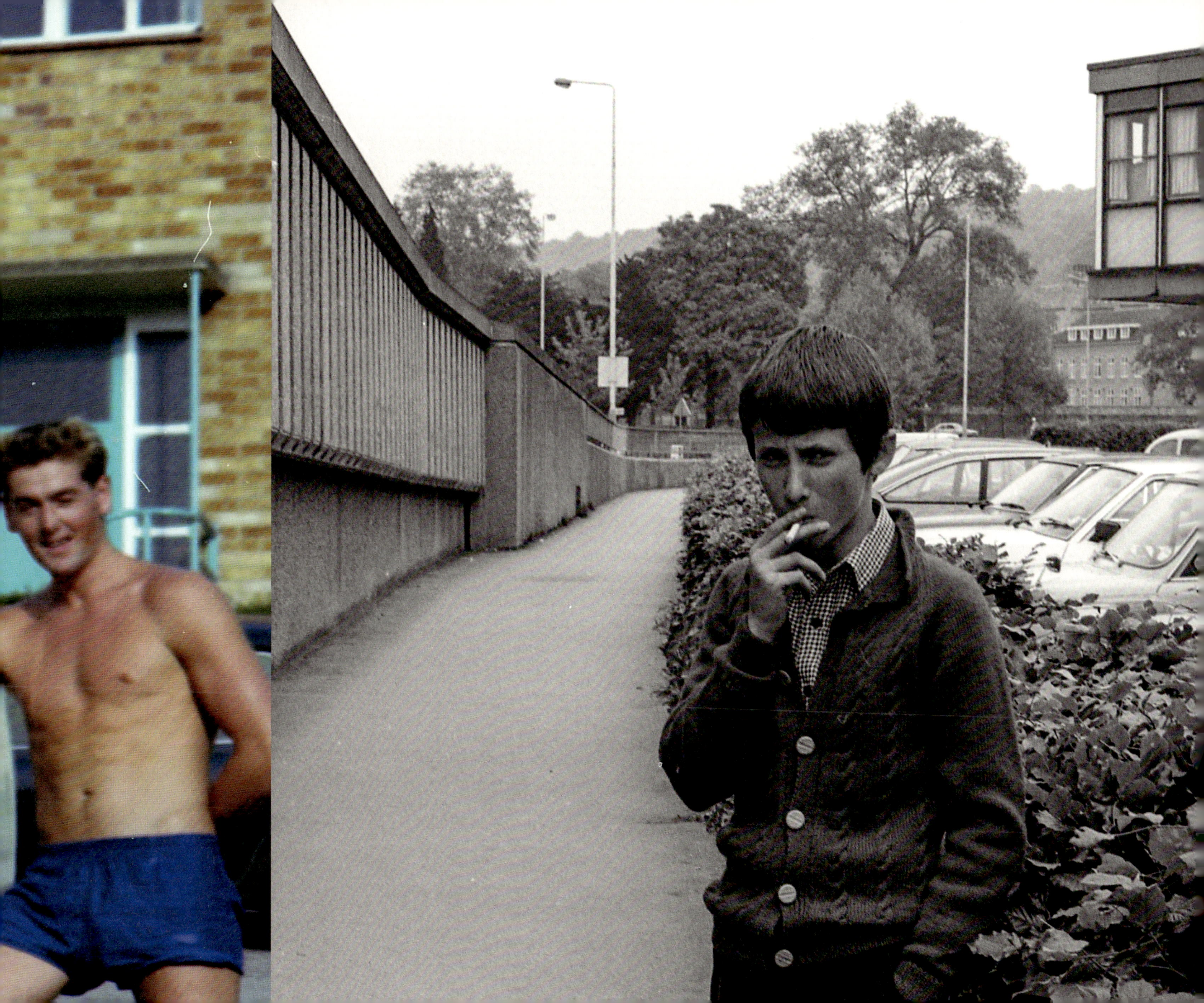

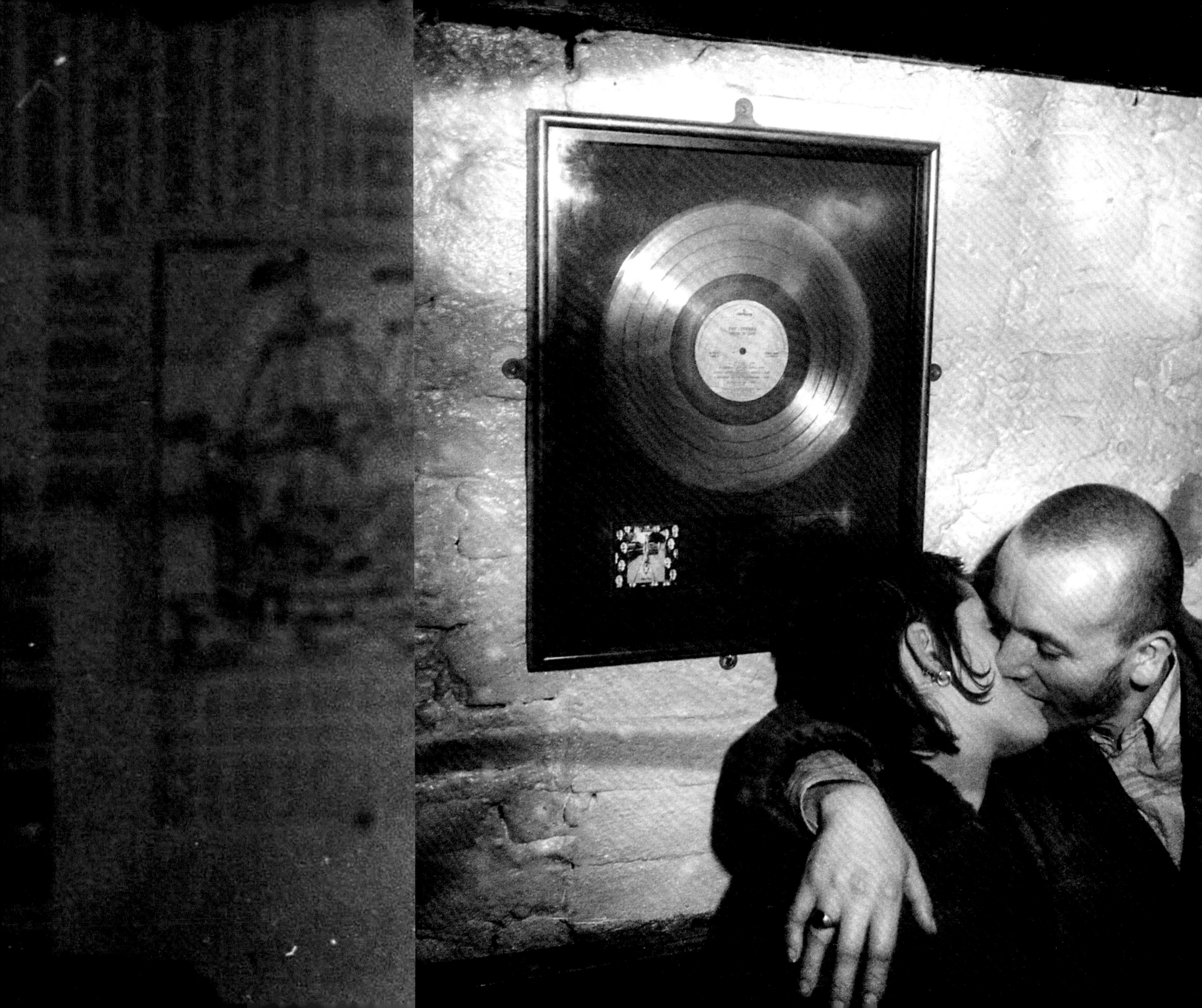

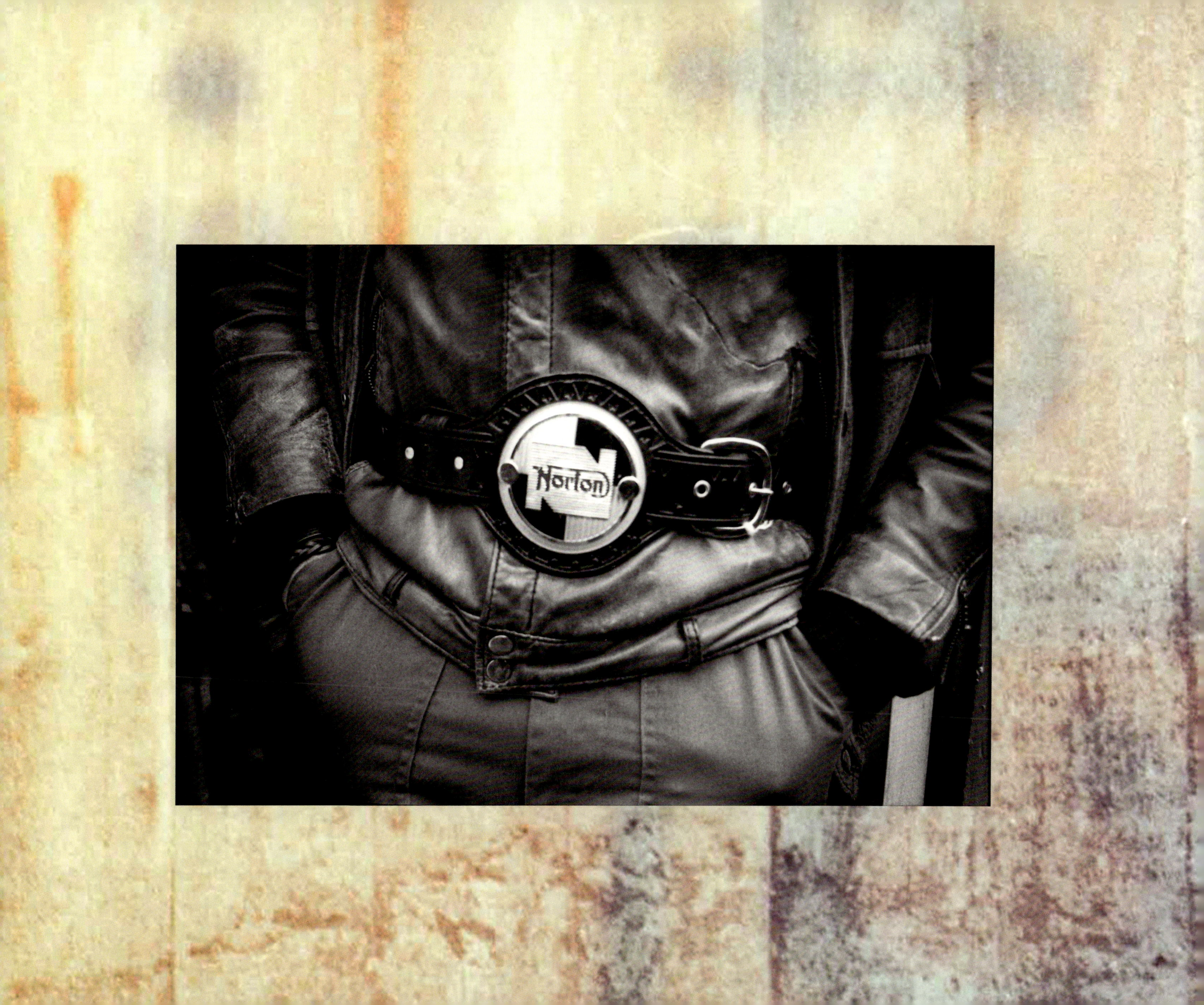
Norton

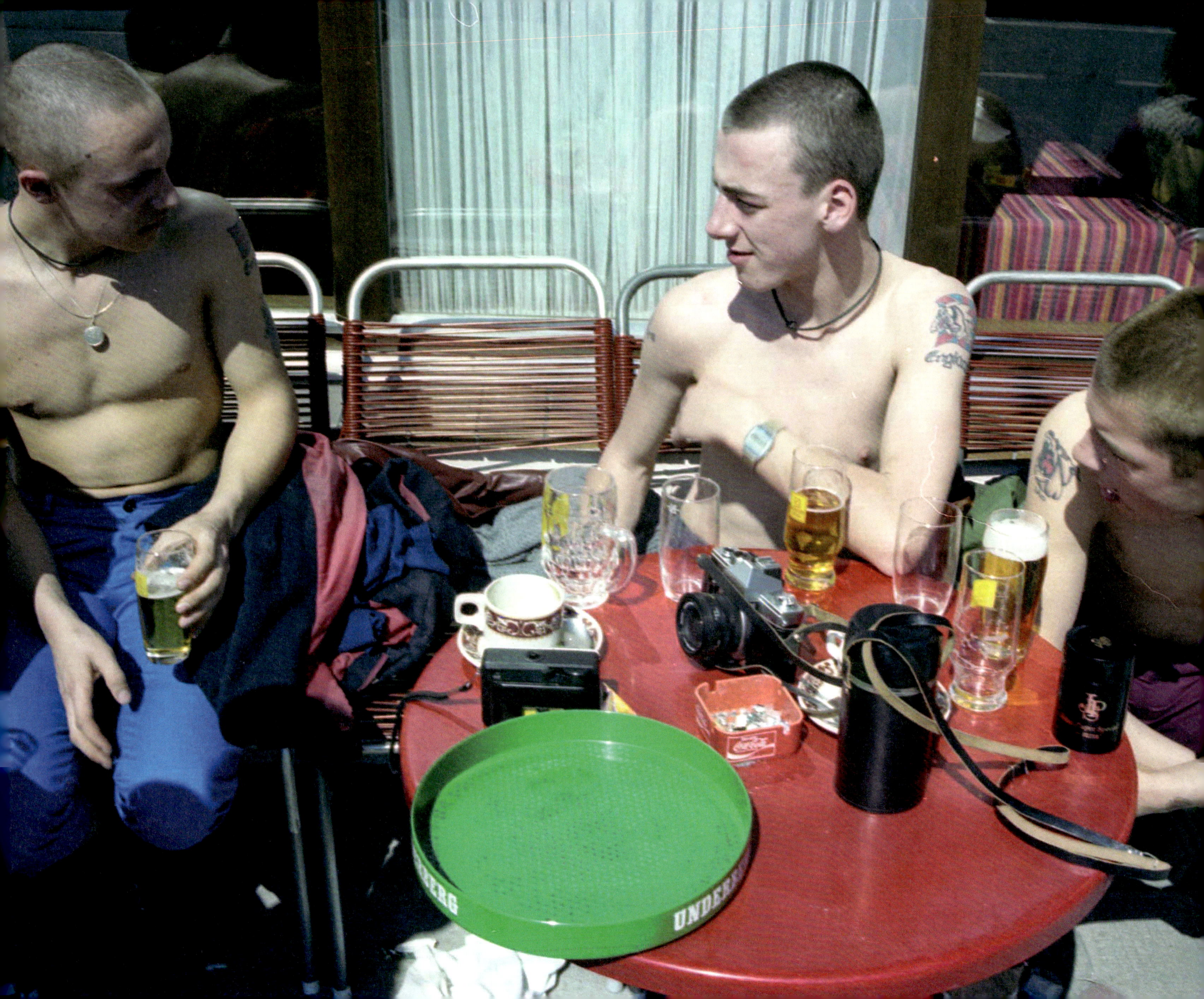

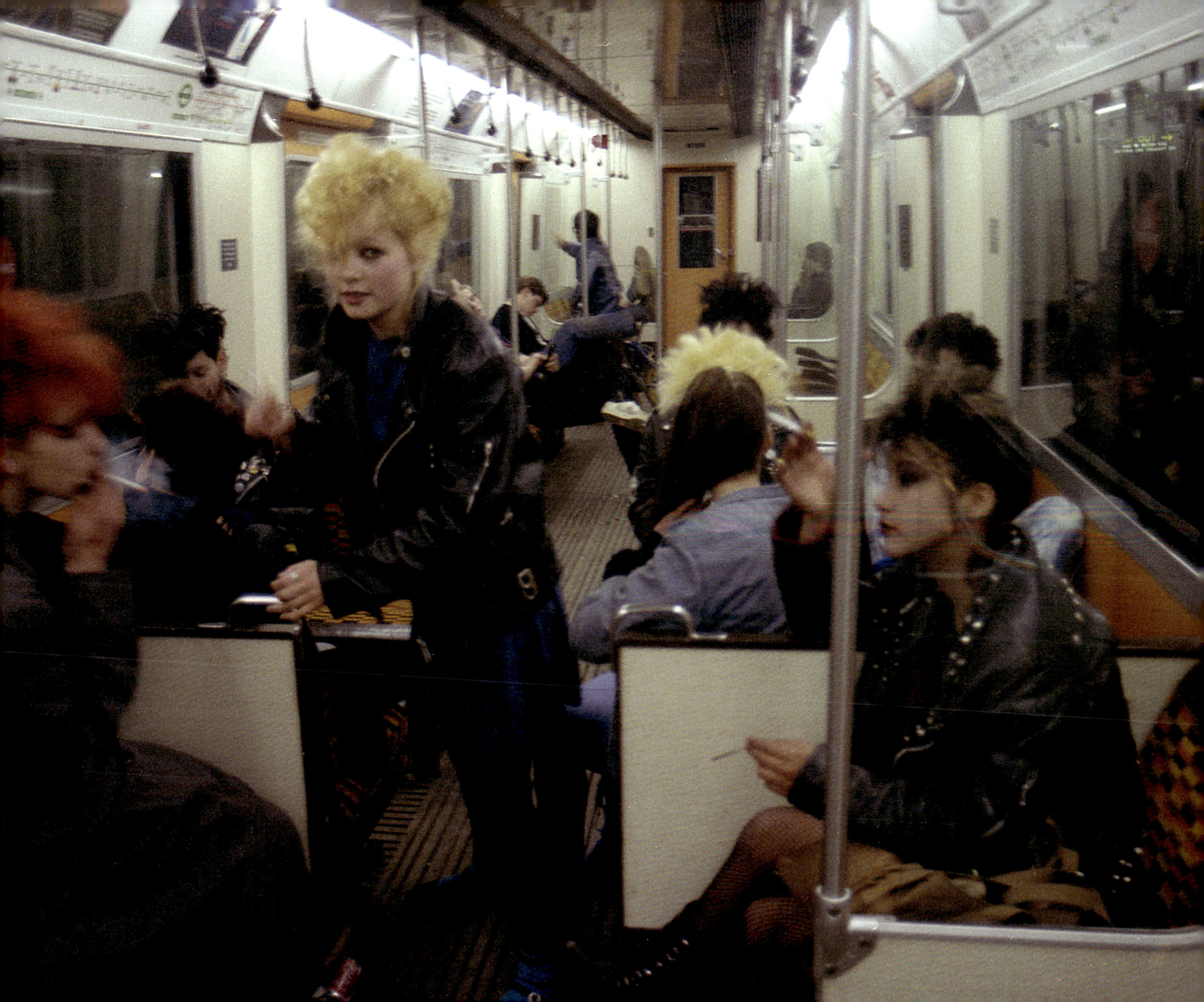

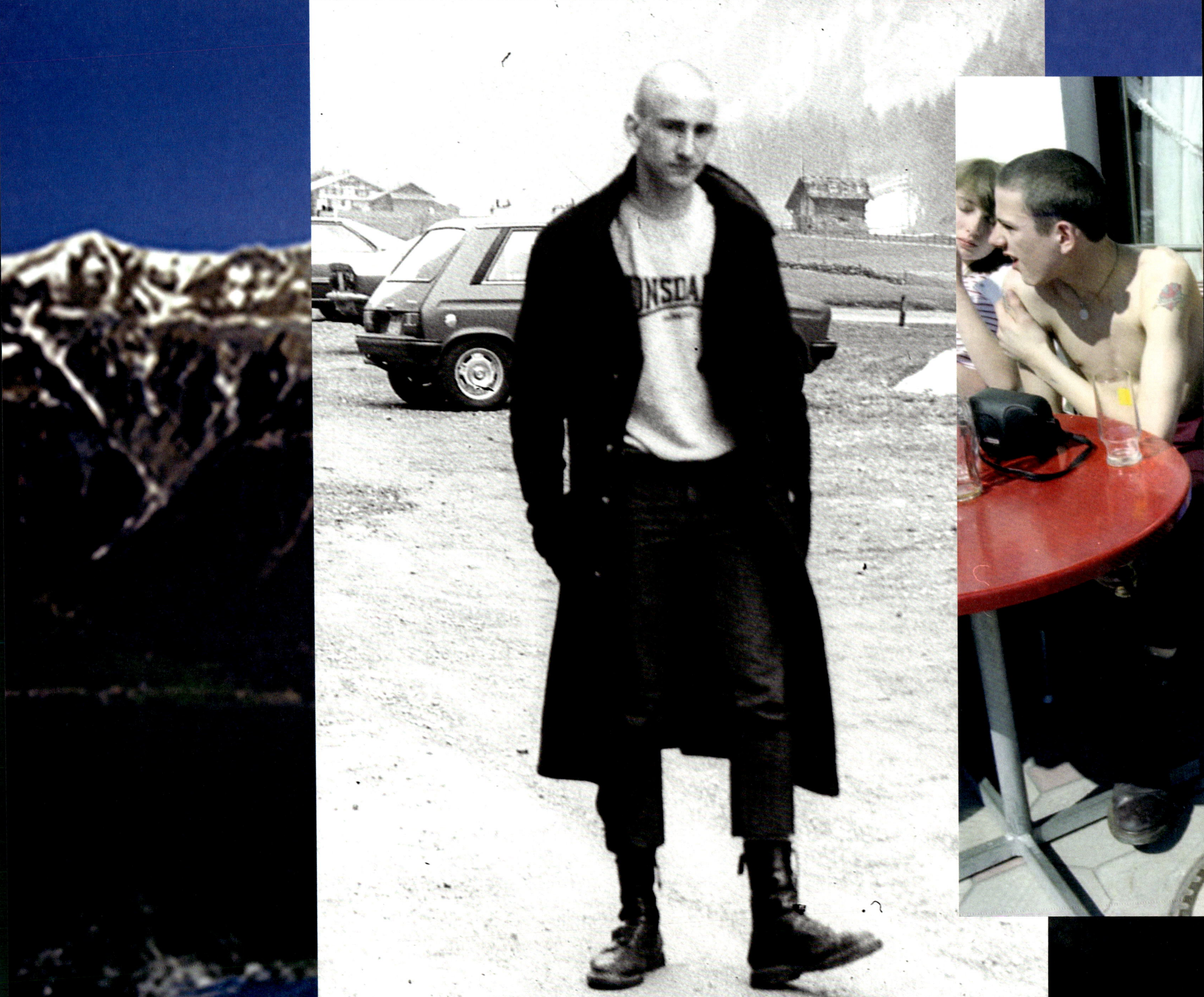

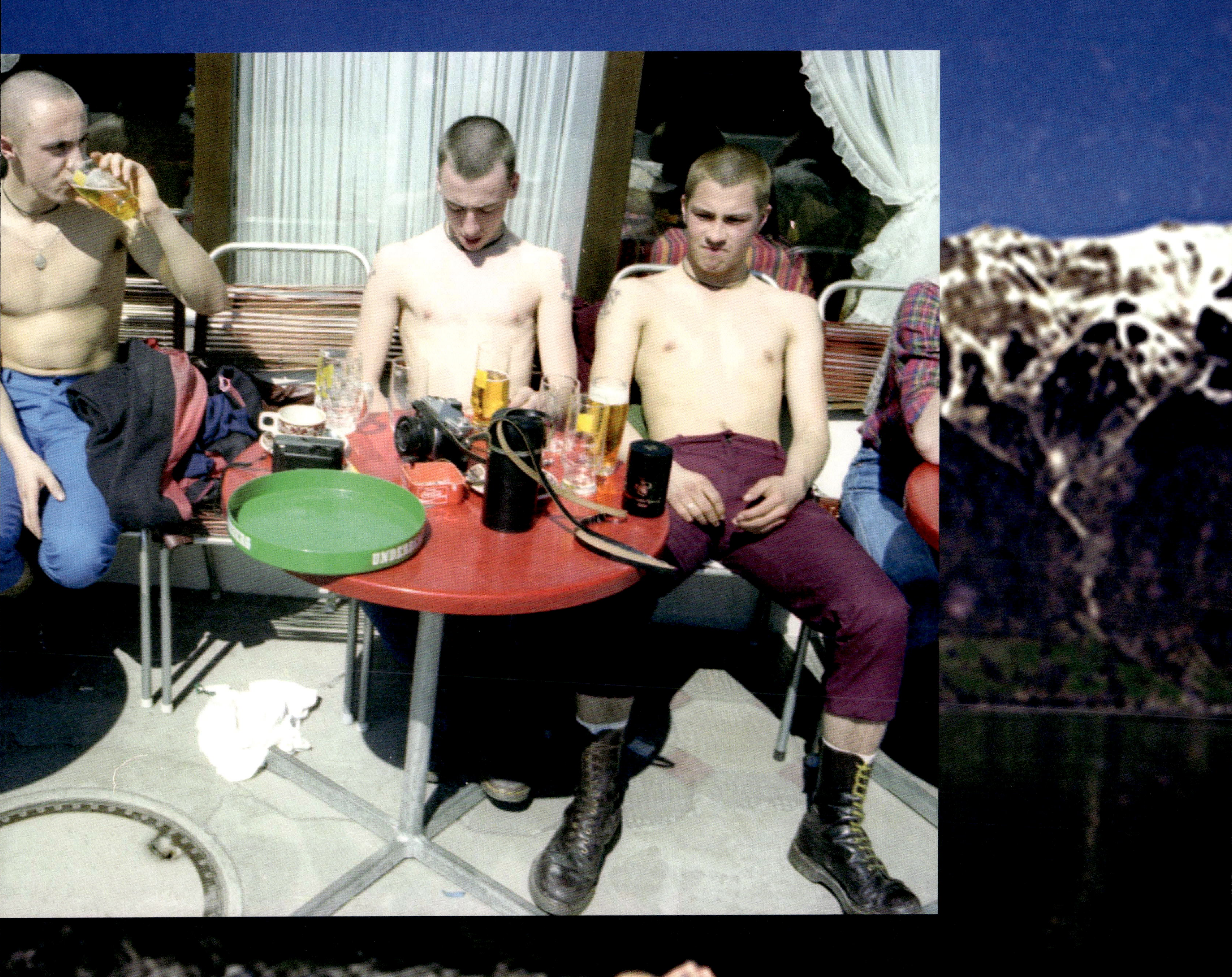

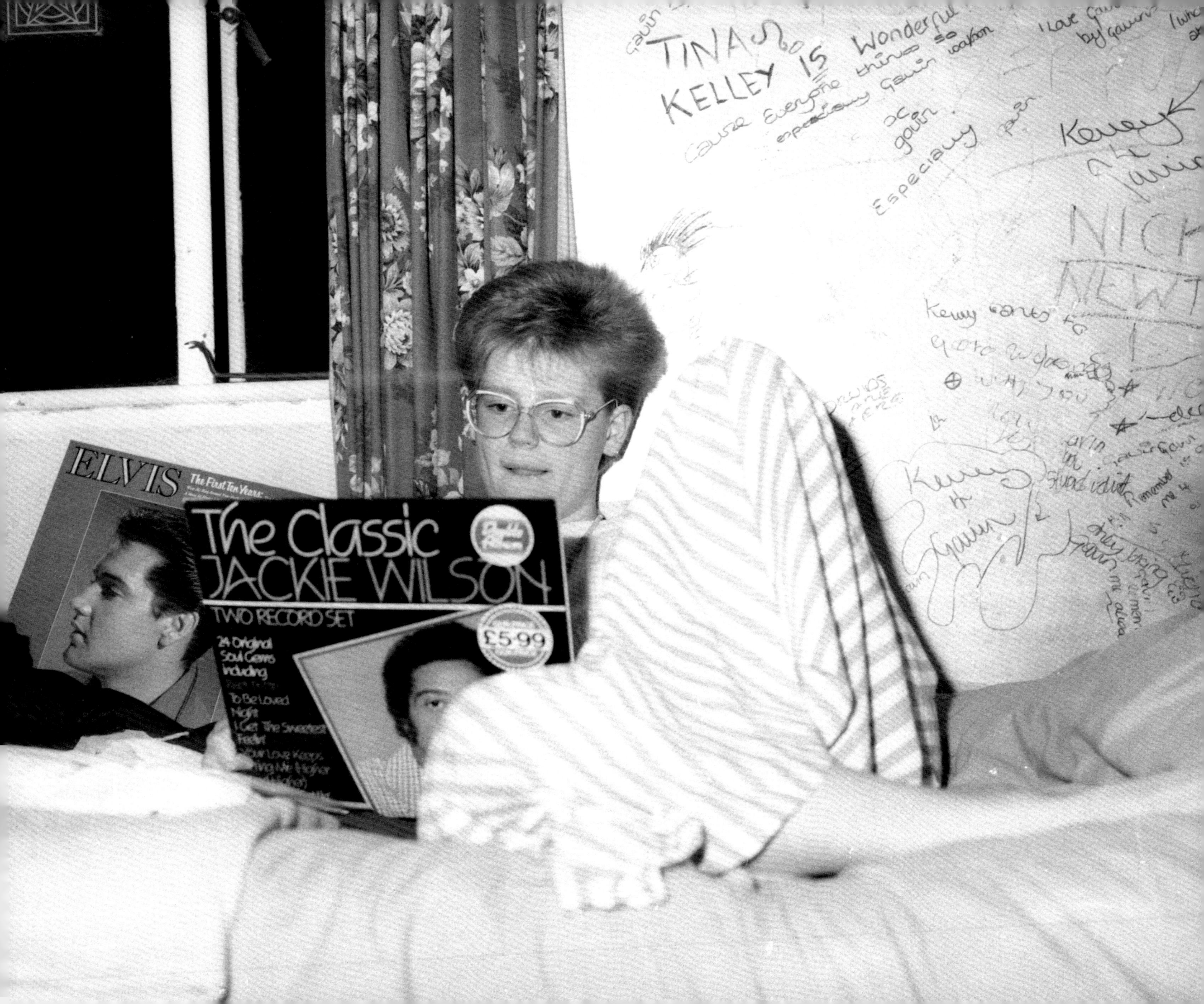
ELVIS
The Classic
JACKIE WILSON
TWO RECORD SET
24 Original
Soul Gems
Including
To Be Loved
Night
I Get The Sweetest
Feelin'
£5·99
TINA
KELLEY IS Wonderful

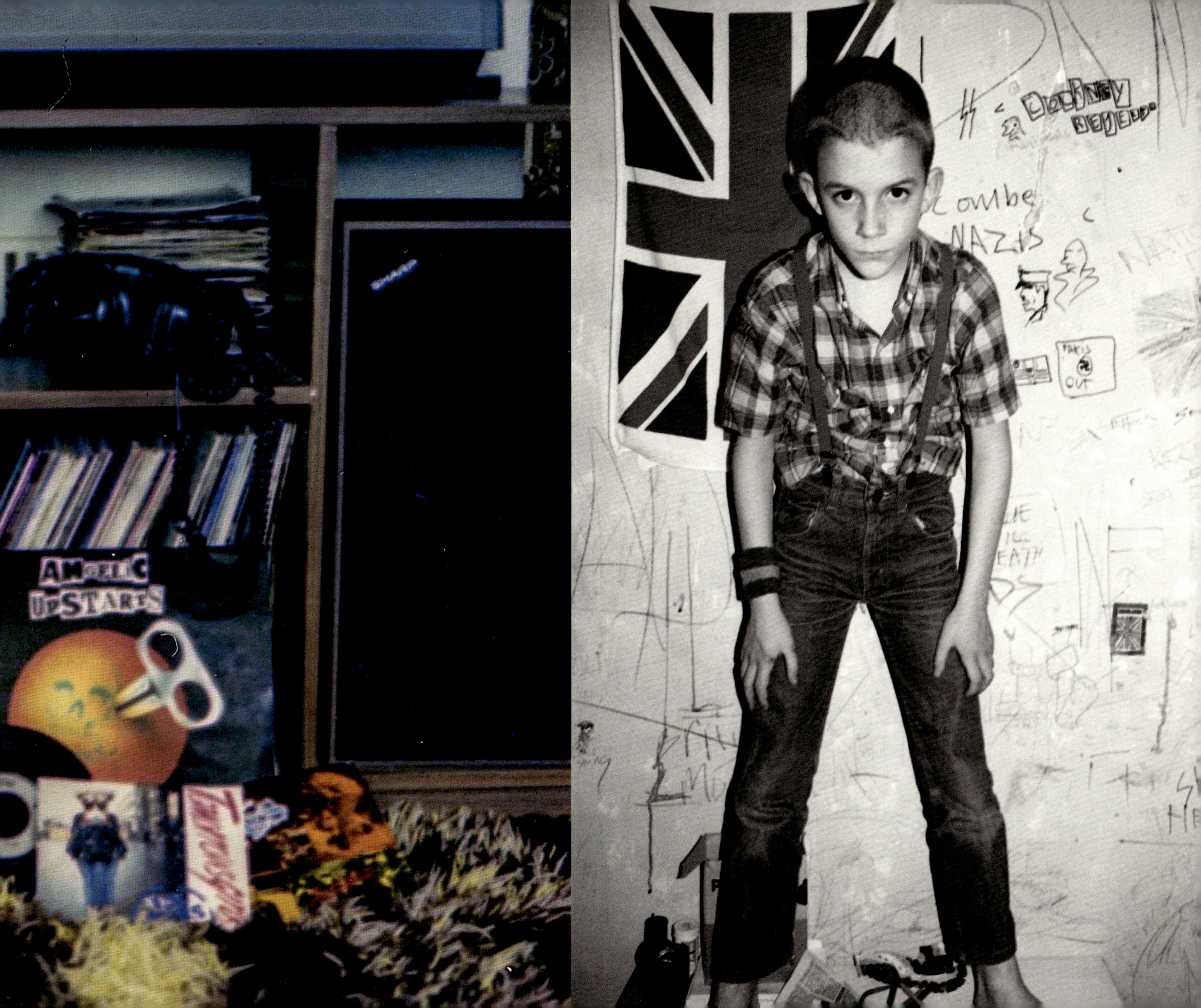
UPSTARTS
COCKNEY REJECTS
NAZIS

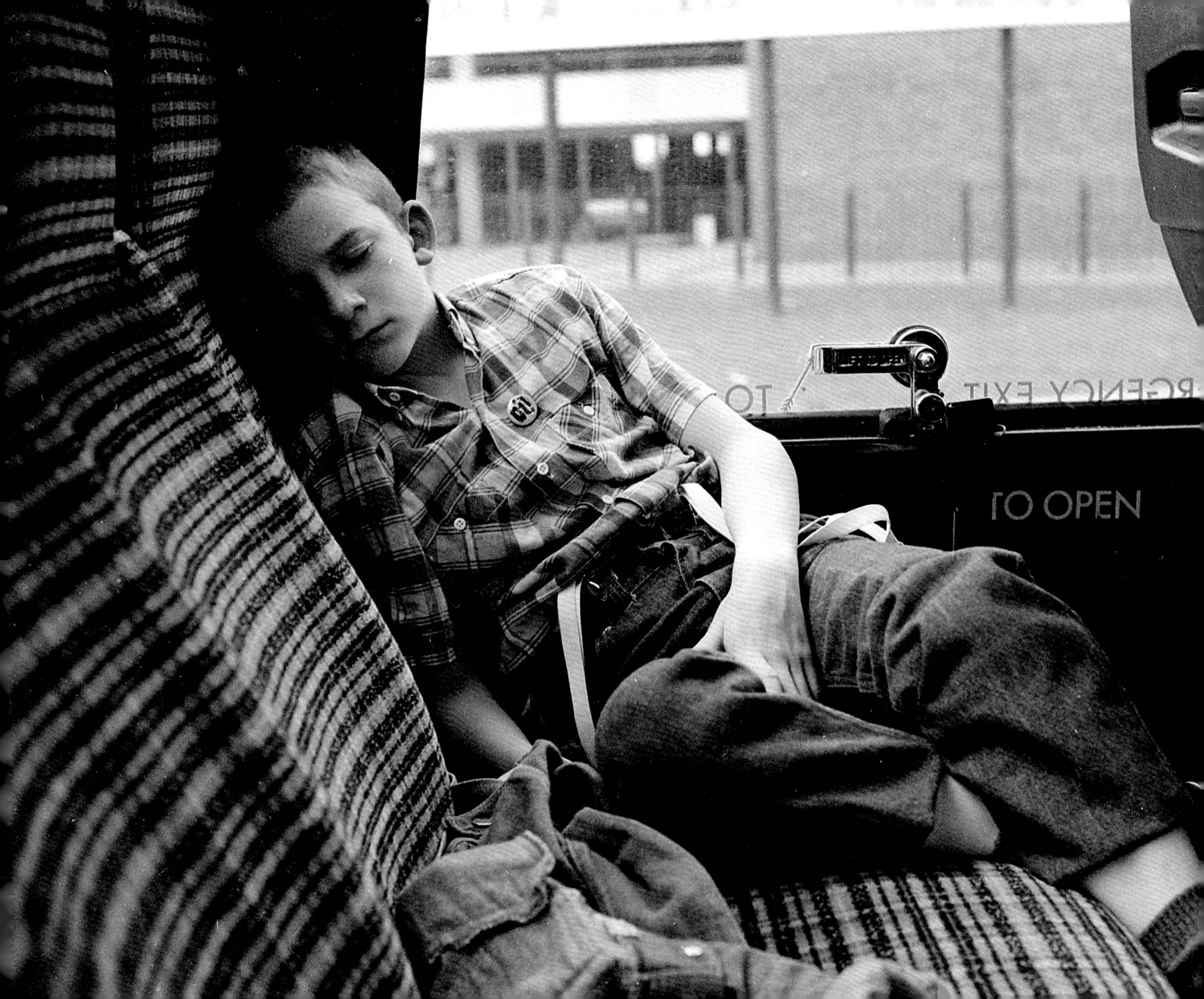
TO OPEN

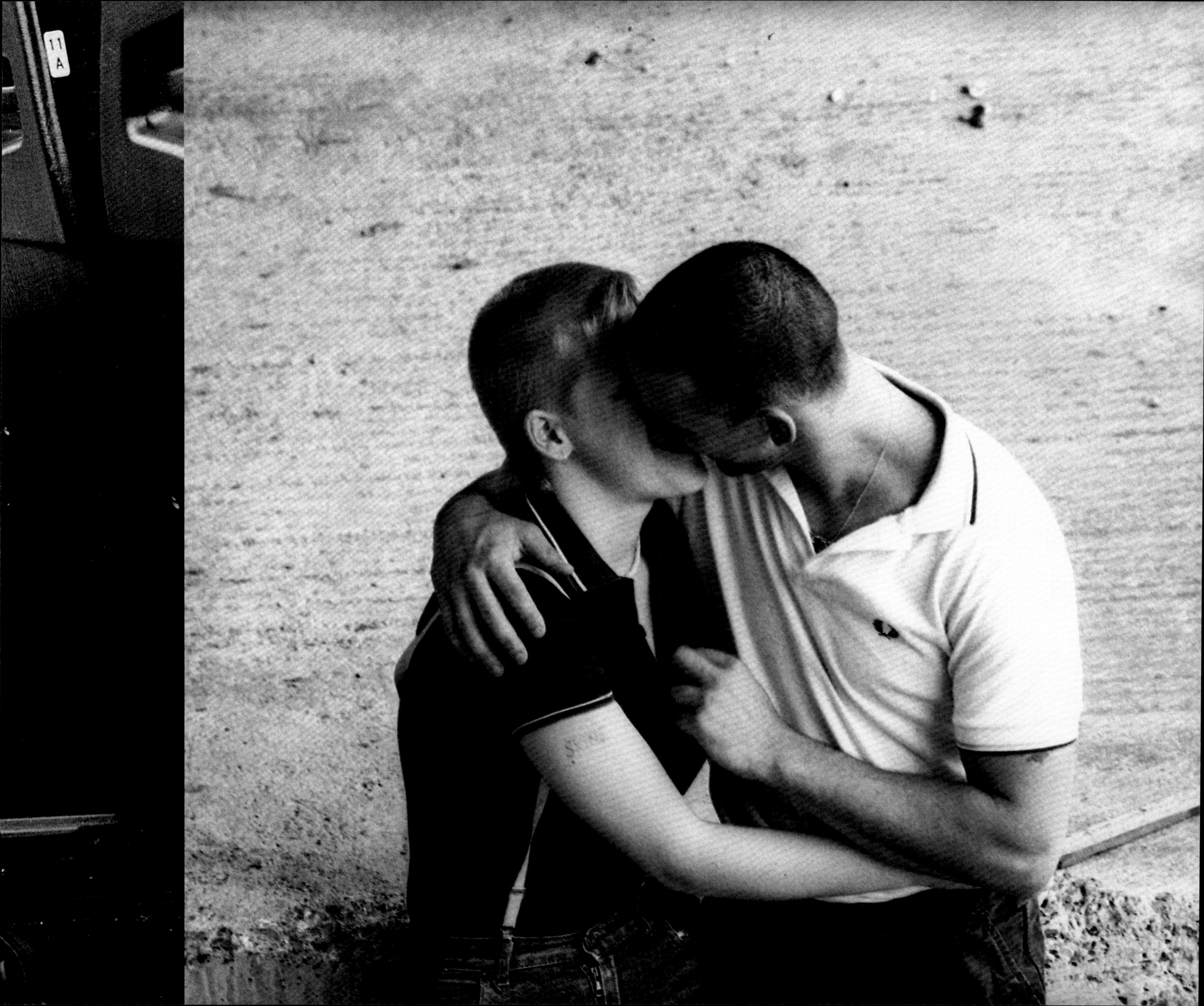
11
A

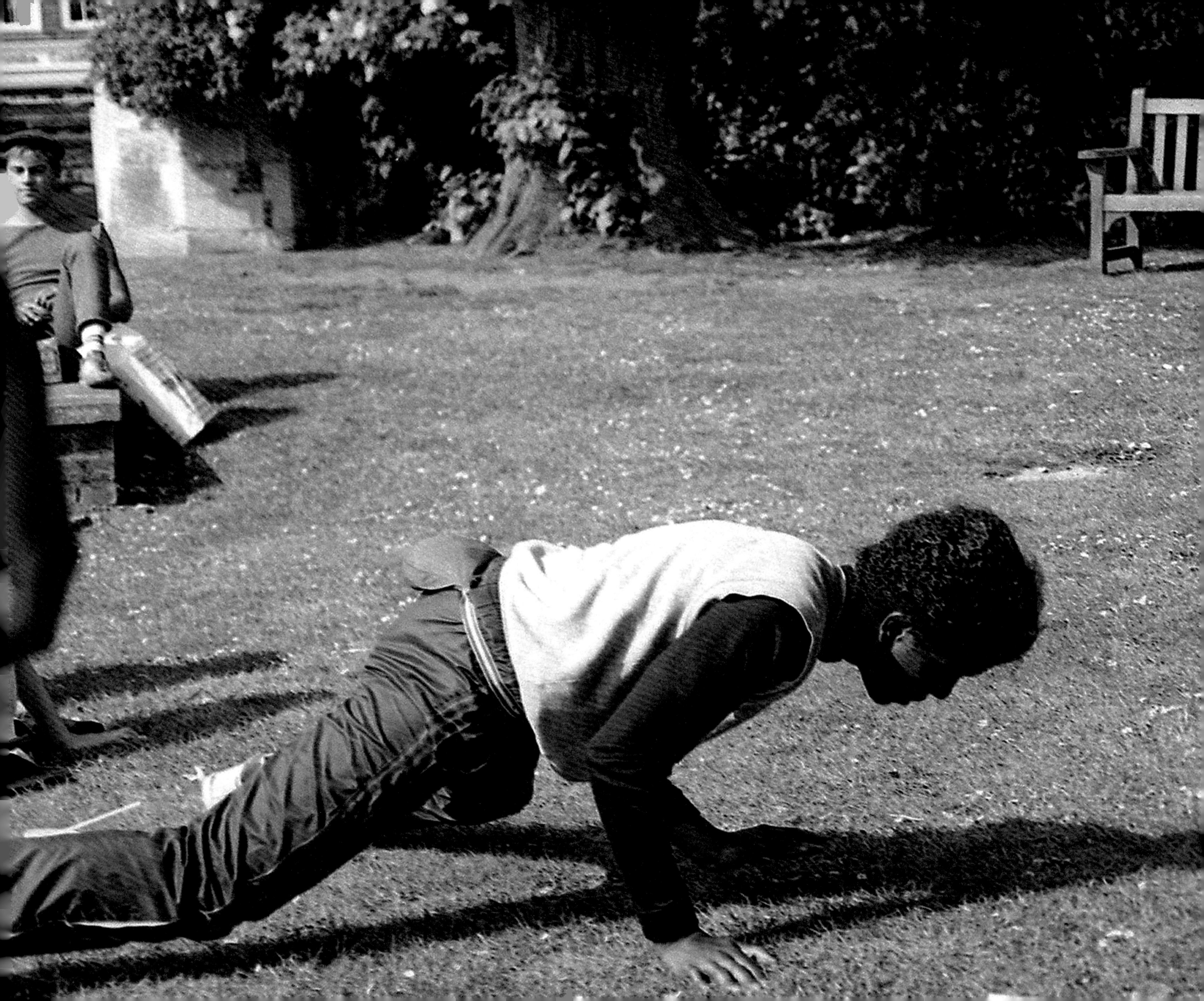

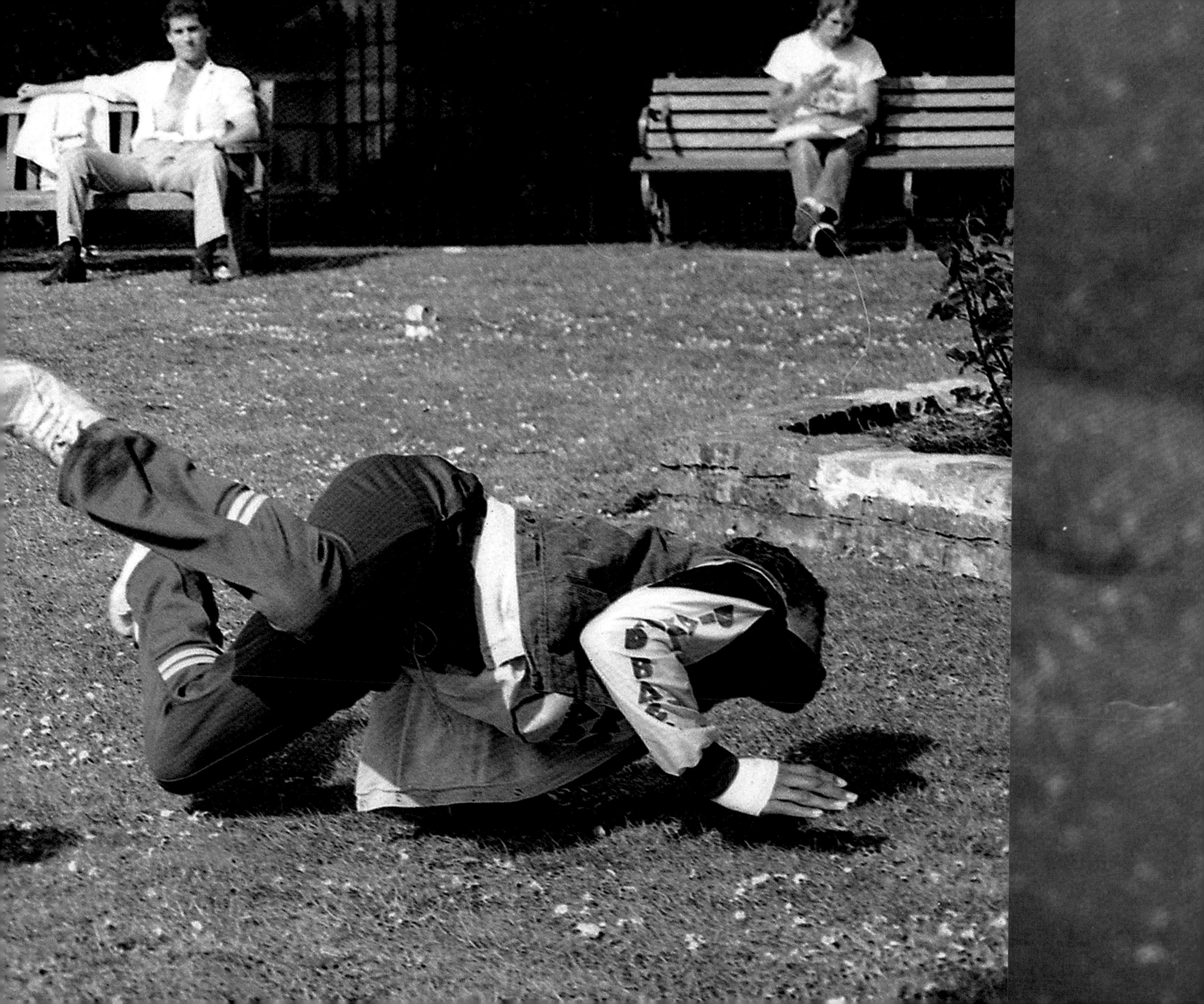

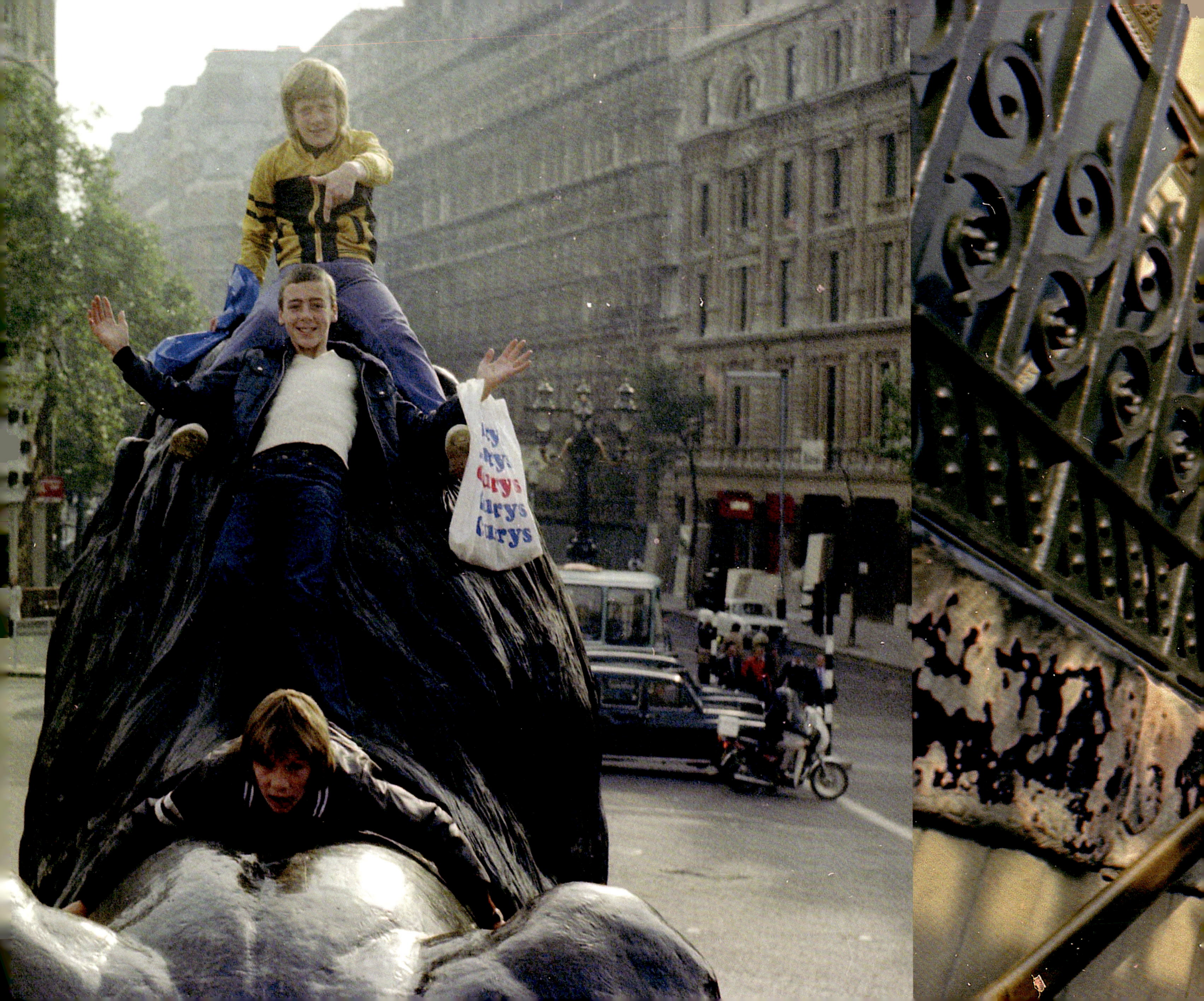

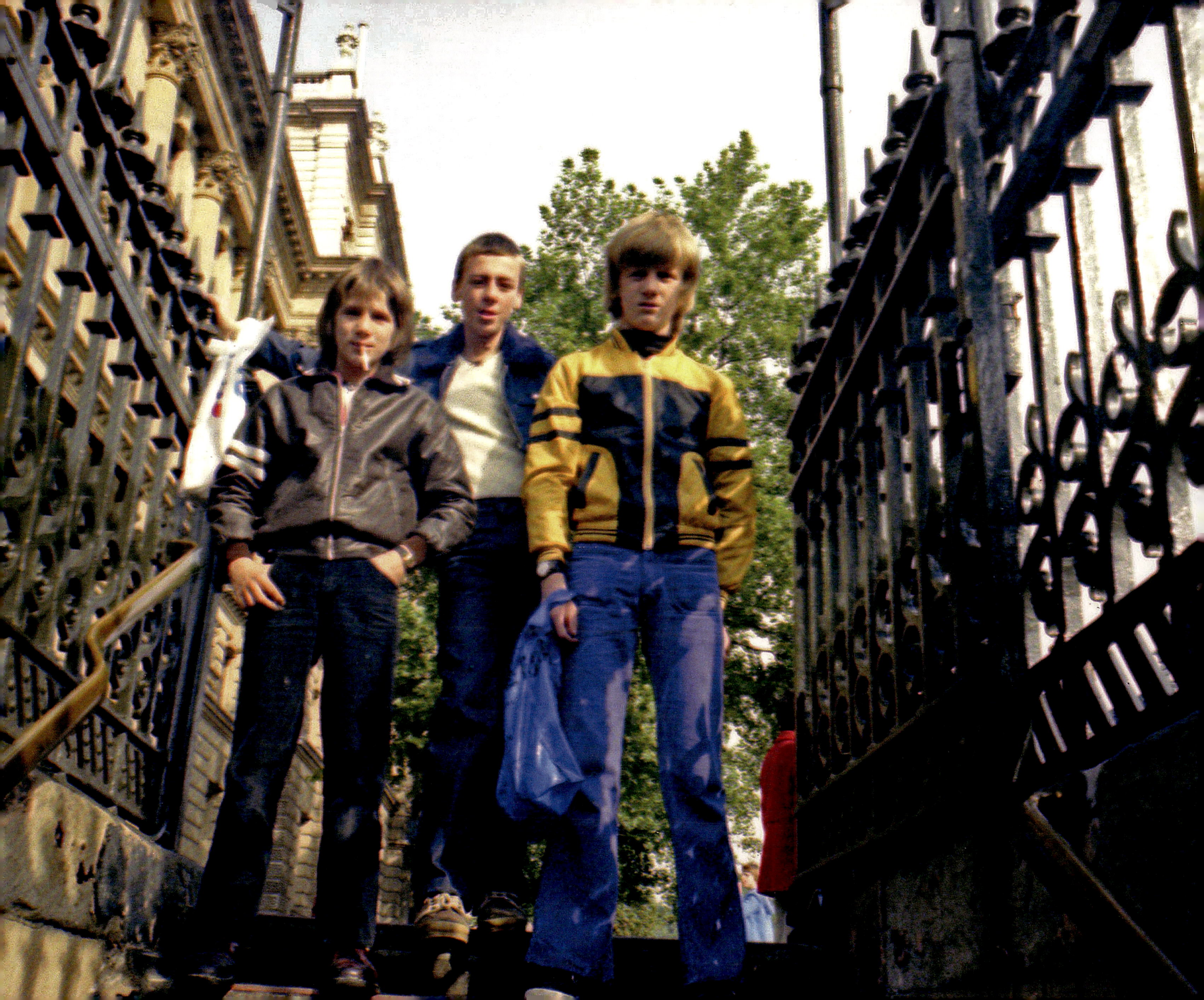

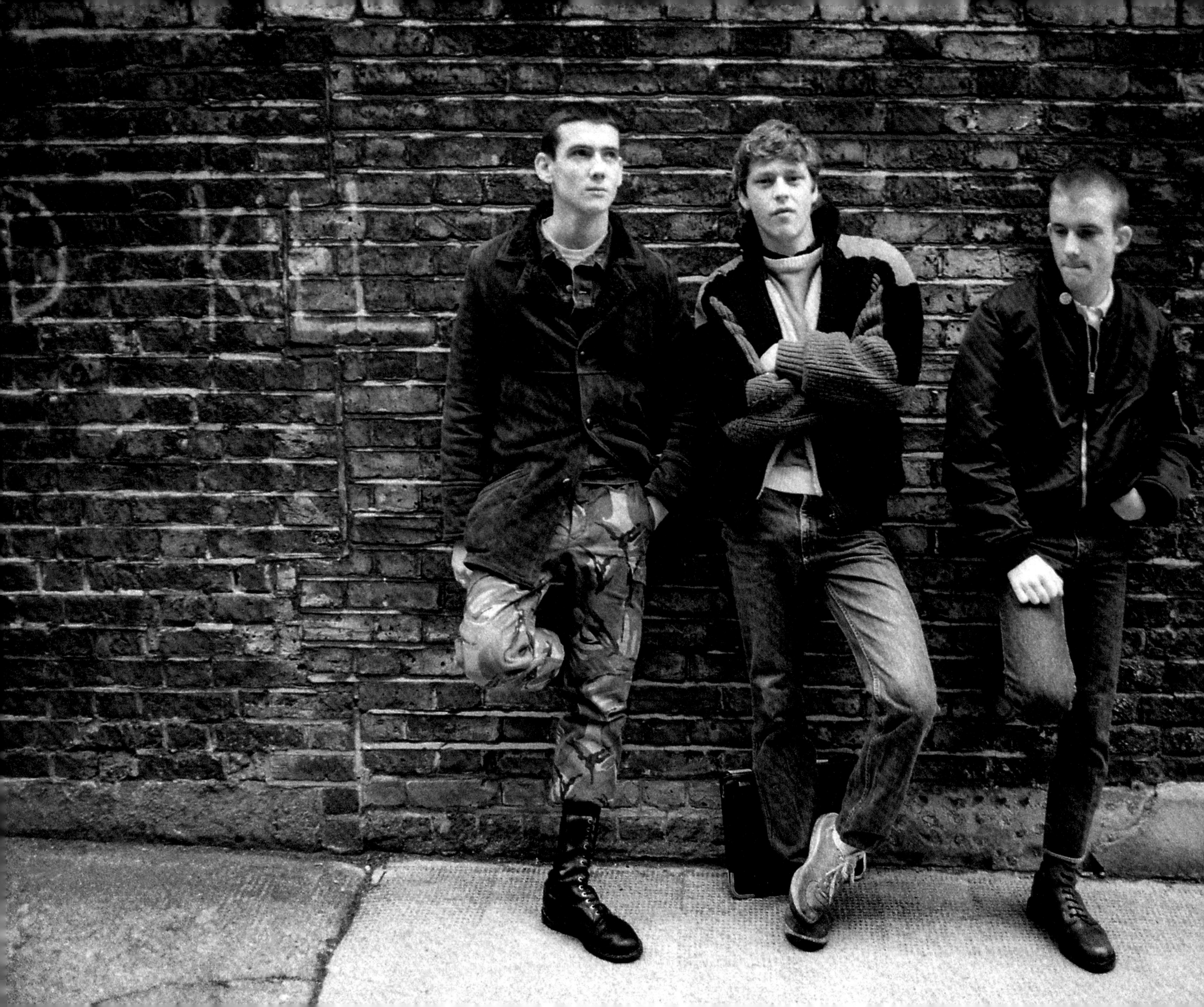

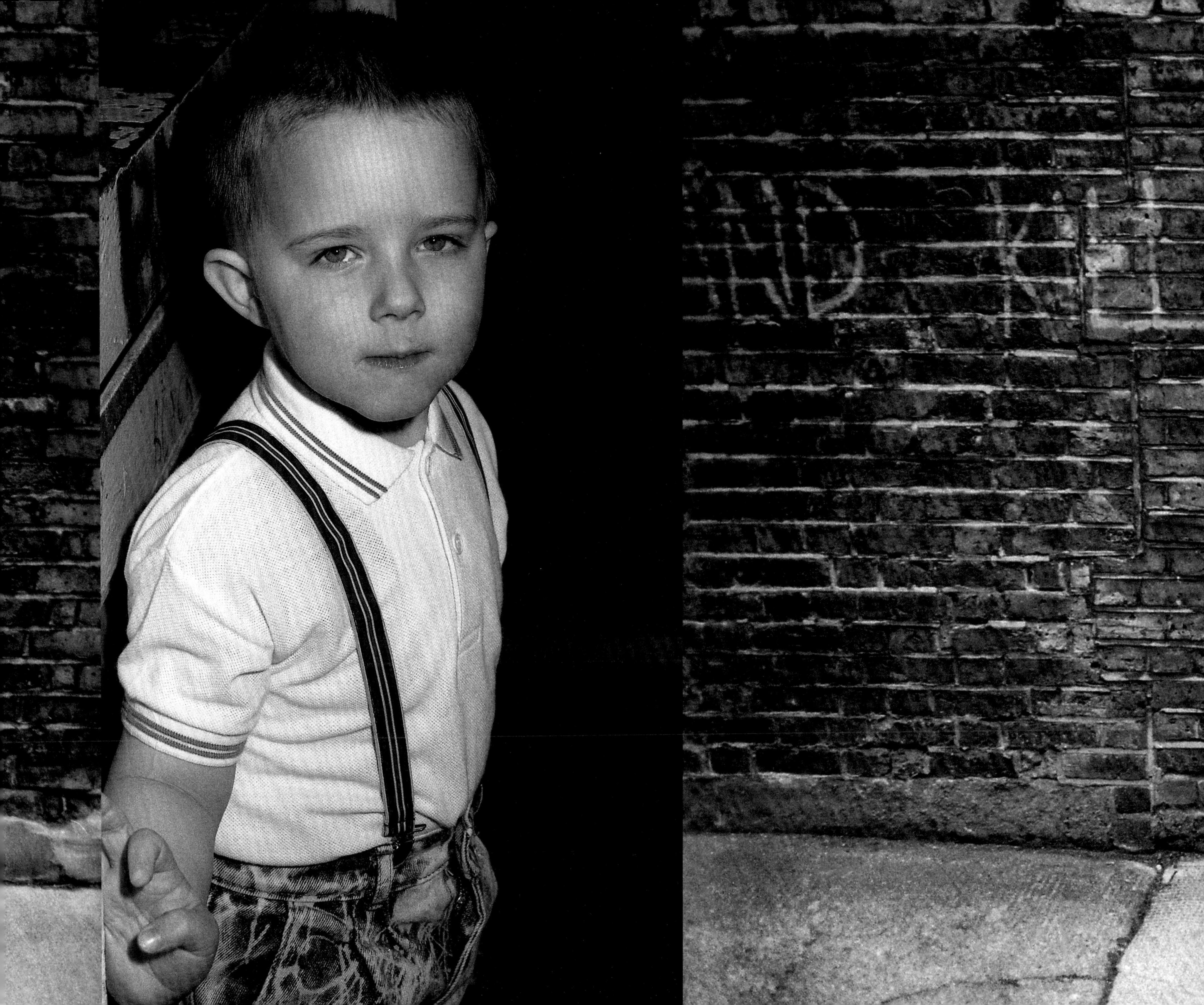

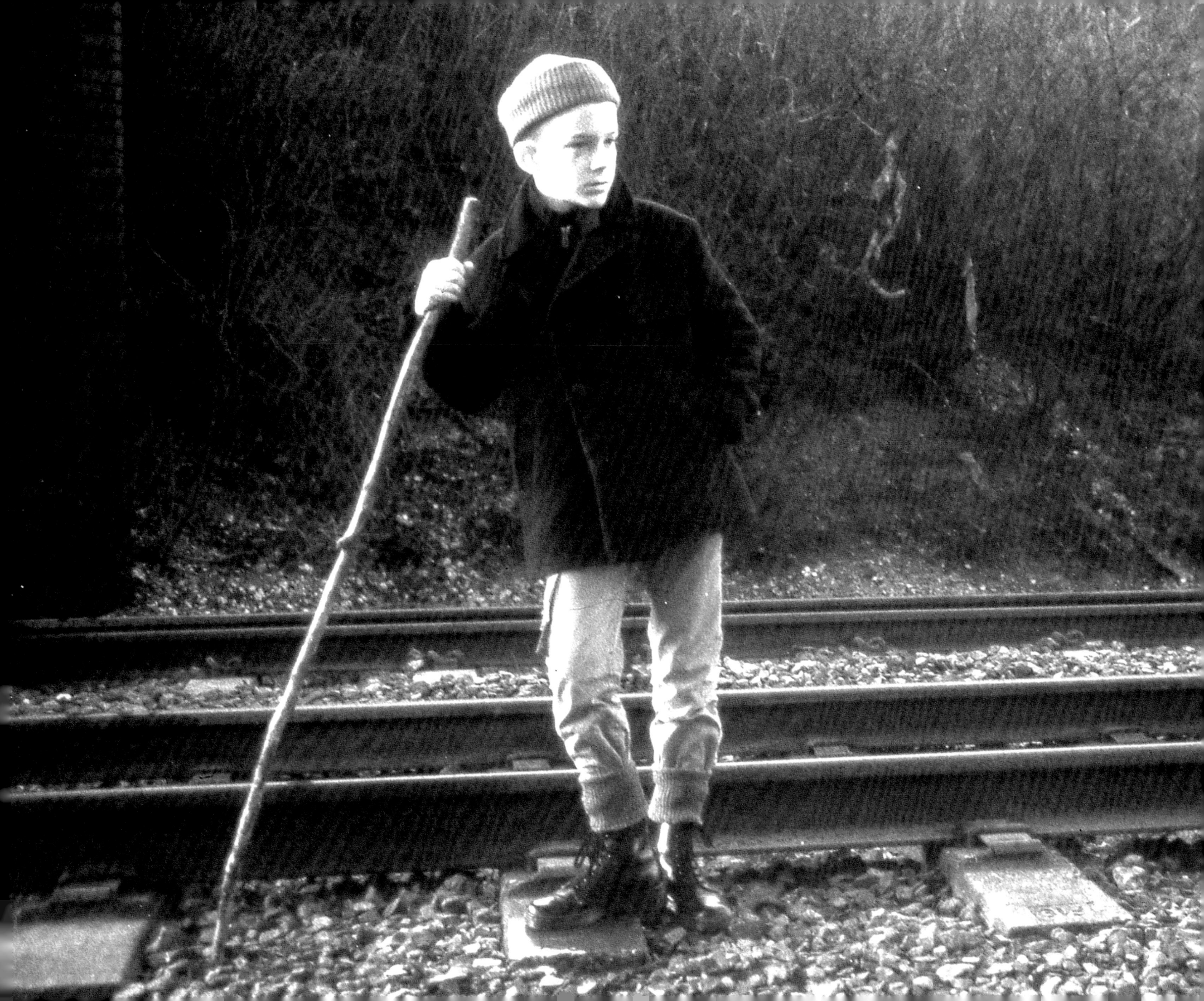

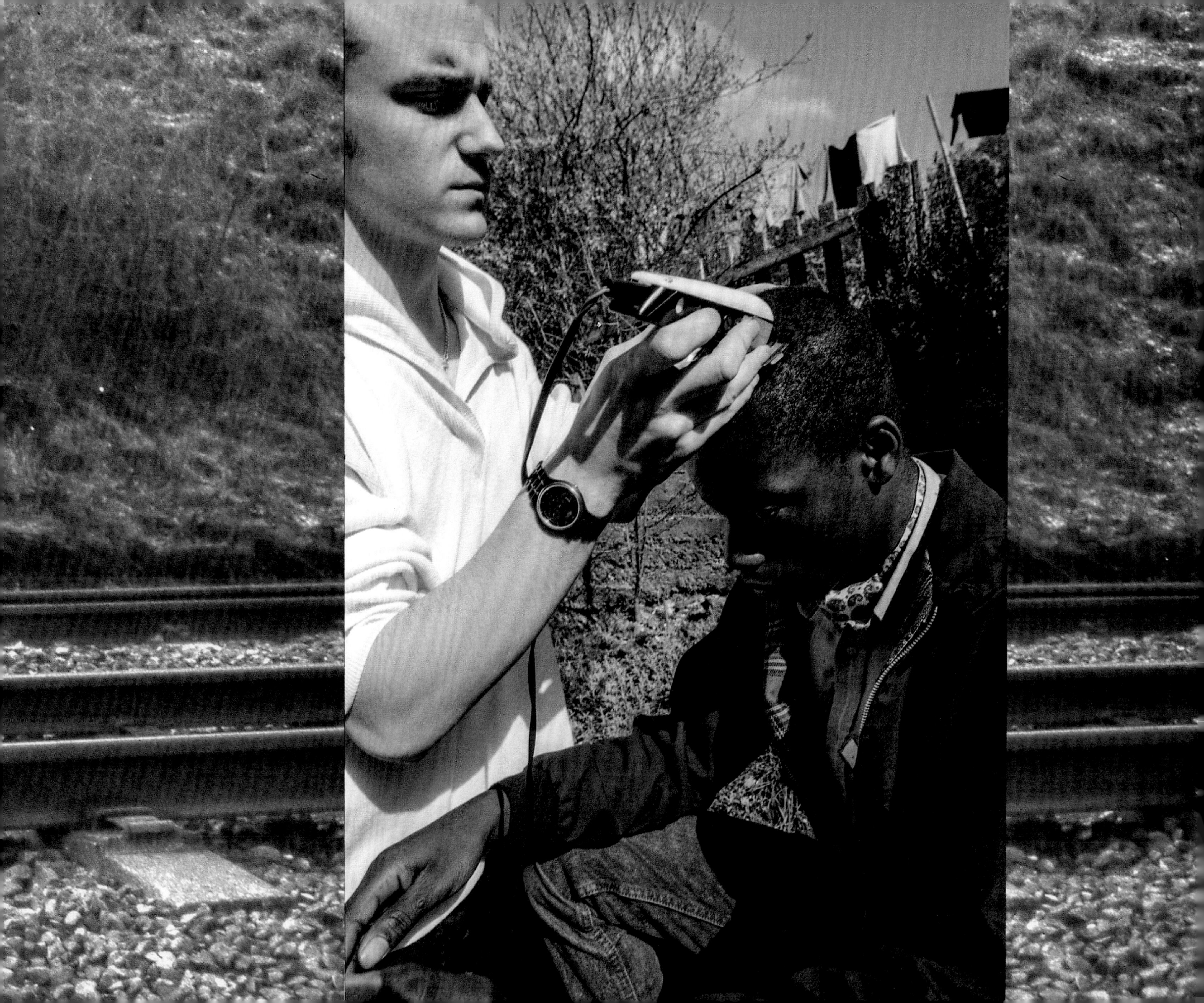

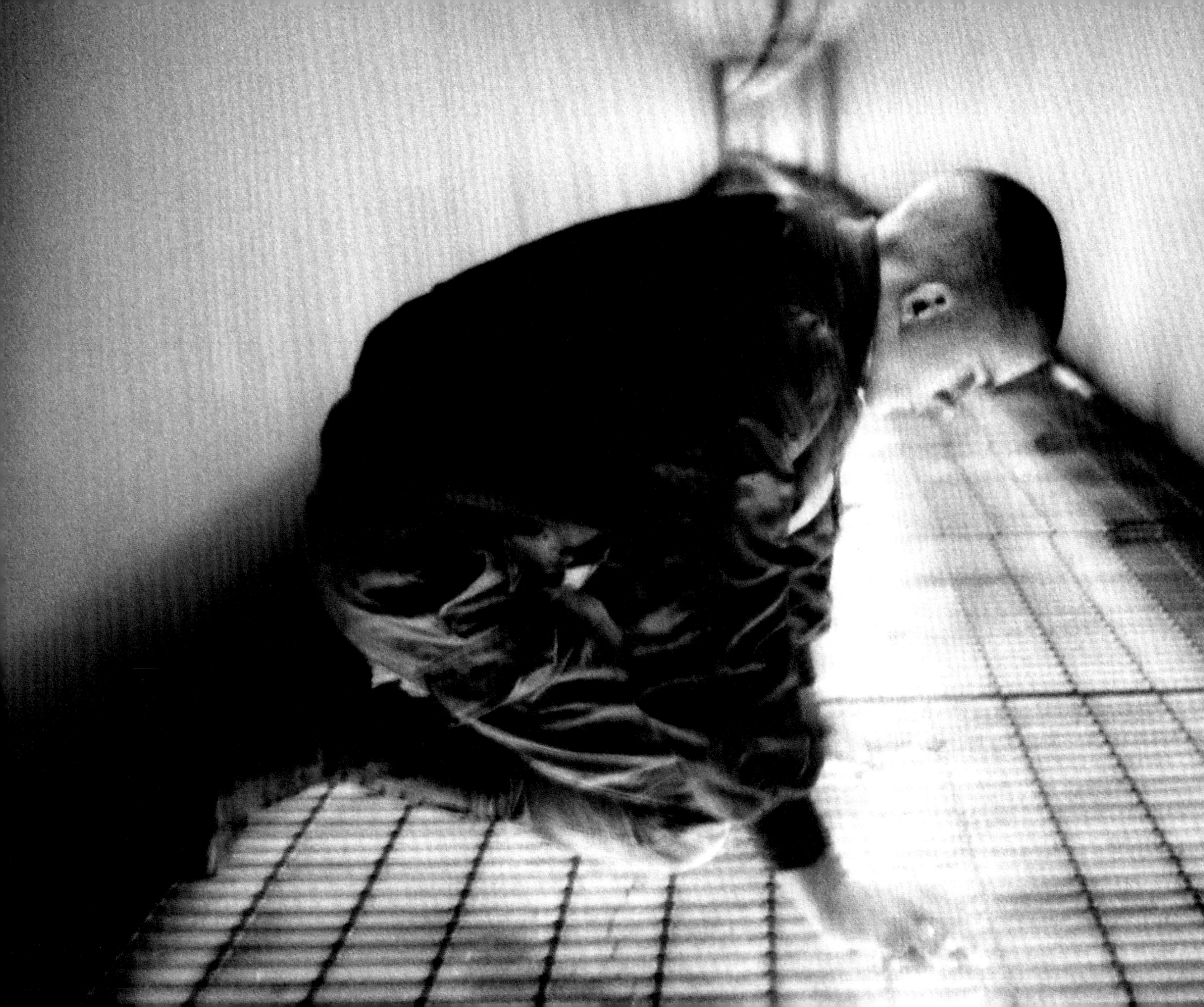

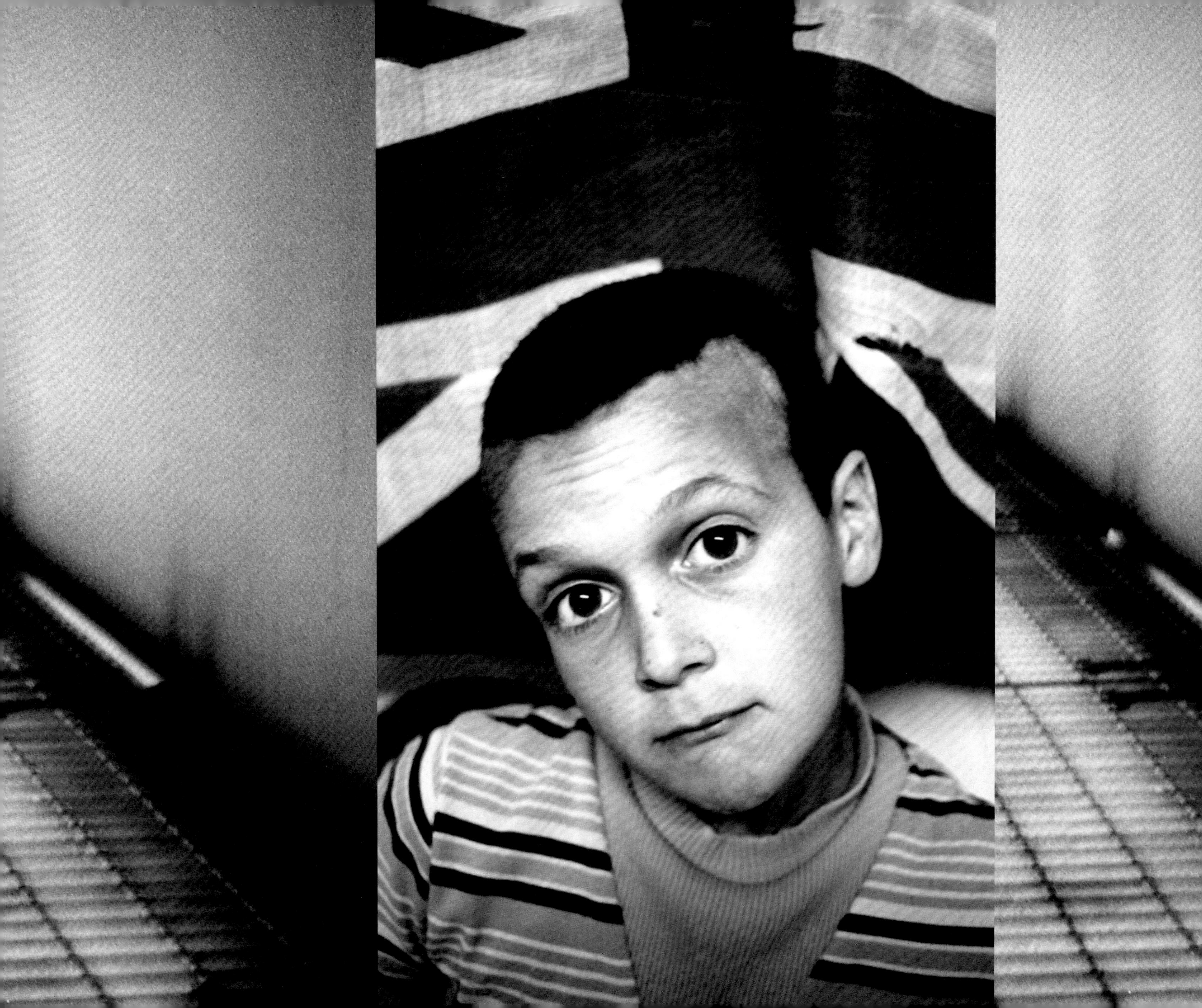

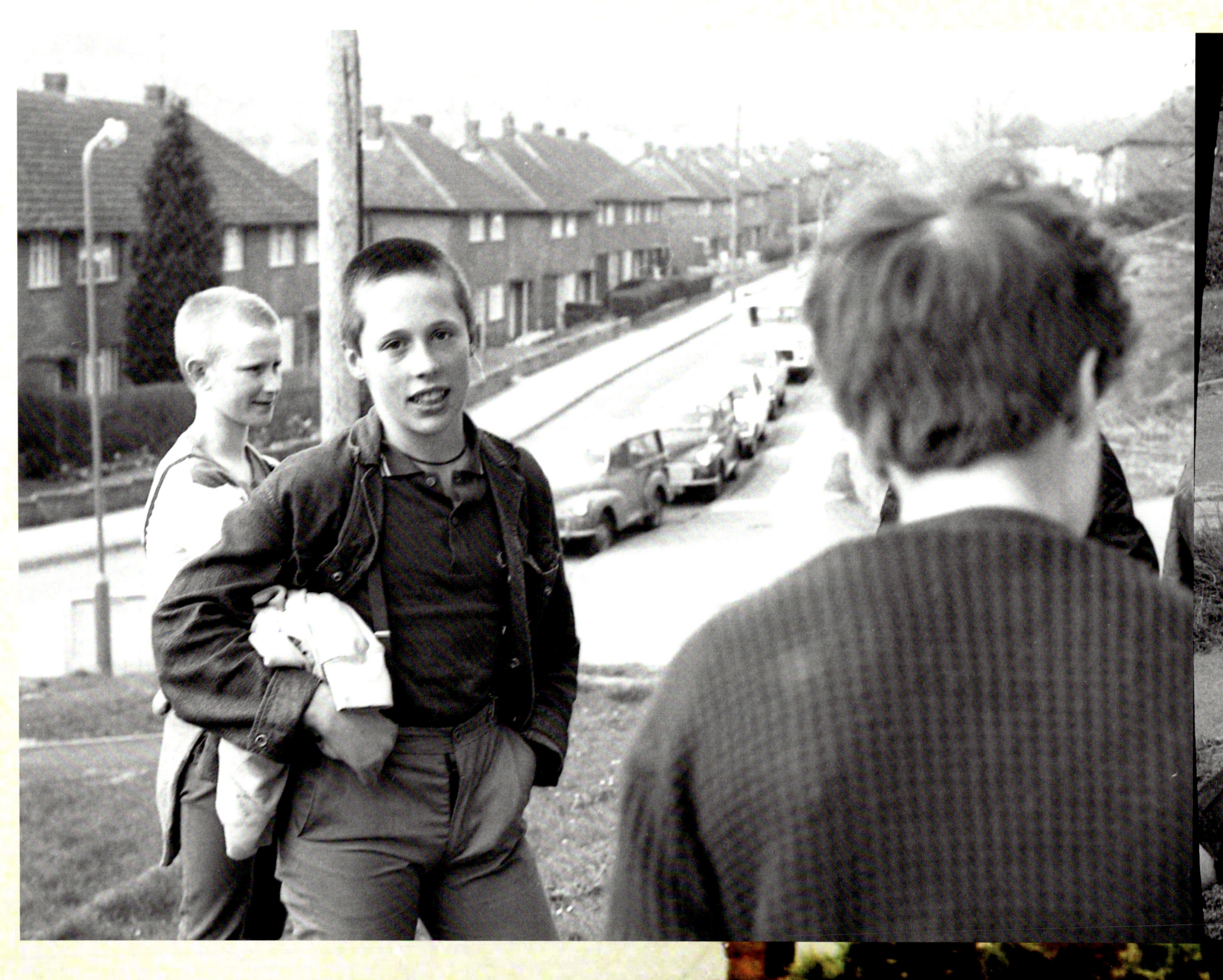

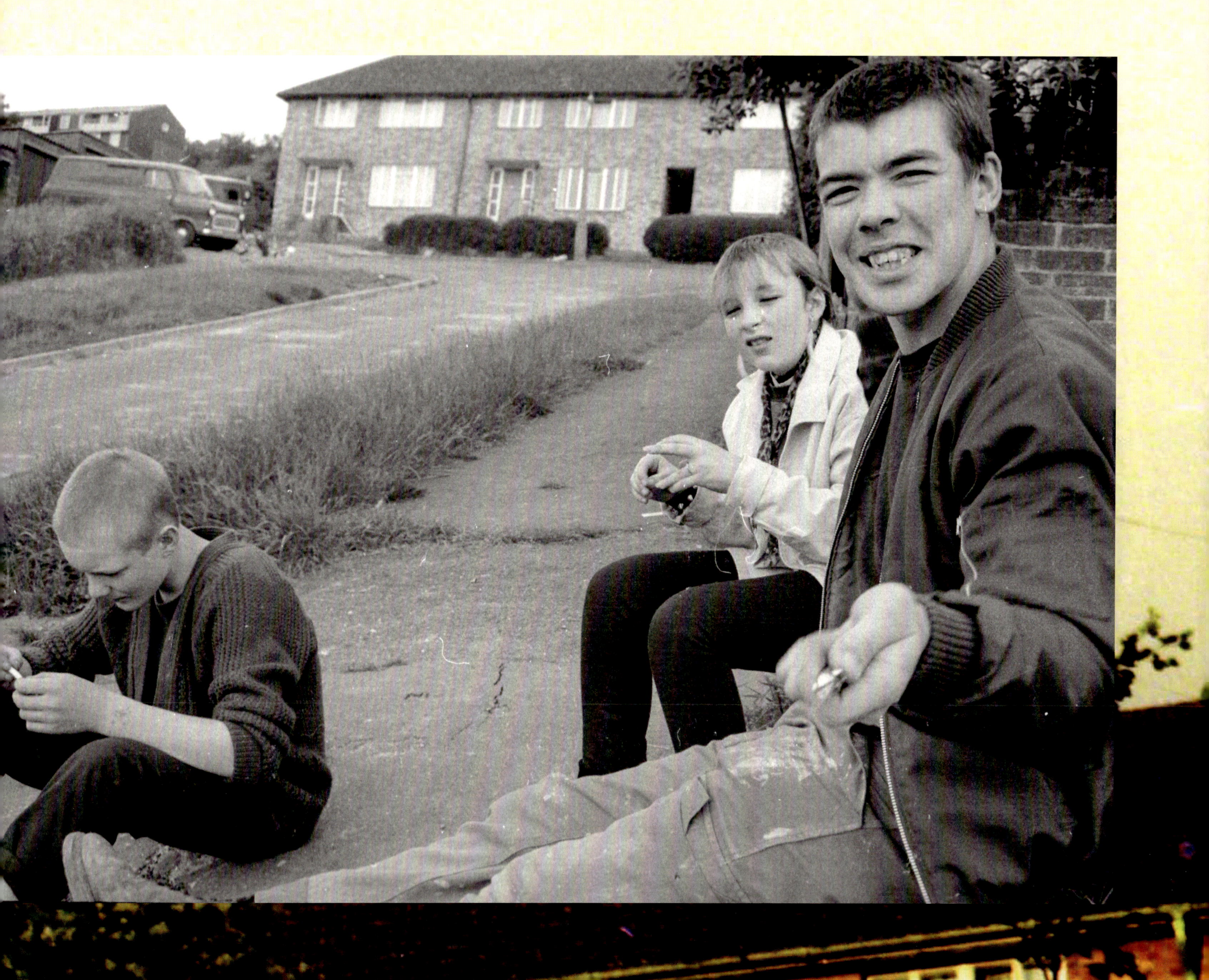

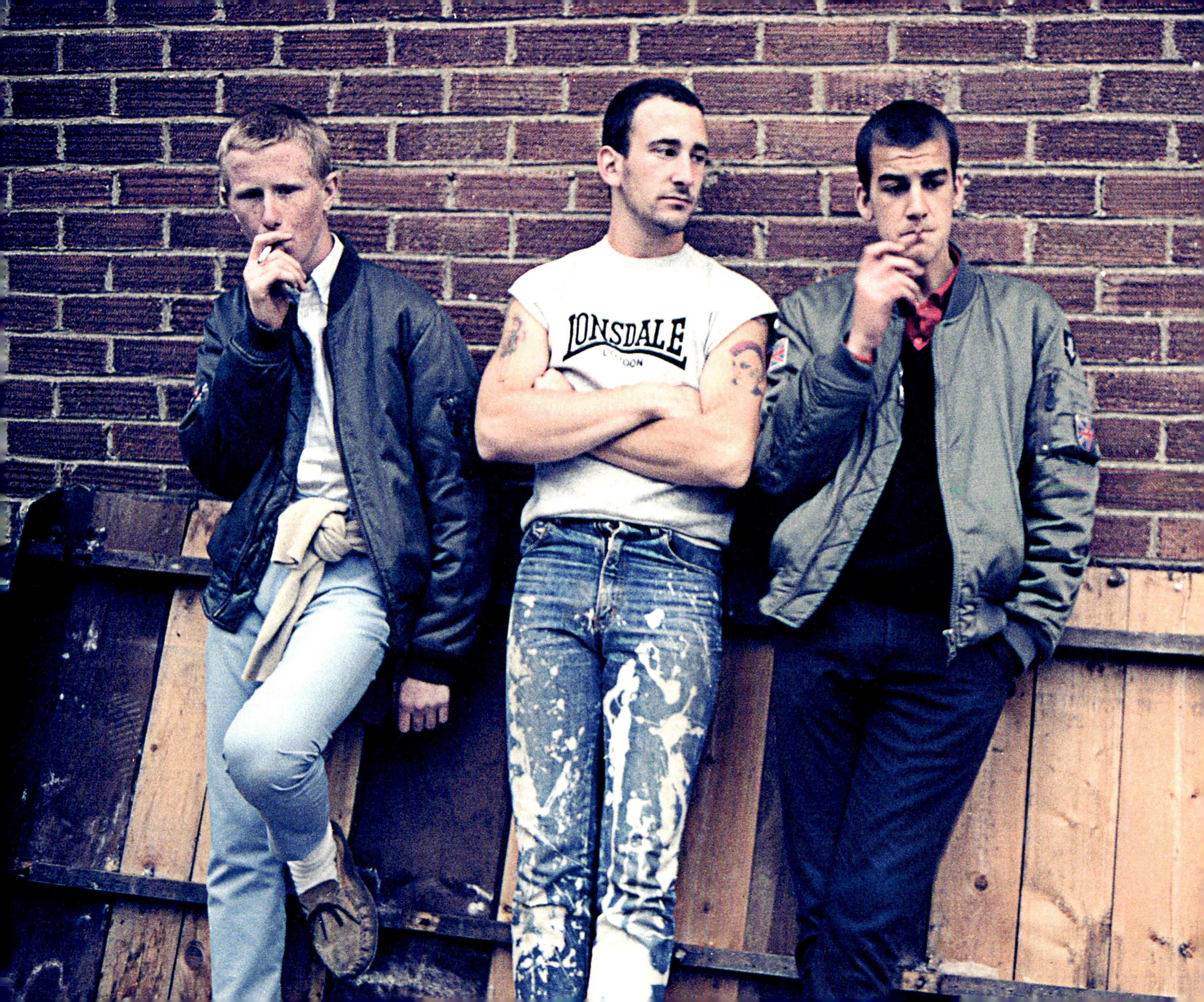
LONSDALE

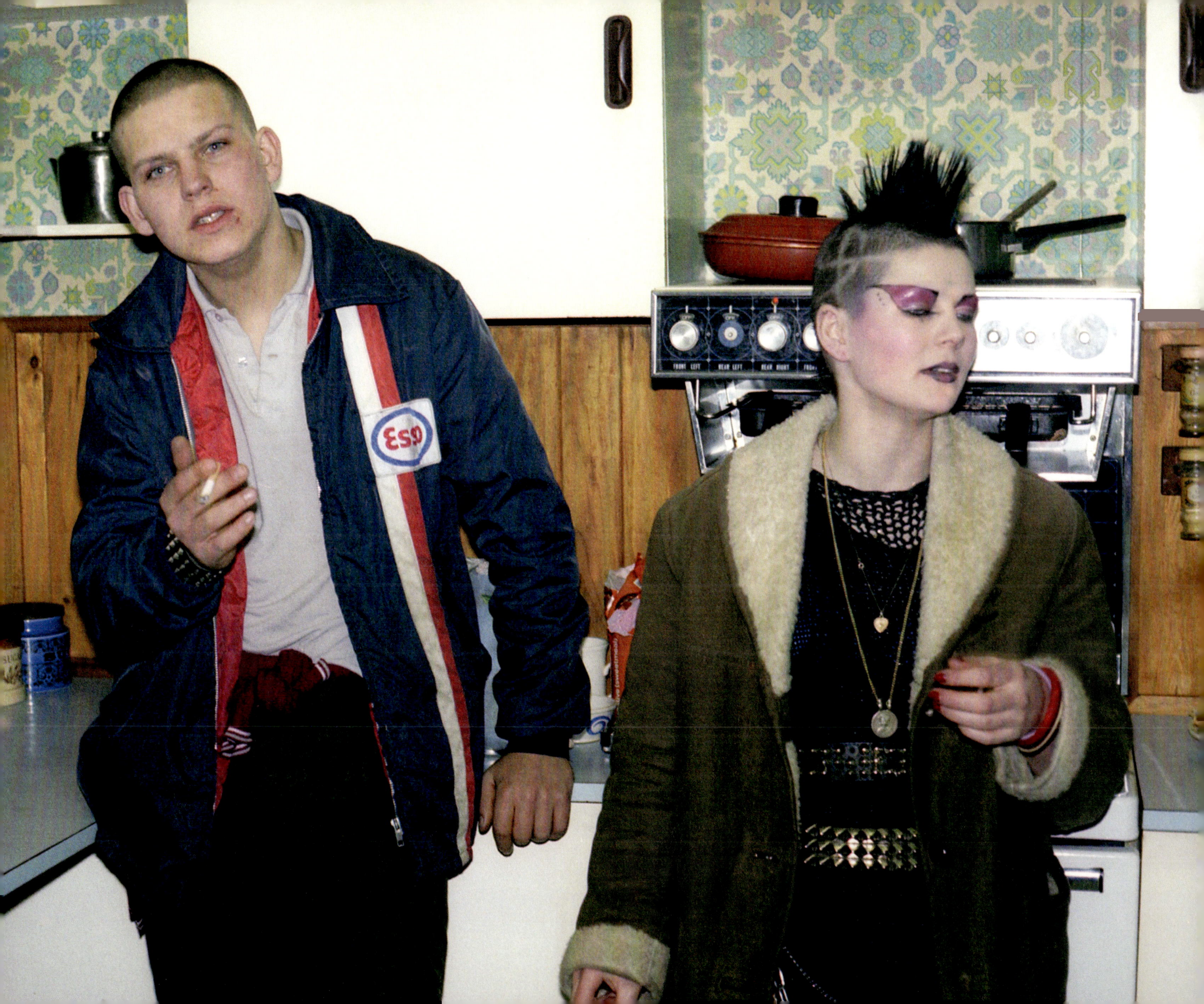
FRONT LEFT
REAR LEFT
REAR RIGHT

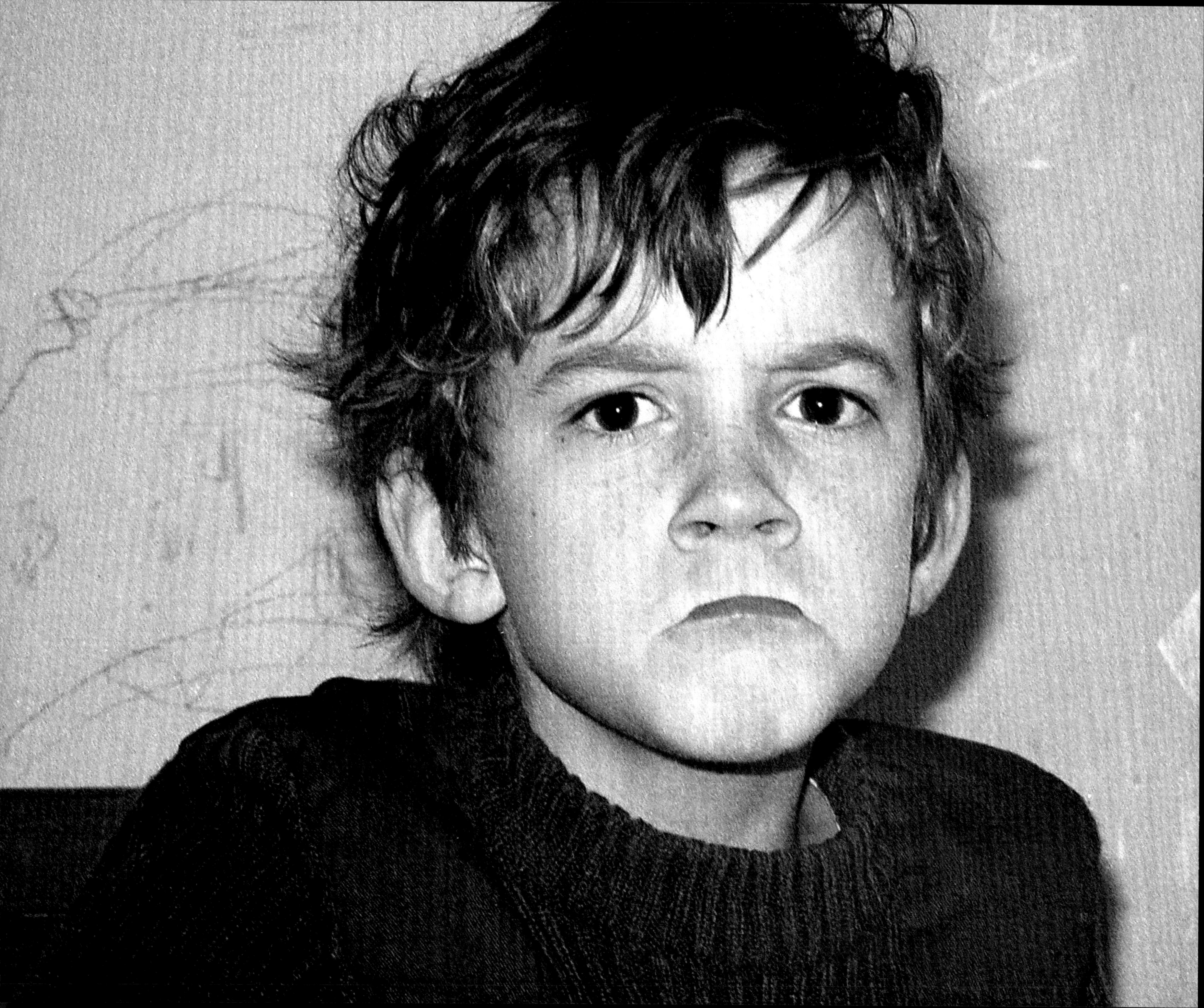

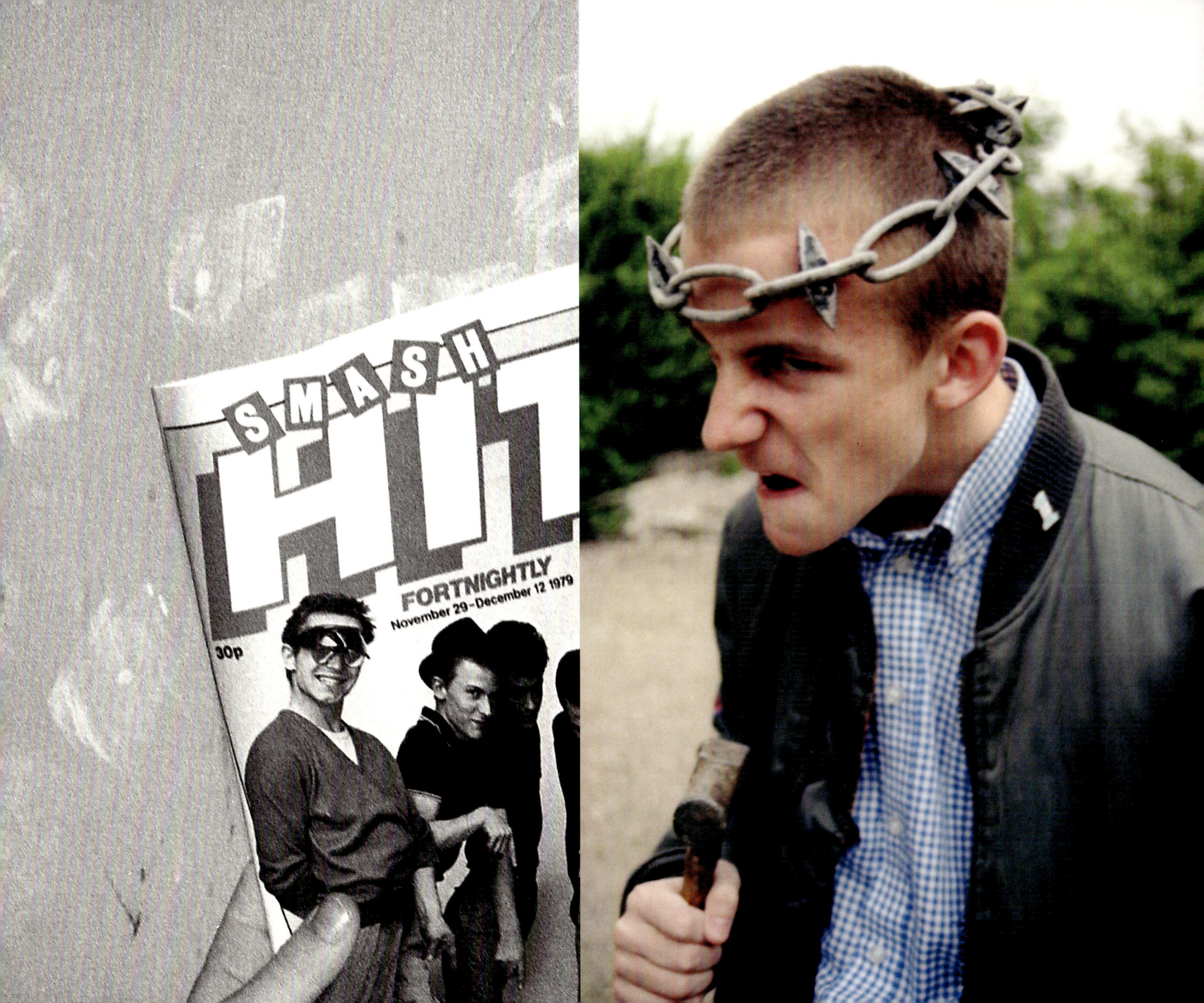
SMASH
HIT
FORTNIGHTLY
November 29 - December 12 1979
30p

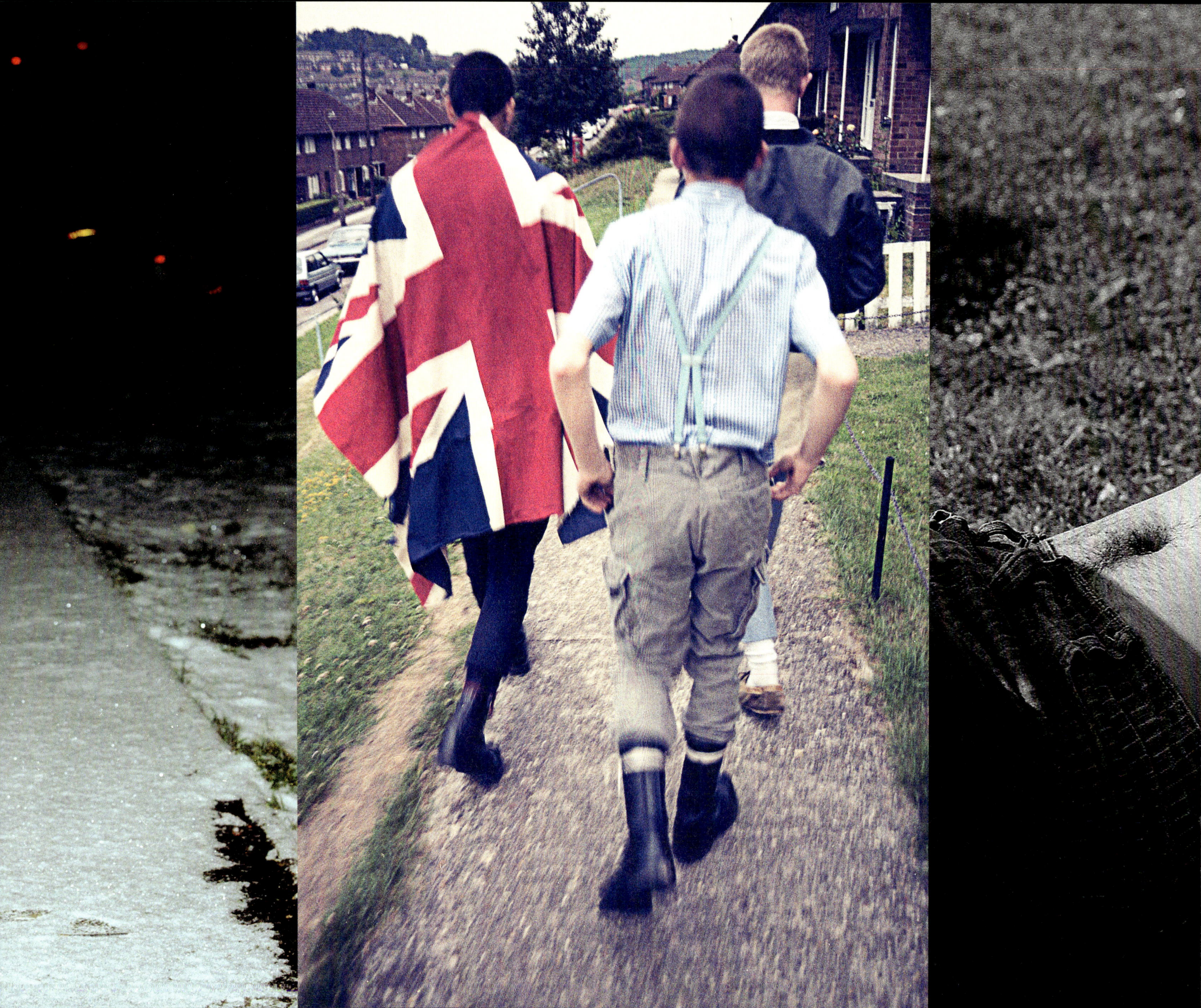

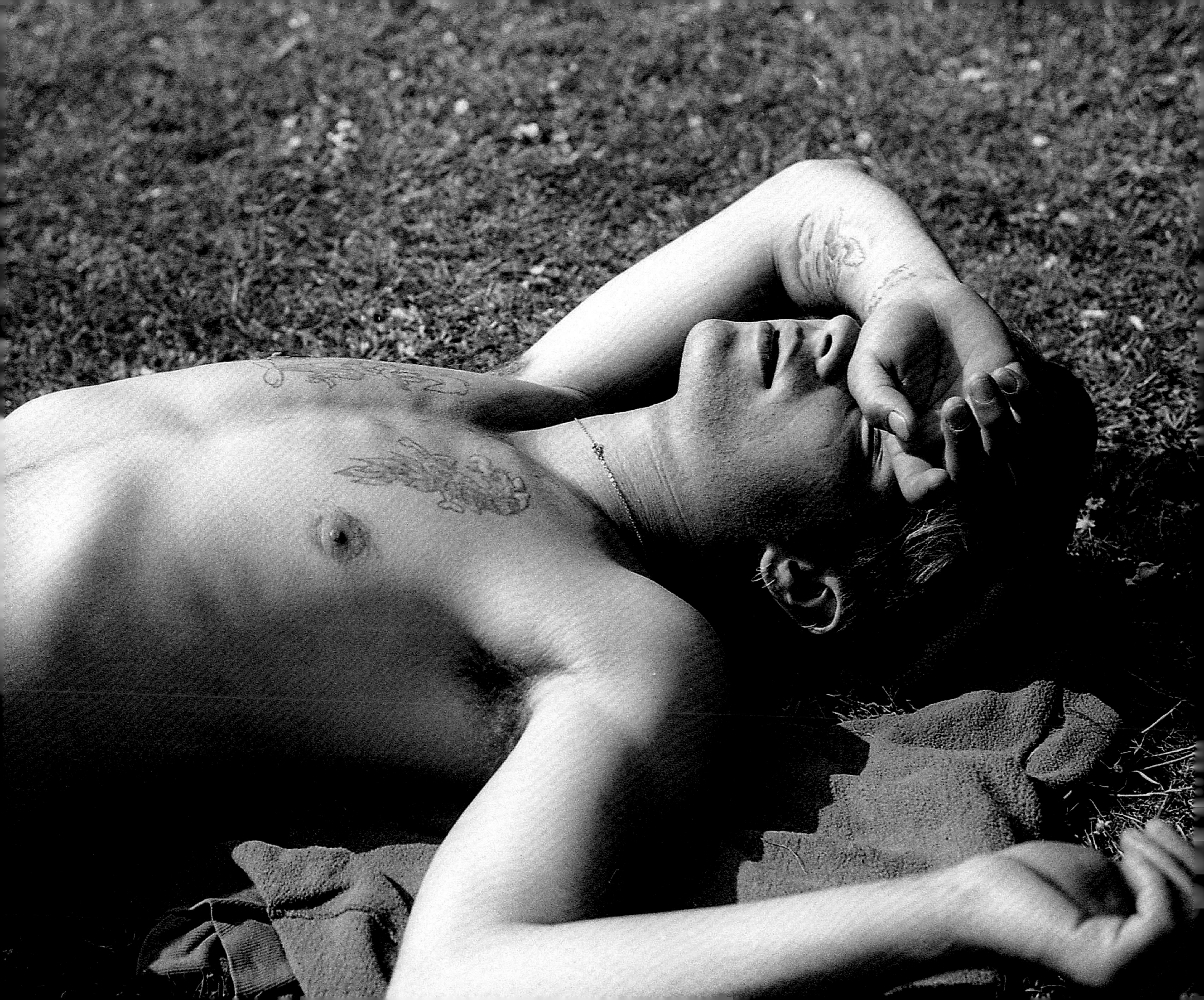

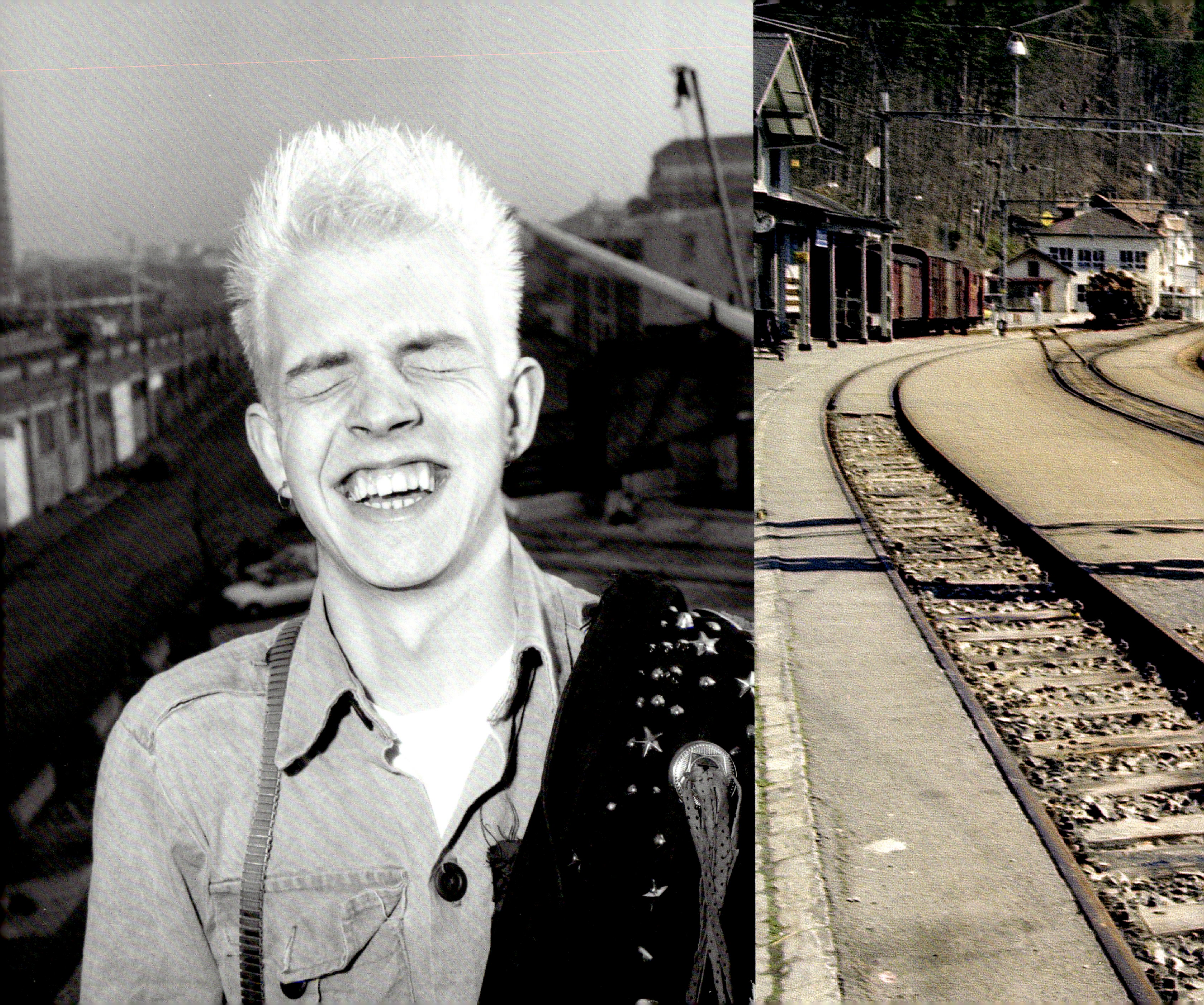

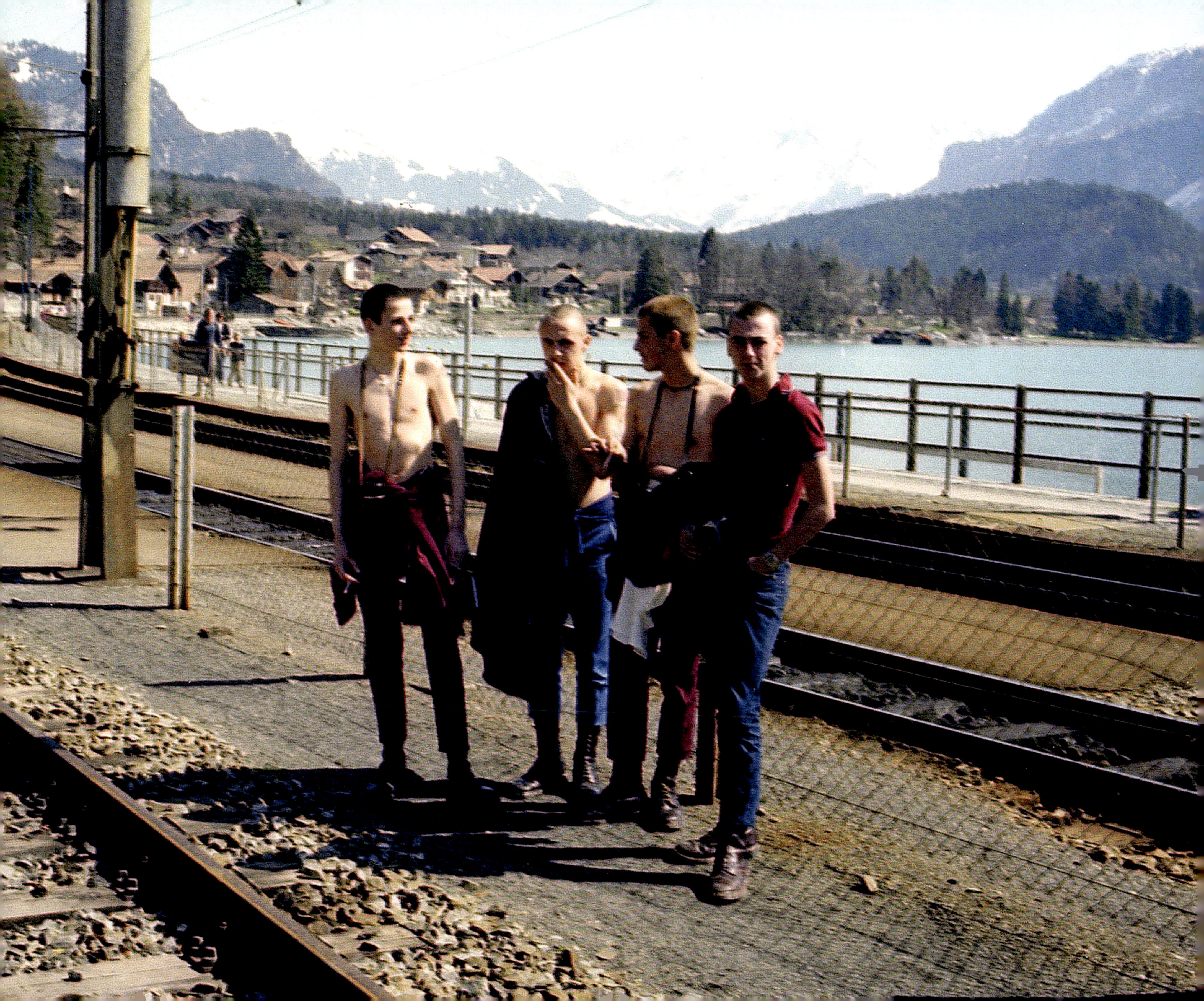

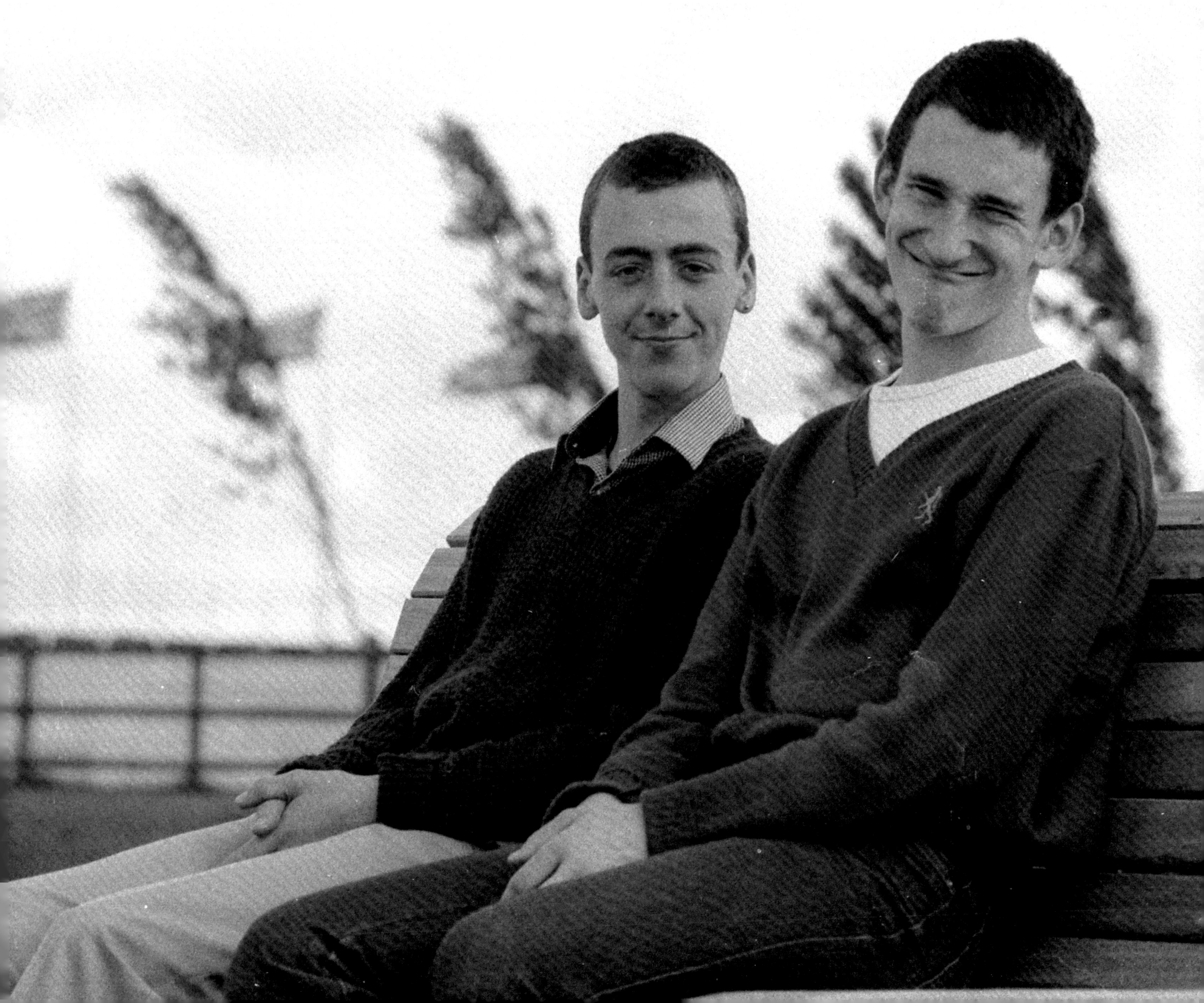

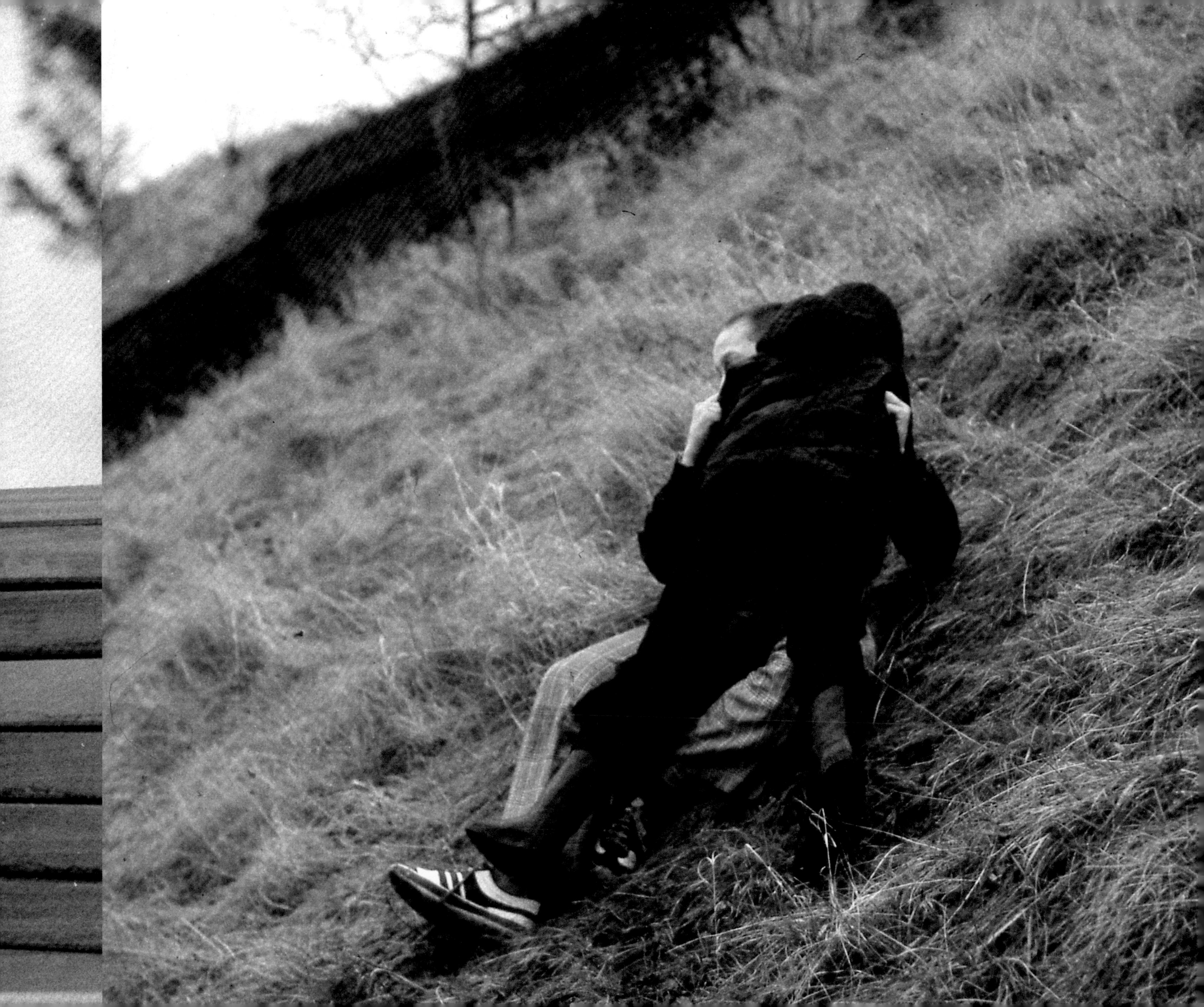

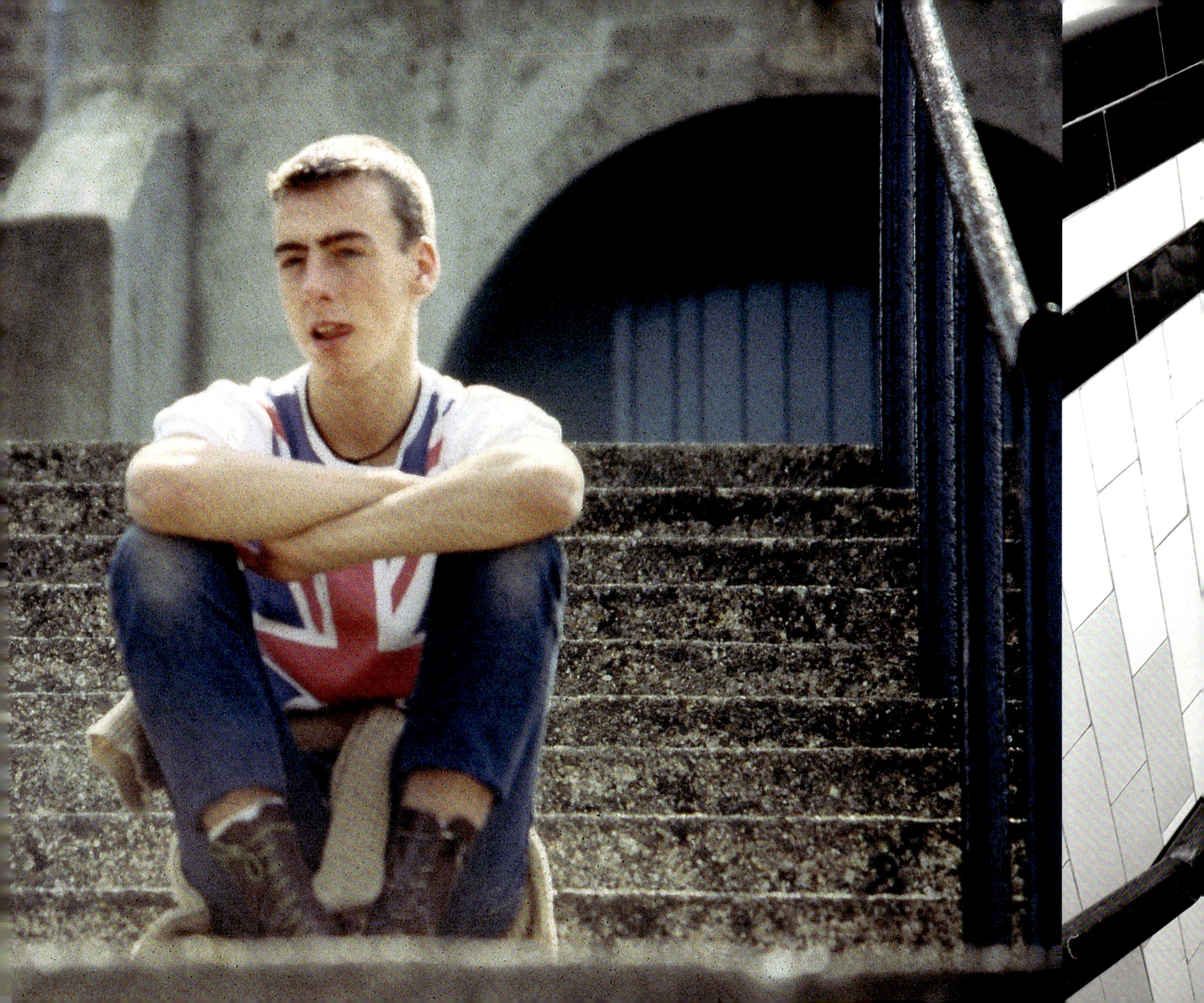

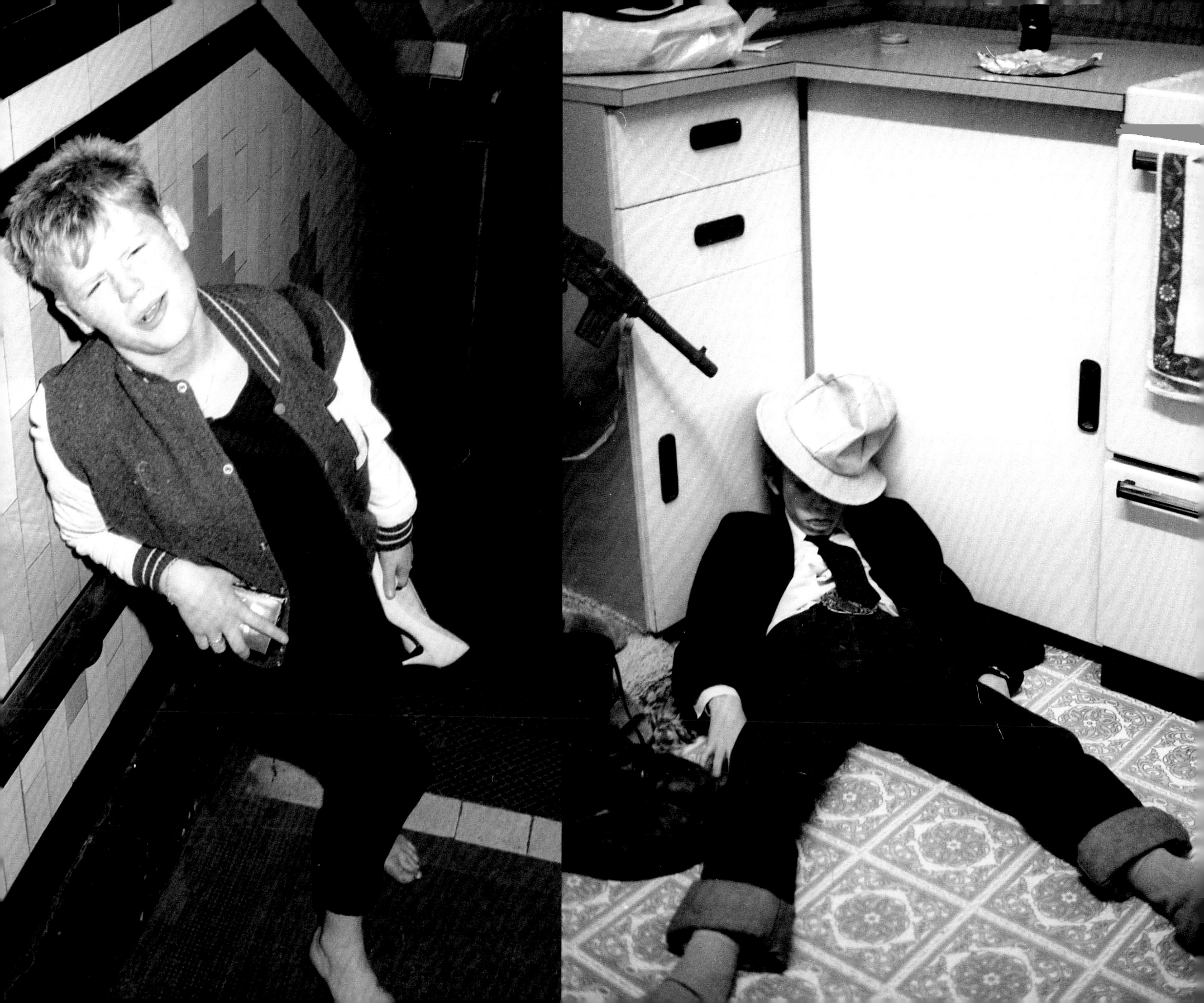

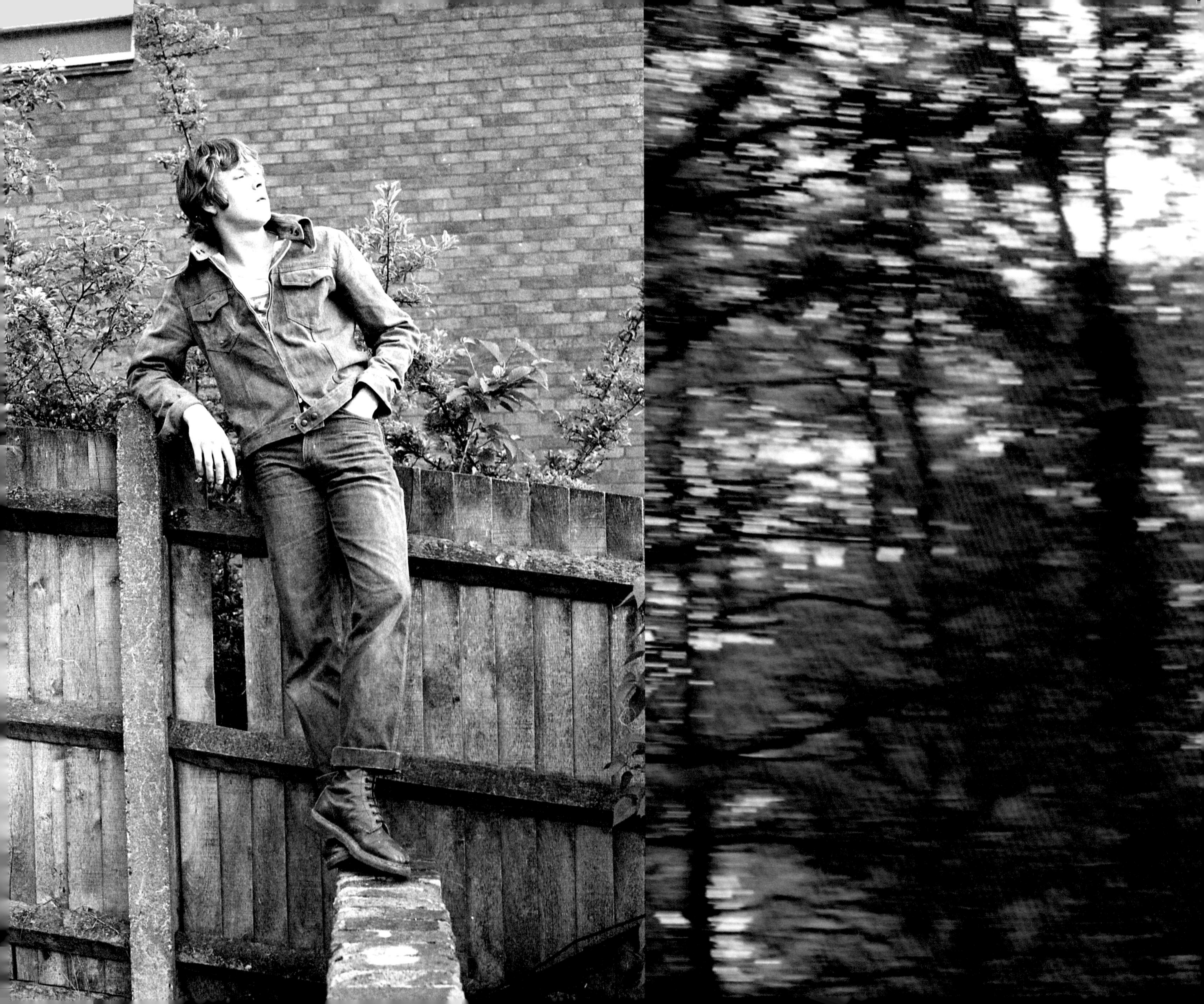

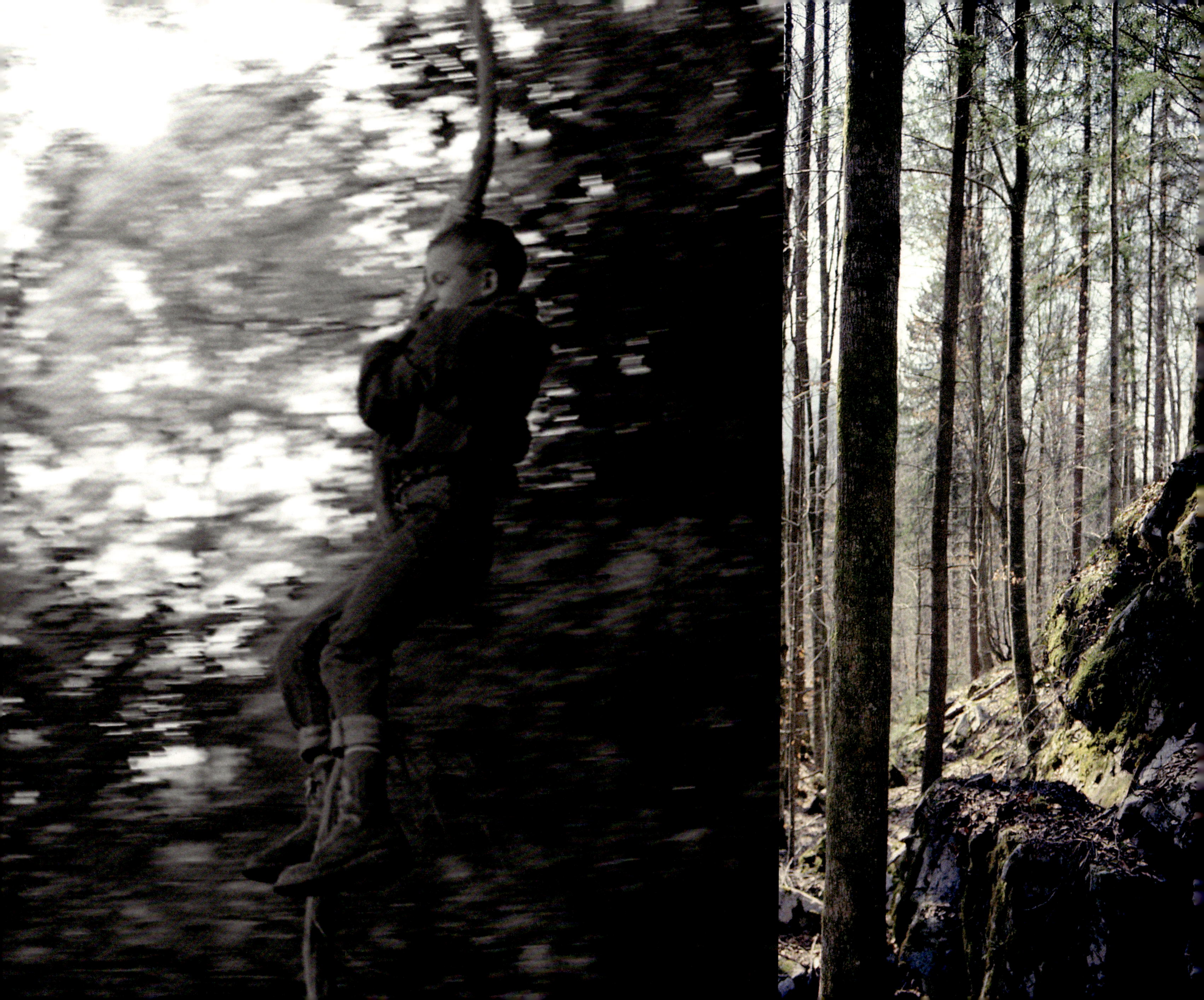

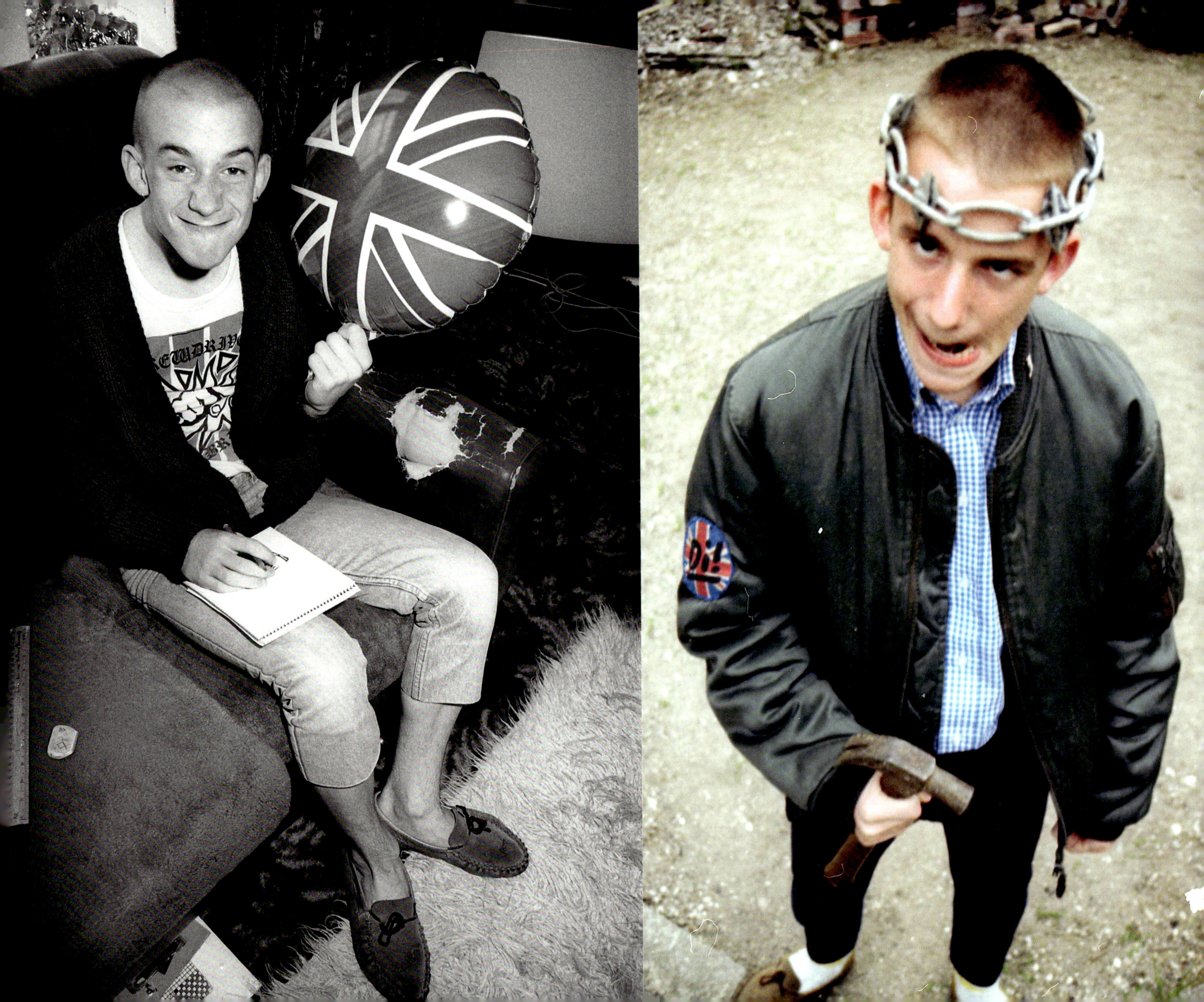

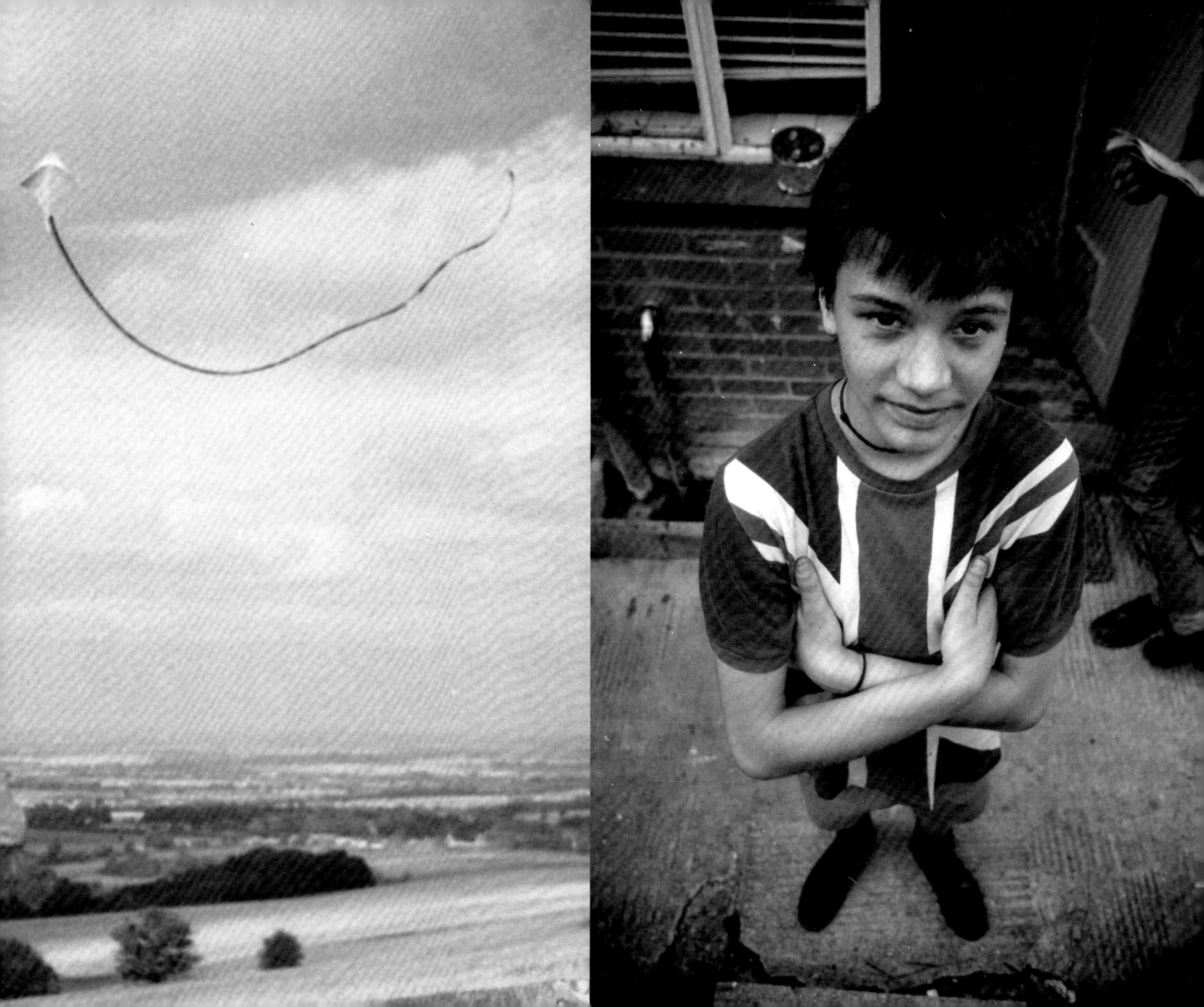

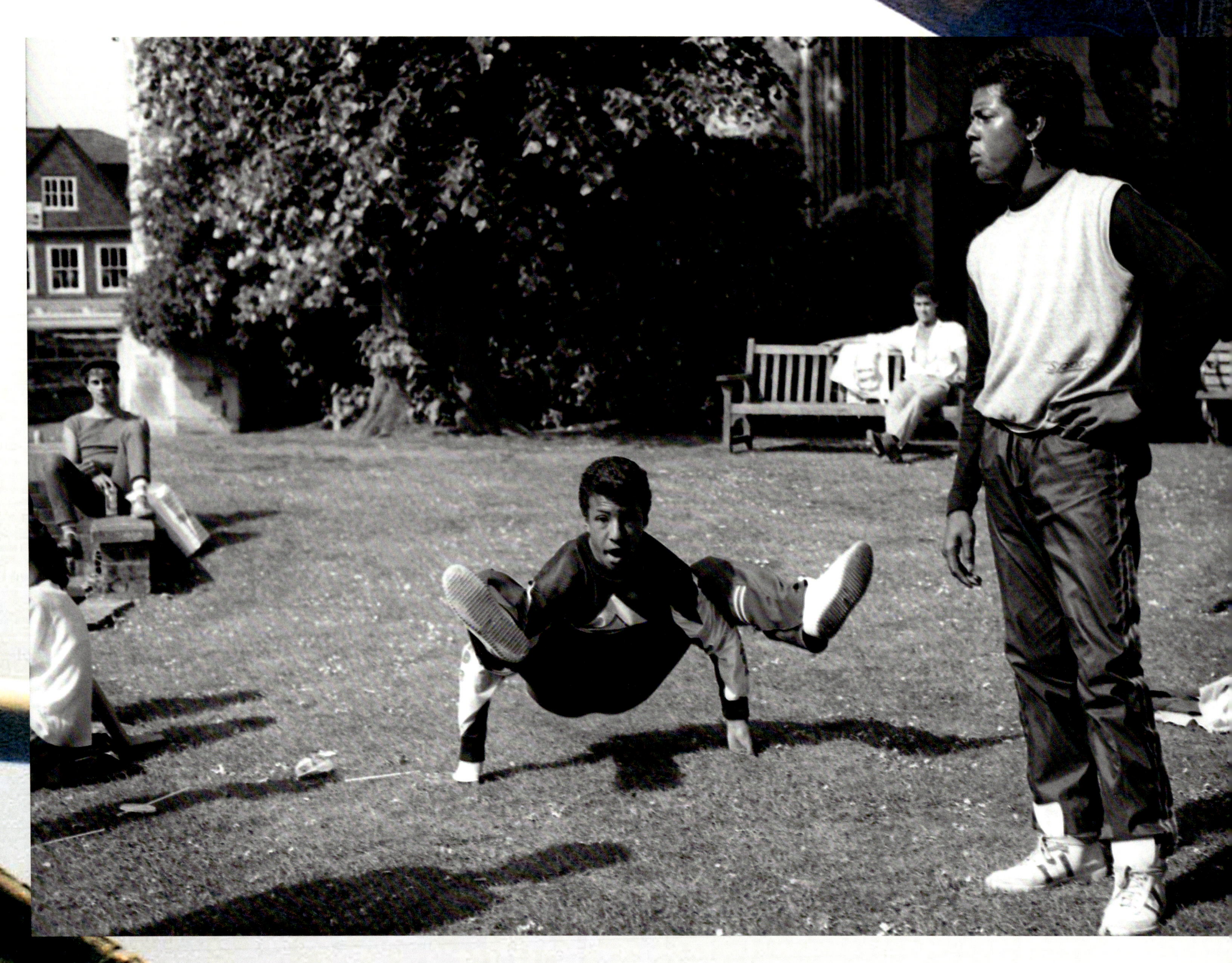

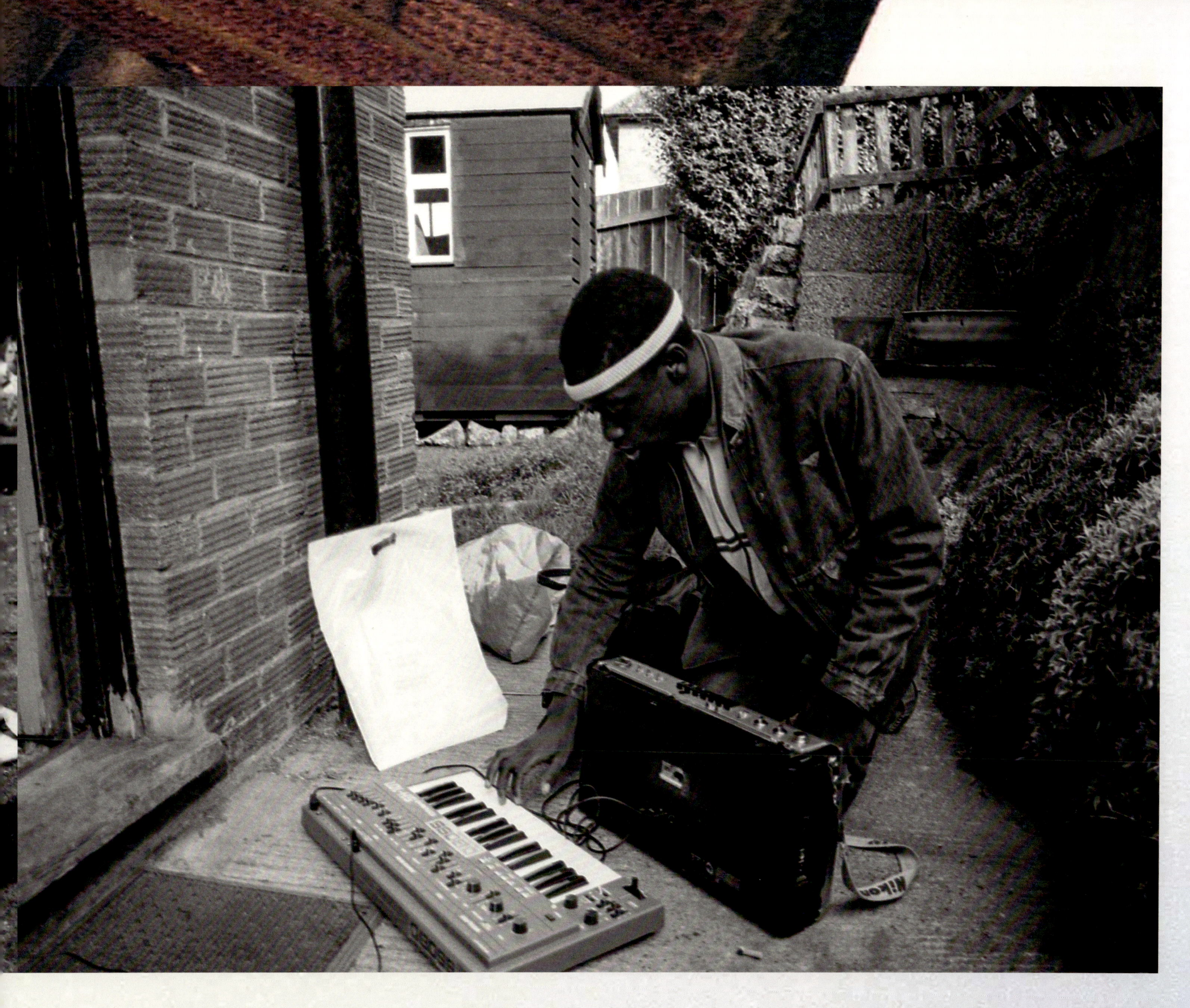
Nikon

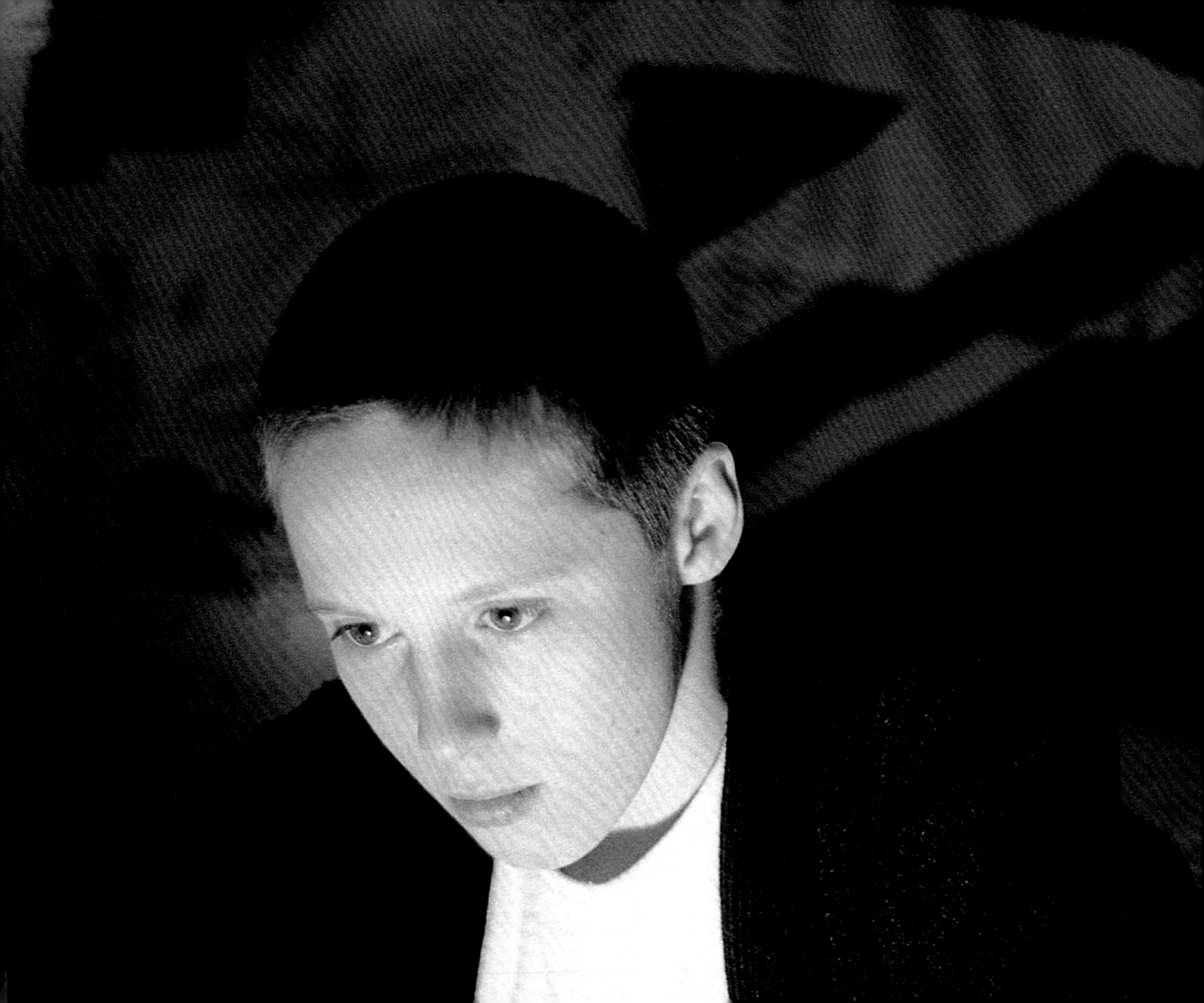

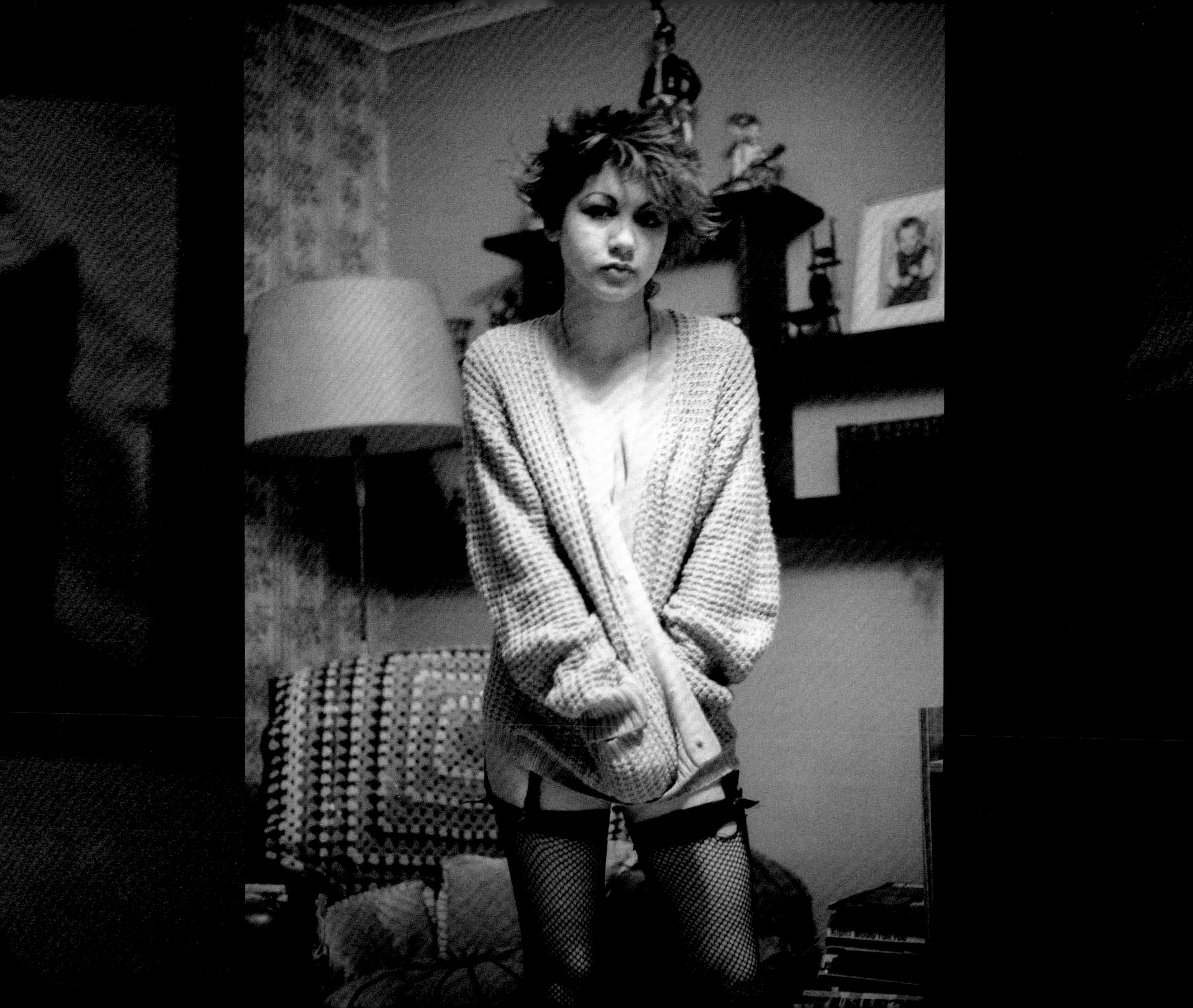

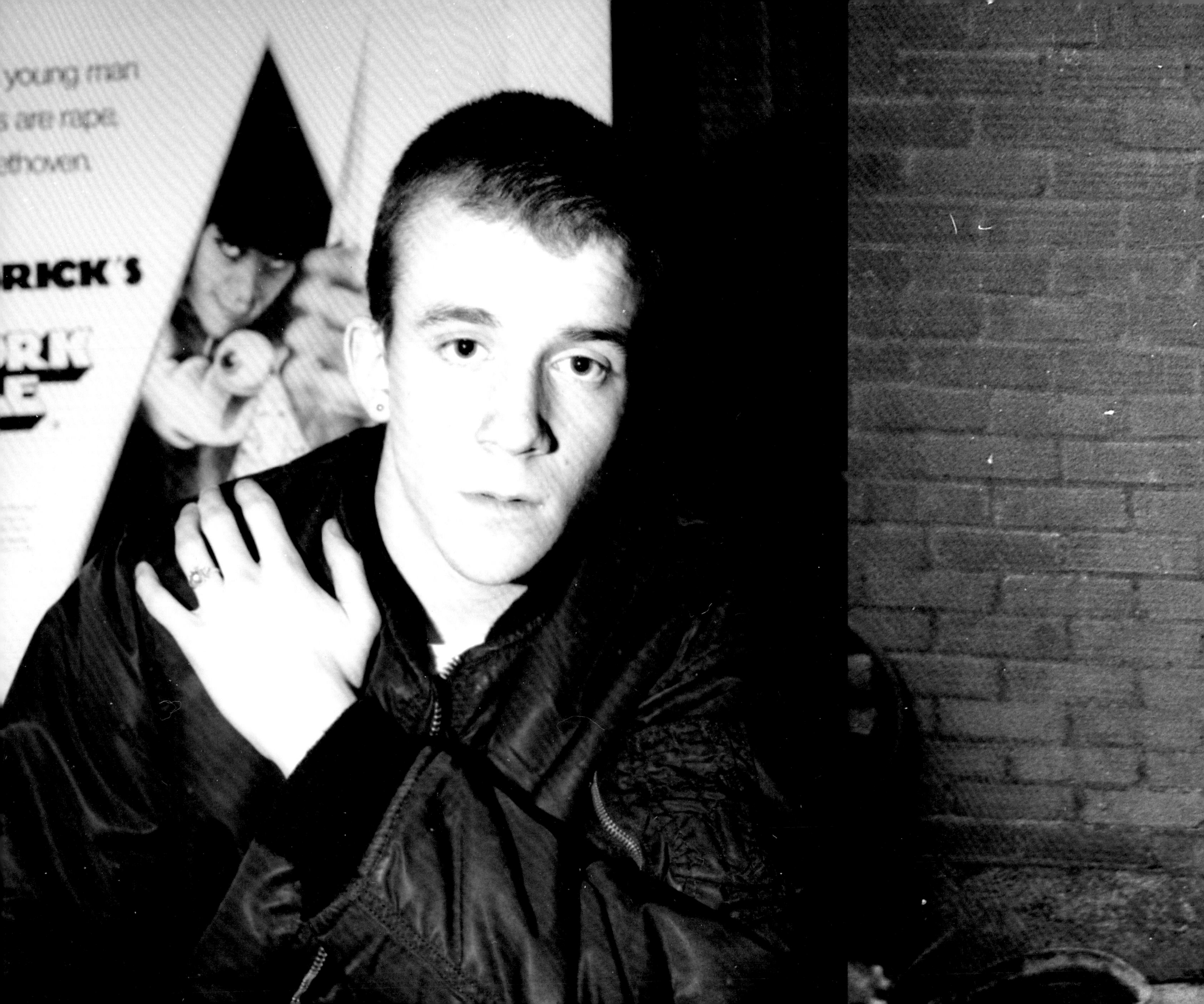
young man
s are rape
ethoven
RICK'S

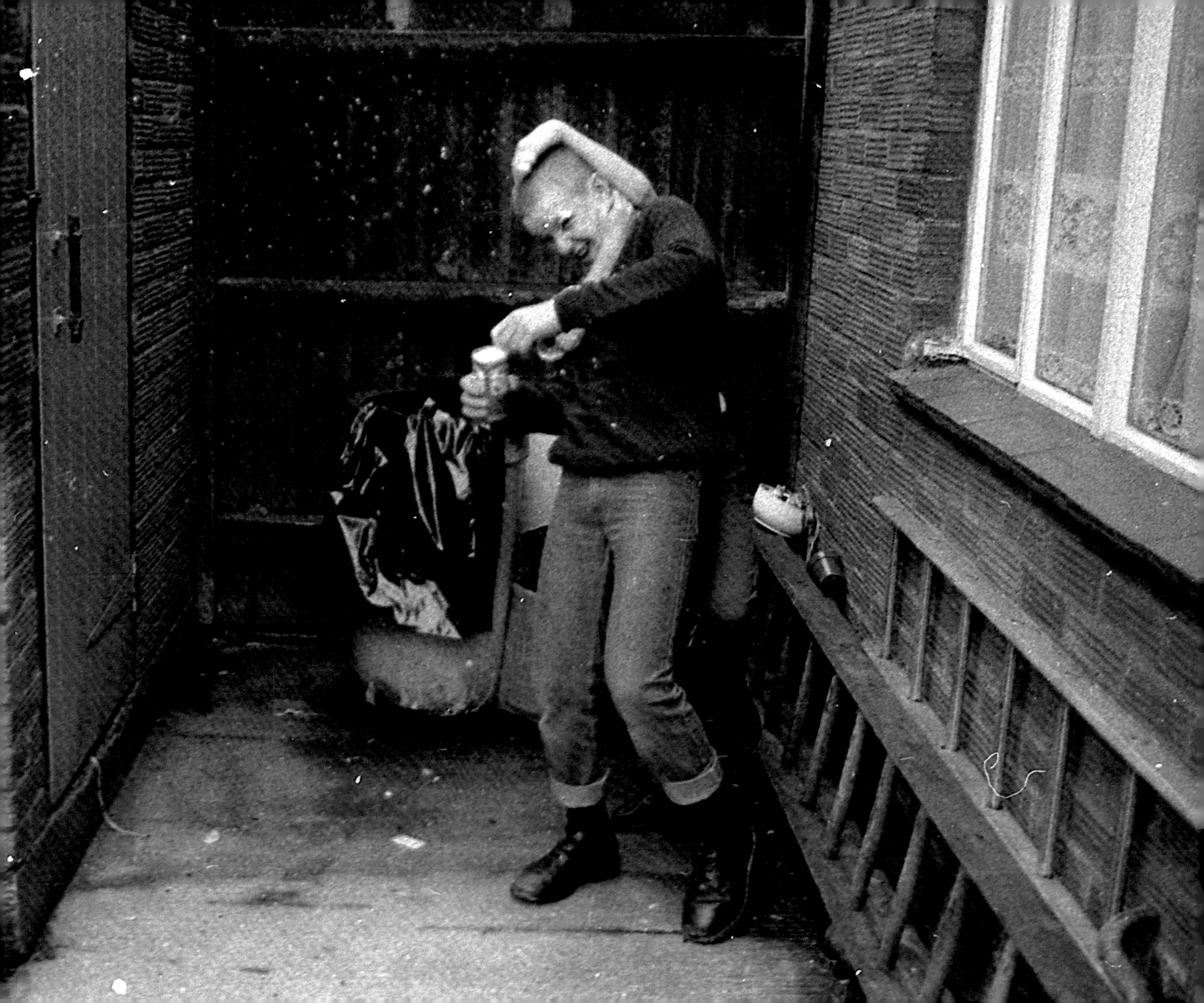

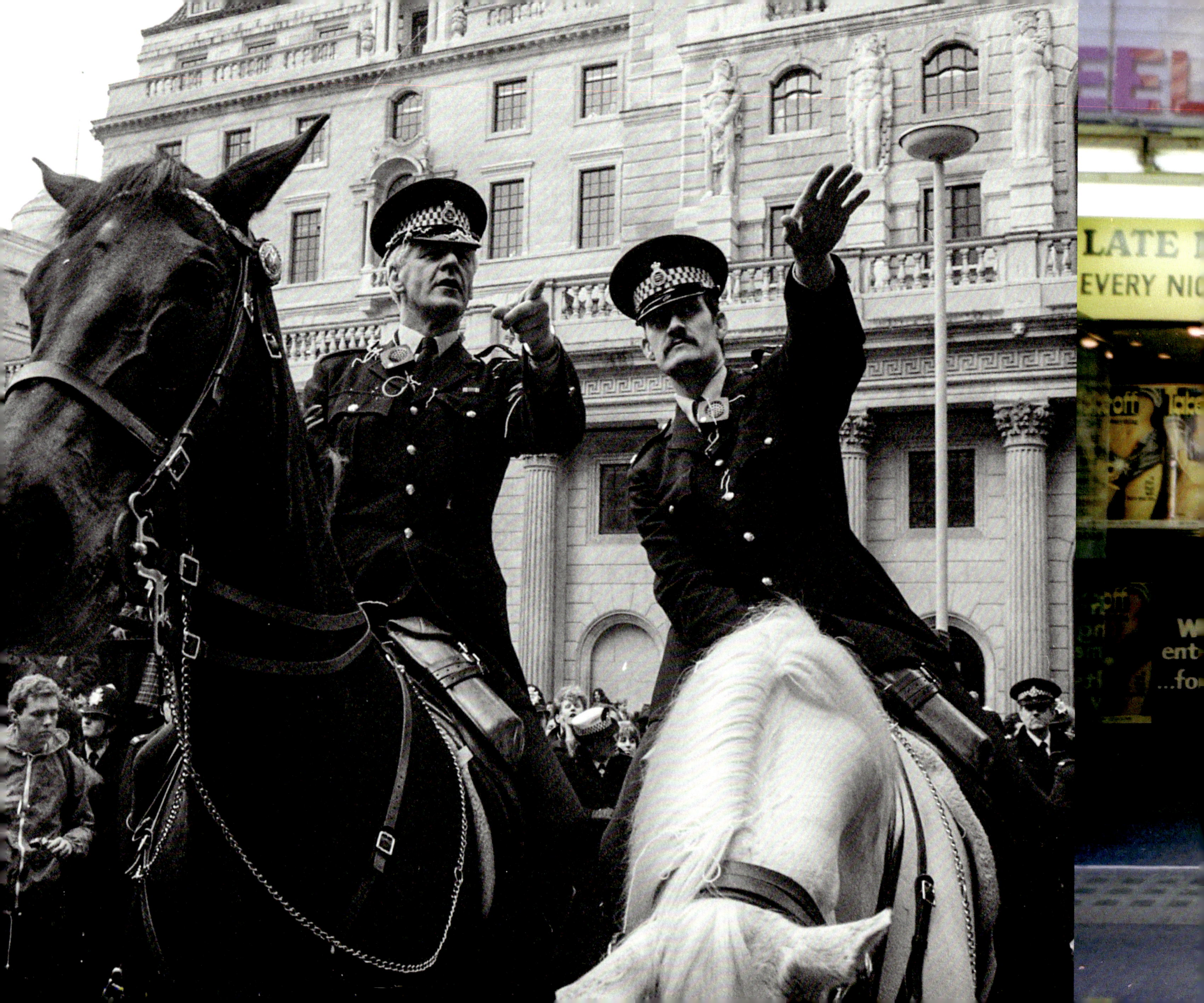
LATE
EVERY

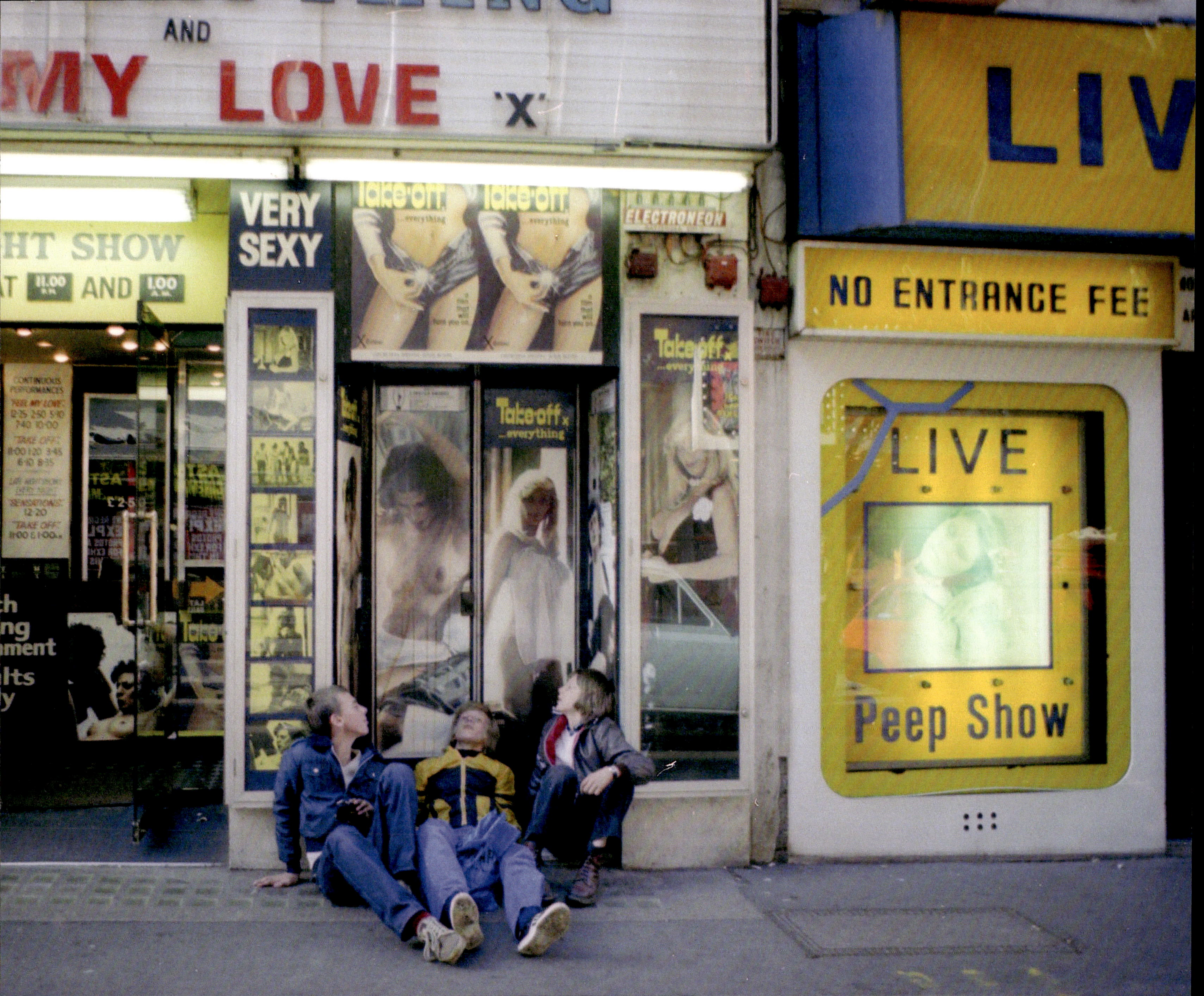

AND
MY LOVE
'X'
VERY SEXY
Take-off
...everything
ELECTRONEON
NO ENTRANCE FEE
LIVE
Peep Show

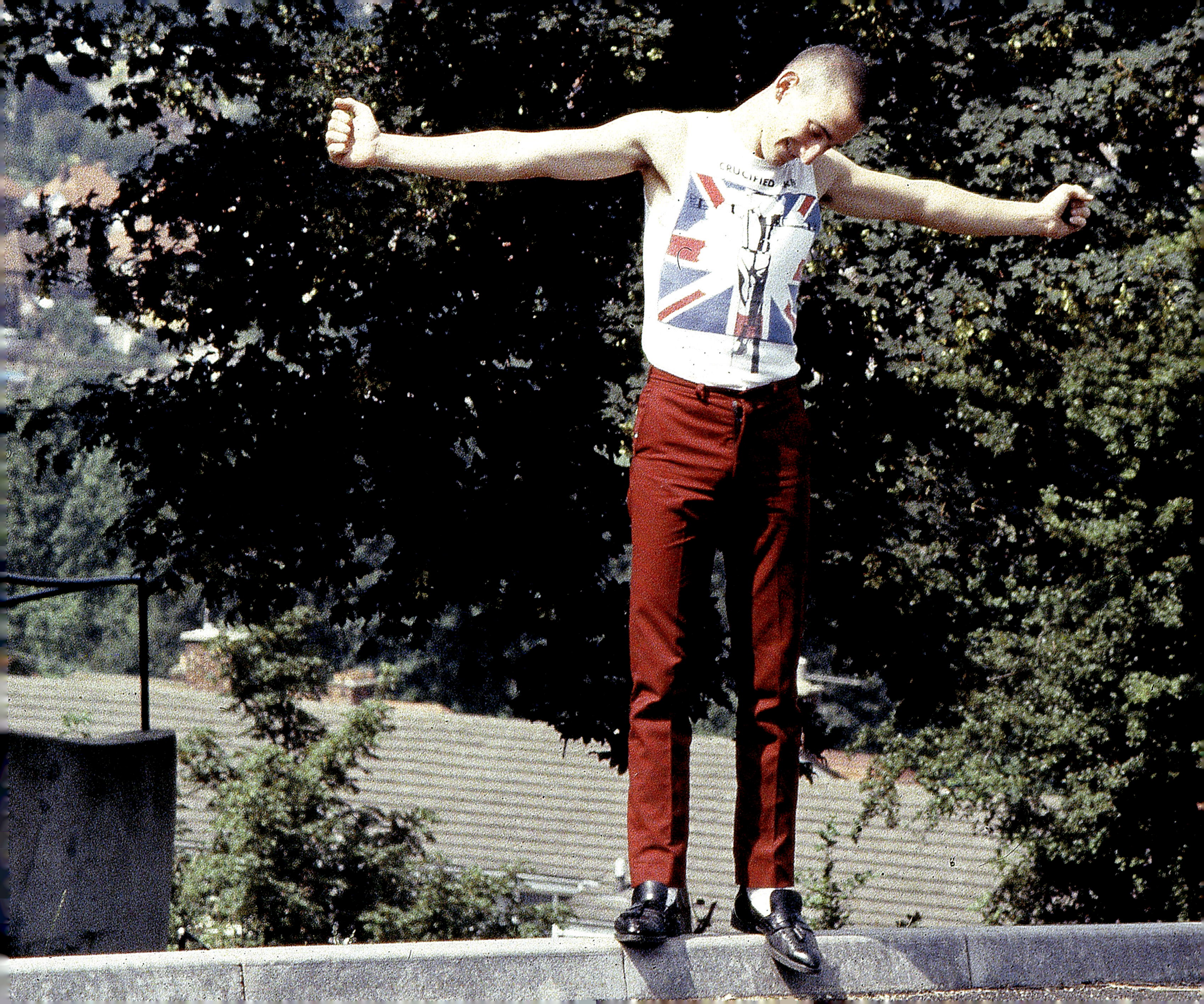
CRUCIFIED

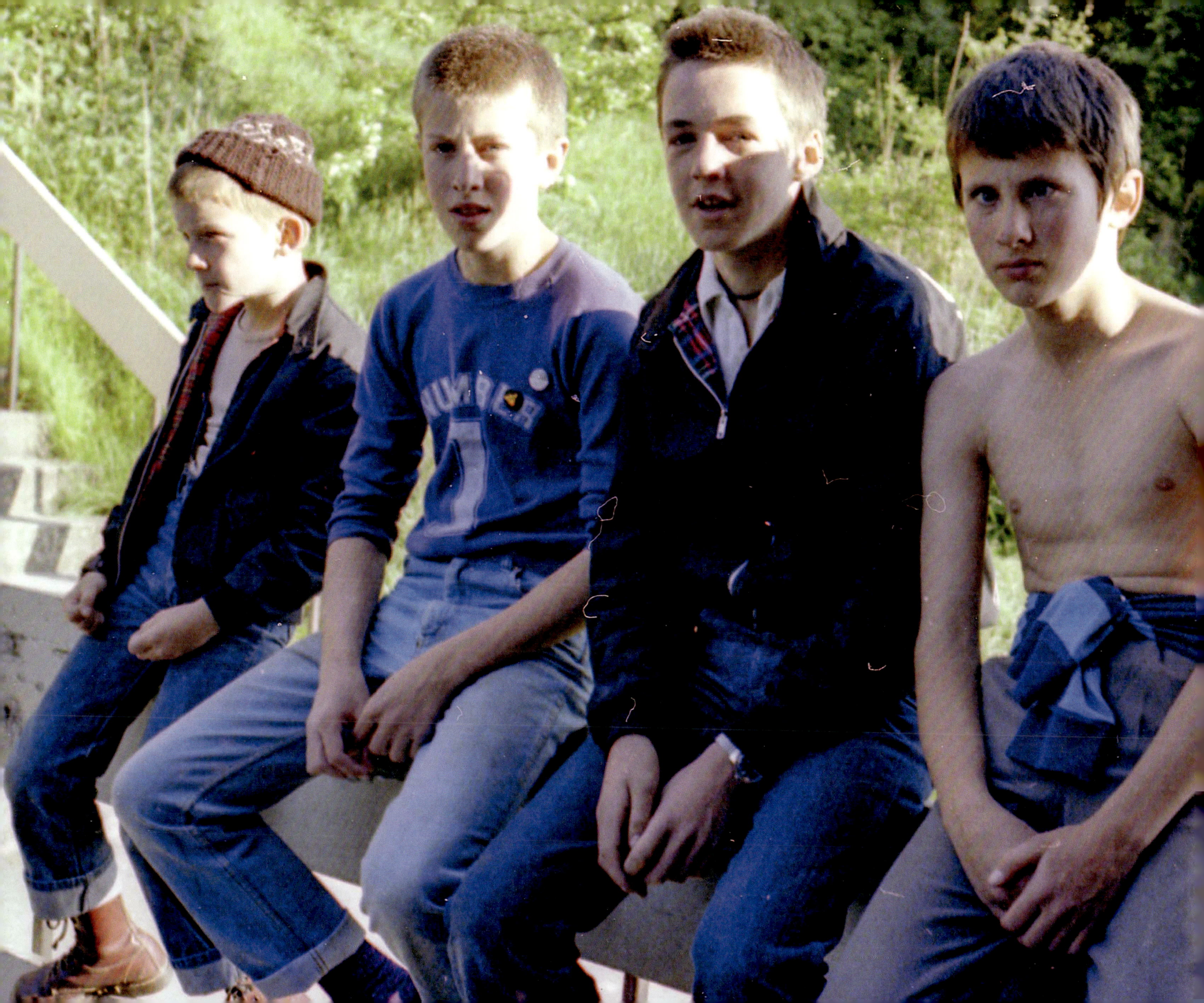

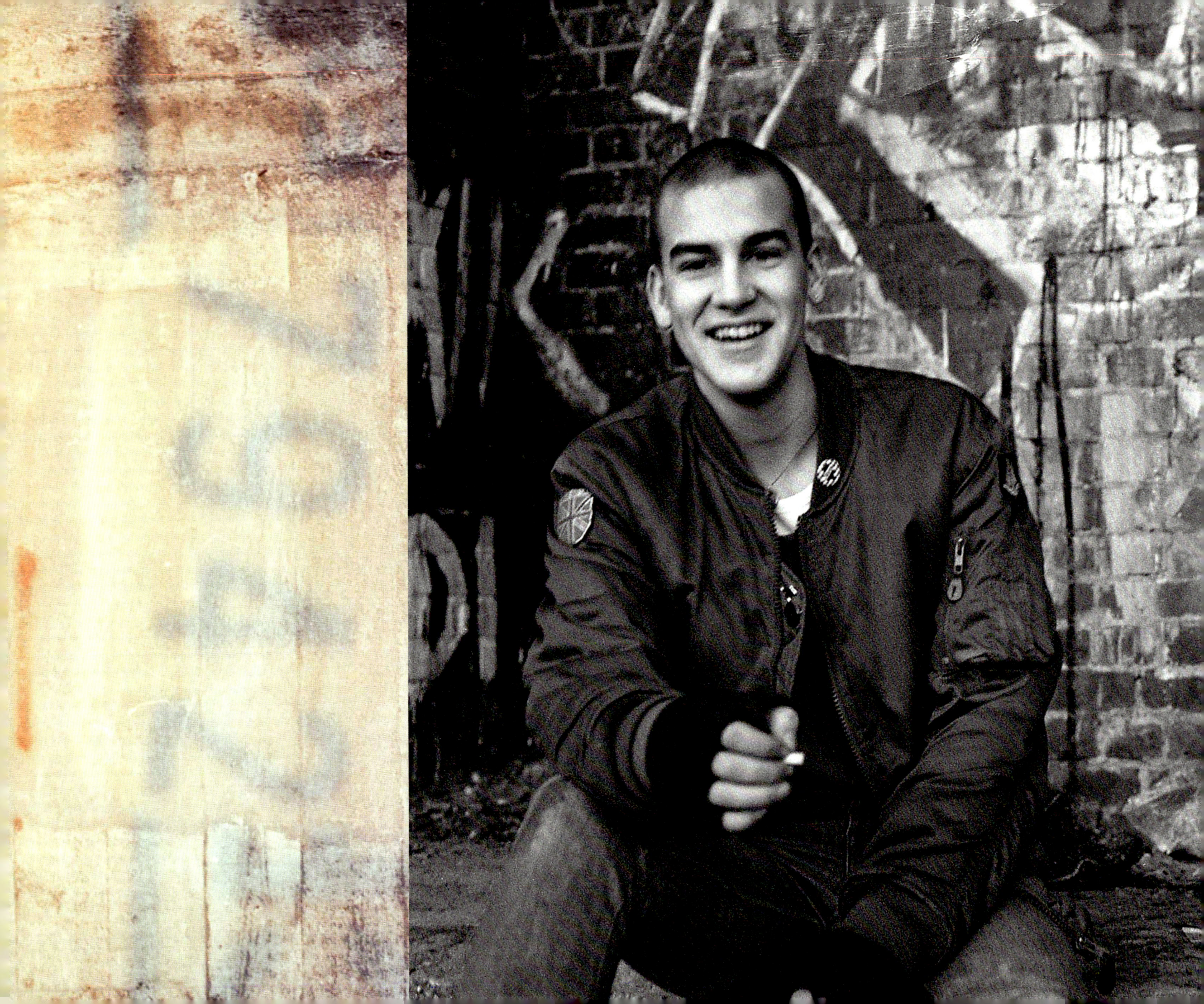

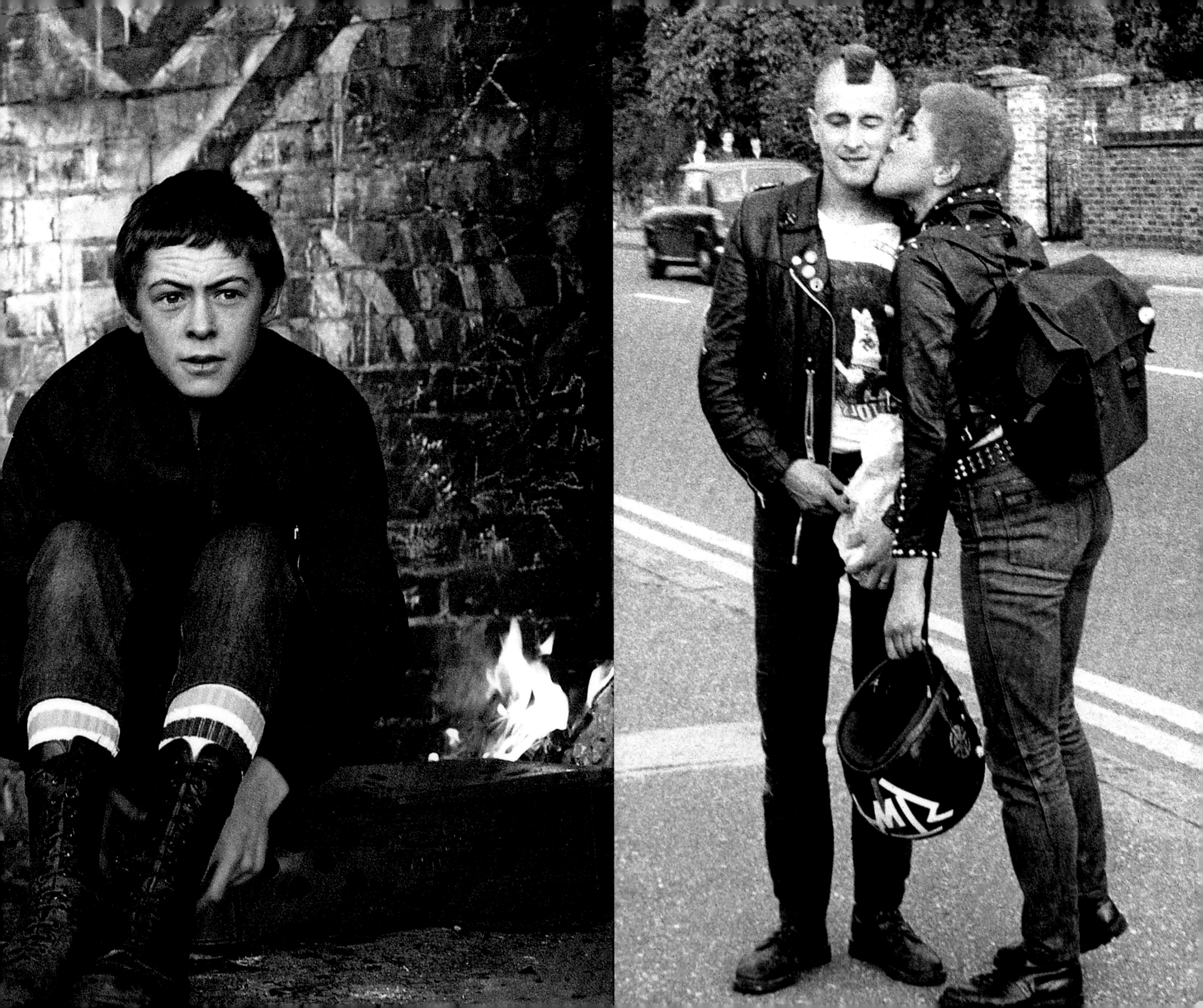

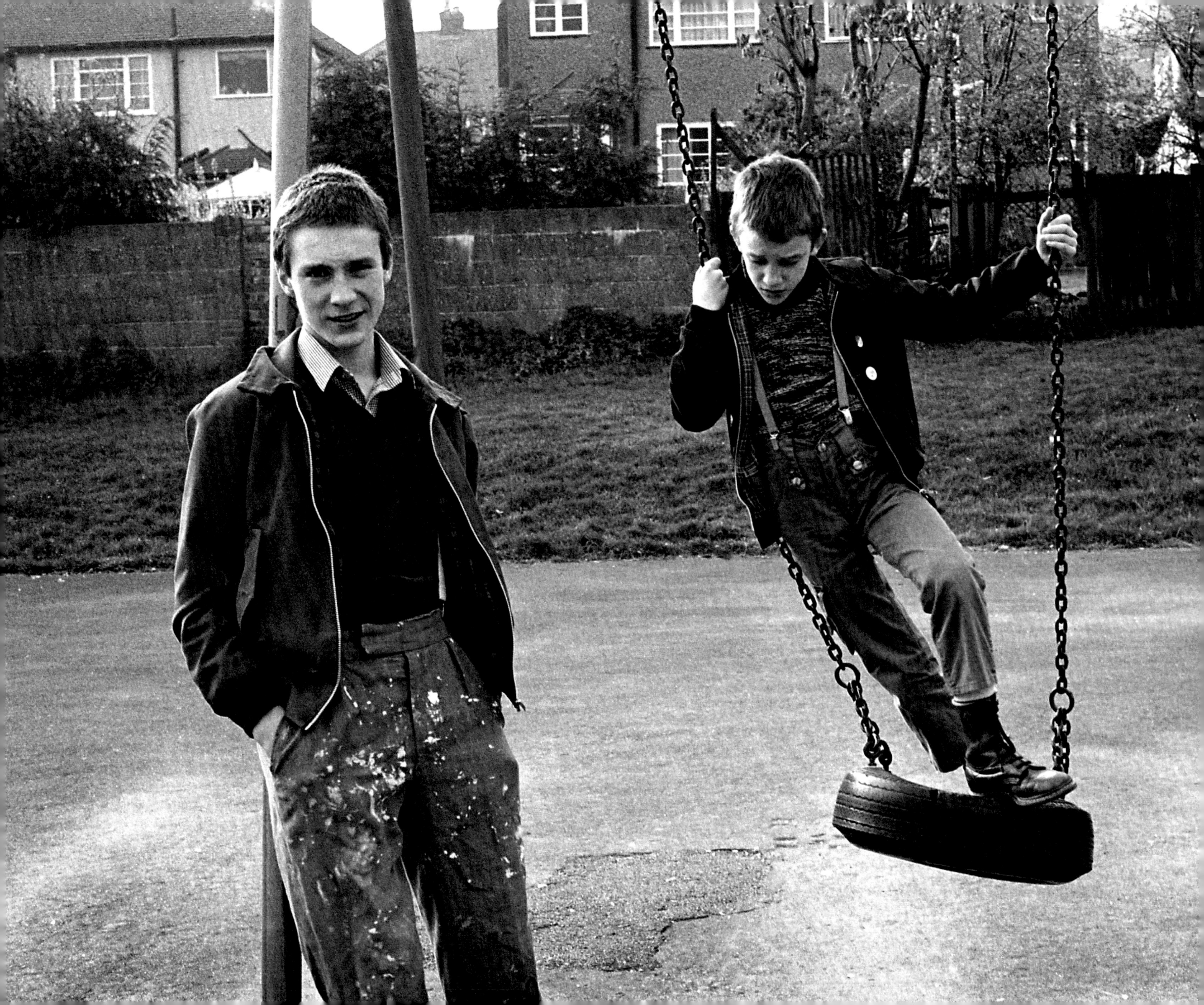

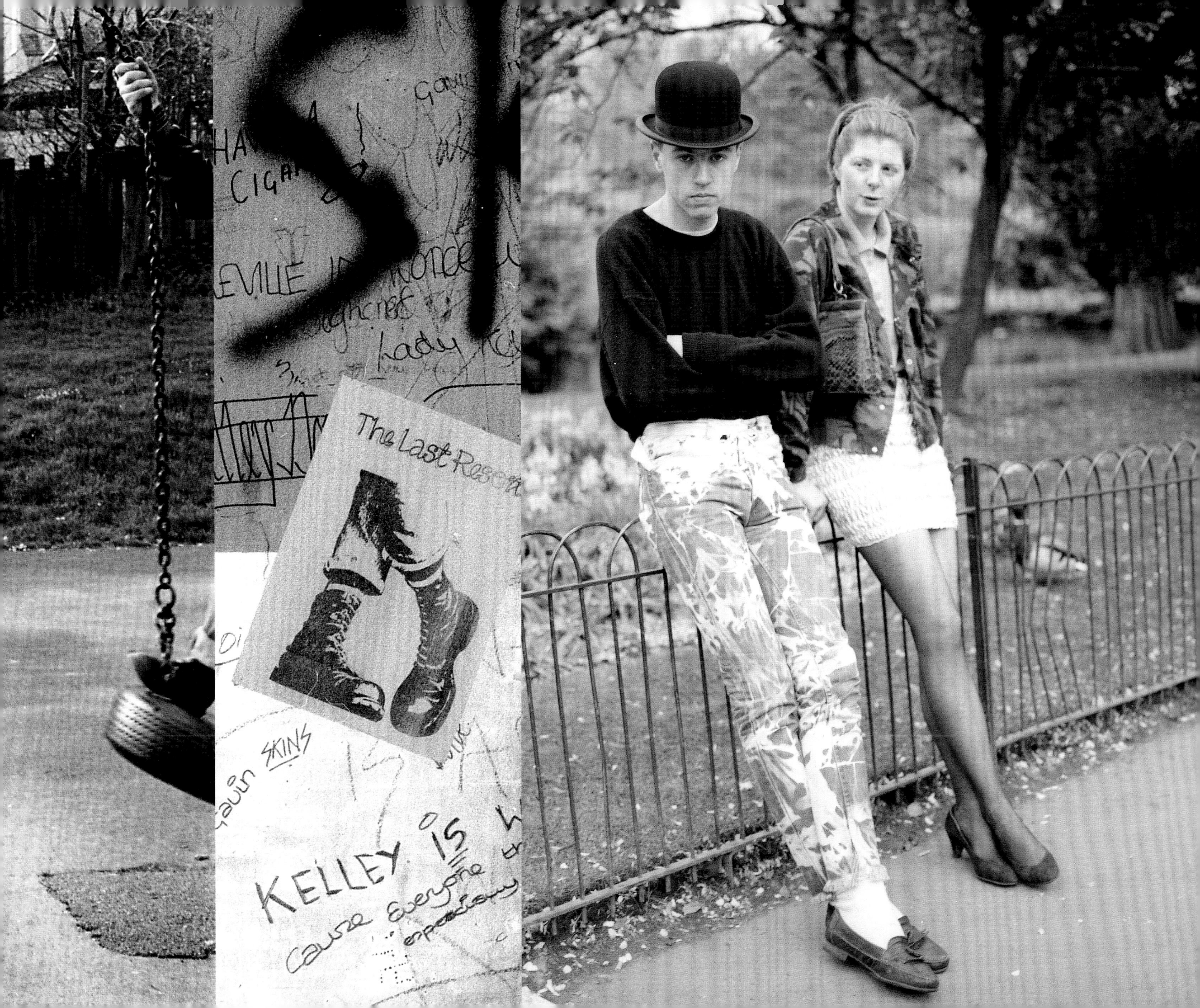
SKINS
KELLEY IS
Cause everyone

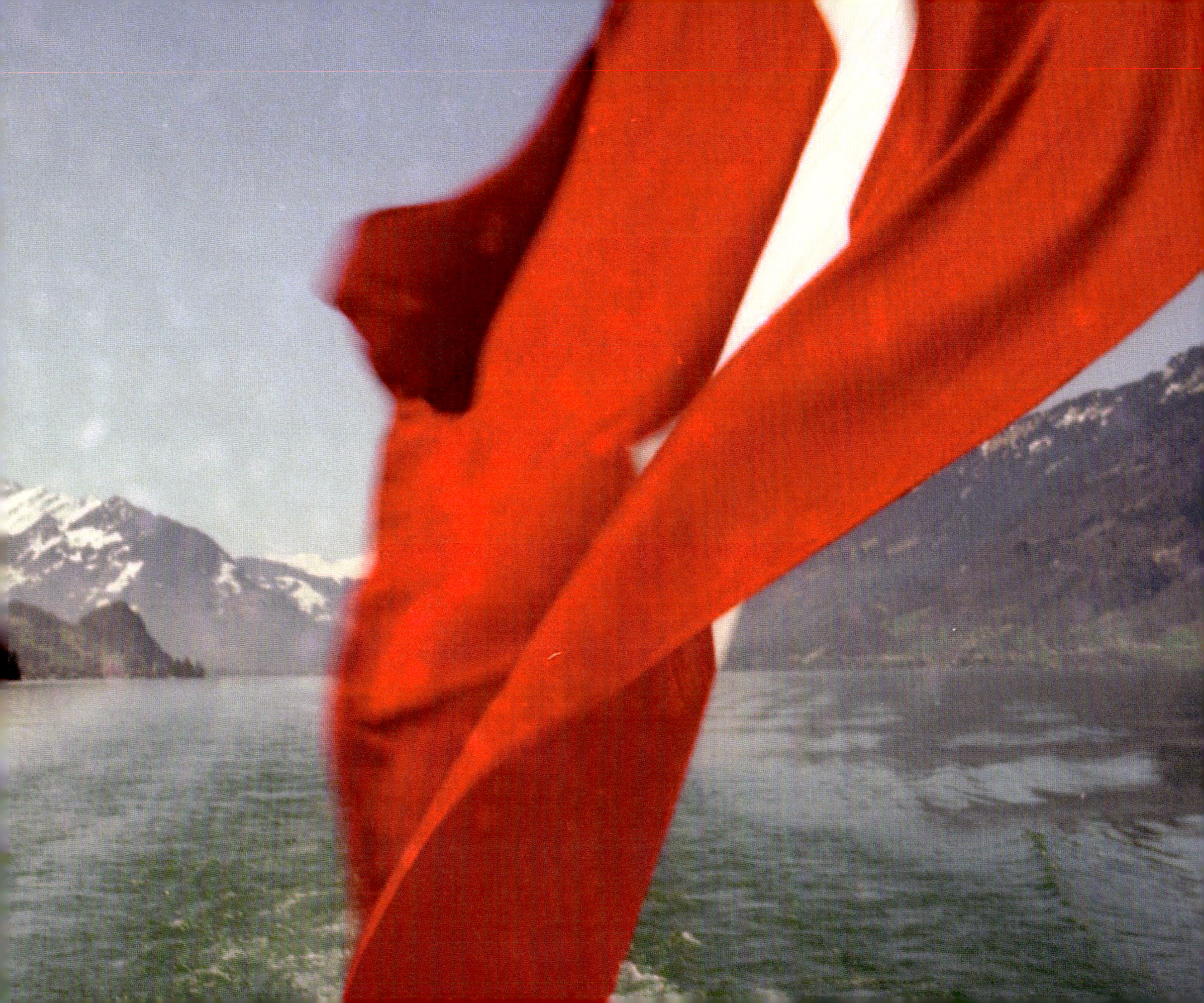

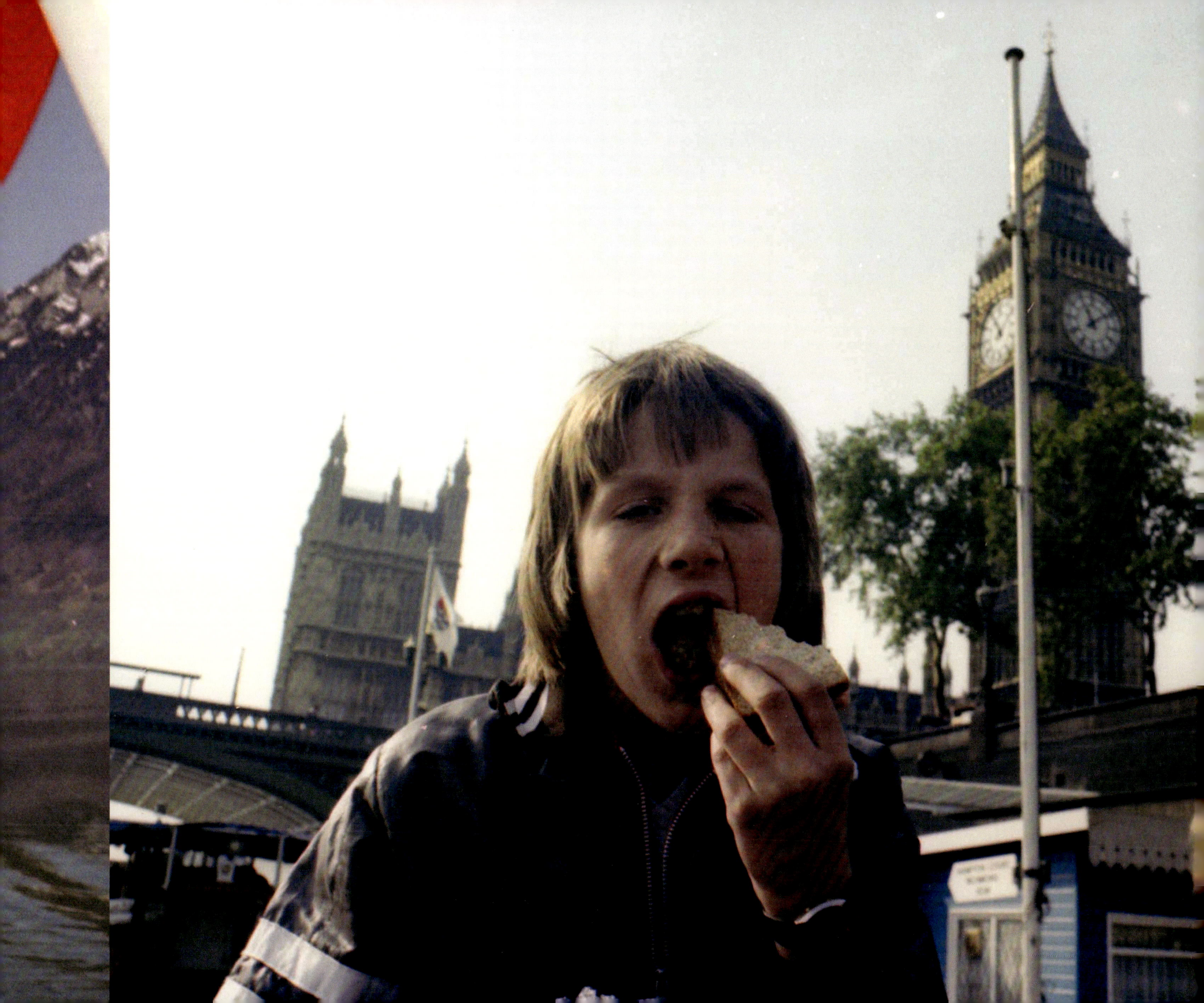

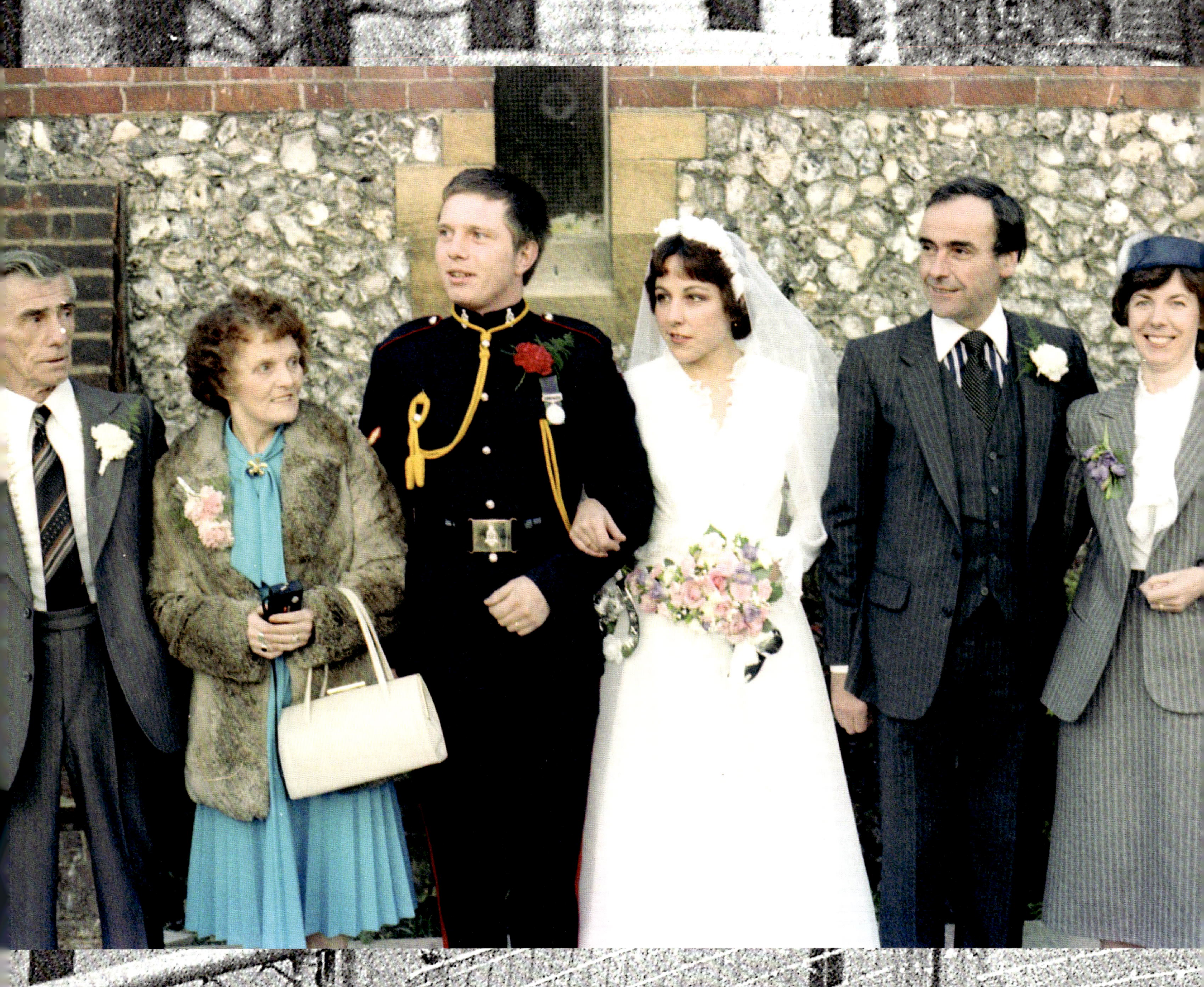

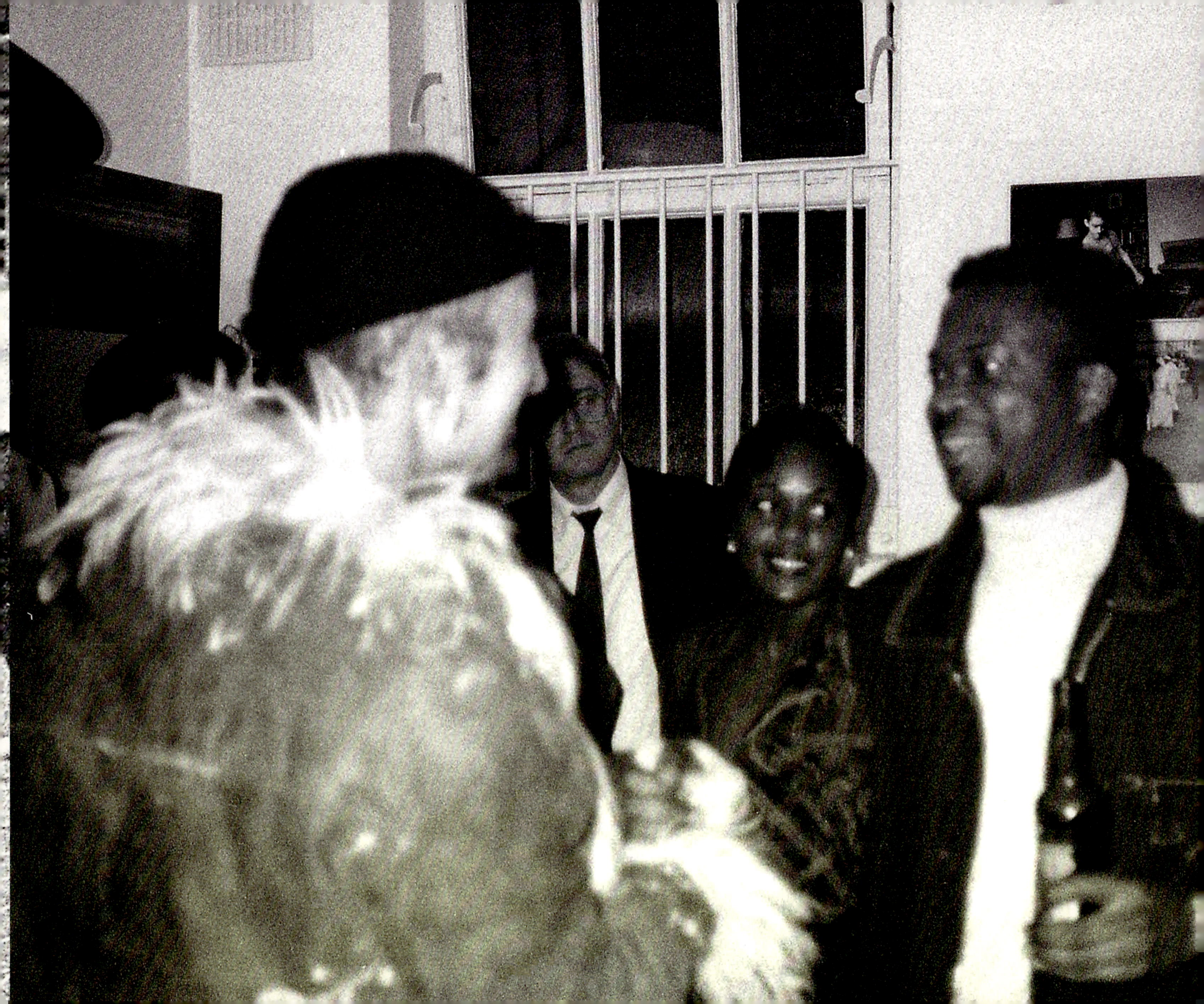

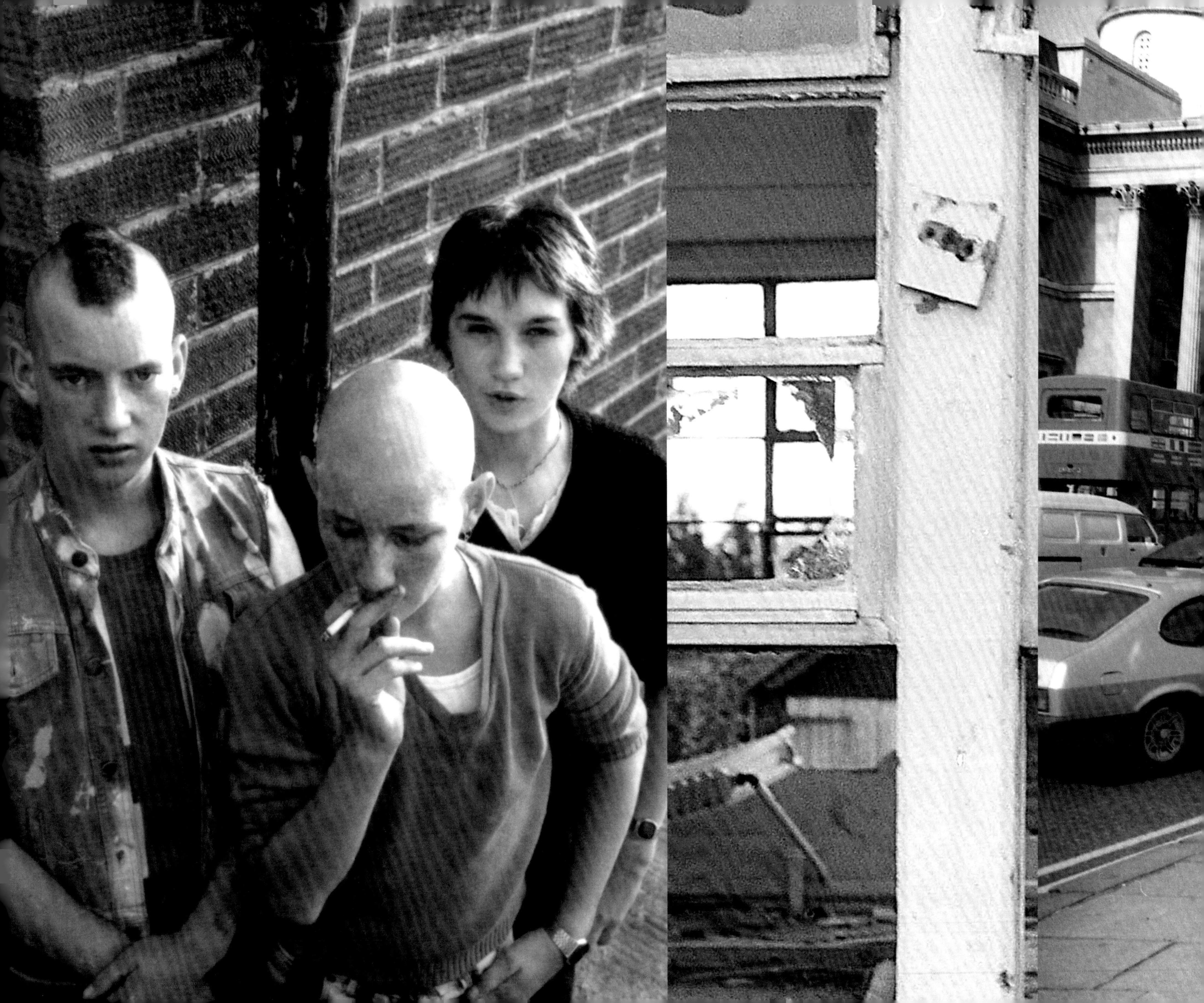

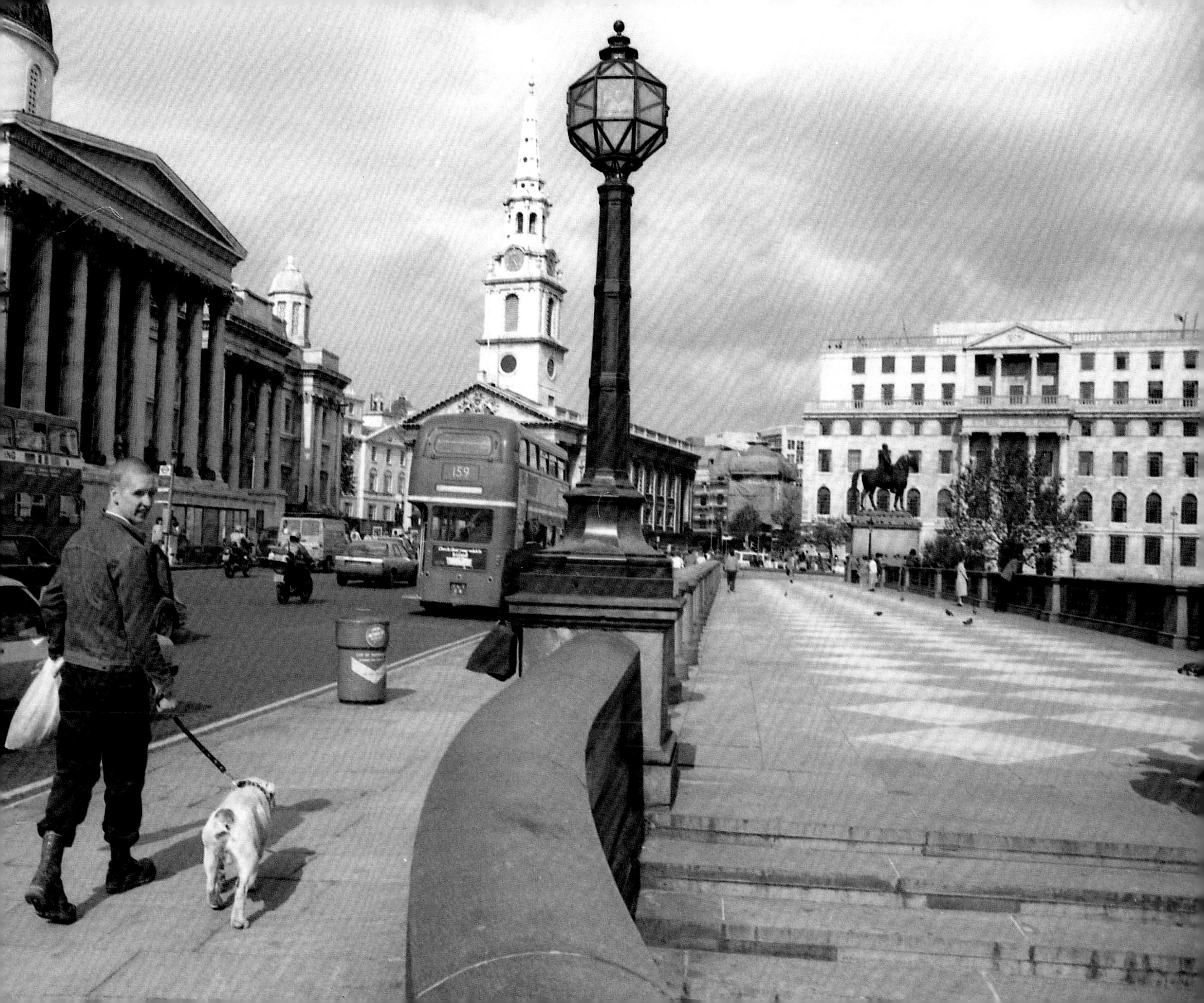
159

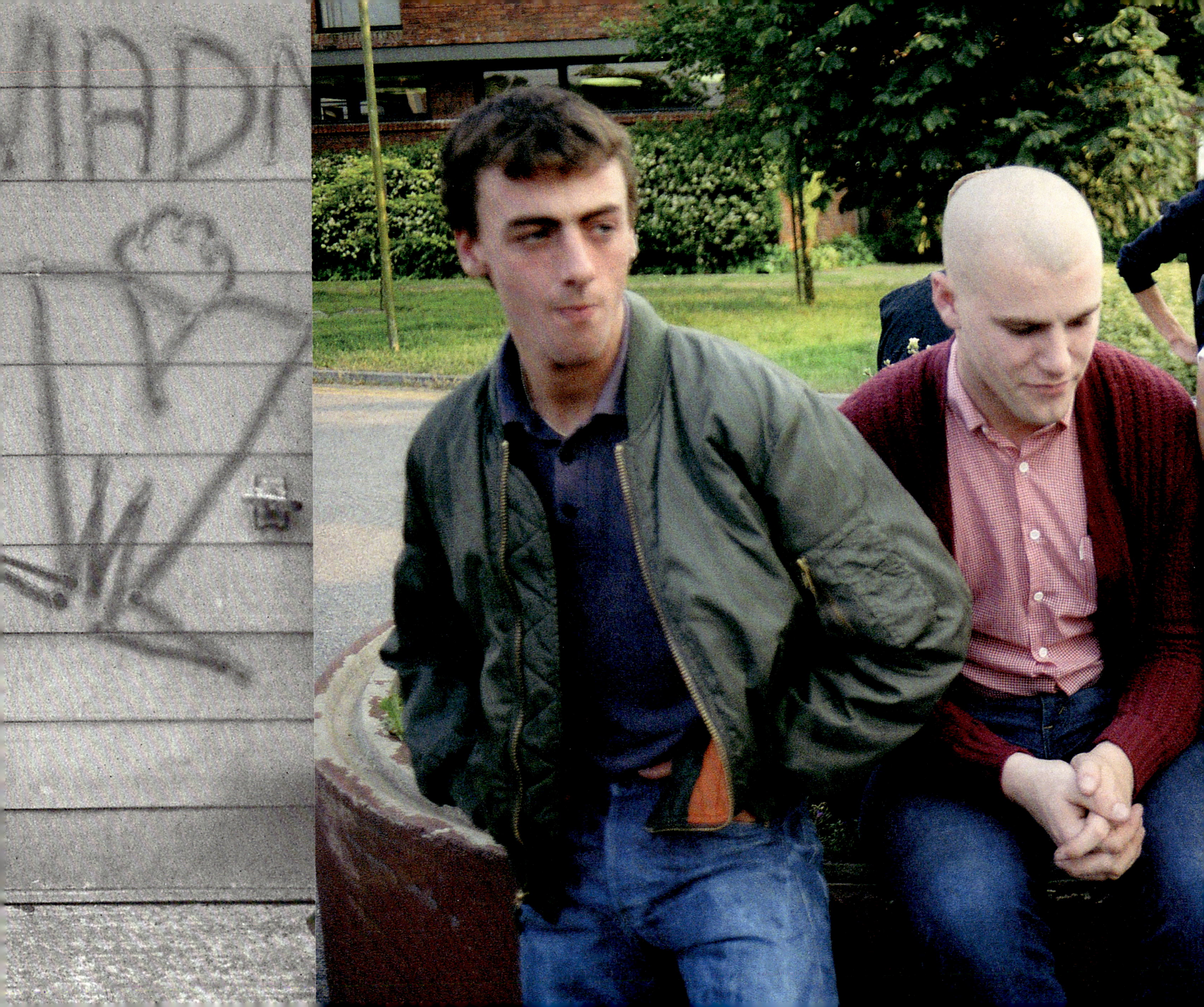

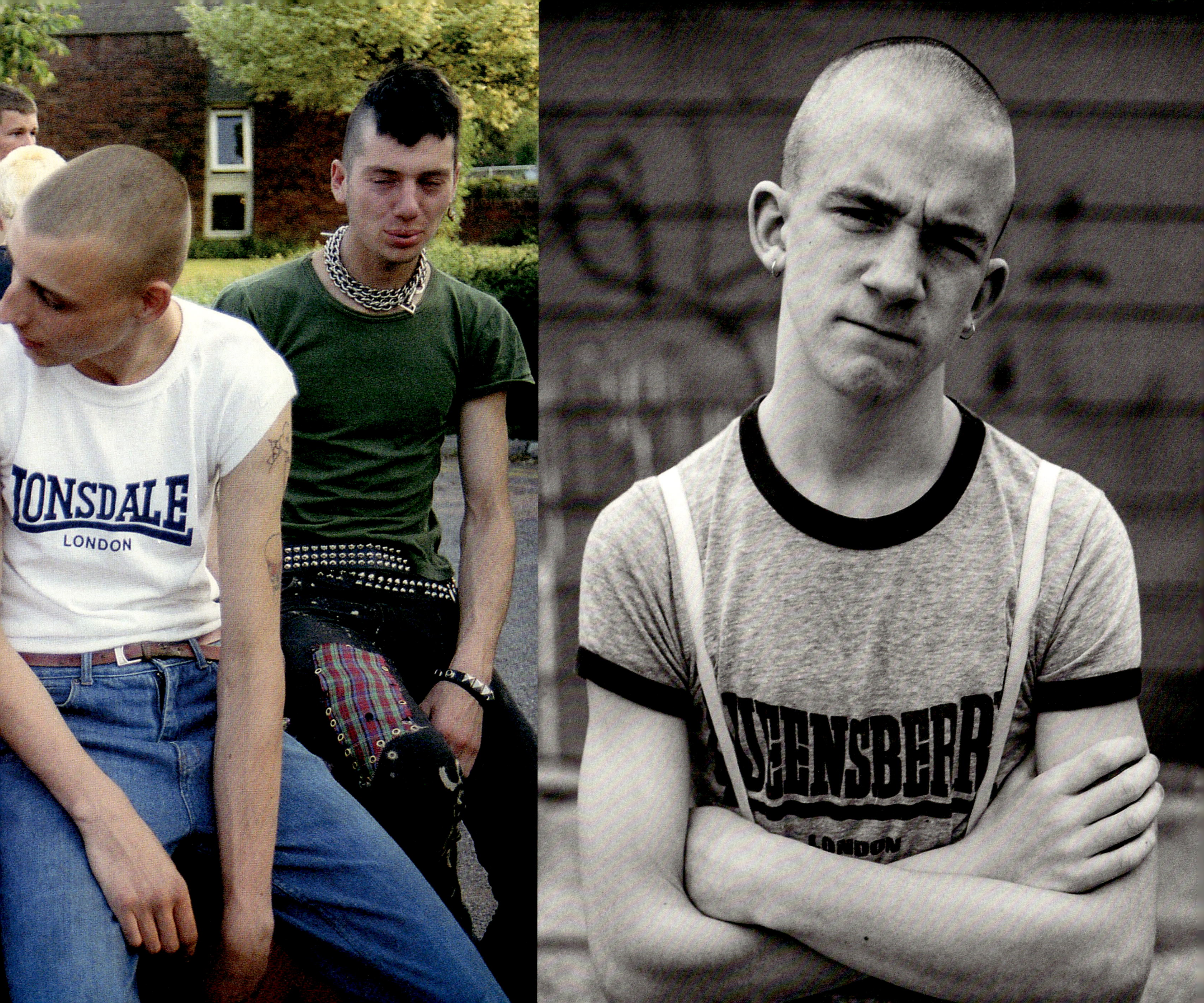
LONSDALE
LONDON
LONDON

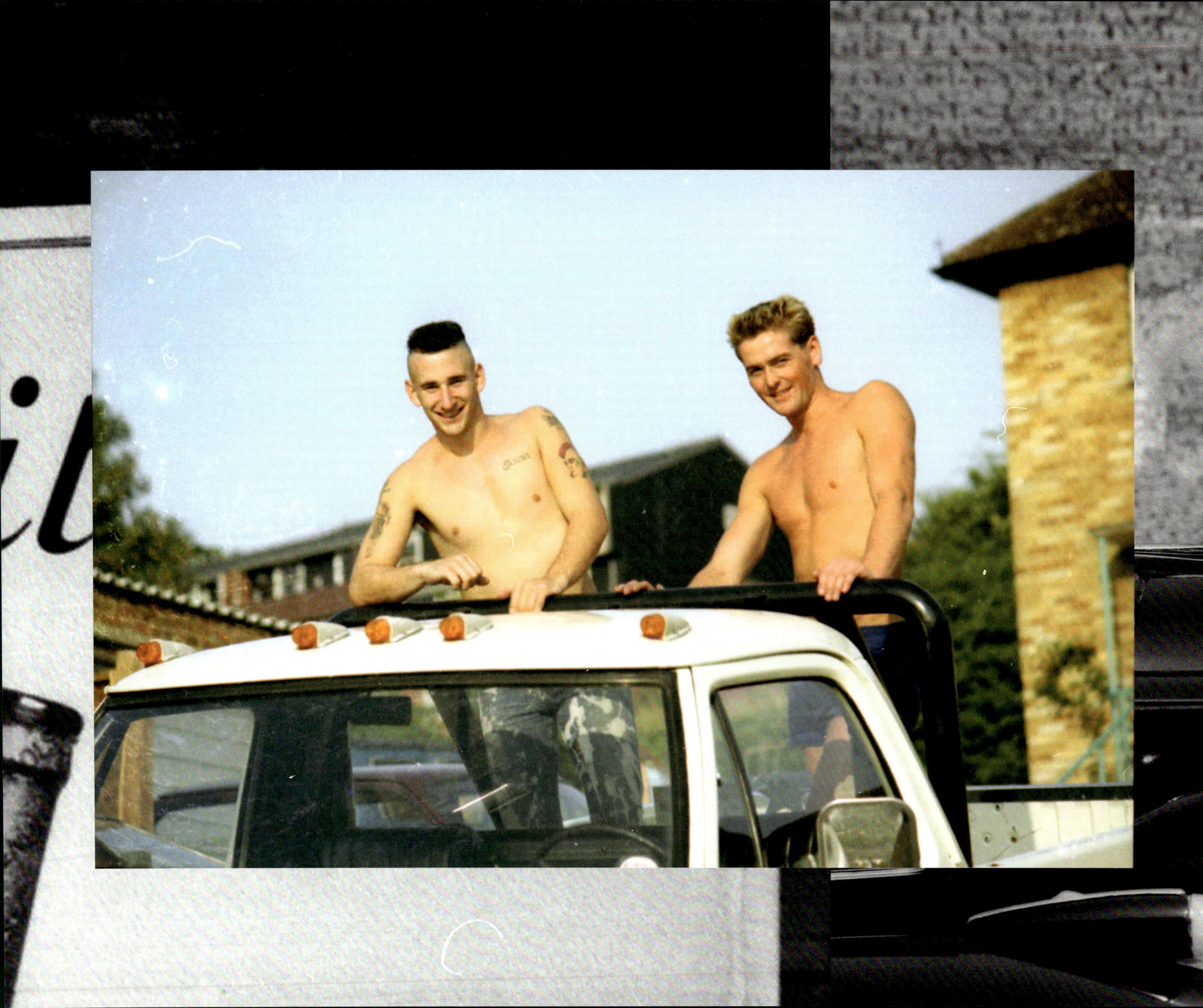

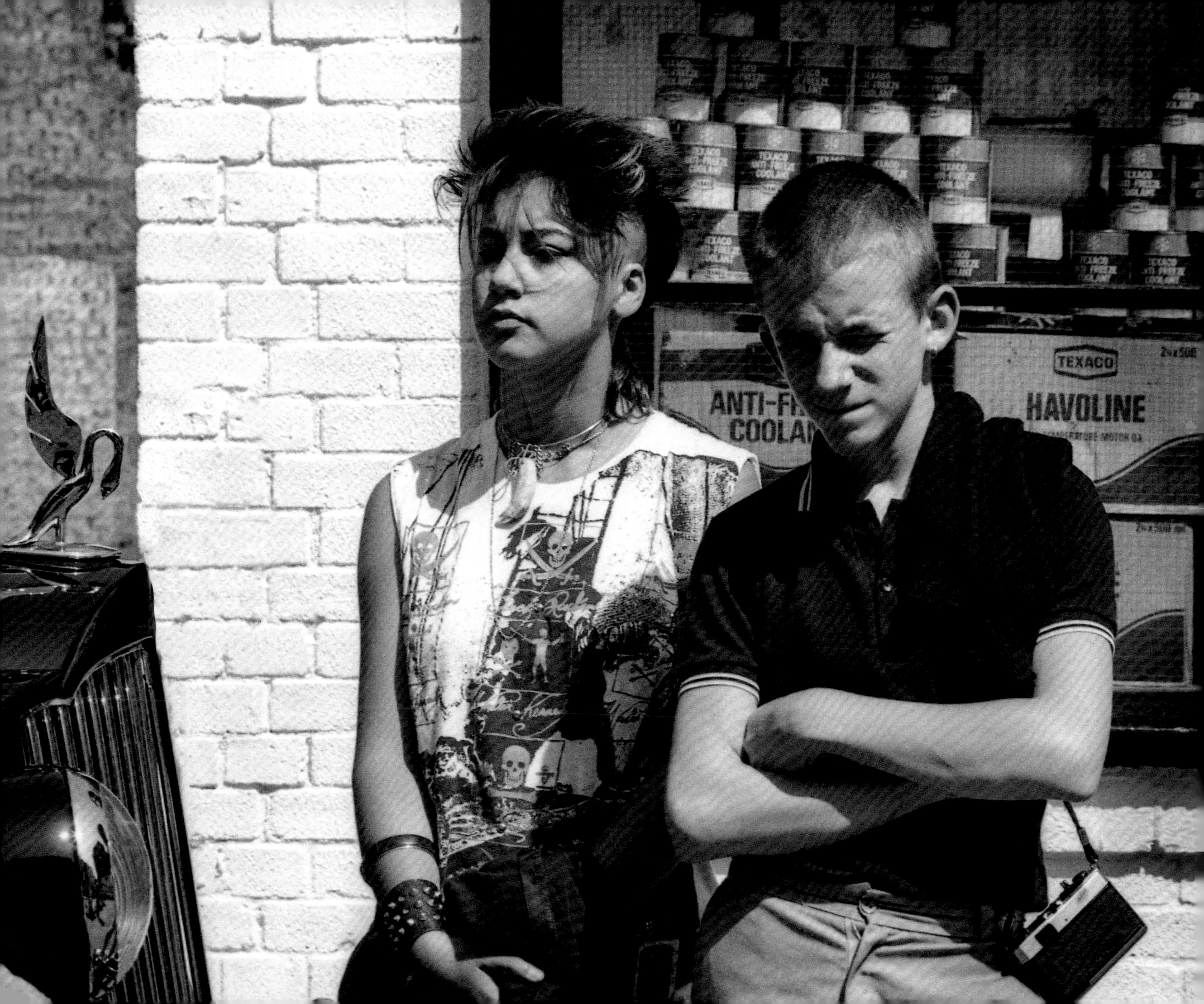
TEXACO
HAVOLINE

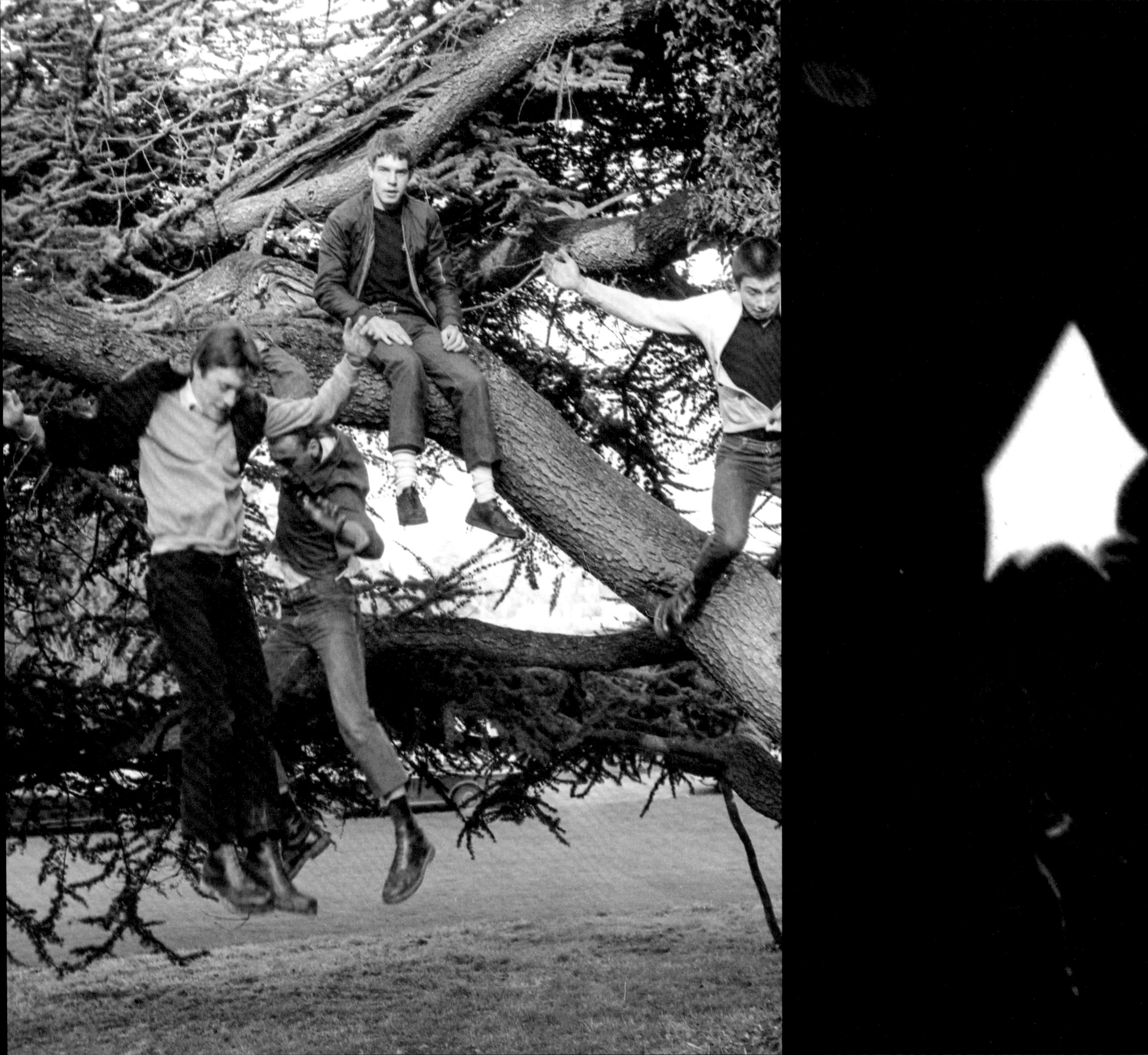

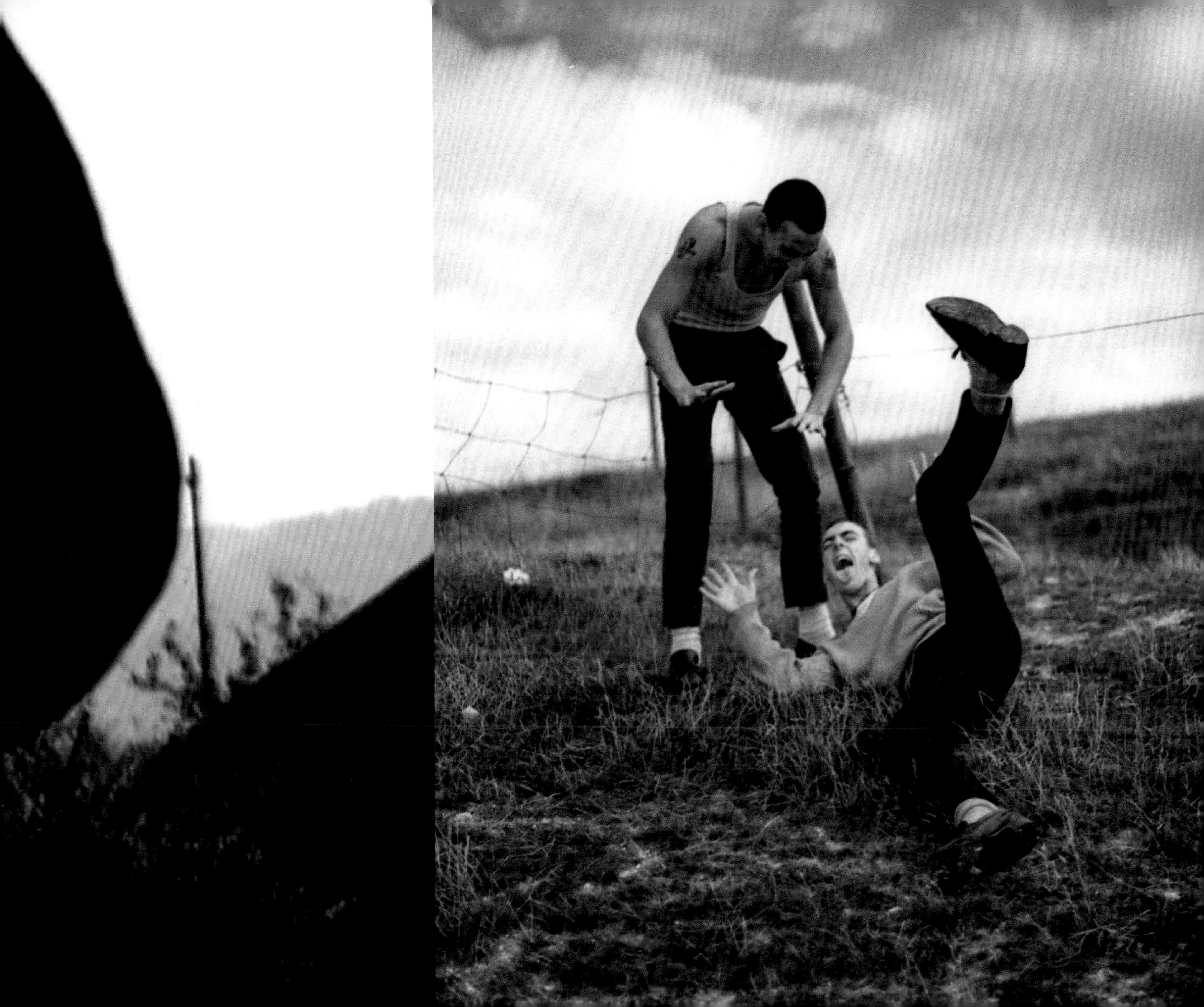

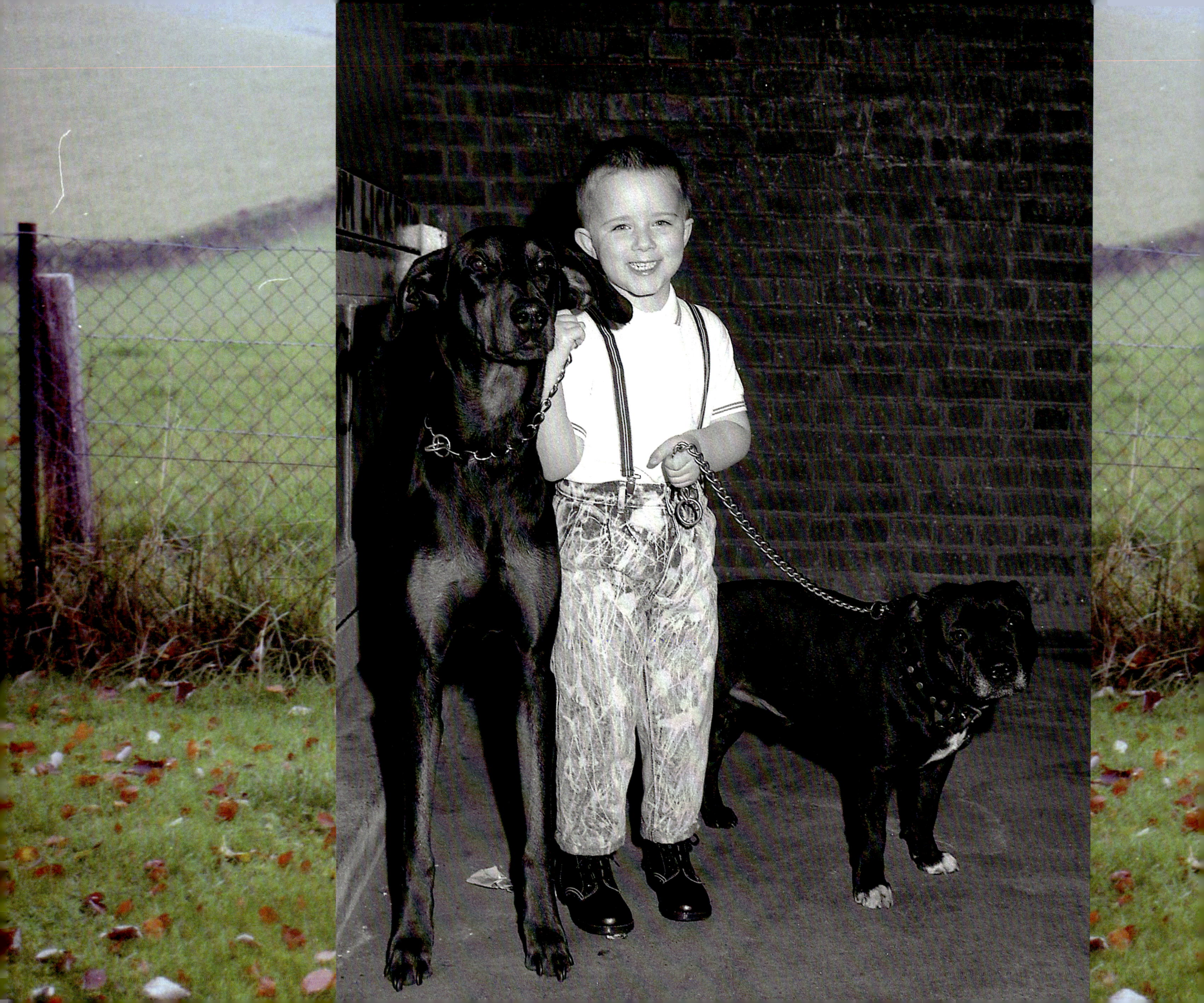

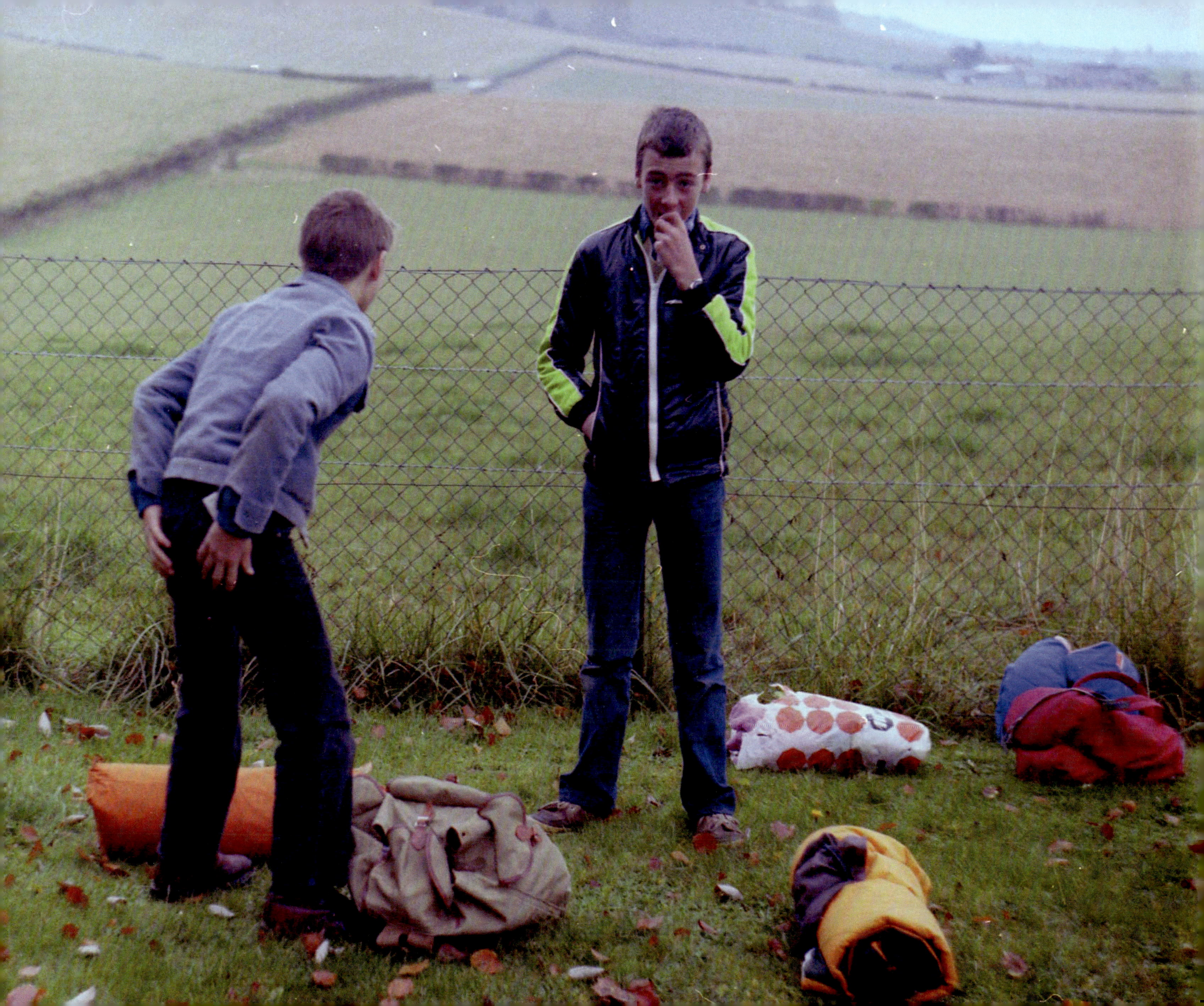

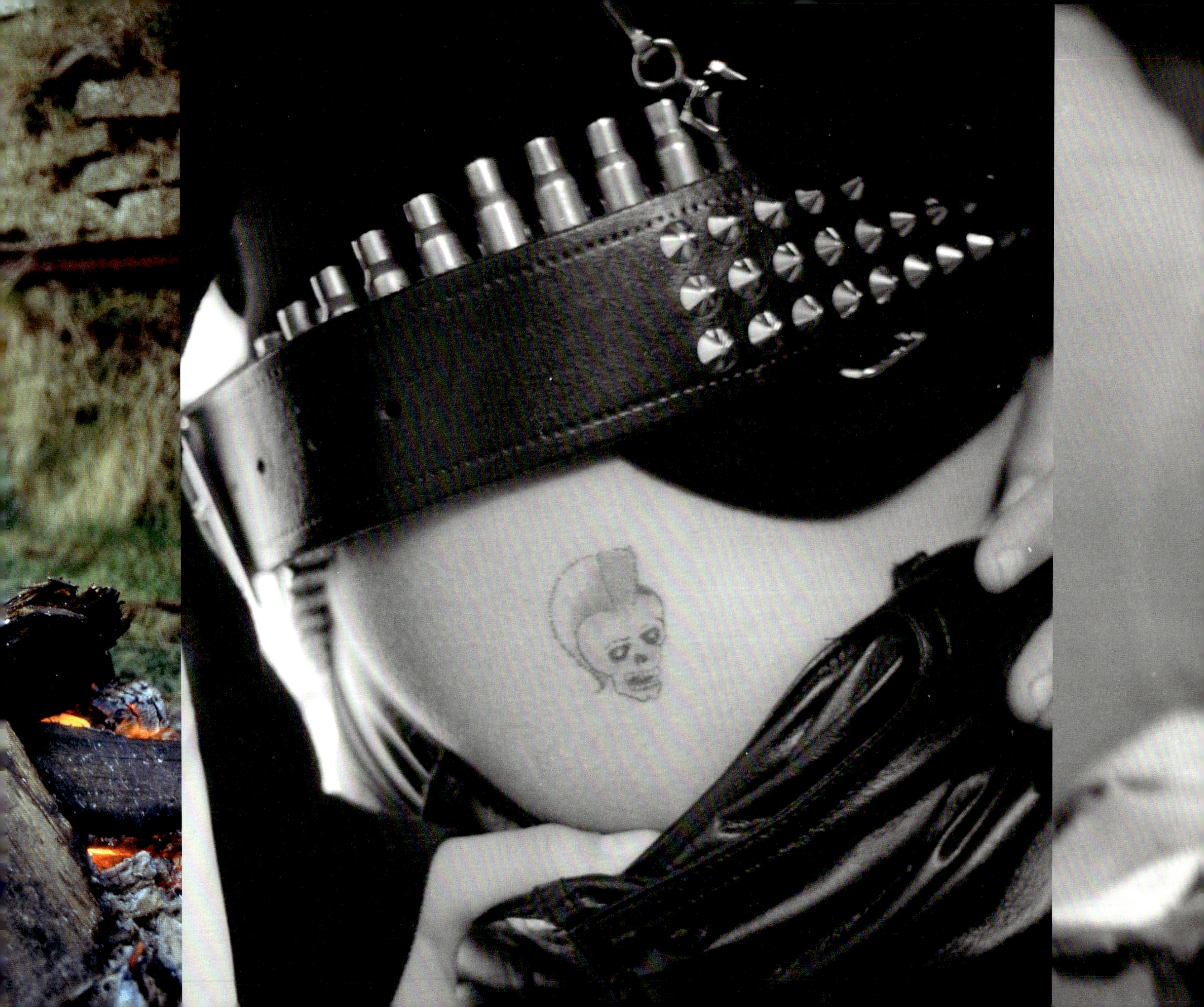

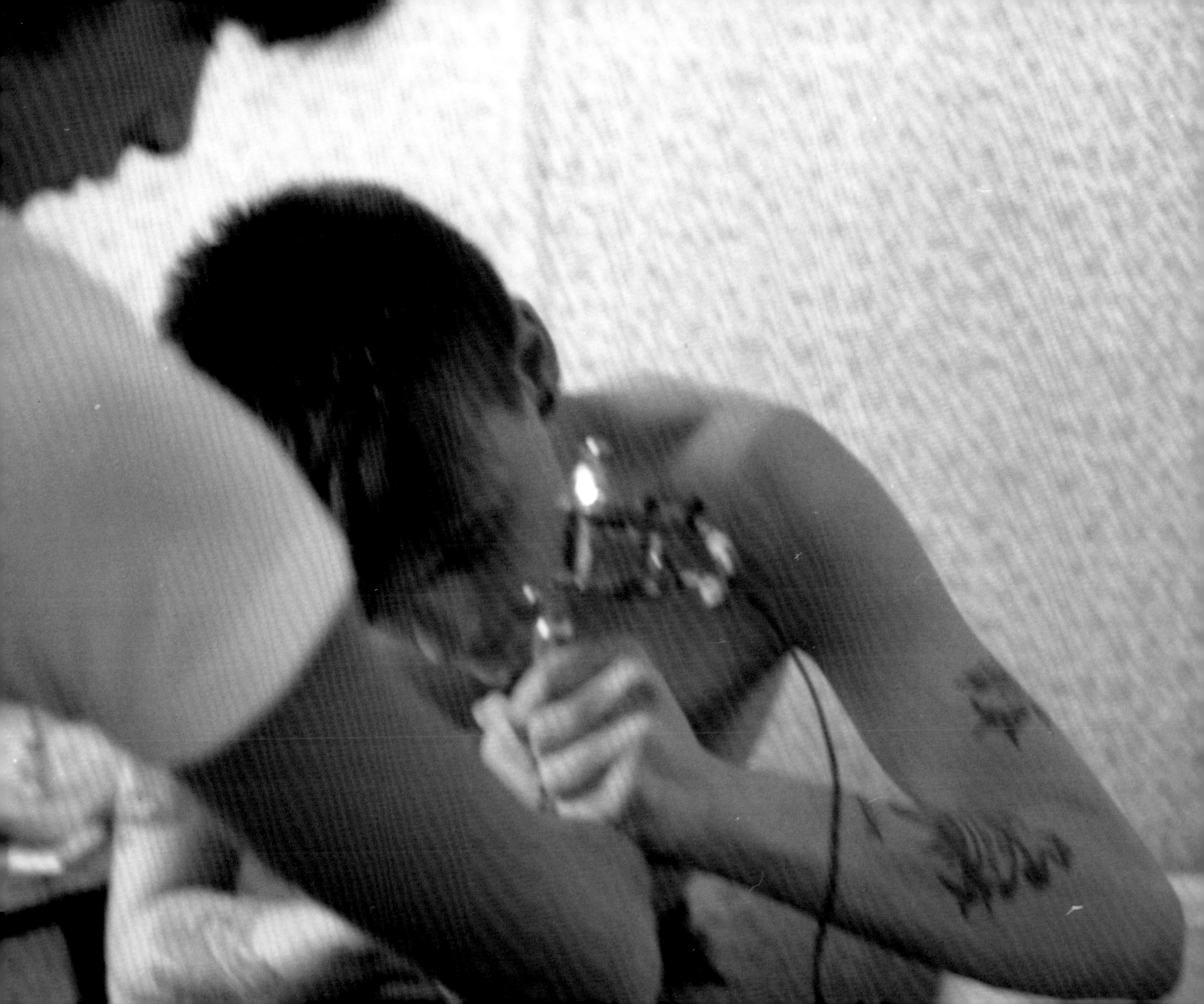

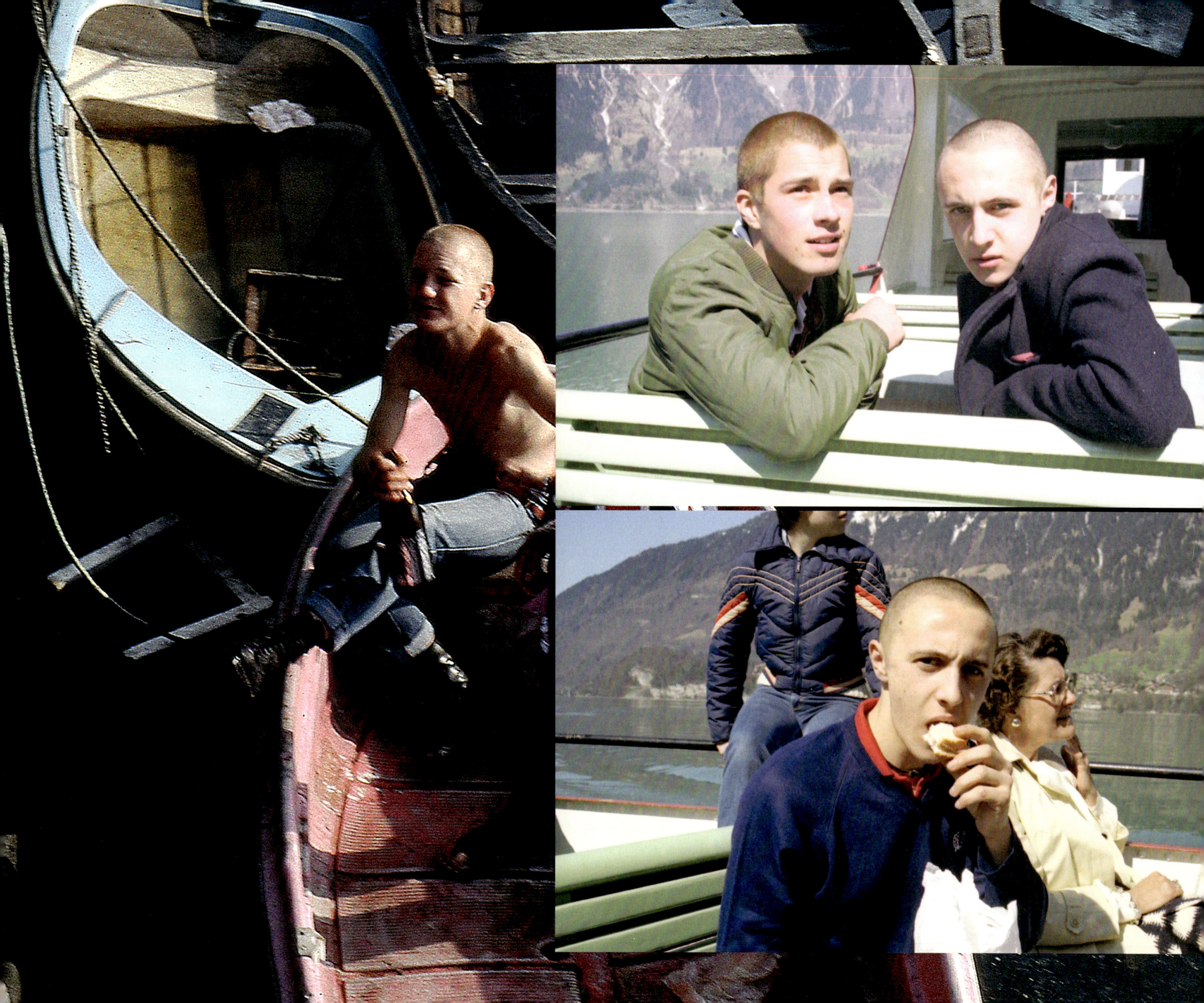

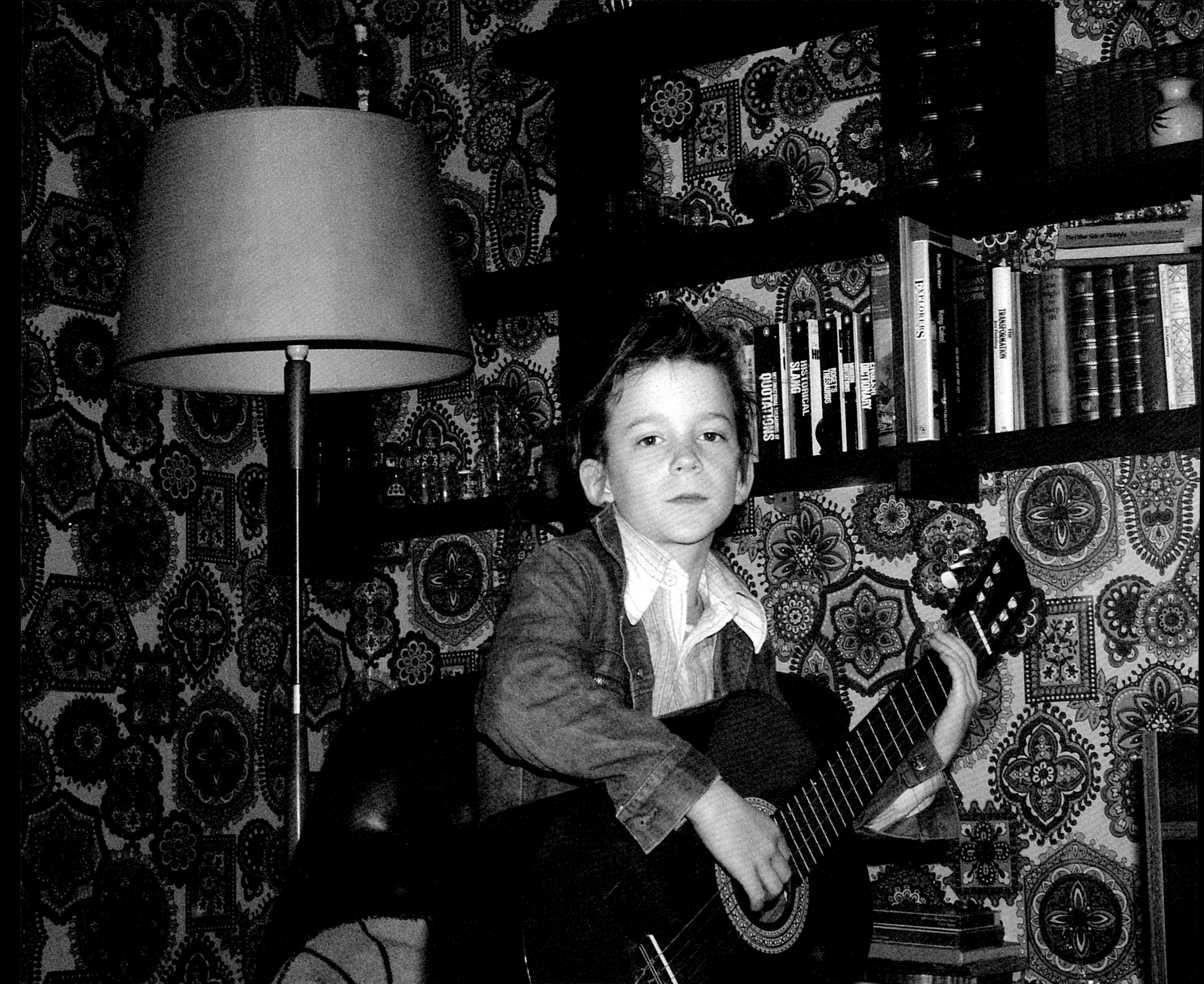
INTERNATIONAL THESAURUS OF QUOTATIONS
HISTORICAL SLANG
ROGET'S THESAURUS
MODERN QUOTATIONS
ENGLISH DICTIONARY
EXPLORERS
Ruth Winter
Keep Calm!
THE TRANSFORMATION
The Other Side of Midnight

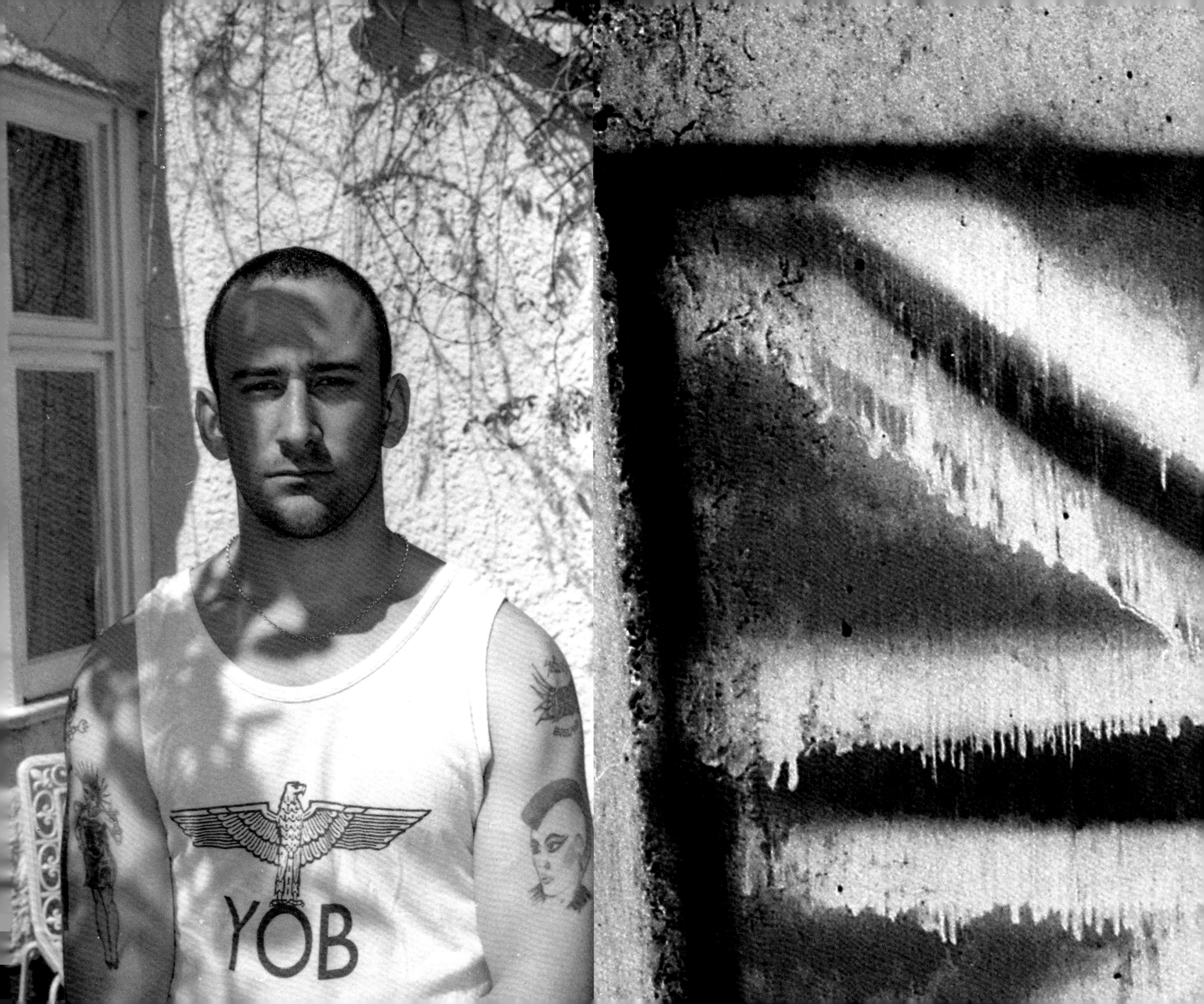
YOB

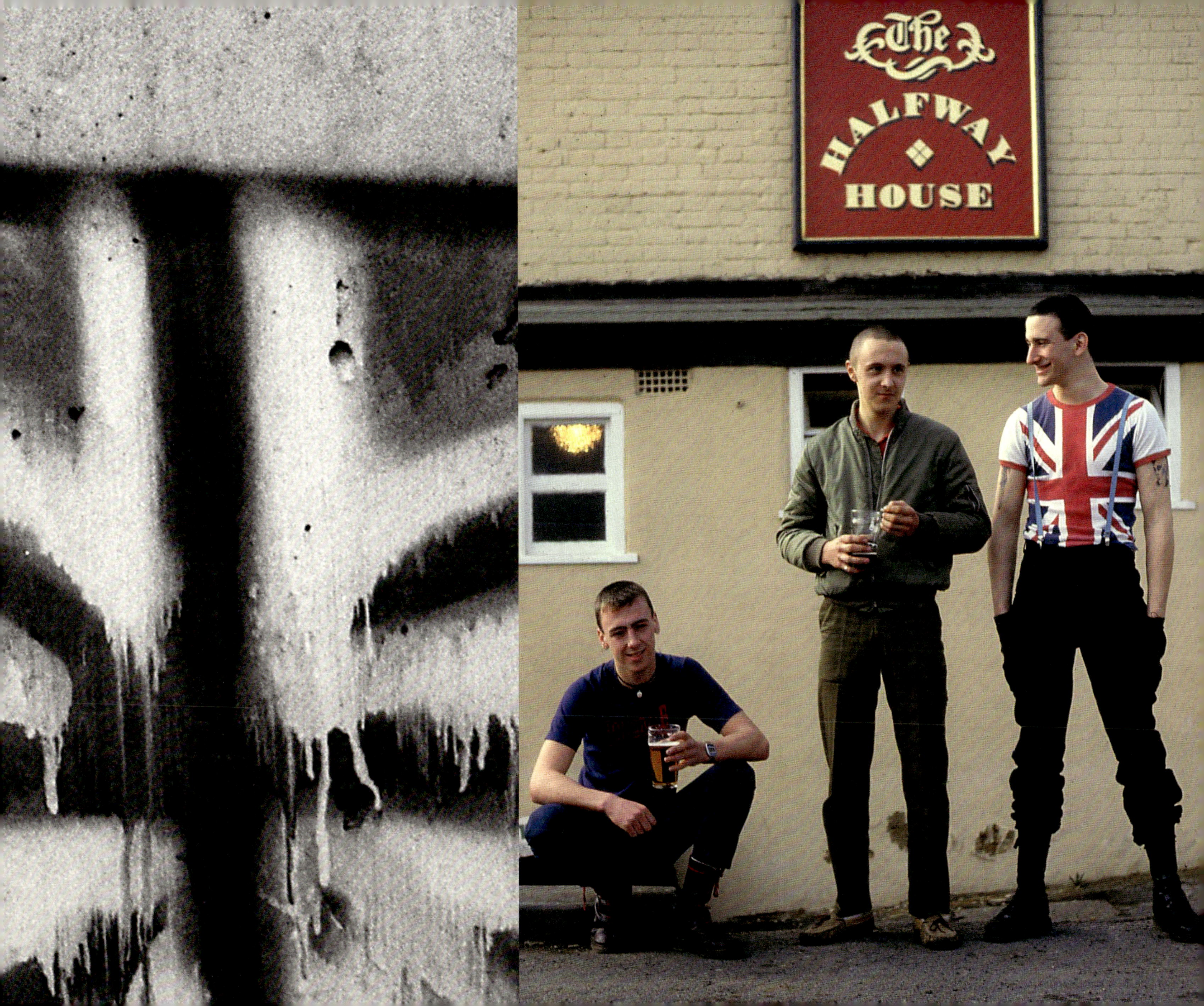
The
HALFWAY
HOUSE

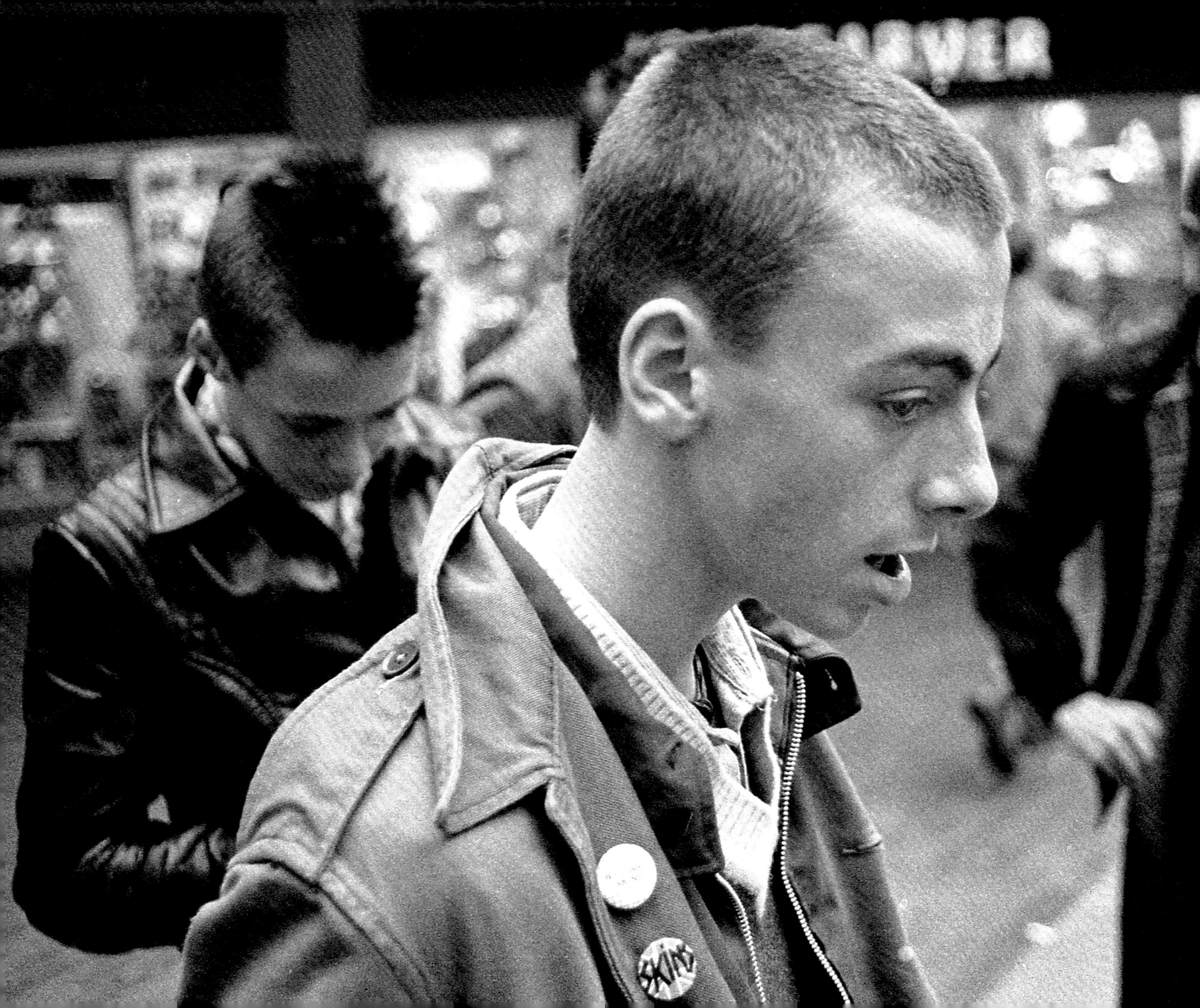

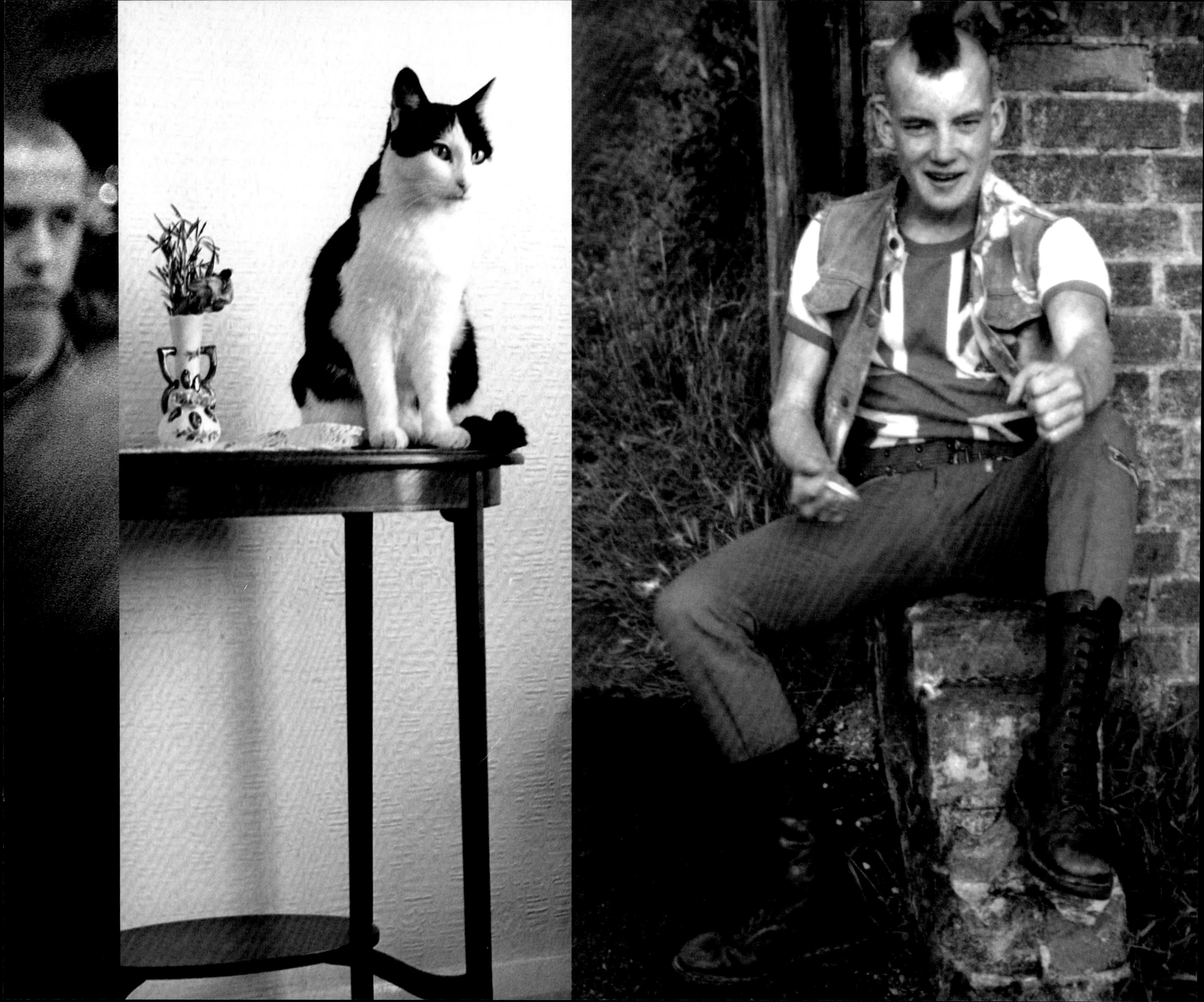

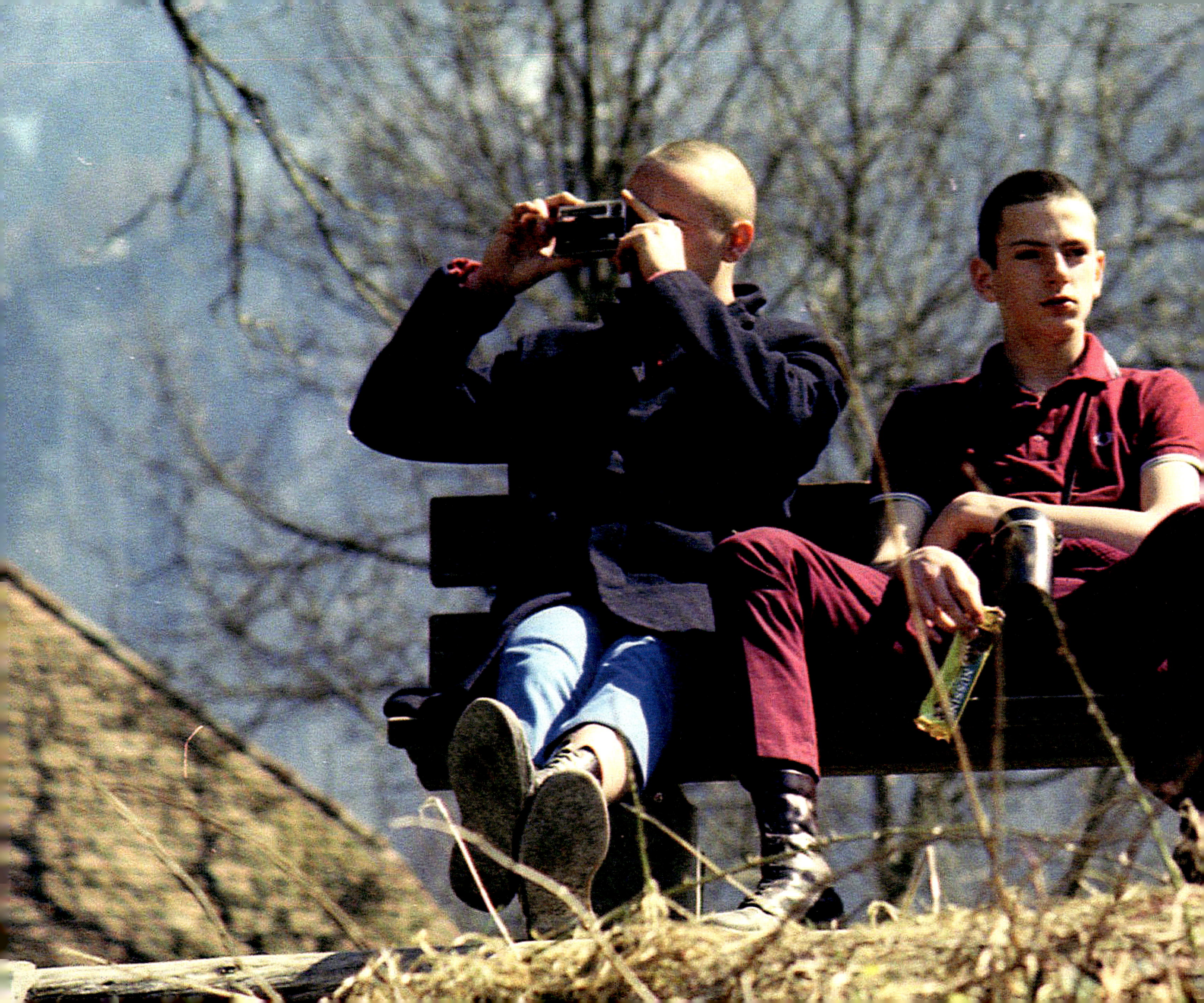

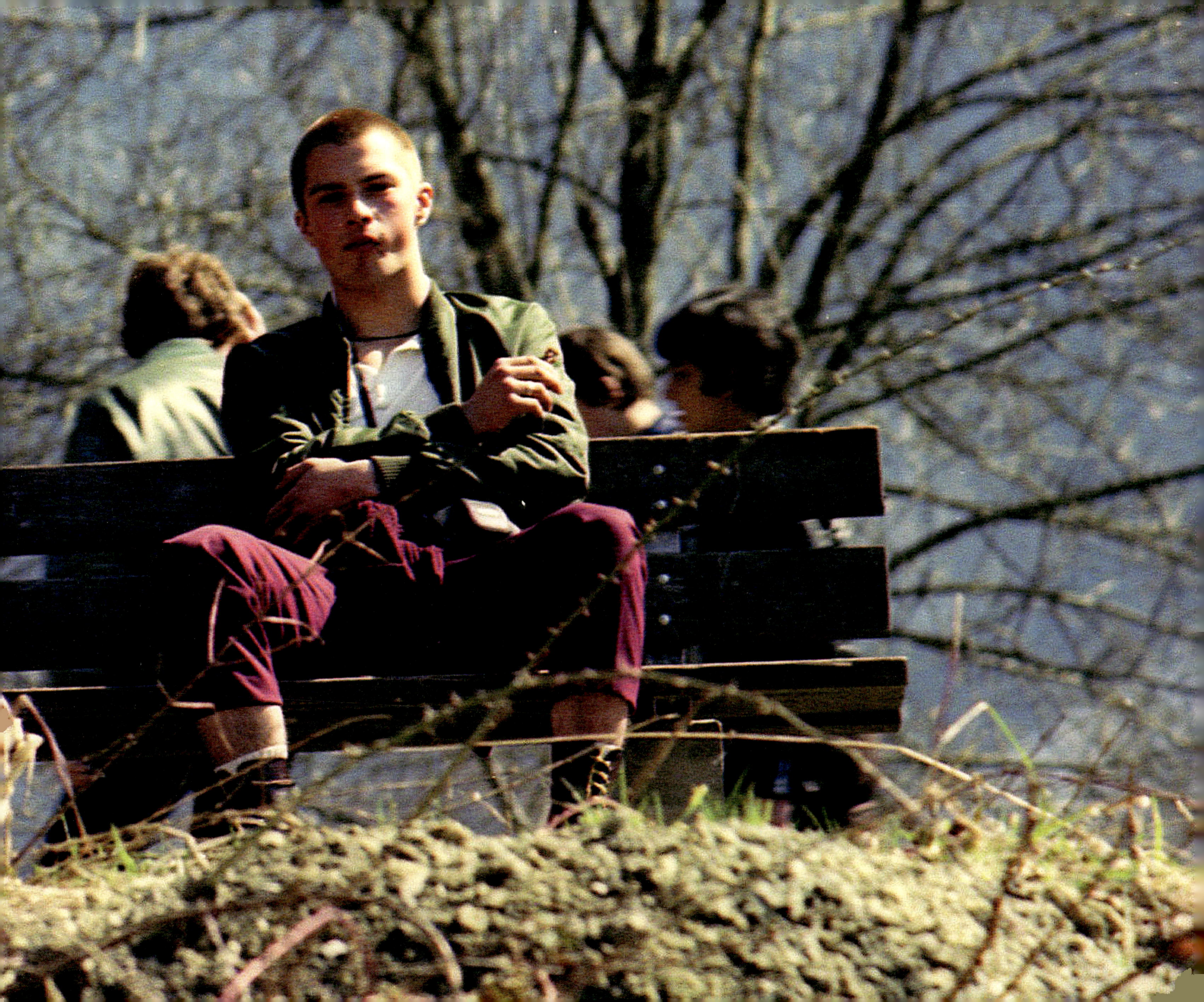

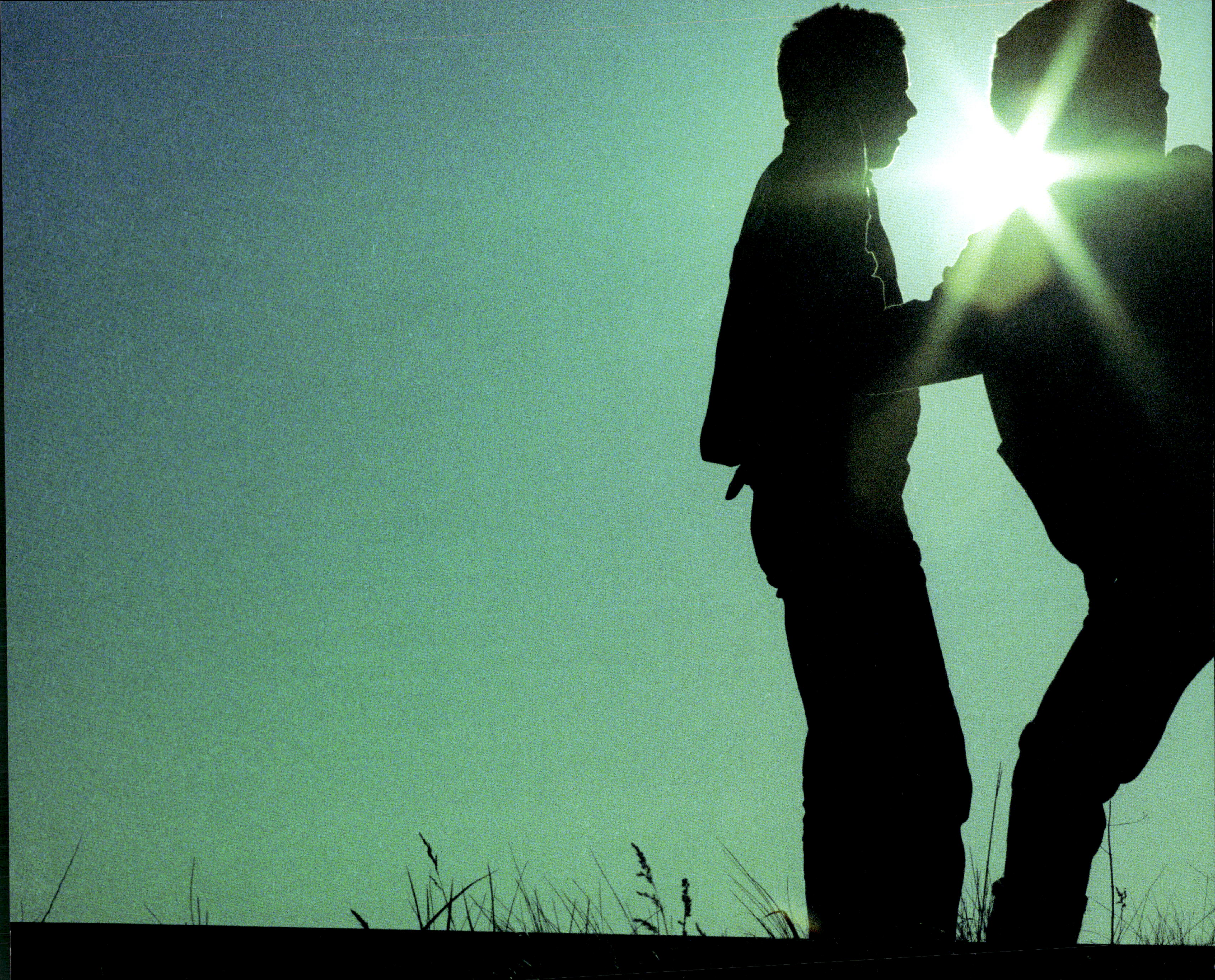

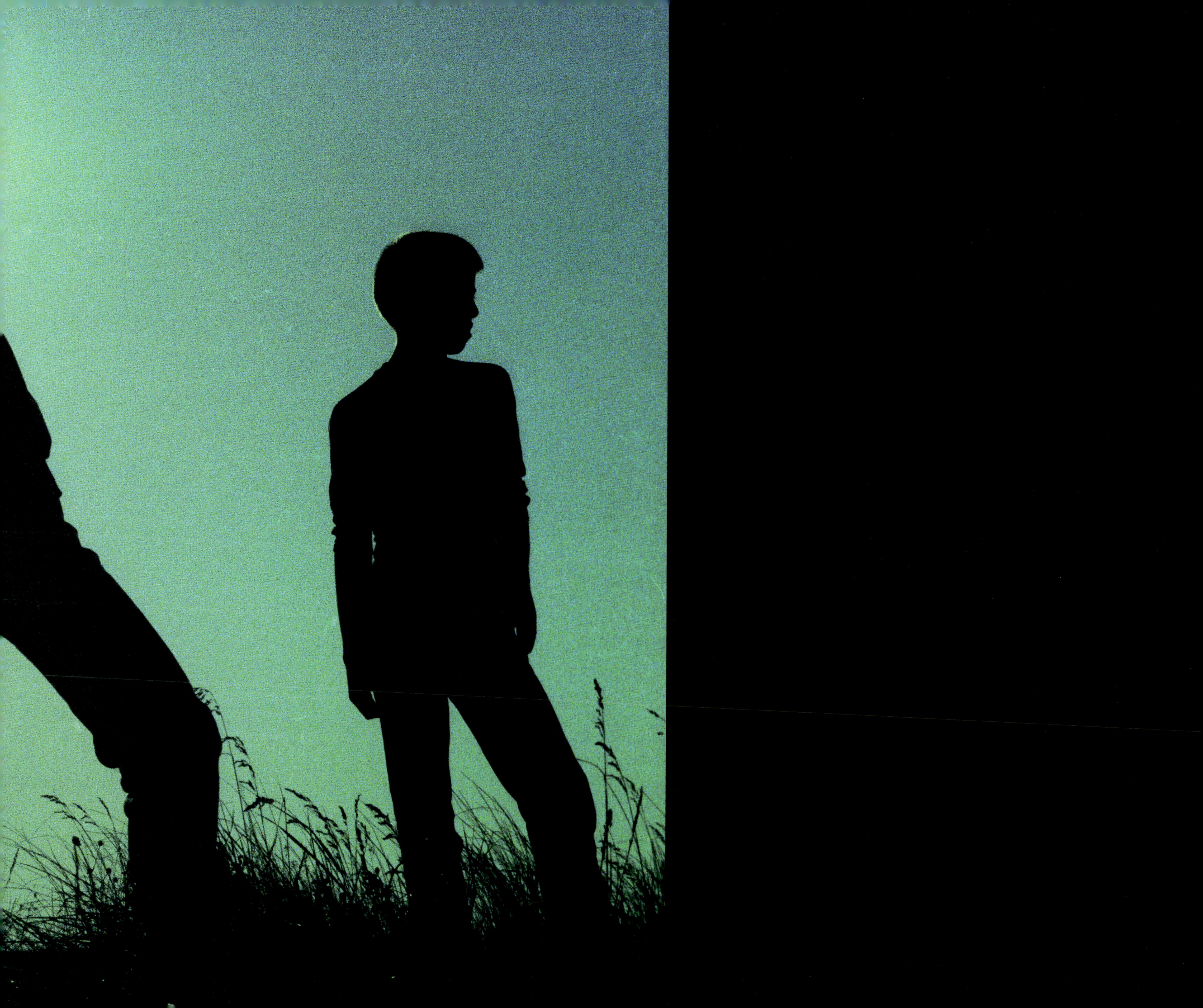

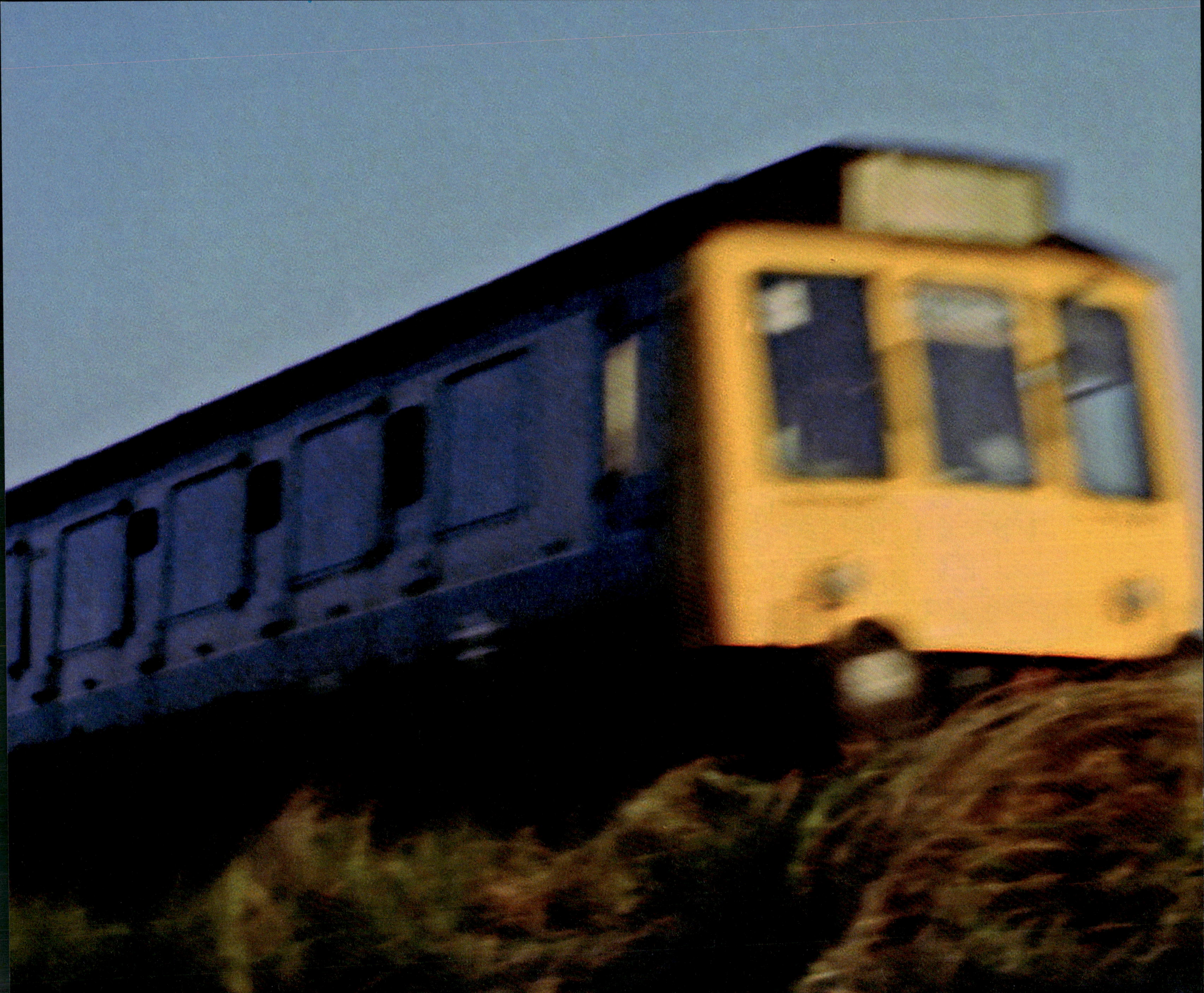

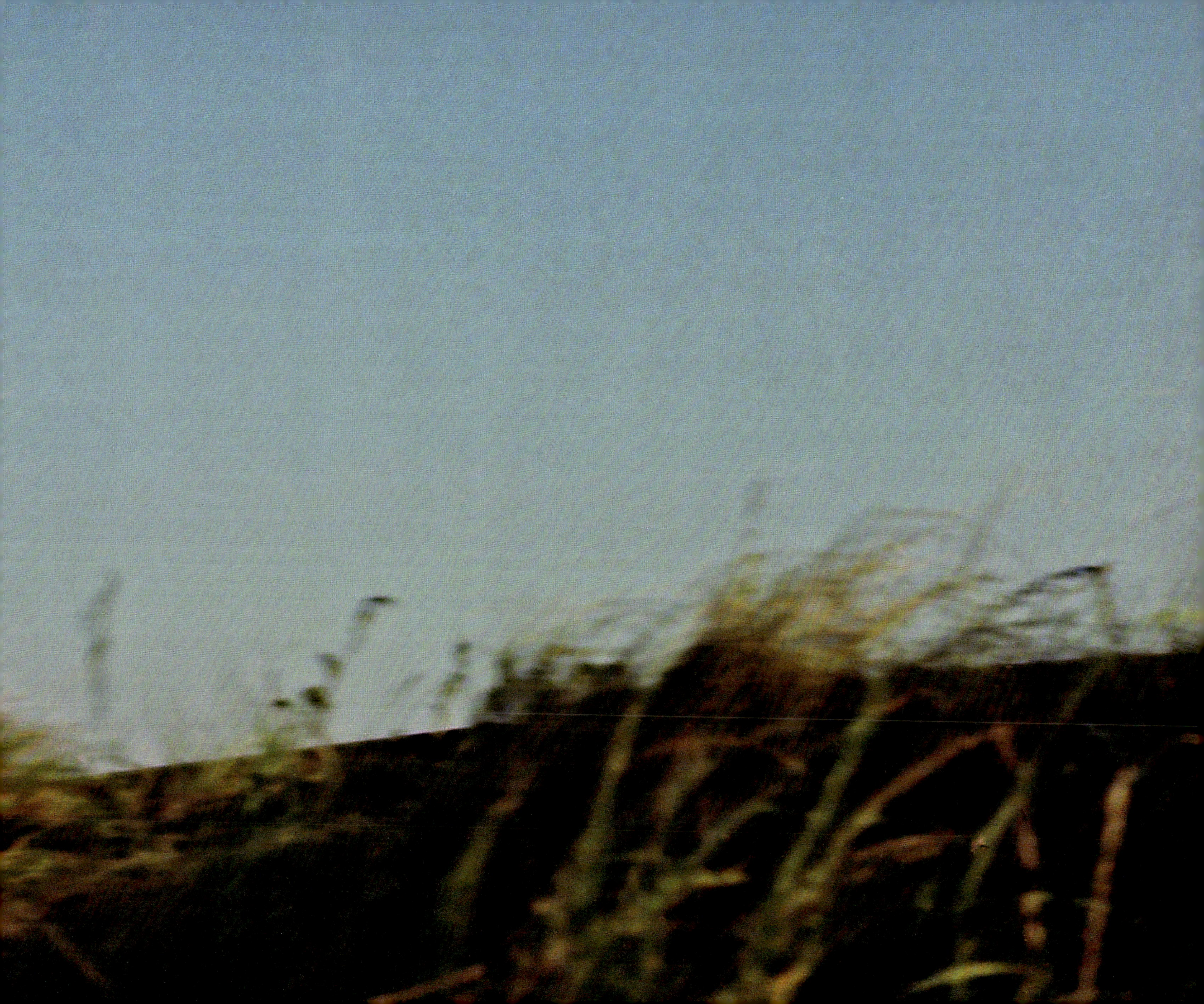

Gavin Watson was born in London in 1965 and grew up on a council estate in High Wycombe, Buckinghamshire. He bought a Hanimex camera from Woolworths in his early teens and began to take photographs. Upon leaving school at the age of sixteen, Watson moved back to London and became a darkroom assistant at Camera Press. He continued to photograph his younger brother Neville and their group of skinhead friends in High Wycombe.

The 'Wycombe Skins' were part of the working-class subculture brought together by a love of ska music and fashion. Although skinhead style had become associated with the right-wing extremism of political groups like the National Front in the 1970s, Watson's photographs document a time and place where the subculture was racially mixed and inclusive.

His photographs were published in the books *Skins* (1994) and *Skins and Punks* (2008); director Shane Meadows cited them as an inspiration for his film, *This is England* (2006).

Watson has photographed campaigns for Adidas, Aquascutum, Farah, Lee Cooper, Dr. Martens, to name a few. And he has begun an ongoing project with the singer Plan B.

He continues to exhibit and photograph.

GAVIN WATSON
OH! WHAT FUN WE HAD

Art Direction and Design by
Rini Giannaki

Published by Damiani
info@damianieditore.com
www.damianieditore.com

Printed in February 2019
by Grafiche Damiani – Faenza Group SpA, Italy.

ISBN 978-88-6208-634-9